JESUS

Daily Devotions for Adults

DAVID METZLER

REVIEW AND HERALD® PUBLISHING ASSOCIATION
HAGERSTOWN, MD 21740

The author assumes full responsibility for the accuracy of all facts
and quotations as cited in this book.

Unless otherwise noted, Scripture references are from the New King James Version.
Copyright © 1979, 1980, 1982 by Thomas Nelson, Inc. Used by permission. All rights reserved.
Texts credited to NIV are from the *Holy Bible, New International Version*.
Copyright © 1973, 1978, 1984, International Bible Society. Used by permission of
Zondervan Bible Publishers.
Texts credited to RV are from *The Holy Bible*, Revised Version. Oxford University
Press, 1911.

This book was
Edited by Gerald Wheeler
Copyedited by Jocelyn Fay and Delma Miller
Designed by Bill Tymeson
Electronic makeup by Shirley M. Bolivar
Cover illustration by Nathan Greene
Typeset: Minion 10.5/12.5

PRINTED IN U.S.A.

04 03 02 01 00   5 4 3 2 1

R&H Cataloging Service
Metzler, David Grant, 1951-
    Jesus

    1. Devotional calendars—Seventh-day Adventist.
2. Devotional literature. 3. Jesus Christ—Biography.
I. Title.

242.64

ISBN 0-8280-1444-2

In Appreciation

I wish to thank my wife, Margery, for 25 years of Christian love. Her patience, encouragement, and helpful "suggestions" transformed a vague book idea into reality. Thanks also to my daughters, Jessica and Janna, for showing forbearance while subtly letting me know they also contributed to the writing process—"Dad, are you on the computer . . . again?"

I wish to thank my parents, Richard and Yvonne, for working diligently to send my two sisters and me to church school. They sacrificed much to give us a Christian education, as they thought it worth the effort. Fortunately, before my father died on September 29, 1999, I was able to share the final manuscript of this book with him and personally thank him for the sacrifices both he and my mother gladly faced to see that we children were introduced to Jesus at a young age.

To the members of the Jacksonville Seventh-day Adventist Church in Jacksonville, North Carolina, I also say thank you. Your encouragement kept me on track during periods when other pressures seemed to crowd out spiritual progress and left me discouraged. Though we no longer share Sabbath school lessons on Saturday mornings, you remain in my thoughts and prayers. Thanks to head elder Doc Baysden (now deceased), head deacon Harry Rose, Frank Mattson, Pastor Mario Munoz, and all the rest, for getting me on my feet as a teacher. "Let's talk about Jesus!"

Thank you, Ellen G. White. For me, her prophetic words are inspired and timeless. Mrs. White knew Jesus in a way few of us have ever been privileged to know Him. She richly deserves, but would never have sought, the honor of truly bringing Christ's life and times alive. *The Desire of Ages* is certainly required reading for anyone wishing to know more about the Word made flesh. Her last words, "I know in whom I have believed," testify to her lifelong faith in Jesus. Would that we all might emulate a faith such as hers.

Most important, I wish to thank our Lord for the assistance He gave me as I prayerfully struggled at times to complete this humble rendering of His story. Without His love and sacrifice, there would be no story to tell. Because Jesus *did* come and die for each of us, we have the opportunity to echo at last the words of Paul, who said: "I have fought the good fight, I have finished the race, I have kept the faith. Now there is in store for me the crown of righteousness, which the Lord, the righteous Judge, will award to me on that day—and not only to me, but also to all who have longed for his appearing" (2 Tim. 4:7, 8, NIV). Amen. Even so, come, Lord Jesus!

Dedication

We shall ever be students. In the New Earth the love of God and Christ's sacrifice will be our eternal study. To all humble students of truth, who wish a broader experience from the story of our redemption, this book is dedicated. May we continue to encourage each other and learn from the great Teacher.

"It would be well for us to spend a thoughtful hour each day in contemplation of the life of Christ. We should take it point by point, and let the imagination grasp each scene, especially the closing ones. As we thus dwell upon His great sacrifice for us, our confidence in Him will be more constant, our love will be quickened, and we shall be more deeply imbued with His spirit. If we would be saved at last, we must learn the lesson of penitence and humiliation at the foot of the cross" (*The Desire of Ages,* p. 83).

"No other light ever has shone or ever will shine so clearly upon fallen man as that which emanated from the teachings and example of Jesus" (*ibid.,* p. 220).

JESUS

CHILDHOOD AND YOUTH
Christ Our Saviour

First Advent (5 B.C.) to Autumn A.D. 27

Matthew 1:1-2:23

Mark 1

Luke 1:1-2:52

John 1:1-18

The Desire of Ages, pp. 31-92

BEYOND THE BEGINNING

In the beginning was the Word, and the Word was with God, and the Word was God. John 1:1.

The Bible starts with the creation of our world. "In the beginning God created the heavens and the earth" (Gen. 1:1). God created our world, according to Genesis, but what happened before Creation week? While Genesis reveals to us the nature of Creation, John gives us the Creator Himself. He tells us that "in the beginning was the Word" (John 1:1).

As far back as human thought can reach, into the infinite reaches of an eternity we can little comprehend, Christ has always existed. He brought our world into being, "and without Him nothing was made that was made" (verse 3). Before the creation of humanity or angels, God existed. "It was Christ that spread the heavens, and laid the foundations of the earth. It was His hand that hung the worlds in space, and fashioned the flowers of the field. . . . And upon all things in earth, and air, and sky, He wrote the message of the Father's love."[1]

You may recall Moses' concern when told that he must announce to the children of Israel that the God of their fathers had sent him to bring them out of slavery. He thought they might question his credentials. Moses asked for a name that Israel might recognize their God. God replied, "Thus you shall say to the children of Israel, 'I AM has sent me to you'" (Ex. 3:14). A marvelous expression of the continuity of God's existence appears in the name I AM. The Lord has always existed!

John 1:1 contains the fundamental building blocks upon which we build our study of the "Bright and Morning Star." Though distinct from the Father, the Son has been "with the Father from all eternity."[2] "There never was a time when He was not in close fellowship with the eternal God."[3] He has an equality of nature with the Father. "While God's Word speaks of the humanity of Christ when upon this earth, it also speaks decidedly regarding His preexistence. The Word existed as a divine being, even as the eternal Son of God, in union and oneness with His Father."[4] "For God so loved the world that He gave His only begotten Son, that whoever believes in Him should not perish but have everlasting life" (John 3:16).

When we understand the divinity of Jesus we start to appreciate His humanity. Nothing shows the marvelous love of God more than giving us a part of Himself, His Son.

A PLAN: "GOD WITH US"

And the Word became flesh and dwelt among us, and we beheld His glory, the glory as of the only begotten of the Father. John 1:14.

The plan of redemption was not conceived in haste. It reveals God's character that He gave His only Son to ransom us. God is love, and His government rests upon that principle. The great controversy is the selfish system of Satan and the selfless system of God in collision. While Lucifer stated he would "be *like* the Most High" (Isa. 14:14), Christ *is* the Most High. "Who, being in the form of God, did not consider it robbery to be equal with God, but made Himself of no reputation, taking the form of a bondservant, and coming in the likeness of men" (Phil. 2:6, 7). Christ not only lowered Himself to human form but "being found in appearance as a man, He humbled Himself and became obedient to the point of death, even the death of the cross" (verse 8).

"From the days of eternity the Lord Jesus Christ was one with the Father; He was 'the image of God,' the image of His greatness and majesty, 'the outshining of His glory.'" [5] The nature of humanity He took melded with and cloaked His divine image. Had Christ come in His heavenly glory and splendor, humanity would have been unable to bear the brilliance of His being. "In no sense did Christ cease to be God when He became man. The two natures became closely and inseparably one, yet each remained distinct." [6] This mystery staggers us, yet the magnitude of the Incarnation does not end there. The Word was with God from eternity yet He "chose" to become flesh that He might ransom us from sin! We are forever and uniquely linked with God the Father. Through His Son we are again members of the family of God. "Our little world, under the curse of sin the one dark blot in His glorious creation, will be honored above all other worlds in the universe of God. Here, where the Son of God tabernacled in humanity; where the King of glory lived and suffered and died—here, when He shall make all things new, the tabernacle of God shall be with men." [7]

"Redeemed! How I love to proclaim it! Redeemed by the blood of the Lamb; Redeemed through His infinite mercy, His child, and forever, I am." [8]

Christ gave up the courts of heaven that we might henceforth through all eternity be called sons and daughters of God.

TO MAKE HIM KNOWN

No one has seen God at any time. The only begotten Son, who is in the bosom of the Father, He has declared Him. John 1:18.

God did not permit Moses to view Him face-to-face, for to have done so meant instant death for a sinner. Hidden in the cleft of a rock and covered by the hand of God, Moses caught only a glimpse of God's back after He passed by (Ex. 33:18-20). Only in Christ could sinful humans rightly see a representation of the Father. He alone could show the depths of our Father's love, for when God gave the world His Son, He bestowed upon us a unique gift. No angel could have revealed "in the flesh" God's loving mercy and kindness. God's plan to redeem us cost Him His own Son. Christ's favorite topic of conversation while on earth was His Father's love. Jesus was the embodiment of that love. Philip asked, "'Lord, show us the Father, and it is sufficient for us.' Jesus said to him, 'Have I been with you so long, and yet you have not known Me, Philip? He who has seen Me has seen the Father'" (John 14:8, 9).

Fifteen centuries before Christ came, God instructed Israel to build Him a sanctuary that He might "dwell among them" (Ex. 25:8). God's glory hovered above the mercy seat on top of the ark in the Most Holy Place of that sanctuary. We again see that same desire to dwell with humanity expressed in the Incarnation. Upon the Mount of Transfiguration, when divinity flashed through humanity, John witnessed the glory of his Lord. Peter alluded to the same event when he wrote that he was an "eyewitness" to His majesty. "For He received from God the Father honor and glory when such a voice came to Him from the Excellent Glory: 'This is My beloved Son, in whom I am well pleased'" (2 Peter 1:17).

Most Jews did not recognize in Jesus the Messiah. The "lost sheep of the house of Israel" (Matt. 15:24) rejected Him because they had focused on a Messiah who would save them from Roman oppression. But not all were oblivious to the prophecies that portrayed Christ as the suffering servant. Many sincere individuals looked forward to the coming of the Promised One. We are often quick to point a finger at ancient Israel and wonder at their blindness, yet many today shut their eyes to the signs of His second coming.

Will you recognize Him as your Saviour when He comes again? You are invited to know Christ today, and through Him, His Father.

THE GOSPEL WRITERS

All scripture is given by inspiration of God. 2 Tim. 3:16, KJV.

The theme of the four Gospels is Christ—His incarnation, public ministry, death, resurrection, and ascension to heaven; yet each paints a unique picture of the mission and life of the Son of God.

Matthew wrote for Jews and Jewish Christians. He sought to convince a Jewish audience that Jesus was the son of Abraham and David, the King of Israel, the true Messiah. His book presents Christ as the Great Teacher and shows how He fits the bigger picture of Jewish history. To accomplish this, Matthew points to the fulfillment of Old Testament Jewish prophecies that would not have impressed the Gentile reader of his day.

Mark was not an eyewitness to the events he described, though familiar with the gospel because he had heard Peter's accounts of it. Writing his book for non-Jews, he explained Jewish customs (such as the Passover) for readers not familiar with such events. Since wonder-working power impressed the Romans, Mark emphasized miracles.

Luke, colaborer with Paul, was a historian and physician. He traced the lineage of Christ to Adam, the father of humanity, while Matthew, writing for Jews, traced Christ's ancestry to Abraham. Also Luke writes about Christ's interaction with Gentiles and Roman citizens. Because he produced the most complete of the Gospel records, it is from his pen that we learn much concerning Christ's birth and ministry in Perea.

John is a theologian. The youngest of the disciples, he opened his heart to Jesus and spoke of what he saw with his own eyes (1 John 1:1-3). As an eyewitness, John is the only one to document the early ministry of Christ in Judea and His early work with the Jewish leaders. Interestingly, John records the controversies in the Temple but not the miracles. He reveals the Father in the plan of salvation and repeatedly quotes Jesus as saying "He that sent Me." Speaking to the Christian, John presents Jesus as the living Creator and crucified Saviour of the world.

"The Creator of all ideas may impress different minds with the same thought, but each may express it in a different way, yet without contradiction. The fact that this difference exists should not perplex or confuse us. It is seldom that two persons will view and express truth in the very same way. Each dwells on particular points which his constitution and education have fitted him to appreciate. The sunlight falling upon the different objects gives those objects a different hue."[9]

Thank God for the Light.

THE FULLNESS OF TIME

But when the fullness of the time had come, God sent forth His Son.

Gal. 4:4.

Old Testament prophecy had long pointed to a coming Messiah. The promise made to Adam and Eve in the Garden of Eden repeated itself in the prophecies of Daniel and the words of Jacob, who had declared, "The scepter shall not depart from Judah, nor a lawgiver from between his feet, until Shiloh comes" (Gen. 49:10). Many thought the promised scepter would overthrow the Romans, and the coming of the Anointed One became the hope of a nation in bondage. Some accurately understood Daniel's prophecy, but most misinterpreted it. Overlooking scripture that pointed to the humble first advent of Christ, Israel chose instead to dwell upon the prophetic glories of the Second Advent.

"But like the stars in the vast circuit of their appointed path, God's purposes know no haste and no delay. . . . So in heaven's council the hour for the coming of Christ had been determined. When the great clock of time pointed to that hour, Jesus was born in Bethlehem." [10] He came at a most favorable time in history. Greek was the universal language. The world, for the most part, was at peace under Roman rule, and travel was generally safe and rapid in most areas of the empire. Jews dispersed throughout the world could return safely to Jerusalem for annual feasts. Such pilgrims might rapidly spread the news of the Messiah. Palestine remained the center of Jewish thought, and people looked upon the Jewish religion with interest. Many Gentiles knew scriptural prophecies better than some Jewish religious leaders.

While the nation maintained a form of self-government, Rome held the actual power, creating internal strife. The Jews despised Herod's bloody reign, because it used Roman spears to enforce it. Heavy taxation caused widespread discontent. Rome had even placed its own appointees in the position of high priest. Such turmoil caused many to look for a Messiah. "And when the fullness of the time had come, the Deity was glorified by pouring upon the world a flood of healing grace that was never to be obstructed or withdrawn till the plan of salvation should be fulfilled." [11]

The celestial clock now ticks inexorably closer to His second coming! None of us know the hour of the Master's appearing, yet circumstances seem to favor a soon return. Rest assured that He shall return again "when the fullness of time is come."

"YOU DID NOT BELIEVE MY WORDS"

And Zacharias said to the angel, "How shall I know this?"

Luke 1:18.

King David divided the priesthood into 24 courses. Each course of priests served twice a year for one week, commencing on Sabbath at the 3:00 p.m. service and ending on the following Sabbath at the 9:00 a.m. service. On special occasions all 24 courses were expected to attend the Temple. The priests gathered in a semicircle and cast lots to determine who would participate. Each man held up one or more fingers to be counted. The president of the course chose a random number and started counting fingers until he had reached that number. The first chosen cleansed the altar of burnt offering and prepared the sacrifice. The second cleansed the candlestick and altar of incense. The third offered incense and prayed—the most important task. The fourth burned the pieces of the sacrifice on the altar and concluded the service.

"The privilege of officiating at the golden altar on behalf of Israel was considered a high honor, and Zacharias was in every respect worthy of it. This privilege usually came to each priest but once in a lifetime, and was therefore the great moment of his life."[12] Choosing a helper to remove the old coals from the altar and another to lay new ones, Zacharias spread incense on the coals. As the sweet fragrance of the smoke ascended before the Most Holy Place, he prayed for Israel.

Suddenly the angel of the Lord appeared to the right of the altar, the side signifying favor. Stunned, Zacharias failed to notice this sign of approval and "fear fell upon him." The angel's first words are "Do not be afraid" (Luke 1:13). Gabriel, the same angel who gave the time of the Messiah's coming to Daniel, now appeared to announce the birth of a son to Zacharias and Elizabeth. (Zacharias had expressed doubt that he and his wife could have a son at their advanced age.) Although he knew the story of Isaac, he had forgotten that God accomplishes what He promises. As a result of his disbelief, the angel declared that Zacharias would be mute until the promised child's birth.

"The birth of a son to Zacharias, like the birth of the child of Abraham, and that of Mary, was to teach a great spiritual truth, a truth that we are slow to learn and ready to forget. In ourselves we are incapable of doing any good thing; but that which we cannot do will be wrought by the power of God in every submissive and believing soul."[13]

11

"I AM GABRIEL"

And the angel answered and said to him, "I am Gabriel, who stands in the presence of God." Luke 1:19.

The angel Gabriel holds the position next in honor to the Son of God. To "stand in the presence" is an expression reserved in Old Testament times for a minister or high official with duties in the royal court. Christ Himself said that in heaven angels always "see the face of My Father" (Matt. 18:10). The Bible and writings of Ellen G. White have much to say regarding Gabriel. "Before his fall, Lucifer was the first of the covering cherubs, holy and undefiled." [14] After Lucifer's fall, Gabriel took his place. Gabriel in Hebrew means "man of God." "It was Gabriel, the angel next in rank to the Son of God, who came with the divine message to Daniel. It was Gabriel, 'His angel,' whom Christ sent to open the future to the beloved John." [15]

Gabriel talked with Daniel (Dan. 8:16; 9:21) and announced the coming of the Messiah. He spoke with Zacharias (Luke 1:19) and Mary (verses 26, 27). Probably he also appeared to Joseph (Matt. 1:20). Later the angel comforted Christ in Gethsemane [16] and protected Him from the mob. [17] He rolled back the stone of the tomb and called the Saviour forth. [18] The angel was one of two who accompanied Christ during His ministry here on earth, [19] and appeared to the disciples as Christ ascended to heaven. [20] Finally, Gabriel announced himself to John on Patmos, [21] calling himself "your fellow servant, and of your brethren the prophets" (Rev. 22:9).

What do angels do? "Are they not all ministering spirits sent forth to minister for those who will inherit salvation?" (Heb. 1:14). Angels have always had a part to play in God's plans. Conversing with Adam and Eve and then guarding access to the tree of life, they later shut the door to the ark, sealing faithful Noah and his family inside. They visited with Abraham and Lot. Repeatedly they intervened in battle for Israel. In the New Testament they formed the star the Magi followed and comforted the disciples as Christ ascended. Today they watch over us.

"Although we may not be conscious of the constant presence of angels in our lives, we may know of a surety that we are always under their loving watchcare." [22]

THE MAID-SERVANT OF THE LORD

Then the angel said to her, "Do not be afraid, Mary, for you have found favor with God." Luke 1:30.

Once again Gabriel appeared with a message, this time to a young girl engaged to a previously married man of the same village. Her betrothed was a carpenter named Joseph, a direct descendant of King David and thus of the house of Judah. We know little of Joseph except that he was poor (Luke 2:24) and had at least four sons by the previous marriage (Matt. 12:46; 13:55).

The sudden appearance of an angel to Mary and, more important, what he had to say, were a high honor; yet she was engaged to Joseph. Why had God chosen her and how would it affect her future? She knew Scripture and quickly reviewed the Messianic prophecy. It must have been familiar to her, especially since the promised Messiah was to arise from her own tribe. Her prayers and those of a nation were about to be fulfilled.

Mary belonged to the house of David, and through her Jesus would be the literal "seed of David" (Rom. 1:3). Whereas Elizabeth and Zacharias were of priestly descent, Mary and Joseph could both trace royal descent. The angel's words mystified Mary: "The Holy Spirit will come upon you, and the power of the Highest will overshadow you; therefore, also, that Holy One who is to be born will be called the Son of God" (Luke 1:35). The birth of Christ would link deity with humanity. The ambassador of God, the Holy Spirit, would be the agency through which God exercised His power to fulfill the Messianic prophecy.

Mary's reaction differed from Zacharias's, for he questioned whether God could cause Elizabeth to conceive at her advanced age. Mary, in simple faith, did not doubt. She knew that "with God nothing will be impossible" (verse 37). As soon as she understood what God's will in the matter was, and she had gained sufficient information on how to carry out her part in the plan, Mary submitted to her part.

"God first let Mary become fully conscious of the fact that the anticipated event was beyond human power, that it was impossible from man's point of view, before presenting to her the means by which it would be brought about. It is thus that God leads us to appreciate His goodness and His power and teaches us to have confidence in Him and in His promises." [23]

"HIS NAME IS JOHN"

And they made signs to his father, how he would have him called. And he asked for a writing table, and wrote, saying, His name is John. Luke 1:62, 63, KJV.

The angel Gabriel came to Mary with the announcement of Jesus' birth when Elizabeth was in her sixth month of pregnancy. Mary immediately left Nazareth to visit her relation. Zacharias and Elizabeth probably lived in the city of Hebron. The girl remained with Elizabeth for three months (Luke 1:56), quite possibly staying until her aunt delivered John. But Mary did not visit Elizabeth to prove what the angel said regarding the future birth of Jesus or to confirm the angel's message about Elizabeth's pregnancy. She went because she believed his words. As soon as she arrived, Mary was confirmed in her faith, for she found Elizabeth pregnant. What wonderful stories and hopes the two devout women must have shared as they prepared for the births of their respective sons. Christian fellowship is one of the greatest gifts found in life. "No Christian should ever be too busy to fellowship with those who may be in need of help he is in a position to give." [24]

When Elizabeth gave birth, her neighbors and relatives rejoiced with her. Middle Eastern culture considered childlessness as a curse, and Elizabeth's had been broken. Zacharias still could not speak. On the eighth day the parents took their boy to be circumcised. The ceremony was important, for it symbolized entrance into a covenant relationship with God. At the time of the rite the child would receive a name. Usually it perpetuated the family name and was especially important with the firstborn son, for it showed continuity and respect for previous generations.

Many of those present at the ceremony were undoubtedly fellow priests with their families. Perhaps a close friend performed the priestly function of the day. The friends sought to honor Zacharias by naming his son for him, but Elizabeth said, "No, he shall be called John." Her statement amazed them, for it was not the usual custom. They questioned Zacharias to know what name he wanted. He called for a writing tablet and wrote "His name is John." Then, after nine months of contemplative silence, Zacharias suddenly could speak. His first words were ones of praise to God.

Fitting that his last words of doubt have been changed to praise! "With every other voice hushed, and waiting in quietness and humility before God, Zacharias found that 'the silence of the soul' had made 'more distinct the voice of God.'" [25]

A "Just" Man

And she will bring forth a Son, and you shall call His name Jesus. Matt. 1:21.

Matthew omits much of the human side of the birth of Christ, concentrating rather on the fulfillment of Old Testament prophecies. Luke, however, traces the birth and childhood of Jesus in great detail. Some believe Luke learned the events of Jesus' infancy from Mary herself. His narrative certainly takes a mother's view, while Matthew takes Joseph's.

Mary returned to Nazareth following her three-month visit with Elizabeth. Though still bound by solemn covenant to wed Joseph, she was pregnant. Joseph had no idea Mary was the recipient of a miracle. He therefore decided to "put her away secretly." We know little about Joseph, but the Bible calls him a "just" man. In other words, he strictly observed the laws of Moses and the traditions of his people. Joseph wondered whether he could be "righteous" and yet marry a supposed adulterer. To divorce, Joseph had only to state that the bride "does not please." A man could do it for any reason. But Joseph did not want to embarrass Mary by going public with what would soon be obvious to everyone in Nazareth. Many might think that she was carrying his child, conceived before the formal marriage. The situation presented a tough moral and ethical dilemma for a "just" man. What should he do? After all, the baby was not his. Then God revealed His will in a dream. The angel calmed Joseph's fears and told him he must in faith take Mary as his wife, for she would "bring forth a son."

The angel had told Zacharias that *his* wife would bear *him* a son, but Gabriel explained to Joseph only that Mary would have a son. Joseph would be that son's earthly father, but Jesus would be born the Son of God, not the son of Joseph. Now Joseph must name the child Jesus on the eighth day according to custom. "Great significance was attached to the names given by Hebrew parents to their children. Often these stood for traits of character that the parent desired to see developed in the child."[26] God's chosen name for His Son is significant: "Jehovah is salvation!" Joseph acts in faith. "The role of Joseph was humble yet indispensable, and his prompt compliance with the angel's instructions made a great deal of difference, both to Mary and to public opinion."[27]

What must have been his qualities, this earthly father God chose for His Own Son? We may learn much from that quiet, obedient servant of the Lord.

LEGS OF IRON

And it came to pass in those days that a decree went out from Caesar Augustus that all the world should be registered. Luke 2:1.

His rivals assassinated Julius Caesar because many felt he wanted to be a king. Most Romans hoped that Consul Mark Antony would reorganize the nation into a more democratic government, but Octavian, the 18-year-old grand-nephew of Caesar, showed up in Rome to claim his position as adopted heir. In 43 B.C. a triumvirate comprising Antony, Octavian, and Lepidus divided the empire among themselves. During this alliance Herod, governor of Coele-Syria and fleeing an uprising in Palestine, arrived in Rome. After he found favor with Antony and then Octavian, the Roman Senate, in 40 B.C., unanimously voted Herod the kingship of Judea. "Although Herod had the help of Roman arms, it took him three years to gain possession of his throne. . . . Herod was now (37 B.C.) 'master of a city in ruins and king of a nation that hated him.'"[28]

Antony forgot his duties when Cleopatra VII, queen of Egypt, planted in his head the dream of kingship. In 32 B.C. Octavian declared war against Antony, defeating his naval forces off the coast of Actium in western Greece. Antony and Cleopatra fled to Egypt where both committed suicide. By 30 B.C. Egypt, the last great Greek monarchy to rise out of Alexander the Great's empire, became only a Roman province. Daniel's interpretation of Nebuchadnezzar's dream of the image was complete (Dan. 2:40). The legs of Roman iron now ruled the civilized world. Octavian took care not to repeat his granduncle's mistake. He had the Senate vote him the new title Augustus ("majestic") and he ruled as "first citizen." "Augustus was a wise and moderate ruler who brought peace and prosperity to his vast empire. It was during a census decreed by him that the New Testament era was ushered in at Bethlehem."[29]

Palestine was a thorn in the side of Imperial Rome. The Senate punished high-ranking officials by posting them to the frontier—especially Palestine. The Jews bitterly resisted the census, for it meant registration of property as well as of names and formed the basis for assessment of hated property taxes. "As in old time Cyrus was called to the throne of the world's empire that he might set free the captives of the Lord, so Caesar Augustus is made the agent for the fulfillment of God's purpose in bringing the mother of Jesus to Bethlehem."[30]

Prophecy is fulfilled as nations and rulers rise and fall. God still guides human affairs and nations to His ends.

CITY OF DAVID

But you, Bethlehem Ephrathah, though you are little among the thousands of Judah, yet out of you shall come forth to Me the One to be Ruler in Israel.

Micah 5:2.

Bethlehem Ephrathah lies about five miles south of Jerusalem in Judea. Scripture calls it Ephrathah to distinguish it from Bethlehem in Zebulun. Micah leaves no doubt as to which town his prophecy refers to by telling us that it is "Ephrathah" and "little among the thousands of Judah." Bethlehem figures repeatedly in the Bible, which first mentions it as the place to where Jacob was traveling when Rachel died giving birth to Benjamin (Gen. 35:16-20). Boaz came from Bethlehem, where Ruth gleaned in the wheat and barley fields (Ruth 2). Perhaps the name Bethlehem, meaning "house of bread," had its origin in the fields of wheat surrounding the town.

It is easy to imagine the grazing herds of sheep covering the surrounding hillsides. Here David watched his father's flocks. "Now David was the son of that Ephrathite of Bethlehem Judah, whose name was Jesse, and who had eight sons" (1 Sam. 17:12). The three sons of Zeruiah—Joab, Abishai, and Asahel—came from David's hometown and supported him in his bid to be king of Judah. When Abner, the commander of Saul's army, killed Joab's brother Asahel, Joab took his younger brother home to Bethlehem to be buried (2 Sam. 2:12-32).

Later the Philistines took and garrisoned Bethlehem. David longed for a drink from the well of his hometown. "So the three mighty men broke through the camp of the Philistines, drew water from the well of Bethlehem that was by the gate, and took it and brought it to David. Nevertheless he would not drink it, but poured it out to the Lord" (2 Sam. 23:16). Small wonder that Scripture referred to Bethlehem as the "city of David." It certainly had a rich history.

"But in the city of their royal line, Joseph and Mary are unrecognized and unhonored. Weary and homeless, they traverse the entire length of the narrow street, from the gate of the city to the eastern extremity of the town, vainly seeking a resting place for the night. There is no room for them at the crowded inn. In a rude building where the beasts are sheltered, they at last find refuge, and here the Redeemer of the world is born."[31]

Bethlehem—city of David, city of the heavenly King!

HER FIRSTBORN SON

And she brought forth her firstborn Son, and wrapped Him in swaddling cloths, and laid Him in a manger, because there was no room for them in the inn. Luke 2:7.

The trip from Nazareth to Bethlehem was no doubt a difficult one for a woman in her ninth month of pregnancy. Roads in Palestine were rarely level, and terrain was rough. Arriving in Bethlehem, Mary and Joseph had no relatives to stay with. To turn away a fellow of one's own tribe without first offering food and lodging was a grave breach of etiquette, but the homes and the inn were full. Descendants of Judah, Benjamin, and Levi packed the town.

Tradition states the Nativity took place in a cave in the vicinity of Bethlehem, but Ellen White mentions "a rude building where the beasts are sheltered." "Hebrew children, at birth, were washed in water, rubbed in salt, and wrapped in 'swaddling clothes.' . . . These were strips of cloth wound loosely about the body and limbs of the infant. According to the usual custom, the baby was laid diagonally on a square piece of cloth, two corners being folded over its body, one over its feet, and the other underneath its head. This was held in place by bands loosely wound around the outside."[32] The Child of God had no nursery, no crib, no rocker, no place of honor in the home. The Son of God laid His head in a manger filled with straw for oxen and donkeys.

Roman law did not require Mary to appear in Bethlehem. Knowing her time was near and aware of the prophecy regarding Bethlehem as the birthplace of the Messiah, perhaps she chose to accompany Joseph. Whatever the reason, the King of kings descended from the courts of heaven and the throne room of God to a rustic building where beasts took shelter on a darkened, sin-filled earth. "In contemplating the incarnation of Christ in humanity, we stand baffled before an unfathomable mystery, that the human mind cannot comprehend. The more we reflect upon it, the more amazing does it appear. How wide is the contrast between the divinity of Christ and the helpless infant in Bethlehem's manger! How can we span the distance between the mighty God and a helpless child? . . . Looking upon Christ in humanity, we look upon God, and see in Him the brightness of His glory, the express image of His person."[33]

Praise God! The Bright and Morning Star is born!

THOSE WHO DID HUNGER AND THIRST

Then the angel said to them, "Do not be afraid, for behold, I bring you good tidings of great joy which will be to all people." Luke 2:10.

Heaven dispatches an angel to the earth to see who is ready to welcome Jesus. Priests continue their rituals, Pharisees make loud demonstrations of piety in prayer, and kings go about governing the people. In Palestine's religious schools the rabbis continue to teach the same prophecies with no thought to their impending fulfillment. The angel returns disappointed. "All the people should have been watching and waiting that they might be among the first to welcome the world's Redeemer. But, lo, at Bethlehem two weary travelers from the hills of Nazareth traverse the whole length of the narrow street to the eastern extremity of the town, vainly seeking a place of rest and shelter for the night. No doors are open to receive them. In a wretched hovel prepared for cattle, they at last find refuge, and there the Saviour of the world is born."[34]

A small but faithful number were watching and waiting for the coming Messiah. Shepherds living in the fields day and night during grazing season prayed for the King that would occupy David's throne. Winter in Judea is cold and wet in the mountains, and shepherds would not live with their sheep during the period of heavy winter rain. Late spring to autumn best seems to fit the time when these devout but simple men would gather under the stars to discuss the coming of their future King.

The fields where the boy David had watched his father's flocks would now witness the greatest news ever given to humanity. As they talked quietly in the silence of the darkness while gazing up into the starry sky, suddenly the veil between the invisible world and ours parted and they saw an angel. We often fail to realize that the message the shepherds received is "good tidings" for us as well. It speaks of God's redeeming love for fallen humanity. The gospel story is good news! And it is "to those who eagerly wait for Him" that Christ will "appear a second time, apart from sin, for salvation" (Heb. 9:28).

Like the shepherds, all who find Christ will spread their great joy to others (Luke 2:17).

THE CHOSEN AND THE PROPHECIES

For unto us a Child is born, unto us a Son is given; and the government will be upon His shoulder. And His name will be called Wonderful, Counselor, Mighty God, Everlasting Father, Prince of Peace. Isa. 9:6.

Adam and Eve first received the promise of a Redeemer. "And I will put enmity between you and the woman, and between your seed and her Seed; He shall bruise your head, and you shall bruise His heel" (Gen. 3:15). God would break Satan's power. Abraham had a revelation of the coming Messiah. "Your father Abraham rejoiced to see My day, and he saw it and was glad," Jesus said (John 8:56). As Jacob lay dying he called his sons to him and spoke to Judah. "Judah, you are he whom your brothers shall praise.... The scepter shall not depart from Judah, nor a lawgiver from between his feet, until Shiloh comes; and to Him shall be the obedience of the people" (Gen. 49:8-10).

Moses declared: "The Lord your God will raise up for you a Prophet like me from your midst, from your brethren. Him you shall hear" (Deut. 18:15). When called to curse Israel, Balaam spoke of the Redeemer: "I see Him, but not now; I behold Him, but not near; a Star shall come out of Jacob; a Scepter shall rise out of Israel" (Num. 24:17). David foresaw the arrival of Christ as "the light of the morning, when the sun rises, a morning without clouds" (2 Sam. 23:4). Hosea added that "His going forth is established as the morning" (Hosea 6:3). As dawn pushes back darkness so Malachi told them that "the Sun of Righteousness shall arise with healing in His wings" (Mal. 4:2).

The Jews had studied the prophecies but without spiritual insight. By paying attention to the minutiae of the law, they thought to build a reputation of godliness, and in boastful pride they waited for the time when their nation would prevail. Matthew wrote to convince those same Jews that the Man they had crucified had already fulfilled the prophecies in His life. They failed to interpret correctly the prophecies pointing to the Messiah's humiliation and death at His first advent because they chose to focus on the glory accompanying His second advent. Danger exists in any interpretation of the Bible that serves self-interest.

"Oh, what a lesson is this wonderful story of Bethlehem! . . . How it warns us to beware, lest by our criminal indifference we also fail to discern the signs of the times, and therefore know not the day of our visitation." [35]

BORN UNDER THE LAW

Now when the days of her purification according to the law of Moses were completed, they brought Him to Jerusalem to present Him to the Lord. Luke 2:22.

At 8 days of age Jesus underwent circumcision in obedience to the covenant law. Born "under the law" (Gal. 4:4), now He must be dedicated to the Lord as "firstborn." Jews redeemed or bought back the first male child for the fee of five shekels, approximately five days' wages. The code of Levi stipulated that a mother's "uncleanness" for a male child was to last 40 days, then she should appear at the Temple to be "purified" and the child "presented." Had Joseph and Mary been wealthy, they would have brought a lamb for an offering. Instead, they had only two turtledoves, one for the burnt and the other for the sin offering. "As man's substitute, Christ must conform to the law in every particular."[36]

Entering the Temple with their meager offering, dressed in humble peasant clothing, the couple handed their Infant to the priest. The priest held the Baby before the altar, returned Him to His mother, and asked the Child's name for the roll of firstborn. The first of Joseph's duties as legal father was to name the Child. "The priest went through the ceremony of his official work. . . . Little did he think, as the babe lay in his arms, that it was the Majesty of heaven, the King of glory. . . . He did not think that this babe was He whose glory Moses had asked to see. But One greater than Moses lay in the priest's arms; and when he enrolled the child's name, he was enrolling the name of One who was the foundation of the whole Jewish economy. . . . This was Shiloh, the peace giver. It was He who declared Himself to Moses as the I AM. . . . This was He whom seers had long foretold. He was the Desire of all nations, the Root and the Offspring of David, and the Bright and Morning Star."[37]

The Child for whom the couple paid this ransom money would one day pay the ransom for all sinners. The priest failed to recognize the Saviour of the world. He only saw two poor Galileans blessed with a son to help them earn their daily bread. As he unwittingly dedicated God's Son to His great work for humanity, the event passed almost unrecognized.

It is our privilege today to look for "the blessed hope and glorious appearing of our great God and Savior Jesus Christ" (Titus 2:13).

"My Eyes Have Seen Your Salvation"

Lord, now You are letting Your servant depart in peace, according to Your word; for my eyes have seen Your salvation. Luke 2:29, 30.

Simeon, a just and devout man living in Jerusalem, had been faithfully looking for the Messiah. His constant study of the Scriptures had convinced him that he would see the prophecies confirmed in his lifetime. Unlike the priest whose eyes did not behold the Desire of nations, even when he held Him in his hands, Simeon had lived by the principles found in Scripture. It was therefore not luck that drew Simeon to the Temple on the day Joseph and Mary presented Jesus. The Spirit led him there at just the right moment. Advancing toward the little scene, he felt deeply impressed that the Child was special. "To the astonished priest, Simeon appears like a man enraptured. The child has been returned to Mary, and he takes it in his arms and presents it to God, while a joy that he has never before felt enters his soul." [38]

Mary and Joseph were both aware of the divinity of their child, but it nonetheless startled them that a complete stranger should recognize the secret they kept. Simeon described Jesus as a light to the Gentiles and the glory of Israel, words echoing the message to the shepherds. His birth was a joy to *all* peoples. Simeon seemed to ignore Joseph and spoke only to Mary. "Behold, this Child is destined for the fall and rising of many in Israel, and for a sign which will be spoken against (yes, a sword will pierce through your own soul also), that the thoughts of many hearts may be revealed" (Luke 2:34, 35). It is Mary's first inkling of Calvary. The shadow of a cross lies ahead for the Child's mother.

Anna, a prophet who faithfully attended services morning and evening, heard Simeon's pronouncement. Her heart touched, she too came forward to praise God. "These humble worshipers had not studied the prophecies in vain. But those who held positions as rulers and priests in Israel, though they too had before them the precious utterances of prophecy, were not walking in the way of the Lord, and their eyes were not open to behold the Light of life." [39]

If our eyes would be opened during the last days, we must, like Anna and Simeon, walk in the way of the Lord.

A STAR OUT OF JACOB

When they saw the star, they rejoiced with exceedingly great joy. Matt. 2:10.

The Messianic story had spread with the Jews to the farthest parts of the civilized world. On the night of the Nativity a strange and mysterious light appeared in the western sky. It persisted even though no astrologer had charted it before. Impressed, Eastern Magi studied their scrolls to find the symbol's meaning. Perhaps they read Numbers 24:17: "A Star shall come out of Jacob." A dream instructed them to search for the Messiah. "Like Abraham, they knew not at first where they were to go, but followed as the guiding star led them on their way."[40]

The people of the Mediterranean regarded the East in those days to be Syria, Arabia, and Mesopotamia. To reach Jerusalem would have taken more than a month of walking or several weeks if they rode. The time was probably longer, as they could travel only by night, when the star was visible. "That star was a distant company of shining angels, but of this the wise men were ignorant."[41] The Magi arrived in Jerusalem near the time of Christ's Temple dedication. Cresting the Mount of Olives they gazed down at Jerusalem. Surely here they would find someone who could tell them of the Messiah and His star. God had directed them to Jerusalem rather than Bethlehem to call attention to Christ's birth among Jewish leaders. Their visit did arouse interest, but it offended the Jewish leaders that Gentiles should know about it first.

Herod sensed another plot against him. His ancestry was Idumean but this new Prince belonged to the Davidic line. Calling his chief priests and scribes or "keepers of the law," Herod asked them about the Messianic prophecy. At first they hesitated, but when he threatened, they dug deeper into Scripture. "So they said to him, 'In Bethlehem of Judea, for thus it is written by the prophet: "But you, Bethlehem, in the land of Judah, are not the least among the rulers of Judah; for out of you shall come a Ruler who will shepherd My people Israel"'" (Matt. 2:5, 6). The priests and rulers might have sought and found the birthplace themselves, or did they treat the shepherd's story as below their dignity to investigate? Rich Gentiles and shepherds with stories were not enough to get them to go five miles to Bethlehem! "Here began the rejection of Christ by the priests and rabbis."[42]

It requires effort on the part of God's people to search for Him. But we can find Him, for He is not far from any of us.

Herod the Not So Great

When Herod the king heard this, he was troubled, and all Jerusalem with him. Matt. 2:3.

Herod was first and foremost a politician. It took fine perception and skill to survive when the political situation in Rome had been as twisted and changing as the Jordan River. He could also be brutal, as when he cornered the last who fought his rule in the Temple. They held out for three months before he slaughtered them with the help of Roman arms. The life of anyone he felt posed a threat to his throne was forfeit. Gradually he came to trust no one, and was constantly on the lookout for family plots. Mere suggestions were enough to cause him to murder his closest relatives and best friends. His own two sons (Aristobulus and Alexander), educated in Rome, returned to find that another son (Antipater) had conspired against them. They and 300 who sympathized with them died from stoning.

The arrival of the Wise Men threw Jerusalem into a frenzy of excitement. Herod heard the news as well. Anyone who boldly came into the city stating he was looking for the King of the Jews after seeing His star in the east and now wanted to worship Him would have gotten Herod's immediate attention. "The advent of Christ was the greatest event which had taken place since the creation of the world. The birth of Christ, which gave joy to the angels of heaven, was not welcome to the kingly powers of the world. Suspicion and envy were aroused in King Herod, and his wicked heart was planning his dark purposes for the future."[43]

The indifference of the priests to divulge information regarding the Messiah seemed proof of a plot. "It is little wonder the whole city was 'troubled' also, because its residents were too familiar with the atrocities of which Herod was capable. Fearing a popular tumult, he might well decree the slaughter of hundreds or thousands of the people."[44] "This was the reception the Saviour met as He came to a fallen world."[45]

The misinterpretation of the Messianic prophecies by priests and scribes now placed the infant Jesus in danger. The common belief proclaimed a temporal Messiah who would reign in power and glory over the entire world. Satan encouraged this misinterpretation. Herod determined to kill Christ as soon as he found Him.

Today misrepresentation of Scripture is still as dangerous to our spiritual survival as it was to Christ's physical security.

DREAMS

Then, being divinely warned in a dream that they should not return to Herod, they departed for their own country another way. Matt. 2:12.

Herod met with the Magi privately to enlist their aid in finding the Child. Unaware of the atrocities Herod inflicted upon any threat to his throne, the unsuspecting foreigners agreed to help. Leaving Jerusalem at dusk, they were overjoyed to see the star again. Five miles distant lay Bethlehem and the object of their search. No fanfare marked the location, and no guards protected the newborn King. Instead they discovered Him in a humble house. Unpacking their gifts, they entered and fell upon their faces in respect and reverence. A visit to a high official or prince required a gift of homage. Thus they bestowed three expensive gifts on Jesus: frankincense, myrrh, and gold. Frankincense smelled sweet when burned for sacred incense. The ancients used myrrh in holy oil, perfume, and for embalming bodies.

Joseph received a dream warning him to flee to Egypt with the Child and Mary. Egypt was now a Roman province and beyond Herod's reach. The Egyptian border was the Wadi-el-Arish, 100 miles southwest of Bethlehem. Joseph made haste. "And through the gifts of the magi from a heathen country, the Lord supplied the means for the journey into Egypt and the sojourn in a land of strangers." [46]

The Wise Men intended to report their success, but a dream told them to avoid Herod, so they headed homeward by another route. Herod, however, impatiently awaited their return. As the days passed he began to suspect they weren't coming. Possibly his reluctant priests had warned them away. There must be a plot, since the Magi had outwitted him. Subtlety had failed, but cruel force remained. The king dispatched hardened soldiers to Bethlehem to slay every male child below 2 years of age. The culture considered a child 1 year old at birth, so these infants had not yet reached their first birthday. "Such was the Saviour's reception when He came to the earth. There seemed to be no place of rest or safety for the infant Redeemer. God could not trust His beloved Son with men, even while carrying forward His work for their salvation. He commissioned angels to attend Jesus and protect Him till He should accomplish His mission on earth, and die by the hands of those whom He came to save." [47]

We must never forget that from cradle to cross the Father was also an active participant in our salvation.

HOME-COMING

Arise, take the young Child and His mother, and go to the land of Israel, for those who sought the young Child's life are dead. Matt. 2:20.

The killing of Bethlehem's infants capped the long and bloody reign of Herod. When he died about 4 B.C. his will divided his kingdom among his remaining sons. Archelaus, the oldest, received Judea, Samaria, and Idumaea, becoming an "ethnarch" or "ruler of the people." Herod Antipas became "tetrarch" of Galilee and Perea or "ruler of a fourth part of a province." Philip, also a "tetrarch," ruled the six northeastern districts. A Jewish deputation to Augustus pleaded with him to place Palestine directly under a Roman governor rather than have the nation submit to rule by Herod's sons. That independence-minded Jewish leaders were willing to go to such lengths to avoid life under the rule of Herod's offspring speaks volumes. Unfortunately, Augustus upheld Herod's will.

Archelaus was a tyrant and every bit as brutal as his father. In A.D. 6 Augustus banished him to Gaul and placed Judea and Samaria under a Roman procurator (Pontius Pilate became procurator about A.D. 26). Antipas ruled well, for he was cunning. Jesus referred to him as "that fox" for his ability to avoid pitfalls and intrigue. The son was in great favor with Tiberias, who succeeded Augustus as emperor in A.D. 14. To honor the emperor, Antipas built a city named Tiberias on the western shore of the Sea of Galilee and tried to rename the sea itself as the "Sea of Tiberias." Philip became the best ruler. His marriage to Salome, daughter of Herodias, cemented ties with his brother Antipas in Galilee. Philip built his capital city near one of the sources of the Jordan and called it Caesarea in honor of the emperor. A town by that name already existed on the Mediterranean, so Philip's town became known as Caesarea Philippi.

During this political turmoil Joseph received his third recorded dream. It told him he was free to return home. "Regarding Jesus as the heir of David's throne, Joseph desired to make his home in Bethlehem; but learning that Archelaus reigned in Judea in his father's stead, he feared that the father's designs against Christ might be carried out by the son."[48] Joseph chose instead to go to his hometown of Nazareth in Galilee, then governed by Herod Antipas. His return fulfilled the prophecy: "When Israel was a child, I loved him, and out of Egypt I called My son" (Hosea 11:1).

Tracing each Old Testament prophecy and noting the exact way each met its fulfillment reaffirms the Christian's trust in God's Word.

A NAZARENE

And he came and dwelt in a city called Nazareth, that it might be fulfilled which was spoken by the prophets, "He shall be called a Nazarene." Matt. 2:23.

High in the Galilean hills, just north of Samaria and several days' travel north of Jerusalem, sits the small mountain village of Nazareth roughly halfway between the southern tip of the Sea of Galilee to the east and the Mediterranean to the west. It probably occupied the western slope of a small depression one mile across and opening southward by a narrow, winding, steep ravine down to the Esdraelon plain. To the north rose the mountains of Lebanon and snow-capped Mount Hermon.

Nazareth was so small it was not even among the 200 towns listed by the historian Josephus. At the time of Christ Galilee was a rural province containing a mixture of Jew and Gentile. Many looked upon it as "backward" and generally considered it to be "less sophisticated" than Judea. Even among Galileans, Nazareth had a reputation for wickedness. Nathaniel merely voiced the commonly held low opinion of Nazarenes when he asked, "Can anything good come out of Nazareth?" This was the area to which Jesus and His parents arrived after leaving Egypt. "How great must be the humiliation of the Son of God, that He should live in the despised and wicked town of Nazareth. The most holy place upon earth would have been greatly honored by the presence of the world's Redeemer a single year. The palaces of kings would have been exalted to receive Christ as a guest. But the Redeemer of the world passed by the courts of royalty and made His home in a humble mountain village, for 30 years, thus conferring distinction upon despised Nazareth."[49]

We know little of Christ's childhood. Surrounded by nature and trained by His mother, He passed His early life continually exposed to temptations. He had to remain constantly on guard in order to remain pure and spotless amid so much sin and wickedness. "Christ did not select this place Himself. His Heavenly Father chose this place for Him, where His character would be tested and tried in a variety of ways. The early life of Christ was subjected to severe trials, hardships, and conflicts, that He might develop the perfect character which makes Him a perfect example for children, youth, and manhood."[50]

Dedication to God and devotion to duty make any place honorable.

THE SUNLIGHT OF HIS FATHER'S COUNTENANCE

And the Child grew and became strong in spirit, filled with wisdom; and the grace of God was upon Him.
Luke 2:40.

"I n the days of Christ the town or city that did not provide for the religious instruction of the young was regarded as under the curse of God. Yet the teaching had become formal."[51] Jesus did not receive His education in the synagogue. Useful work, the study of nature, searching the Scriptures, and the everyday experiences of life in a small town served as God's lesson books, developing His active and penetrating mind. He presented a wisdom and thoughtfulness that went beyond His contemporaries.

The scribes and elders felt that they should easily be able to sway a child so gentle and meek to their interpretations. Yet the more they tried to mold Him, the more they realized His understanding was superior to theirs. "Failing to convince Him, they sought Joseph and Mary, and set before them His course of noncompliance. Thus He suffered rebuke and censure."[52] On occasion Mary would plead with Him to conform to their teachings, but nothing could cause Him to swerve from principle, and because of it the rabbis made His life exceedingly bitter. "Even in His youth He had to learn the hard lesson of silence and patient endurance."[53]

"The life of Christ was marked with respect and love for His mother."[54] He loved His brothers, but they looked down on Him; and they were not alone. "There were those who tried to cast contempt upon Him because of His birth, and even in His childhood He had to meet their scornful looks and evil whisperings. If He had responded by an impatient word or look, if He had conceded to His brothers by even one wrong act, He would have failed of being a perfect example."[55] Failure to join in forbidden plans caused His friends to label Him narrow and straitlaced. But He bore each insult patiently. Although He avoided controversy, His sterling example was a constant rebuke to those around Him who chose to sin. "The perfect character development of Jesus from infancy to manhood, without sin, is, perhaps, the most amazing fact of His entire life. It staggers the imagination."[56]

"Satan was unwearied in his efforts to overcome the Child of Nazareth. From His earliest years Jesus was guarded by heavenly angels, yet His life was one long struggle against the powers of darkness. . . . [Satan] left no means untried to snare Jesus."[57]

"No child of humanity will ever be called to live a holy life amid so fierce a conflict with temptation as was our Saviour."[58]

28

AFTER THE CUSTOM

And when He was twelve years old, they went up to Jerusalem according to the custom of the feast. Luke 2:42.

The twelfth year separated a Jewish boy from childhood. At 13 (the end of the twelfth year), Hebrew youth become personally responsible for observing the commandments. During Christ's time all the men of Israel had to appear before the Lord at Jerusalem during the annual feasts of Passover, Pentecost, and Tabernacles. Devout Jews flocked to the Temple from every part of the land, and the high point of the religious year was always Passover. They might miss other feasts but usually attended Passover.

Although Nazareth was only 64 miles north of Jerusalem, Samaria lay between it and the pilgrim's destination. "In the time of Christ, Jews traveling between Galilee and Judea avoided, if possible, the more direct route through Samaria, because of hostility between Jews and Samaritans."[59] To do that required taking a detour through the Jordan valley. Most walked down steep gorges to the river and then back up steep trails to Jerusalem, an ascent of more than 3,000 feet.

Passover time occurred late March or early April. The weather was temperate and the land wore the bloom of spring. Pilgrims traveled together for safety and companionship, and often a caravan consisted of inhabitants from a single town. Neighbors planned the excursion for weeks. Once worshipers arrived in Jerusalem, they told and retold stories of the deliverance from Egypt. The priests slew the Passover lamb on the fourteenth day, and the people ate it after sunset on the fifteenth. The fifteenth day corresponded with the first day of the seven-day Feast of Unleavened Bread. On the sixteenth day the priest presented the wave sheaf before the Lord. Both the fifteenth and twenty-first days were celebrated as Sabbaths regardless of the day of the week on which they fell. The fourteenth to the sixteenth days were considered most important. Following the sixteenth day, those who absolutely had to return home might do so.

"All the ceremonies of the feast were types of the work of Christ. The deliverance of Israel from Egypt was an object lesson of redemption, which the Passover was intended to keep in memory. The slain lamb, the unleavened bread, the sheaf of first fruits, represented the Saviour. With most of the people in the days of Christ, the observance of this feast had degenerated into formalism. But what was its significance to the Son of God!"[60]

Has your religious experience become mere formalism? Pray that God might open your eyes that you might gain a deeper understanding and richer experience in the things of God.

"MY FATHER'S BUSINESS"

Now so it was that after three days they found Him in the temple, sitting in the midst of the teachers, both listening to them and asking them questions. Luke 2:46.

Joseph and Mary completed the required Passover attendance and started home. Neither had the slightest reason to doubt that Jesus was in their homeward bound group. Villagers watched each others' children during such trips. "Jesus had never given His parents a valid reason for anxiety. They presumed that He was acquainted with their plans to return with 'the company,' and that He knew the proposed time for departure."[61] Day after day as the priests performed the Passover services, Jesus saw how their meanings applied to Him, and the mystery of His mission became clear. Realizing that He was the Son of God, He lingered in the Temple to gather deeper understandings of His mission and to commune with God in solitude.

During this period of meditation He was drawn to one of the roofed porches of the Temple mount. Here the rabbis seated their pupils on the ground while they taught from Scripture. Asking and answering their questions led to a discussion of the selected passage. Jesus joined them and listened. He questioned them pointedly, wishing to know their interpretation of the prophecies that foretold the advent of the Messiah. It soon became evident to the older men that He was a gifted student. His insightful answers to their challenging questions amazed them. Jesus' grasp of Scripture was broad, His depth of understanding profound. He explained Scripture with freshness and insight. Immediately they saw in Him a future great teacher in Israel. Each wanted to tutor Him, to mold His mind.

Mary and Joseph finally missed their son as the caravan stopped to rest. Remembering Herod's attempt to kill Him, fear gripped their hearts. How could they have been so negligent? Quickly they retraced their steps to Jerusalem. The next day they heard a familiar voice, and finding Him in the rabbinical school, His mother scolded Him for causing her to worry. His answer showed that He understood for the first time His special relationship to God. "'How is it that ye sought Me? . . . Wist ye not that I must be about my Father's business?' And as they seemed not to understand His words, He pointed upward. On His face was a light at which they wondered. Divinity was flashing through humanity."[62]

He did not deserve censure, for He had not left them, but they had left without Him. He never leaves us, either. Instead, we choose to desert Him.

SON OF A CARPENTER

Then He went down with them and came to Nazareth, and was subject to them. Luke 2:51.

In the Temple Mary realized Jesus had in mind His relationship with His heavenly Father and not Joseph. "These words Mary had pondered in her heart; yet while she believed that her child was to be Israel's Messiah, she did not comprehend His mission."[63] As Jesus had been lost to her for three days, He would again be lost to her when offered up for the sins of the world. Although His mission was now clear, Jesus was ever faithful to His parents. Returning with Joseph and Mary to their home, for 18 years He kept the mystery of His mission in His heart. Each morning found Him in meditation, searching the Scriptures and praying.

Jesus became known as the "carpenter's son" (Matt. 13:55). "He was doing God's service just as much when laboring at the carpenter's bench as when working miracles for the multitude."[64] His work was as perfect as His character. "Throughout His life on earth, Jesus was an earnest and constant worker. He expected much; therefore He attempted much."[65] Each job found Him laboring cheerfully and diligently. Often His family heard the sound of a psalm or a song coming from where He labored. "He worked at the carpenter's trade with His father Joseph, and every article He made was well made, the different parts fitting exactly, the whole able to bear test."[66] Joseph had died by the time Jesus responded to John the Baptist, for "in Nazareth it was told in the carpenter shop that *had been* Joseph's, and One recognized the call."[67]

Each day the King of glory walked the streets of the small town going to and from His work at the carpenter's shop. "Christ had been the Commander of the heavenly host; but He did not because of this excuse Himself from labor, allowing His parents to support Him. While still quite young, He learned a trade, and faithfully discharged His daily duties, contributing to the support of the family. Christ was the light and joy of the family."[68] Angels marveled that Jesus should stoop to take human form and assume a life of obscurity and toil.

Christians should expect much, attempt much, and accomplish much, for in following His example we may draw strength for our daily labors.

Growing in Favor

And Jesus increased in wisdom and stature, and in favor with God and men. Luke 2:52.

The first 30 years of His life Jesus spent in a little mountain village preparing for His brief three-and-one-half-year ministry. During that time He performed no miracle, gave no sermon, and healed no illness. "The life of Christ had been so secluded at Nazareth that the world did not know Him as the Son of God—their Redeemer. He was regarded as nothing more than the son of Joseph and Mary. His life in childhood and youth was remarkable. His silence in regard to His exalted character and mission contains an instructive lesson to all youth."[69] Jesus' simple life developed His spiritual, mental, and physical powers. Early in the morning He would find a secluded spot in which to read the Scriptures, meditate, and pray. Surrounded by scenes of nature, He developed illustrations that would later become parables. "Every prophecy concerning His work and mediation was familiar to Him, especially those having reference to His humiliation, atonement, and intercession. In childhood and youth the object of His life was ever before Him, an inducement for His undertaking the work of mediating in behalf of fallen man."[70]

From His first understanding at age 12 of the mission He was to fulfill, until the moment He surrendered His spirit to His Father, the weight of responsibility for human salvation never lifted. Who can appreciate the burden He carried without complaint? His life was one of self-denial and sacrifice. Ever willing to serve, "He lived to bless others."[71] Always kind and considerate, He took the part of the downtrodden. When His brothers dealt harshly with someone, Jesus would seek that person out and encourage the individual. "To those who were in need He would give a cup of cold water, and would quietly place His own meal in their hands."[72]

It was a joy to be in Jesus' company. Ever patient, tactful, courteous, cheerful, sympathetic, and tender, He walked among the short-tempered, rude, discourteous, mean, unsympathetic, and cruel citizens of Nazareth. His unselfish religion brought the goodness of His Father to those who needed encouragement. "Jesus is our example. There are many who dwell with interest upon the period of His public ministry, while they pass unnoticed the teaching of His early years. But it is in His home life that He is the pattern for all children and youth."[73]

When we increase in the wisdom of the Lord, we will serve others as He did.

JESUS

EARLY MINISTRY
Christ Our Example

Autumn A.D. 27 to Spring A.D. 28

Matthew 3:1-4:11

Mark 1:2-13

Luke 3:1-4:13

John 1:19-2:12

The Desire of Ages, pp. 97-153

GREAT IN THE SIGHT OF THE LORD

So the child grew and became strong in spirit, and was in the deserts till the day of his manifestation to Israel.

Luke 1:80.

The Old Testament closes (Mal. 3:1; 4:5, 6) and the New Testament opens (Luke 1:16) on the theme of Israel turning to the Lord their God. Greed, lust, gluttony, and a diminished ability to discern spiritual things had reduced God's people from the exalted state He desired for them. They looked forward to a Messiah who would deliver Israel from Roman rule. John the Baptist read the same Scriptures and believed Israel would be a holy nation only when the people awakened from their slumber. They must have something in which to believe! The central purpose of John's ministry was to lay the framework for a belief in Jesus of Nazareth as the Messiah. Before the children of Israel could accept the gospel of Jesus they first had to recognize their need for salvation.

John's parents died during his childhood, and God called him to the Wilderness of Judea to fulfill His mission for his life. "He will be great in the sight of the Lord. . . . He will also be filled with the Holy Spirit. . . . And he will turn many of the children of Israel to the Lord their God" (Luke 1:15, 16). In the rugged, wild, unpopulated area between the Dead Sea and the highlands of southern Palestine he established his home. John listened for the voice of God in the stillness of the desert evening. The stars expanded his mind to God's limitless love. Surrounded by wild ravines, rocky cliffs, deep canyons, and dry barren hills, John the Baptist learned that silent meditation upon God's will was essential to focus one's affections upon eternal subjects. "When every other voice is hushed, and in quietness we wait before Him, the silence of the soul makes more distinct the voice of God."[74]

From birth John's mission lay before him. As a Nazarite he had vowed consecration to God. Satan sought to tempt him even in the solitude of the wilderness, but he resisted and with the help of the Holy Spirit could detect the approach of the evil one. Not a hermit, John often traveled to nearby towns to observe people so that he might better approach them with his message.

John's original message, delivered at Jesus' first advent, will again be proclaimed by every Christian just before His second coming: "Repent, for the kingdom of heaven is at hand!" (Matt. 3:2).

CHARACTER AND LIFE

John came baptizing in the wilderness and preaching a baptism of repentance for the remission of sins. Mark 1:4.

Judea was in turmoil. Rome had finally removed Herod the Great's tyrant son Archelaus and placed Judea directly under a Roman governor. The people now chafed under practices introduced by pagan governors. The Pharisees preached strict observance to the law while fanatical resistance fighters preached revolution. Then suddenly a new and different message came from the wilderness. Its presenter dressed as an ancient prophet and appeared at the river Jordan in the power of Elijah. His message of "Repent, for the kingdom of heaven is at hand" carried the people back to earlier prophets. Aroused, the nation flocked to the Jordan.

The Jordan River meanders 200 miles to cover 65 straight-line miles from the Sea of Galilee to the Dead Sea. Although only 30 yards wide and three to 10 feet deep, it can still be swift and treacherous in spots. It was the muddy river Naaman objected to bathing in when Elisha told him to do so to cure his body of leprosy (2 Kings 5:1-15). The same muddy watercourse, once miraculously parted for the conquest of Canaan, now again became the center of attention for God's people.

Multitudes flocked to hear John fearlessly call upon the nation to rid itself of sin and prepare for the Messiah. Many confessed their spiritual state and asked to be baptized. The baptism was only a symbol. Without true repentance it was a meaningless gesture. Yet many scribes, Sadducees, and Pharisees, in an attempt to curry favor with the coming Prince, sought baptism. John, seeing through their shallowness, rebuked them. "Brood of vipers! Who warned you to flee from the wrath to come? Therefore bear fruits worthy of repentance" (Matt. 3:7, 8). They did not help the needy, care for the widow, protect the helpless, feed the hungry, or reach out to the stranger. "John declared to the Jews that their standing before God was to be decided by their character and life. Profession was worthless. If their life and character were not in harmony with God's law, they were not His people."[75]

"God does not send messengers to flatter the sinner. He delivers no message of peace to lull the unsanctified into fatal security. He lays heavy burdens upon the conscience of the wrongdoer, and pierces the soul with arrows of conviction."[76]

THE VOICE OF ONE CRYING IN THE WILDERNESS

For this is he who was spoken of by the prophet Isaiah, saying: "The voice of one crying in the wilderness: 'Prepare the way of the Lord; make His paths straight.'" Matt. 3:3.

Old Testament prophets had foretold John's mission when they wrote, "Behold, I send My messenger, and he will prepare the way before Me" (Mal. 3:1). "The voice of one crying in the wilderness: 'Prepare the way of the Lord; make straight in the desert a highway for our God'" (Isa. 40:3). John referred to himself as the "voice" of Isaiah 40:3 (John 1:23) and Jesus called him the "messenger" of Malachi 3:1 (Matt. 11:7-14).

Ancient kings sent messengers to tell their subjects that they were planning to visit. They expected the villages to organize work details to "prepare" the route over which the king would travel. Roads were usually in desperate shape, so the work crews filled ditches and leveled the highway until it was smooth enough for the king's chariot. The people understood John's message: their Prince was coming and they must prepare for His arrival; but the work John spoke of involved a preparation in their hearts. He "looked for the high places of human pride and power to be cast down."[77]

John's ministry started in Judea to give the priests and rulers first opportunity to hear and accept his message. Crowds grew as those who heard him carried back favorable reports. The power of the message as well as curiosity caused people to travel into the wilderness to hear and be baptized by the new prophet. Baptism was not new, and John did not invent the rite. Jews had proselytes totally immerse their bodies. That baptism was accepted is a given, for the deputation sent to question John "the Baptist" did not challenge the rite but merely his authority to perform it (John 1:19-28). People in Old Testament times understood baptism to symbolically wash away sin. John's message was vastly different from the commonly accepted New Testament concept that reserved it for Gentiles converting to Judaism. John was calling upon Jews to be baptized! Being a descendent of Abraham was no longer enough for a Jew. "All who became the subjects of Christ's kingdom, he said, would give evidence of faith and repentance. . . . In the daily life, justice, mercy, and the love of God will be seen."[78]

The true test of conversion, then as now, is a transformed life.

THE BAPTISM

Then Jesus came from Galilee to John at the Jordan to be baptized by him.

Matt. 3:13.

The message of the wilderness prophet reached the small carpenter shop in Nazareth. For six months John had presented his message, and now the autumn feasts of Rosh Hashanah, Yom Kippur, and the Feast of Tabernacles were about to begin. It was A.D. 27, and Jesus recognized His time had come. "Turning from His daily toil, He bade farewell to His mother, and followed in the steps of His countrymen who were flocking to the Jordan." [79] Jesus and John were cousins, yet neither had communicated directly with the other through the years. "Providence had ordered this. No occasion was to be given for the charge that they had conspired together to support each other's claims." [80] John had heard of Jesus' visit to the Temple in Jerusalem as a boy. He believed Jesus to be the Messiah, yet the fact that his cousin had spent so many years in Nazareth without announcing His mission raised doubt in his mind. Having been told the Messiah would seek baptism by his hand and that a divine sign would accompany the act, John waited patiently for God's Son to manifest Himself.

One day as John preached, Jesus presented Himself and asked for baptism. The Baptist recognized in Him a purity of soul he had never seen. "The very atmosphere of His presence was holy and awe-inspiring." [81] How could John baptize One so holy? He shrank from the task, saying, "I need to be baptized by You, and are You coming to me?" (Matt. 3:14). How could he offer the baptism of repentance to One so pure and undefiled? "With firm yet gentle authority, Jesus answered, 'Suffer it to be so now: for thus it becometh us to fulfill all righteousness.' " [82] John yielded, and Jesus stepped into the Jordan River. Identifying Himself with sinners, Jesus set the example for all who would follow Him.

"Christ's submission to baptism by John was the seal that confirmed John's ministry and placed Heaven's stamp of approval upon it." [83] The baptism of the Messiah was the crowning act of John's ministry. From that point on John saw that Christ must increase and he must decrease in importance. Coming up out of the water, Jesus bowed in prayer upon the bank of the river. "A new and important era was opening before Him." [84] No longer a simple man from Nazareth, Jesus now began His public ministry.

Do you pray just before starting out on a new endeavor?

"MY BELOVED SON"

When all the people were baptized, it came to pass that Jesus also was baptized; and while He prayed, the heaven was opened.

Luke 3:21.

Luke is the only Gospel writer to mention Christ's prayer on the Jordan riverbank. Jesus knew the Jews were not looking for the type of kingdom He was bringing. He recognized that He would face strife, lies, distrust, discord, and woe. "Alone He must tread the path; alone He must bear the burden. Upon Him who had laid off His glory and accepted the weakness of humanity the redemption of the world must rest. He saw and felt it all, but His purpose remained steadfast. Upon His arm depended the salvation of the fallen race, and He reached out His hand to grasp the hand of Omnipotent Love."[1] His life from then on would be vastly different from the one left behind in Nazareth.

Jesus would have to draw continually upon the Father's love to face the task ahead. There upon the riverbank He sought evidence from His Father that God accepted His humanity. Tearfully He pleaded for us. "Never before have the angels listened to such a prayer. They are eager to bear to their loved Commander a message of assurance and comfort. But no; the Father Himself will answer the petition of His Son. Direct from the throne issue the beams of His glory."[2] For a moment the gates of the unseen world opened and Jesus saw the Holy Spirit descend in the likeness of a dove of light. The dove is significant, as it represents the rabbinical symbol for Israel as a nation. As Christ prayed for strength, wisdom, and help with His mission, the Holy Spirit anointed Him with special power to accomplish the task ahead.

Few other than John saw the heavenly manifestation. Those gathered upon the riverbank silently looked upon the kneeling figure. A light they had never before seen glorified the upturned face, and they heard a voice saying, "You are My beloved Son; in You I am well pleased." When God said, "You are My beloved Son," He included all humanity. God accepted His Son as our representative. God still loves us. "By sin, earth was cut off from heaven, and alienated from its communion; but Jesus has connected it again with the sphere of glory. His love has encircled man, and reached the highest heaven."[3]

"The light which fell from the open portals upon the head of our Saviour will fall upon us as we pray for help to resist temptation."[4]

INTO THE WILDERNESS

*Then Jesus, being
filled with the Holy
Spirit, returned
from the Jordan and
was led by the Spirit
into the wilderness.
Luke 4:1.*

Jesus now drew apart to meditate and contemplate the sacrifice He must make for humanity. His success would regain the dominion Adam had lost in Eden. The great struggle between God and Satan for the inhabitants of this earth was about to intensify. "At the birth of Jesus, Satan knew that One had come with a divine commission to dispute his dominion. He trembled at the angel's message attesting the authority of the newborn King. Satan well knew the position that Christ had held in heaven as the Beloved of the Father. That the Son of God should come to this earth as a man filled him with amazement and with apprehension. He could not fathom the mystery of this great sacrifice. His selfish soul could not understand such love for the deceived race."[5]

Satan found it hard to believe that the commander of the heavenly host would stoop so low as to take upon Himself the limitations of degenerate humans. Why would Christ give up the halls of heaven for the hills of earth? Why did the Father and the Son place such value on human beings that They would seek to rescue them? The deceiver decided to attack when Jesus was physically weak, hungry, and worn with mental fatigue. After being shut in by His Father's glory for 40 days, Jesus found Himself alone when it departed. Now He was His most vulnerable before the tempter's subtle power.

"Satan's temptations continued during the entire 40 days of Jesus' fast; the three mentioned in [Luke 4:3-13] represented the climax of the temptations and came at the close of the period."[6] "Many claim that it was impossible for Christ to be overcome by temptation. . . . But our Saviour took humanity, with all its liabilities. He took the nature of man, with the possibility of yielding to temptation. We have nothing to bear which He has not endured."[7] From birth Jesus' childhood had been one of continual temptation to sin. Had not Jesus assumed human liabilities, His trials would have been meaningless to us. Overcoming by divine power would prove nothing, for we do not possess that asset. The power of the Word sustained Him and the indwelling of the Holy Spirit strengthened Him, but the trial was severe.

"Not even by a thought did He yield to temptation. So it may be with us."[8]

"MAN SHALL NOT LIVE BY BREAD ALONE"

But He answered and said, "It is written, 'Man shall not live by bread alone, but by every word that proceeds from the mouth of God.'" Matt. 4:4.

We do not know the exact location of the temptation, but tradition places it in the barren and rugged area west of Jericho. It is also possible Jesus went east of the Dead Sea to a spot near Mount Nebo. Jesus did not invite temptation or place Himself on Satan's ground. "Before He came to earth, the plan lay out before Him, perfect in all its details. But as He walked among men, He was guided, step by step, by the Father's will."[9] After 40 days without food He was physically weak. Satan had witnessed Jesus' baptism, seen the glory of the Father come down upon His Son, and heard God proclaim Him to be His beloved Son. Knowing the stakes involved, Satan realized that he could not trust the temptation of God's Son to one of his evil angels. He must personally oversee the seduction of heaven's special ambassador to humanity.

As he had in the Garden of Eden thousands of years before, Satan now attempted to separate human beings from their God forever. The temptation of self-indulgence by which Adam fell is one of the severest tests. Cloaking his appearance, Satan approached Jesus. "Now when the tempter came to Him, he said, 'If You are the Son of God, command that these stones become bread'" (Matt. 4:3). "Though he appears as an angel of light, these first words betray his character. 'If thou be the Son of God.' Here is the insinuation of distrust."[10] Satan wishes Jesus to disbelieve the words spoken at His recent baptism.

The test grows more subtle as Satan mixes truth with error in an attempt to confuse a weakened Jesus. "One of the most powerful of the angels, he [Satan] says, has been banished from heaven. The appearance of Jesus indicates that He is that fallen angel, forsaken by God, and deserted by man."[11] Jesus recognized Satan immediately and refused to be drawn into controversy. He would perform no miracle to prove His divinity. "Neither here nor at any subsequent time in His earthly life did He work a miracle in His own behalf. His wonderful works were all for the good of others."[12]

"Every promise in God's word is ours. . . . When assailed by temptation, look not to circumstances or to the weakness of self, but to the power of the word. All its strength is yours."[13]

"THEY SHALL BEAR YOU UP"

If you are the Son of God, throw yourself down. For it is written: "He shall give His angels charge over you," and, "In their hands they shall bear you up, lest you dash your foot against a stone." Matt. 4:6.

Satan increased the pressure on Jesus. The site of temptation shifted to the outer wing of the Temple in Jerusalem. The devil now gave evidence that he was a student of Scripture. If Jesus placed Himself in a situation from which His Father must intervene to save Him, the deceiver would have shown Jesus' weak human nature. To experiment with the Father's mercy, in a needless exhibition of His protecting care, would misplace trust and destroy Christ's perfect example.

"The sin of presumption lies close beside the virtue of perfect faith and confidence in God."[14] Had Jesus thrown Himself from the Temple, no one but Satan and the holy angels would have witnessed the act. The deceiver twisted the Word of God in such a way that it appeared to approve of a sinful deed. By leaving out the key element of Psalm 91:11, 12 ("to keep you in all your [God's] ways") Satan shrouded the quotation's intent. God will protect only when we remain faithful to the path of His choosing.

"The tempter can never compel us to do evil. He cannot control minds unless they are yielded to his control. The will must consent, faith must let go its hold upon Christ, before Satan can exercise his power upon us. But every sinful desire we cherish affords him a foothold."[15] Jesus declared, "It is written again, 'You shall not tempt the Lord your God' " (Matt. 4:7). Originally Moses spoke these words to the children of Israel as they murmured for water in the Sinai despite the fact that God had dramatically provided for them already. Their deliverance, the crossing of the Red Sea, the manna provided for food—all should have built their faith in His ability to deliver them. Yet in just a short period of time they mistrusted God's concern for their welfare and doubted His protective care.

Christ's faith never wavered. Manifesting perfect confidence and firm trust in His Father, He didn't need to test God's love. Mature faith led Jesus so to order His life to the will of the Father that He could discern plainly God's love.

"We should not present our petitions to God to prove whether He will fulfill His word, but because He will fulfill it; not to prove that He loves us, but because He loves us."[16]

41

"YOU SHALL WORSHIP THE LORD YOUR GOD"

Then Jesus said to him, "Away with you, Satan! For it is written, 'You shall worship the Lord your God, and Him only you shall serve.'" Matt. 4:10.

Satan now stood forth as the prince of the world. "He is a mighty angel, though fallen." [17] Taking Jesus to a high mountain, he passes the world's kingdoms before His gaze. Hiding the effects of sin, he displays the beautiful fields, forests, temples, and cities of the world. Satan now whispers, "All these things I will give You if You will fall down and worship me." But the deceiver had stolen these things—they were not his to give. Christ was the earth's true owner for "all things were made through Him" (John 1:3). If Jesus simply would bow in worship to Satan, the devil would surrender the earth to Christ with no further need of sacrifice. All Satan wanted in return was for Jesus to transfer His allegiance from God the Father. But for Jesus to do so would be blasphemy

Christ confronted the devil with Scripture. "Away with you, Satan! For it is written, 'You shall worship the Lord your God, and Him only you shall serve.'" "Satan trembles and flees before the weakest soul who finds refuge in that mighty name." [18] Just as Jesus overcame temptation we are likewise admonished to "submit to God. Resist the devil and he will flee from you" (James 4:7).

We cannot conceive of the intense interest the angels had in the struggle between Christ and Satan as they watched their Commander's trial. Exhausted by the ordeal, Jesus fell to the ground. "He had endured the test, greater than we shall ever be called to endure. The angels now ministered to the Son of God as He lay like one dying. He was strengthened with food, comforted with the message of His Father's love and the assurance that all heaven triumphed in His victory." [19] "The cost of the redemption of the race can never be fully realized until the redeemed shall stand with the Redeemer, by the throne of God." [20]

Satan approaches us with similar temptations. The promises of God seem far away at times, while the glories of our world are tempting and near. Once Satan has the human affection, he has captured them. No one can love the things of this earth and be saved.

We must keep our eyes on the prize of the high calling of God in Christ Jesus.

COME BOLDLY BEFORE THE THRONE OF GRACE

For we do not have a High Priest who cannot sympathize with our weaknesses, but was in all points tempted as we are, yet without sin. Heb. 4:15.

Jesus took upon Himself human nature and with it the possibility of yielding to sin. "[God] permitted Him to meet life's peril in common with every human soul, to fight the battle as every child of humanity must fight it, at the risk of failure and eternal loss."[21] Only thus might Christ claim to have been tested in all points *as we are.* Christ met trials only in His humanity. "This agony He must not exert His divine power to escape. As man He must suffer the consequences of man's sin. As man He must endure the wrath of God against transgression. . . . As Christ felt His unity with the Father broken up, He feared that in His human nature He would be unable to endure the coming conflict with the powers of darkness. In the wilderness of temptation the destiny of the human race had been at stake. Christ was then conqueror."[22]

Jesus recognized Satan from the outset, for He had seen him fall from heaven as lightning (Luke 10:18). Today "Satan deals with men more guardedly than he dealt with Christ in the wilderness of temptation, for he is admonished that he there lost his case. He is a conquered foe. He does not come to man directly and demand homage by outward worship. He simply asks men to place their affections upon the good things of this world."[23] Our Saviour knows the limits of our endurance and has promised to temper our trials to what we can successfully bear. "No temptation has overtaken you except such as is common to man; but God is faithful, who will not allow you to be tempted beyond what you are able, but with the temptation will also make the way of escape, that you may be able to bear it" (1 Cor. 10:13). Our only salvation is in the name of God and His Word. "The name of the Lord is a strong tower; the righteous run to it and are safe" (Prov. 18:10). From childhood Jesus fortified His mind with the Word. By quoting three texts from Deuteronomy, He resisted and refuted the wiles of the evil one.

Here was the secret of His ability to resist temptation. "And this is the victory that has overcome the world—our faith" (1 John 5:4). "So then faith comes by hearing, and hearing by the word of God" (Rom. 10:17).

THE DELEGATION FROM JERUSALEM

Now this is the testimony of John, when the Jews sent priests and Levites from Jerusalem to ask him, "Who are you?" John 1:19.

John was preaching not far from Jericho. His fame had spread beyond the common people and reached the religious and political leaders. The Sanhedrin could no longer evade the questions people had been asking about John's message. Priests, teachers, and the chief rulers of the nation met under the leadership of the high priest in their quarters on the Temple mount in Jerusalem. To belong to the special assembly a man had to be mature in years, possess a general knowledge of more than Jewish religion, be without physical blemish, be married, and have children. Exercising the right to control public teaching, the men alone could validate John's credentials to teach. Only a true prophet, speaking directly from God, would not need their sanction.

The assembly dispatched a deputation to meet with the new teacher. The group of predominately Pharisees traveled the 25 miles from Jerusalem to the Jordan and approached the crowd surrounding the Baptist. The people parted to let the rabbis pass. The rich robes of the priests and the camel's hair robe of John provided a stark contrast. The delegation asked John, "Who are you?" It was not a question of identity but one of authority to teach or preach. John knew that many believed him to be the Messiah, so he answered, "I am not the Christ." Tradition said that Elijah would appear in person to proclaim the Messiah and that Moses "the prophet" would rise from the dead. Following this line of popular thought, the priests asked, "'What then? Are you Elijah?' He said, 'I am not.' 'Are you the Prophet?' And he answered 'No.' Then they said to him, 'Who are you, that we may give an answer to those who sent us? What do you say about yourself?'" (John 1:21, 22). John plainly stated, "I am the *voice* of one crying in the wilderness: 'Make straight the way of the Lord'" (verse 23). Isaiah had foretold John's coming (Isa. 40:3).

The Pharisees had their answer. John claimed to be God's voice, His spokesman. The central issue of authority to baptize remained. "The Jewish nation could have paid John no higher compliment; it could have borne no more eloquent testimony to the power of his message. Indeed, his proclamation of the coming of the Messiah was so effective that the people mistook him for the Messiah Himself!"[24]

Do others see Jesus' reflection in you? It is His work to change you and yours to submit.

PHARISEES + SADDUCEES = VIPERS

But when he saw many of the Pharisees and Sadducees coming to his baptism, he said to them, "Brood of vipers! Who warned you to flee from the wrath to come? Therefore bear fruits worthy of repentance." Matt. 3:7, 8.

Most scholars believe that the name Pharisee means "separatist." The conservative Jewish sect adopted the name "Hasidim," or "pious ones," for they advocated separation of Jewish religion from civil government. They felt the priestly lineage should concern itself with religion only and leave ruling to political organizations. Also they believed that political entanglements weakened the high priesthood and detracted from its traditional responsibility of interpreting the law. The Pharisees were nevertheless popular and formed the majority party.

They were the "doctors of the law" (experts in religious law) and theologians, the self-proclaimed spiritual guides for the nation. Their views included belief in a future life in which the righteous would be rewarded for virtue and the wicked punished in perpetual torment. One might describe them as being legalistic, nationalistic, and Messianic.

The Sadducees, on the other hand, were more concerned with the civil, political, and secular national interests. They sought political stability through alliances that might advance the nation toward their goals. Most were aristocratic. Extremely conservative, they accepted the Pentateuch but rejected most of the rest of the Old Testament and denied the value of tradition. In this, they were the exact opposite of the Pharisees. The Sadducees rejected any teaching of a future life, future rewards, or future punishments, since such concepts did not appear in the Pentateuch. They were also skeptical about angels and spirits. In some ways the Sadducees relied upon self, not God.

Neither group approached baptism for the right reason. Both groups sought out John's baptism to advance their credibility with the people and to hedge their bets against a coming Messiah who might embrace the Baptist's ministry. "By the word 'vipers' John meant those who were malignant and antagonistic, bitterly opposed to the expressed will of God. John exhorted these men to 'bring forth therefore fruits meet for repentance.' That is,

Show that you are converted, that your characters are transformed. . . . Neither words nor profession, but fruits—the forsaking of sins, and obedience to the commandments of God—show the reality of genuine repentance and true conversion." [25]

THE LAMB OF GOD

The next day John saw Jesus coming toward him, and said, "Behold! The Lamb of God who takes away the sin of the world!" John 1:29.

Few heard God's voice at the baptism of Jesus, but John recognized it as the promised sign identifying the Redeemer. Deeply moved, he knew he had baptized the Messiah. During the time Jesus was in the wilderness, John had studied anew the Messianic prophecies. Although he still did not understand the scriptural distinction between the first and second advents, he realized there must be a deeper meaning. Now, looking over the crowd by the river, he spotted Jesus. When Jesus did not proclaim Himself as the Messiah, John directed the people's attention to Him. "I baptize with water, but there stands One among you whom you do not know. It is He who, coming after me, is preferred before me, whose sandal strap I am not worthy to loose" (John 1:26, 27). The deputation from Jerusalem reacted in surprise. The Messiah—here, now, in their presence?

"The words of John could apply to no other than the long-promised One. The Messiah was among them! In amazement priests and rulers gazed about them, hoping to discover Him of whom John had spoken. But He was not distinguishable among the throng."[26]

The next day John again saw Jesus in the crowd and identified Him as the Lamb of God. Some believed while others questioned or rejected the idea outright. The Man the Baptist pointed to was dressed as a peasant. He gave no outward sign of being a deliverer. His time in the wilderness had changed His appearance. He was paler, more gaunt and thin than when He first came to John to be baptized. But the face of Christ was unique, for He exuded a love that could be seen even though not spoken. The people felt the compassion He expressed for their condition. He was humble, gentle, unassuming, and yet a confident aura of power radiated from Him. "Was this the Christ? With awe and wonder the people looked upon the One just declared to be the Son of God!"[27] This Messiah was no king who would lead them to victory against the Romans. "The words which the priests and rabbis so much desired to hear, that Jesus would now restore the kingdom to Israel, had not been spoken."[28] No king they knew would show such humility. Their Messiah would not associate with the poor or converse with the downtrodden!

Appearances, even today, may be misleading. Do you focus on the message or the appearance of the messenger?

"WHAT SEEK YE?"

One of the two who heard John speak, and followed Him, was Andrew, Simon Peter's brother. John 1:40.

For John the Baptist this day had been special. It was the last time we know for certain that John was in the presence of His Saviour. Among the Baptist's disciples were two men seeking truth. Both had heard John address Jesus as "the Lamb of God," but what had he meant? Neither was sure, but they followed Jesus and left the Jordan. Although Andrew and John wished to speak with Him, they held back. "Jesus knew that the disciples were following Him. They were the first fruits of His ministry, and there was joy in the heart of the divine Teacher as these souls responded to His grace. Yet turning, He asked only, 'What seek ye?' He would leave them free to turn back or to speak their desire."[29] "What do you seek?" are the first words of Jesus that the disciple John recorded in his Gospel. The two men desired more than a simple exchange of words by the side of the road. Wishing to sit at His feet and hear what He had to say, they asked simply, " 'Rabbi' (which is to say, when translated, Teacher), 'where are You staying?'" (John 1:38).

During Christ's time people broke daylight into 12 hours. As the tenth hour (4:00 p.m.) approached, Jesus said, "Come and see" (verse 39). Many of John the Baptist's disciples had been present on the riverbank that day and heard him refer to Jesus as "the Lamb of God," yet only these two followed Him. "To them the words of Jesus were full of freshness and truth and beauty. A divine illumination was shed upon the teaching of the Old Testament Scriptures. The many-sided themes of truth stood out in new light."[30] They had come not as the scribes and Pharisees to criticize the message or to trap the speaker, but because they recognized in Jesus a subtle glory and truth they could not deny.

Neither would follow Jesus fully until He issued His call for permanent discipleship, but they would visit with their "Rabbi" and learn from Him for another year and a half. They had accepted Him as the Messiah.

"It is contrition and faith and love that enable the soul to receive wisdom from heaven. Faith working by love is the key of knowledge, and everyone that loveth 'knoweth God' (1 John 4:7, KJV)."[31] Acceptance builds faith, and faith creates trust.

"WE HAVE FOUND THE MESSIAH"

"We have found the Messiah" (which is translated, the Christ). John 1:41.

The Greek "Messias" is a transliteration of the Hebrew term *mashiach,* meaning "an anointed one." Scripture applied *mashiach* to the high priest in Leviticus 4:3, 5 and also to Cyrus, king of Persia, in Isaiah 45:1. "In Old Testament times the high priest (Ex. 30:30), the king (2 Sam. 5:3; cf. 1 Sam. 24:6), and sometimes prophets (1 Kings 19:16) were 'anointed' upon consecration to holy service, and were therefore *mashiach.* . . . In Messianic prophecy the term came to be applied specifically to *the* Messiah, who, as Prophet (Deut. 18:15), Priest (Zech. 6:11-14), and King (Isa. 9:6, 7), was the One ordained to be our Redeemer (Isa. 61:1; Dan. 9:25, 26)."[32]

The term *Messiah* rarely appears in the New Testament, though the Greek term *Christos,* from *chrio,* meaning "to anoint," occurs hundreds of times. John 1:41 used the Old Testament term *Messias* to convince those Jews who still looked for the Promised One to appear in John's day that the promise had been fulfilled. Before His resurrection Scripture generally referred to Jesus as *the* Christ. It was His title—the Anointed One. After His resurrection the New Testament dropped the article, and the title also became His name. In several instances it used the two names Jesus and Christ together. In such cases the combination indicates an acceptance by the user of both the human Jesus ("Jehovah is salvation") and the divine "Christ" or "Anointed One." John refers to our Lord for the first time in John 1:17 by both names—Jesus Christ. The Christ of the New Testament is the Messiah of the Old Testament.

Individuals who had been studying Daniel's 70-weeks prophecy knew that time was drawing near for the Anointed One to appear. "'The Anointed One'—Christ had received the anointing of the Spirit after His baptism by John in Jordan."[33] Few recognized the significance, but Peter later wrote "how God anointed Jesus of Nazareth with the Holy Spirit and with power" (Acts 10:38). Jesus said: "The Spirit of the Lord is upon Me, because He has anointed Me to preach the gospel to the poor" (Luke 4:18). One Sabbath when Jesus told the hearers in Nazareth that He fulfilled the prophecy of Isaiah, His neighbors tried to throw Him off a cliff for blasphemy.

Few accepted that the Anointed One had come in their time, and relatively few of the world's population acknowledge Him even today.

"COME AND SEE"

And Nathanael said to him, "Can anything good come out of Nazareth?"
Philip said to him, "Come and see."
John 1:46.

Simon Peter had heard the Baptist. Now Andrew, his brother, sought him to bring him to Jesus. Needing no second invitation, Peter immediately trusted Andrew. Jesus recognized Peter at once. "His impulsive nature, his loving, sympathetic heart, his ambition and self-confidence, the history of his fall, his repentance, his labors, and his martyr's death—the Saviour read it all."[34] After spending another day with Andrew, Peter, and John, Jesus then returned to Galilee on the third day. Arriving at the northern shore, Jesus searched for a man named Philip, a resident of Bethsaida Julias—hometown of Andrew and Peter. Perhaps the brothers had recommended Philip. For the first time Jesus issued the call "Follow Me." Philip obeyed and immediately brought someone else to Jesus.

Nathanael had been in the crowd when John the Baptist pointed to Jesus as "the Lamb of God." He and Philip often prayed and studied together in seclusion. Philip now found his friend praying beneath the leaves of a fig tree and told him that he had found the Messiah. He was Jesus of Nazareth, the son of Joseph. Nathanael was a resident of Cana, a small town not far to the north and east of Nazareth. Being acquainted with the town and its reputation, he was skeptical. "Can anything good come out of Nazareth?" he asked. Philip did not argue, but simply said, "Come and see." Jesus welcomed Nathanael, saying, "Behold, an Israelite indeed, in whom is no deceit!" (John 1:47). Jesus knew that Nathanael was looking for the Messiah and truly aspired to live in conformity with God's will. Surprised, Nathanael asked, "How do You know me?" Jesus answered, "Before Philip called you, when you were under the fig tree, I saw you" (verse 48). His reply convinced Nathanael. "Rabbi, You are the Son of God! You are the King of Israel!" (verse 49).

"While they trust to the guidance of human authority, none will come to a saving knowledge of the truth. Like Nathanael, we need to study God's Word for ourselves, and pray for the enlightenment of the Holy Spirit."[35] Be willing to see for yourself whether the message is from God. Go prepared, having studied the Scriptures, so that you might discern truth. Once you have found it, share it with others.

The Baptist's influence directed two of his own disciples to Christ. Andrew sought his brother and Philip his friend. We must invite others to "come and see."

UNDER THE FIG TREE

Nathanael said to Him, "How do You know me?" Jesus answered and said to him, "Before Philip called you, when you were under the fig tree, I saw you."

John 1:48.

In Palestine the fig tree is a common sight. In rough ground the tree more nearly resembles a vine, but in good soil it can grow to be a tree reaching 20 to 30 feet in height. Nathanael had been praying under just such a tree. He felt the need to understand the promises of the coming Messiah and wanted to know for himself what was truth. He wished to know more about why John the Baptist had referred to Jesus as "the Lamb of God." Only by secluding himself could he meditate and read the promises of the coming Messiah. "Never should the Bible be studied without prayer. Before opening its pages we should ask for the enlightenment of the Holy Spirit, and it will be given." [36]

The Holy Spirit led Nathanael to check for himself who this prophet was, and in doing so he became a believer. "How do You know me?" he asked. Jesus answered him by revealing where and what he was doing at the moment of the call to "come and see." It should encourage us that Jesus watches and listens when we pray. "And Jesus will see us also in the secret places of prayer if we will seek Him for light that we may know what is truth. Angels from the world of light will be with those who in humility of heart seek for divine guidance." [37]

"The prayer which Nathanael offered while he was under the fig tree came from a sincere heart, and it was heard and answered by the Master. . . . The Lord reads the hearts of all and understands their motives and purposes. 'The prayer of the upright is his delight.' He will not be slow to hear those who open their hearts to Him, not exalting self, but sincerely feeling their great weakness and unworthiness." [38] We are not to be surprised that Jesus hears our prayers. "Prayer is the opening of the heart to God as to a friend." [39] Nathanael had the privilege to see more and greater examples of Jesus' divinity during the years he walked with his Master.

We too may lean on Jesus—our dearest friend—for "the Lord is faithful, who will establish you and guard you from the evil one" (2 Thess. 3:3).

A SOCIABLE MAN

Now both Jesus and His disciples were invited to the wedding. John 2:2.

Jesus had been staying near Bethabara, one of the many fords in the Jordan area (John 1:28). Leaving the Jordan and traveling by way of Bethsaida, Jesus arrived in the small village of Cana. Cana, or the "place of reeds," was home to the new disciple, Nathanael. The 65-mile journey took three days. He had been gone from Nazareth for two months. A wedding ceremony was taking place in Cana, and Jesus' mother attended it.

Mary had heard of her Son's baptism, and she recognized that the lives of John and Jesus had touched each other. She remembered the promise of John the Baptist and had watched his mission with interest. Her heart thrilled when she heard that the Baptist had proclaimed Jesus as the Lamb of God. Her husband, Joseph, had died, and she could not share her feelings with any other person who had witnessed the miracle of Jesus' birth. A dread had filled her when Jesus entered into the wilderness and she had received little news about His fate. During those weeks she had anxiously awaited His return and fearfully recalled Simeon's prophecy.

When people learned that Jesus was in the town, He and His disciples, John, Andrew, Peter, Philip, and Nathanael, received invitations to the wedding. Such a wedding feast took place in the home of the groom and usually continued for several days. The families involved were relatives of Mary and Joseph and possibly also related to some of the disciples. Jesus did not perform His first miracle for the Sanhedrin or in the Temple. It took place at a small gathering in a little village to bring joy to common people. "Jesus reproved self-indulgence in all its forms, yet He was social in His nature. He accepted the hospitality of all classes, visiting the homes of the rich and the poor, the learned and the ignorant, seeking to elevate their thoughts from questions of commonplace life to those things that are spiritual and eternal."[40] Christ saw a potential citizen for His kingdom in every person He met. He passed among them on city streets, dined in private houses, rode in their boats, worshiped in their synagogues, taught by the shores of their lake, and socialized with them at their joyful weddings.

"We should not seclude ourselves from others. In order to reach all classes, we must meet them where they are. They will seldom seek us of their own accord. . . . Let all who profess to have found Christ minister as He did for the benefit of men."[41]

"MY HOUR HAS NOT YET COME"

Jesus said to her, "Woman, what does your concern have to do with Me? My hour has not yet come." John 2:4.

Mary had heard rumors coming from the Jordan. "John, one of the new disciples, had searched for Christ and had found Him in His humiliation, emaciated, and bearing the marks of great physical and mental distress. Jesus, unwilling that John should witness His humiliation, had gently yet firmly dismissed him from His presence. He wished to be alone; no human eye must behold His agony, no human heart be called out in sympathy with His distress. The disciple had sought Mary in her home and related to her the incidents of this meeting with Jesus, as well as the event of His baptism." [42] She now saw that Jesus had changed during those two months. While His face bore traces of the intense struggle in the wilderness He also showed evidence of a new sense of purpose and power. "With Him is a group of young men, whose eyes follow Him with reverence, and who call Him Master." [43] The guests had heard of Jesus and they gathered in small groups to talk and glance at Him. Mary was encouraged that Jesus was the Son of God.

Custom called for the father or a near relative to choose an eligible bride for the young man, pay a dowry to the bride's father or brothers, and host a feast that lasted several days in the groom's home. Mary had been involved in the preparations for the wedding feast. Unfortunately the wine ran out before the end of the party. Mary suggested that perhaps Jesus might supply their need, but He replied, "Woman, what does your concern have to do with Me? My hour has not yet come." Though His words might have sounded harsh, Jesus' tone, look, and manner interpreted them as He addressed His mother with respect. He who gave the commandment "Honor your father and your mother" was ever mindful of His mother's feelings. Yet, as at the Temple while still a child, He must subject everything to His reason for coming to earth.

"The words, 'Mine hour is not yet come,' point to the fact that every act of Christ's life on earth was in fulfillment of the plan that had existed from the days of eternity. Before He came to earth, the plan lay out before Him, perfect in all its details. But as He walked among men, He was guided, step by step, by the Father's will." [44]

"The claims of God are paramount even to the ties of human relationship." [45]

HIS GIFTS ARE FRESH AND NEW

Every man at the beginning sets out the good wine, and when the guests have well drunk, then the inferior. You have kept the good wine until now!

John 2:10.

Mary did not understand Jesus' mission, but she did trust her Son explicitly. "To this faith Jesus responded. It was to honor Mary's trust, and to strengthen the faith of His disciples, that the first miracle was performed."[46] Doing whatever she could to prepare the way, she ordered, "Whatever He says to you, do it." Near the entrance to the dwelling stood six stone jars used for ritual purification. Servants washed the hands and feet of the guests before and after meals with water from the containers. John described the jars so non-Jews would understand Jewish ceremonial ritual. Each jar is thought to have contained "about 12-29 gallons."[47] A large number of guests must have been in attendance.

Jesus told the servants to "fill the water pots with water." "All that human power could accomplish was to be done by human hands. . . . Divine power was about to be revealed, but conscientious human effort was to be united with it. God never does for men what they can do for themselves, as this would make spiritual weaklings out of them. . . . We are to utilize fully the resources we have at hand if we expect God to add His blessing."[48] The servants filled the jars to the brim. The transformation took place after the water left the jars, for the servants who *brought the water* knew it was water when they drew it from the cistern or well.

The guests were unaware the wine supply had failed, and the master of ceremonies of the feast feared that when they tasted the new wine they would think he had broken custom and saved the best for last. "By calling the groom, he sought to make clear that the responsibility was not his."[49] The drink Jesus provided was superior to any the guests had ever tasted. As the wine was non-alcoholic (this is the "pure juice of the grape"[50]), the guests were clearly able to discern that it was superior. "The gift of Christ to the marriage feast was a symbol. The water represented baptism into His death; the wine, the shedding of His blood for the sins of the world."[51] When the guests realized that a miracle had occurred and looked for Jesus, "He had withdrawn so quietly as to be unnoticed even by His disciples."[52] News of the miracle spread even to Jerusalem.

We would do well to follow Mary's admonition: "Whatever He says to you, do it."

JESUS

MINISTRY IN JUDEA
Christ Our Messiah

Spring A.D. 28 to Spring A.D. 29

Matthew 14:3-5

Luke 3:19, 20

John 2:13-5:47

The Desire of Ages, pp. 154-225

PASSOVER

Now the Passover of the Jews was at hand, and Jesus went up to Jerusalem.

John 2:13.

Jesus returned from Cana and went to Capernaum with His mother, His brothers, and His disciples. From Cana one must descend to Capernaum on the northwest shore of the Sea of Galilee. The distance is not more than 16 miles, but Cana is approximately 1,500 feet higher than Capernaum. Capernaum was home to Simon Peter and Andrew and would soon become headquarters for Jesus' ministry in Galilee. But at the moment Jesus did not spend much time in this border town between the territories of Philip and Herod Antipas, for Passover was at hand.

Jesus joined one of the caravans winding its way down the Jordan Valley and up the steep Wadi Qelt through the barren and arid Wilderness of Judah. No one in the procession paid any attention to Him, because word had not yet spread of His mission. As customary among the religious pilgrims, discussion turned to the promise of the Messiah. Jesus attempted to open the eyes of the travelers to the real meanings of the prophecies, but they already thought they knew what the Messiah would do.

As the travelers crested the rise east of the city, they could see the towers of Jerusalem ahead beyond the Kidron. Jerusalem lay between two valleys—the Kidron and the Hinnom. Rising between them, Jerusalem stretched north along two ridges with a deep valley between that had since been filled with debris. The Temple sat upon a hill on the lower eastern ridge and was visible from the Mount of Olives to the east of the Valley of Kidron.

From the widespread territories of Rome the faithful came to worship at Jerusalem. Many could not bring with them the necessary sacrifices. "For the convenience of these, animals were brought and sold in the outer court of the temple."[53] The money the pilgrims brought was of no use to them. They could use only Temple currency to purchase sacrificial items deemed acceptable for the Temple rituals. "Every Jew was required to pay yearly a half shekel as a 'ransom for his soul;' and the money collected was used for the support of the temple (Ex. 30:12-16, KJV). . . . All foreign coin should be changed for a coin called the temple shekel, which was accepted for the service of the sanctuary. The money changing gave opportunity for fraud and extortion, and it had grown into a disgraceful traffic, which was a source of revenue to the priests."[54]

The deafening noise of commerce shut out God's still voice. How is the spirit of worship in your church lobby?

HEROD'S TEMPLE

And He found in the temple those who sold oxen and sheep and doves, and the money changers doing business.

John 2:14.

Added to the commotion of dealers trying to sell sacrificial animals to the faithful at the top of their voices was the crush of the crowd. Dealers struck sharp bargains to give kickbacks to the priests for endorsements and choice locations. Cattle lowing, sheep bleating, doves cooing, people shouting and arguing, coins clinking, and the murmur of those trying to pray—all caused a huge uproar in the Court of the Gentiles. The Temple was still under construction. Herod the Great had thought to enlarge it, but the Jews, fearing he would tear it down and never get around to rebuilding it, refused permission. In a compromise, Herod agreed to tear down sections and rebuild as he went. By replacing them in this fashion, he could remodel with no interruption to the services. Building still progressed even though Herod was long dead.

The Temple was now twice the size it had been during Solomon's reign. The outer courtyard was open to Jew and Gentile alike. The outer wall had covered porches running along it. The porticoes had gigantic columns arranged in rows of three, forming corridors, with the middle row being higher than the outer two. Eight gates gave access to the outer courtyard. People conducted commerce and trade in the enclosed porches. "As Jesus came into the temple, He took in the whole scene. He saw the unfair transactions. He saw the distress of the poor, who thought that without shedding of blood there would be no forgiveness for their sins. He saw the outer court of His temple converted into a place of unholy traffic. The sacred enclosure had become one vast exchange. Christ saw that something must be done."[55]

The Temple itself stood in the center of the courtyard, elevated by 14 steps. On the higher terrace was a small five-foot wall with pillars atop it. Nine gates entered the enclosure, and signs announced that "no stranger [non-Jew] is to enter within the balustrade and enclosure around the Temple. Whoever is caught will be responsible to himself for his death, which will ensue."[56] "With searching glance, Christ takes in the scene before Him as He stands upon the steps of the temple court. . . . As He beholds the scene, indignation, authority, and power are expressed in His countenance."[57]

We must remember that God's house is not the place for common conversation and everyday concerns.

THE TEMPLE CLEANSED

And He said to those who sold doves, "Take these things away! Do not make My Father's house a house of merchandise!"

John 2:16.

The crowd suddenly became aware of the Man standing on the steps of the inner court. "The confusion is hushed. The sound of traffic and bargaining has ceased. The silence becomes painful. A sense of awe overpowers the assembly. It is as if they were arraigned before the tribunal of God to answer for their deeds. Looking upon Christ, they behold divinity flash through the garb of humanity."[58] His commanding presence made Him seem larger in stature than a common man. Speaking in clear yet forceful tones, His voice resounded through the colonnades and porches. "Take these things away! Do not make My Father's house a house of merchandise!"

Slowly He descended the steps holding a scourge of plaited rushes. He overturned the money changers' tables, and coins clattered to the marble stones. All eyes riveted upon Him, and none dared interfere. "Jesus does not smite them with the whip of cords, but in His hand that simple scourge seems terrible as a flaming sword."[59] The only thought the money changers and priests had was to escape from the presence of the One who had revealed their greed. Panic broke out. "Cries of terror escape from hundreds of blanched lips. Even the disciples tremble."[60] Is this their Master? It is so unlike His normal demeanor they are awestruck. They recall David's prophecy: "For the zeal of thine house hath eaten me up" (Ps. 69:9, KJV).

Cleansing the Temple was Jesus' first act of national importance. Through it He announced His mission as the Messiah. In a larger sense, Jesus had come to cleanse the sinner's heart from sin. Earthly desires, evil habits, lusts, selfishness, evil thoughts, and impurities corrupt and debase the human soul. Only Jesus can clean that soul temple. He does not come with scourge and zeal but must be invited into the heart. "Behold, I stand at the door and knock. If anyone hears My voice and opens the door, I will come in to him" (Rev. 3:20).

Jesus looked at those fleeing with pity as He longed to have them understand the meaning of true worship. But the poor remained behind. Jesus' face now filled with love and compassion for the diseased and suffering. The people crowded in upon Him and pled for a blessing. He welcomed all of them, transforming the outer court into a heaven on earth.

It is not the church's commerce but its communion that the world needs.

"WHAT SIGN DO YOU SHOW US?"

So the Jews answered and said to Him, "What sign do You show to us, since You do these things?" John 2:18.

Many who had witnessed the flight of the priests in terror from the face of divine authority felt impressed that Jesus was the Messiah. The offended priests, however, questioned His authority to interfere with their lucrative Temple business. He had directly challenged their authority. Even worse, what He had done had taken place before the very people they sought to intimidate and control. Unable to shake the thought that perhaps Jesus was a prophet sent to restore Temple sanctity, they fearfully returned to Him and demanded a sign. He had just given them the most convincing evidence of His character as Messiah, but they chose not to understand it. Reading their hearts, He knew they wished Him dead.

"Jesus answered and said to them, 'Destroy this temple, and in three days I will raise it up'" (John 2:19). His saying had two aspects. Christ was speaking of the destruction of the temple service and the destruction of His temple body. The death of Christ would be followed by His glorious resurrection three days later. Misunderstanding Him, the priests replied, "It has taken forty-six years to build this temple, and will You raise it up in three days?" (verse 20). They refused to look for any deeper meaning in His words.

The temple Jesus referred to was His body. "Christ was the foundation and life of the temple. Its services were typical of the sacrifice of the Son of God. . . . Since the whole ritual economy was symbolical of Christ, it had no value apart from Him. When the Jews sealed their rejection of Christ by delivering Him to death, they rejected all that gave significance to the temple and its services. Its sacredness had departed."[61] When the priests crucified Christ, they destroyed their own Temple and its system of sacrificial offerings forever.

Jesus knew that even His disciples would not comprehend His words now. "Being spoken at the Passover, [His words] would come to the ears of thousands, and be carried to all parts of the world. After He had risen from the dead, their meaning would be made plain. To many they would be conclusive evidence of His divinity."[62] But His enemies would twist the same words against Him during His night trial before Caiaphas.

What sign do you require before accepting Him as the foundation of your salvation and life?

NICODEMUS

There was a man of the Pharisees named Nicodemus, a ruler of the Jews.

John 3:1.

Nicodemus, a highly educated and wealthy Pharisee, belonged to the Sanhedrin. Composed of 71 members and headed by the high priest, it met in either the Court of Men, one of the inner Temple courts, or in the southwestern corner of the outer Temple court. The Sanhedrin represented the highest judicial body in the country with control over matters of life and death. The Roman procurator had to confirm any death sentence, however. We know that the Romans placed the responsibility for collection of taxes into the hands of the Sanhedrin, who then sold the rights to tax purchasers or speculators known as publicans.

Nicodemus (from the Greek, "victor over the people") was a sincere seeker of truth. Although a religious teacher, he was not familiar with the kingdom of God as taught by Jesus. But he did not share the feelings of the majority of the priests and national rulers. He feared that killing Jesus would bring additional calamities upon the nation. The murder of past prophets had sent the Jews into bondage as a result of their failure to heed God's warnings. Thus Nicodemus feared that his generation was dooming itself to follow in the footsteps of their ancestors' mistakes.

"He greatly desired an interview with Jesus, but shrank from seeking Him openly. It would be too humiliating for a ruler of the Jews to acknowledge himself in sympathy with a teacher as yet so little known."[63] Should the Sanhedrin hear of his visit, the other members would ridicule and scorn him. A secret meeting was the best course of action. "With many others in Israel he had been greatly distressed by the profanation of the temple. He was a witness of the scene when Jesus drove out the buyers and the sellers; he beheld the wonderful manifestation of divine power; he saw the Saviour receiving the poor and healing the sick; he saw their looks of joy, and heard their words of praise; and he could not doubt that Jesus of Nazareth was the Sent of God."[64] As the city slept, he discovered that Jesus would spend the night on the Mount of Olives just east of the city.

Making his way to Jesus was difficult for the cautious Nicodemus, but truth ought to be worth great risk and possible scorn.

"You Must Be Born Again"

Unless one is born again, he cannot see the kingdom of God. John 3:3.

Nicodemus felt timid before the Master. "Rabbi, we know that You are a teacher come from God; for no one can do these signs that You do unless God is with him" (John 3:2). He here acknowledged that surely God was behind Jesus' miracles and words. Although regarded as a "Master of Israel," a teacher of high regard, he accepted Jesus as his equal even though Jesus had no formal education and the Sanhedrin would not recognize or sanction His teachings.

Jesus knew the reason for the night visit and came to the point immediately. "Most assuredly, I say to you, unless one is born again, he cannot see the kingdom of God" (verse 3). Nicodemus thought he understood the concept of rebirth. Being a descendent of Abraham was a virtual guarantee of salvation. Only non-Jews needed to be saved by adoption or "rebirth" into the family of Abraham. Now Jesus seemed to be saying that Nicodemus himself must be "born again." That the kingdom was too pure for even him.

Jesus' comments unsettled His visitor. The Jewish spiritual leader knew it is impossible for a man to undergo physical rebirth. And it was equally unthinkable that as a Jew he even needed a rebirth experience. *How can a person again enter his or her mother's womb?* he wondered. Jesus did not meet his argument with another. Instead He replied, "Most assuredly, I say to you, unless one is born of water and the Spirit, he cannot enter the kingdom of God" (verse 5), plainly setting the answer before the religious leader. "Nicodemus knew that Christ here referred to water baptism and the renewing of the heart by the Spirit of God. He was convinced that he was in the presence of the One whom John the Baptist had foretold."[65] Anything less than the total change of his life by the Spirit was not enough. Being a son of Abraham was not going to get him into the kingdom.

"The Christian's life is not a modification or improvement of the old, but a transformation of nature. There is a death to self and sin, and a new life altogether. This change can be brought about only by the effectual working of the Holy Spirit."[66] Trying to reach heaven through keeping the law is attempting the impossible.

To be "born of water and of the Spirit" is to be "born from above."

THE INVISIBLE WIND

The wind blows where it wishes, and you hear the sound of it, but cannot tell where it comes from and where it goes. So is everyone who is born of the Spirit. John 3:8.

Since Nicodemus was still confused, Jesus used a parable to illustrate the impact of the Holy Spirit. The wind moves the branches of the trees and rustles the grass, yet it is invisible. No human being can chart the course of a single wind across the face of the earth. Just so, no one can tell the exact moment a heart softens and finally accepts Christ as personal Saviour. But the change is as visible in the life of the converted as the effect of wind upon a bending blade of grass.

"By an agency as unseen as the wind, Christ is constantly working upon the heart. Little by little, perhaps unconsciously to the receiver, impressions are made that tend to draw the soul to Christ. These may be received through meditating upon Him, through reading the Scriptures, or through hearing the word from the living preacher. Suddenly, as the Spirit comes with more direct appeal, the soul gladly surrenders itself to Jesus. By many this is called sudden conversion; but it is the result of long wooing by the Spirit of God—a patient, protracted process." [67]

Nicodemus began to soften toward the "new birth" requirement. *How can such a thing be?* he wondered. Jesus patiently explained that His mission on earth was not to set up a temporal kingdom but rather to establish a spiritual one. Those following only the strict requirements of the law lacked holiness of heart. They needed the change of heart that Christ offered. Slowly light began to dawn on Nicodemus, and he now longed for the new birth.

All that remained was for Jesus to explain how the religious leader might obtain the change. Jesus referred to the serpent Moses had erected in the wilderness (Num. 21:6-9). As the children of Israel died from serpent bites, they gazed at the symbol of Christ and were saved. It was not the bronze serpent that healed them, but their faith in God's ability to save. They looked and lived.

"There are thousands today who need to learn the same truth that was taught to Nicodemus by the uplifted serpent. They depend on their obedience to the law of God to commend them to His favor. When they are bidden to look to Jesus, and believe that He saves them solely through His grace, they exclaim, 'How can these things be?'" [68]

BELIEVE IN HIS NAME

For God so loved the world that He gave His only begotten Son, that whoever believes in Him should not perish but have everlasting life. John 3:16.

The underlying principle of God's government is love. John often repeated the evidence of divine love in his writings. In 1 John 3:1 he wrote: "Behold what manner of love the Father has bestowed on us, that we should be called children of God!" God's love for us caused Him to sacrifice His Son for our salvation. Our only requirement is to believe in Christ and cooperate with His will. Belief comes to different people at different stages in their experience. Nicodemus alone received a glimpse of the coming Crucifixion. Christ spared even His disciples the information that later shattered their hopes and dreams. As the Roman soldiers raised the Saviour up on the cross, Nicodemus recalled the lesson given under the stars on the shadowy Mount of Olives. He remembered the example of the serpent raised in the wilderness and Jesus' words: "And I, if I am lifted up from the earth, will draw all peoples to Myself" (John 12:32). The Crucifixion, more than any other event, convinced Nicodemus of Jesus' divinity, and he believed.

"In the interview with Nicodemus, Jesus unfolded the plan of salvation and His mission to the world. In none of His subsequent discourses did He explain so fully, step by step, the work necessary to be done in the hearts of all who would inherit the kingdom of heaven. . . . Nicodemus hid the truth in his heart, and for three years there was little apparent fruit."[69] During those ensuing years the Sanhedrin leader pondered Jesus' lessons. Repeatedly in the Jewish assembly he thwarted the plans of the priests to destroy Him.

"After the Lord's ascension, when the disciples were scattered by persecution, Nicodemus came boldly to the front. He employed his wealth in sustaining the infant church that the Jews had expected to be blotted out at the death of Christ. In the time of peril he who had been so cautious and questioning was as firm as a rock, encouraging the faith of the disciples, and furnishing means to carry forward the work of the gospel."[70] He endured ridicule and persecution, and became poor in the service of the church, but through all trials he never faltered in his faith. "The Jewish ruler learned the way of life from the lowly Teacher of Galilee."[71]

"The possession of everlasting life is conditional upon Christ's abiding in the heart by faith. He who believes has everlasting life, and 'has passed from death unto life.'" (John 5:24).[72]

INTO THE LAND OF JUDEA

After these things Jesus and His disciples came into the land of Judea, and there He remained with them and baptized. John 3:22.

The public ministries of John and Jesus started in Judea so that the Jewish leaders might be first to accept the Messiah. From April A.D. 28 until April A.D. 29 Jesus took His ministry to the surrounding towns and countryside of Judea. The Scriptures are silent about this period with the exception of the account of the Baptist's disciples found in John 3:22-36. During it Christ chose His first disciples, cleansed the Temple, and performed the first of His public healing miracles in and around Jerusalem. He gained many disciples, but most Jews did not accept Him as the Messiah.

John the Baptist had continued to baptize near the Jordan River in a place called "Aenon near Salim, because there was much water there" (John 3:23). The location of this area is today in doubt, but it is interesting to note that John the apostle mentions "much water there." Such a criteria would be consistent with a practice of baptism by immersion. Were John the Baptist still baptizing in the river Jordan, the reference to "much water" would be redundant. It is likely the location was nearer Nablus and Shechem, for both villages sat at the headwaters of the Wadi Farah, the site of numerous springs.

Jesus now retired to the region about the Jordan. Great crowds flocked to Him. "Many came for baptism, and while Christ Himself did not baptize, He sanctioned the administration of the ordinance by His disciples. Thus He set His seal upon the mission of His forerunner."[73] John's baptism symbolized repentance and a cleansing of sin, thus differing from the typical Jewish rite whereby a Gentile converted through ceremonial purification. John's manner and method were not popular with the scribes and priests. Conflict arose between the disciples of John and other Jews over whether baptism cleansed the soul of sin.

"For a time the Baptist's influence over the nation had been greater than that of its rulers, priests, or princes. . . . Now he saw the tide of popularity turning away from himself to the Saviour. Day by day the crowds about him lessened."[74] Jealousy developed between his disciples and those of Jesus. As John was first to baptize in his particular style, his followers maintained that the baptism of Jesus' disciples differed. They questioned the right of Jesus' disciples to baptize and asserted that the words they used were not proper.

Could you avoid conflict if a fellow church member's ministry became more popular than your own?

DISCIPLE VERSUS DISCIPLE

And they came to John and said to him, "Rabbi, He who was with you beyond the Jordan, to whom you have testified—behold, He is baptizing, and all are coming to Him!" John 3:26.

John's message had stirred a nation. "Unlearned peasants and fishermen from the surrounding country; the Roman soldiers from the barracks of Herod; chieftains with their swords at their sides, ready to put down anything that might savor of rebellion; the avaricious taxgatherers from their toll booths; and from the Sanhedrin the phylacteried priests—all listened as if spellbound; and all, even the Pharisee, and the Sadducee, the cold, unimpressible scoffer, went away with the sneer silenced and cut to the heart with a sense of their sins. Herod in his palace heard the message, and the proud, sin-hardened ruler trembled at the call to repentance."[75]

Had John declared himself to be the Messiah, he could have raised a popular revolt against Rome. An exalted position at the head of the Jewish standard was his for the taking. Now his disciples came to him with their grievances. "Though John's mission seemed about to close, it was still possible for him to hinder the work of Christ. If he had sympathized with himself, and expressed grief or disappointment at being superseded, he would have sown the seeds of dissension, would have encouraged envy and jealousy, and would seriously have impeded the progress of the gospel."[76] Satan sought to tempt John to exalt himself over Jesus as a way of damaging Christ's ministry.

John knew he should welcome Christ and not resent Him. The Baptist had the normal human faults and weaknesses, but he knew his relationship to his Messiah and tolerated no jealousy among his disciples. "The utter humility and selfless submission of John are characteristic traits of the true follower of Christ."[77] We may learn from the Baptist's example. "Those who are true to their calling as messengers for God will not seek honor for themselves. Love for self will be swallowed up in love for Christ."[78] "When we see men firm in principle, fearless in duty, zealous in the cause of God, yet humble and lowly, gentle and tender, patient toward all, ready to forgive, manifesting love for souls for whom Christ died, we do not need to inquire: Are they Christians? They give unmistakable evidence that they have been with Jesus and learned of Him."[79]

Humility and patience must replace jealousy and envy among church members for the Lord's work to move forward united.

THE FRIEND OF THE BRIDE-GROOM

He must increase, but I must decrease.

John 3:30.

In Middle Eastern culture it was customary for a friend of the groom to act as a middleman with the family of the bride. He presented the dowry to the bride's father or brothers and arranged the union. His greatest reward was the joy the bride and groom experienced when they met for the first time face-to-face. John represented himself as a friend of the bridegroom. Now, at the prime of his ministry, God summoned the Baptist to retire and leave the work to others. John had introduced the people to Jesus, the bridegroom. It was now joy for him to witness the success of the union. "He who has the bride is the bridegroom; but the friend of the bridegroom, who stands and hears him, rejoices greatly because of the bridegroom's voice. Therefore this joy of mine is fulfilled" (John 3:29).

That men and women found themselves now attracted to Jesus fulfilled the Baptist's fondest wish. In almost the last recorded words of John prior to his imprisonment, he said, "He must increase, but I must decrease." His disciples reported that many were coming to Christ, but John knew that few among those who flocked to Jesus were ready to accept Him as their Saviour from sin. John reminded his disciples that he himself had told them he was but the Messiah's forerunner. "To Christ, as the bridegroom, belongs the first place in the affections of His people."[80]

Jesus was aware of the division being created between His disciples and John's. He knew that before long one of the greatest prophets ever given to the world would be silenced forever. "Wishing to avoid all occasion for misunderstanding or dissension, He quietly ceased His labors, and withdrew to Galilee. We also, while loyal to truth, should try to avoid all that may lead to discord and misapprehension. For whenever these arise, they result in the loss of souls. Whenever circumstances occur that threaten to cause division, we should follow the example of Jesus and of John the Baptist."[81] God uses human beings as His instruments in reaching others with the plan of salvation. When a person has gone as far as he is qualified, the Lord finds others to carry it forward still further. One must humbly realize, like John, that "He must increase, but I must decrease."

Self has no place in His work.

J-3

65

SAMARIA

He left Judea and departed again to Galilee. But He needed to go through Samaria.
John 4:3, 4.

In the autumn of A.D. 28 Jesus withdrew briefly from Judea. During His last visit to Galilee He had attended the wedding at Cana and sojourned with His family at Capernaum. Much had happened in the past eight months, but He had gained few converts. John the Baptist, with clear insight, was able to say, "No one receives His testimony" (John 3:32). Few in Judea were ready to accept Jesus as their Messiah. The Pharisees attempted to create discord between the followers of Jesus and those of John. Wishing to avoid needless conflict, Jesus prudently shifted His ministry.

On His way to Galilee Jesus took the direct route through Samaria. Most travelers from Judea to Galilee avoided the direct route, since Jews regarded Samaritans as impure and rival nationalists. Upon returning from Babylonian exile in 536 B.C., the Jews had sought to rebuild Jerusalem. But the Jewish leaders rejected Samaritan offers of help. Understanding that their ancestors had gone into captivity because they had forsaken God, these leaders now sought to "purify" their religion. Zerubbabel, Jeshua, and others wanted to avoid the corrupting religious influence of the Samaritans who had mingled the religion of Israel with that of their non-Jewish ancestors. (The Assyrians had brought many non-Jewish settlers into what had been the northern kingdom of Israel.) "As a result of this attitude an increasingly deepening hatred developed between the two nations, which was frequently revealed in hostile acts."[82]

Their offers rejected, the Samaritans did all they could to thwart the rebuilding of Jerusalem. Sanballat, the Samaritan governor, attempted to block the repair of Jerusalem's walls (Neh. 2:10, 19, 20; 4:1, 2; 6:1-14). The Samaritans then built their own temple on Mount Gerizim. They offered sacrifices according to the Mosaic ritual, accepted the Pentateuch, and celebrated their own Passover (which included the sacrifice of Passover lambs), but they did not totally renounce idolatry. During the time of Antiochus IV Epiphanes the Samaritans dedicated their temple to Zeus while Jewish resistance brought Syrian persecution. When the Jews regained control of Palestine, they destroyed the Samaritan temple on Mount Gerizim. The site, however, remained sacred to the Samaritans who continued to worship there. "They would not acknowledge the temple at Jerusalem as the house of God, nor admit that the religion of the Jews was superior to their own."[83] "The Samaritans believed that the Messiah was to come as the Redeemer, not only of the Jews, but of the world."[84]

Although they were correct in this belief, they needed to give up other customs to follow Him. So must we.

JACOB'S WELL

So He came to a city of Samaria which is called Sychar, near the plot of ground that Jacob gave to his son Joseph. Now Jacob's well was there. John 4:5, 6.

Crossing the Jordan, 'Jacob came in peace to the city of Shechem, which is in the land of Canaan' (Gen. 33:18, RV). Thus the patriarch's prayer at Bethel, that God would bring him again in peace to his own land, had been granted. For a time he dwelt in the vale of Shechem."[1] Here Abraham had made his encampment and erected his altar to the Lord. Now Jacob bought land from Hamor, Shechem's father. "It was here also that he dug the well to which, seventeen centuries later, came Jacob's Son and Saviour, and beside which, resting during the noontide heat, He told His wondering hearers of that 'well of water springing up into everlasting life.'"[2] Natural springs abounding in the area would seem to have made a well unnecessary, but Jacob dug his 75- to 100-foot-deep well to avoid water disputes with neighbors, since he was an alien among them.

To the vale of Shechem the Israelites later traveled to renew their covenant of loyalty with God. Stretching from the Carmel Ridge, which juts out into the Mediterranean, toward the east and south lies the hill country of Samaria. The twin peaks of Ebal and Gerizim rise near the middle of the country and approach each other with low spurs that form a pass, the site of the town of Shechem. The southern border of Samaria was approximately 10 miles north of Jerusalem.

Jesus reached the vale of Shechem at the sixth hour or around noon. "The lovely valley, its green fields dotted with olive groves, watered with brooks from living fountains, and gemmed with wild flowers, spread out invitingly between the barren hills."[3] Were it evening, He would have gone into Sychar or continued the short distance to Shechem and sought lodging. Few came to the well at midday because most people drew water early in the morning and again at dusk.

"As Jesus sat by the well side, He was faint from hunger and thirst. The journey since morning had been long, and now the sun of noontide beat upon Him. His thirst was increased by the thought of the cool, refreshing water so near, yet inaccessible to Him; for He had no rope nor water jar, and the well was deep. The lot of humanity was His, and He waited for someone to come to draw."[4]

He still waits for us to do His bidding.

"GIVE ME A DRINK"

Jesus therefore, being wearied from His journey, sat thus by the well. . . . A woman of Samaria came to draw water. Jesus said to her, "Give Me a drink." John 4:6, 7.

Jesus and His disciples had traveled many miles under the warm sun. "Wearied with His journey, He sat down here to rest while His disciples went to buy food."[5] The rabbis allowed trade with Samaritans in the case of necessity but condemned all social contact with them. "The disciples, in buying food, were acting in harmony with the custom of their nation. But beyond this they did not go. To ask a favor of the Samaritans, or in any way seek to benefit them, did not enter into the thought of even Christ's disciples."[6]

A Samaritan woman approached Jacob's well, filled her water pitcher, and prepared to leave, but Jesus suddenly asked her for a drink. "Such a favor no Oriental would withhold. In the East, water was called 'the gift of God.' To offer a drink to the thirsty traveler was held to be a duty so sacred that the Arabs of the desert would go out of their way in order to perform it."[7] His request shocked the woman. "How is it that you, being a Jew, ask a drink from me, a Samaritan woman?" Jesus, seeking an opening, instead of offering a favor, had asked for water. "He who made the ocean, who controls the waters of the great deep, who opened the springs and channels of the earth, rested from His weariness at Jacob's well, and was dependent upon a stranger's kindness for even the gift of a drink of water."[8] "Jesus answered and said to her, 'If you knew the gift of God, and who it is who says to you, "Give Me a drink," you would have asked Him, and He would have given you living water'" (John 4:10).

The woman saw only a dusty, weary Jewish traveler seated before her on the curbside of the well, but she sensed He was different. Changing her tone, she addressed Him with respect. The well was deep and Jesus had no rope or pitcher. Where was His "living water" to come from? No water could be sweeter than that drawn from the well of her ancestor. "She was looking backward to the fathers, forward to the Messiah's coming, while the Hope of the fathers, the Messiah Himself, was beside her, and she knew Him not."[9]

"How many thirsting souls are today close by the living fountain, yet looking far away for the wellsprings of life!"[10]

Everlasting Water

Whoever drinks of this water will thirst again, but whoever drinks of the water that I shall give him will never thirst.

John 4:13, 14.

Jeremiah spoke of Jesus as "the fountain of living waters" (Jer. 17:13), and Isaiah said: "Therefore with joy you will draw water from the wells of salvation" (Isa. 12:3). Because people referred to flowing water as "living water," the woman's thoughts turned to the literal waters of the surrounding springs. Jesus must have access to them. Her interest aroused, she desired the "living water" that He spoke about, but only from a practical standpoint. If she might gain this water, she would no longer have to draw daily from the well.

Jesus gave an example of a soul-winning formula in His dealings with the Samaritan woman. First He awakened in her the *desire* to obtain something better—the "living water." "The need of the world, 'The Desire of all nations,' is Christ. The divine grace which He alone can impart, is as living water, purifying, refreshing, and invigorating the soul."[11] He next *convicted* her of her need when He said to her, "Go, call your husband, and come here" (John 4:16). Jesus knew her checkered past, but she was reluctant to discuss it with a stranger, even if He might be a prophet, as she suspected. Attempting to halt the conversation, she replied with a half-truth: "I have no husband" (verse 17). Discussing the personal details of her life with a stranger was uncomfortable. "Jesus said to her, You have well said, 'I have no husband,' for you have had five husbands, and the one whom you now have is not your husband; in that you spoke truly" (verses 17, 18).

"The listener trembled. A mysterious hand was turning the pages of her life history, bringing to view that which she had hoped to keep forever hidden. Who was He that could read the secrets of her life?"[12] Here was a sinful woman who needed the "living water" Jesus was offering. He had offered to satisfy the thirst of her soul. "The water that Christ referred to was the revelation of His grace in His Word; His Spirit, His teaching, is as a satisfying fountain to every soul. Every other source to which they shall resort will prove unsatisfying. But the word of truth is as cool streams, represented as the waters of Lebanon, which are always satisfying. In Christ is fullness of joy forevermore."[13]

"He thinks of us individually, and knows our every necessity."[14]

IN SPIRIT AND IN TRUTH

God is Spirit, and those who worship Him must worship in spirit and truth. John 4:24.

The Samaritan woman sought to deflect further conversation about her personal life by directing the discussion toward the religious dispute involving the location for true worship. The temple ruins atop Mount Gerizim were close at hand, while the Temple in Jerusalem was closed to her people. She now sought to know from this prophet if He thought the location of worship was significant. Jesus answered, "Woman, believe Me, the hour is coming when you will neither on this mountain, nor in Jerusalem, worship the Father. You worship what you do not know; we know what we worship, for salvation is of the Jews. But the hour is coming, and now is, when the true worshipers will worship the Father in spirit and truth; for the Father is seeking such to worship Him" (John 4:21-23). Jesus repeated the same truth He spoke to Nicodemus: "Unless one is born again, he cannot see the kingdom of God." It is not *where* one worships but *how!*

The Samaritans were just as orthodox as the Jews, but they worshiped God only in form and without any real understanding. All true religion centers in the mind and heart and not on traditions. "And in vain they worship Me, teaching as doctrines the commandments of men" (Mark 7:7). God does not place restraints upon true worship but is interested in the spirit that prompts it.

"Religion is not to be confined to external forms and ceremonies. The religion that comes from God is the only religion that will lead to God. In order to serve Him aright, we must be born of the divine Spirit. This will purify the heart and renew the mind, giving us a new capacity for knowing and loving God. It will give us a willing obedience to all His requirements. This is true worship." [15]

The woman was now convinced that He was a prophet. She knew about the coming Messiah. Her people called Him Taheb, meaning "the returning One" or "the Restorer." When she stated her belief in the coming Taheb, Jesus announced, "I who speak to you am He." "The plain statement made by Christ to this woman could not have been made to the self-righteous Jews." [16] The goods news that He had to hide from the Jews He now revealed to a woman of a despised nation.

Willing obedience to all His requirements is true religion, not adherence to human commandments.

TO DO
HIS WILL

Jesus said to them, "My food is to do the will of Him who sent Me, and to finish His work." John 4:34.

Now excited, the Samaritan woman forgot her errand to fetch water and rushed back to the city to proclaim the arrival of the Taheb. Meanwhile, the disciples had returned with food. When they reached the well they were surprised to see their Master talking with a woman. "Among the Jews it was considered highly improper for a man, and beneath the dignity of a rabbi, to converse with a woman in public. An ancient Jewish literary work . . . advises, 'Let no one talk with a woman in the street, no, not with his own wife.'"[17] The disciples chose not to mention the incident to Jesus out of respect. "They saw Him silent, absorbed, as in rapt meditation. His face was beaming with light, and they feared to interrupt His communion with heaven."[18]

Thinking of His well-being, the disciples urged Him to eat. Knowing they were interested in His welfare, Jesus patiently assured them that doing the will of His Father was far more satisfying than eating. "For I have come down from heaven, not to do My own will, but the will of Him who sent Me" (John 6:38). "To minister to a soul hungering and thirsting for truth was more grateful to Him than eating or drinking. It was a comfort, a refreshment, to Him. Benevolence was the life of His soul."[19]

Christ's four-step process of soul winning was complete. First, He created a desire for the "living water." Second, He brought conviction to the woman. Third, she accepted Jesus as the Taheb, and fourth, He motivated her to bring others to Himself. Such will be the case among all that find the Saviour. Our most earnest desire should be to share our joy with neighbors and friends.

"The most important discourse that Inspiration has given us, Christ preached to only one listener. As He sat upon the well to rest, for He was weary, a Samaritan woman came to draw water; He saw an opportunity to reach her mind, and through her to reach the minds of the Samaritans, who were in great darkness and error. Although weary, He presented the truths of His spiritual kingdom, which charmed the heathen woman and filled her with admiration for Christ. She went forth publishing the news: 'Come, see a man which told me all things that ever I did: is not this the Christ?'"[20]

Each must personally answer to their satisfaction, "Is not this the Christ?"

REAP THE HARVEST

Do you not say, "There are still four months and then comes the harvest"? Behold, I say to you, lift up your eyes and look at the fields, for they are already white for harvest! John 4:35.

While the disciples urged Jesus to eat, the woman gathered her neighbors and led them back to the well. Her excitement was contagious, and they were eager to meet the Messiah. As Jesus sat beside the well He noticed the fields of waving grain. Farmers sowed grain in the autumn in Palestine and harvested it in the spring. It being December or January, the harvest was yet some months distant in April or May. Pointing the scene out to His disciples, Jesus drew a parallel between the harvest of grain and the approaching harvest of the souls pouring out of the city.

Often a literature evangelist or minister first sows spiritual seed, then moves on without seeing any results. Those who follow will reap the harvest of souls. "Here Christ points out the sacred service owed to God by those who receive the gospel. They are to be His living agencies. He requires their individual service. And whether we sow or reap, we are working for God. One scatters the seed; another gathers in the harvest; and both the sower and the reaper receive wages. They rejoice together in the reward of their labor." [21]

Crowding around Jesus, the Samaritans besieged Him with questions. With infinite patience He explained many of the difficulties they perceived in their religious lives. They invited Him to stay with them and for two wonderful days He remained. "Though He was a Jew, Jesus mingled freely with the Samaritans, setting at nought the Pharisaic customs of His nation. In face of their prejudices He accepted the hospitality of this despised people. He slept with them under their roofs, ate with them at their tables—partaking of the food prepared and served by their hands—taught in their streets, and treated them with the utmost kindness and courtesy. And while He drew their hearts to Him by the tie of human sympathy, His divine grace brought to them the salvation which the Jews rejected." [22] The Pharisees wanted a sign, but the Samaritans accepted Him without His performing any miracle.

"The gospel invitation is not to be narrowed down, and presented only to a select few, who, we suppose, will do us honor if they accept it. The message is to be given to all." [23]

INTO GALILEE

So when He came to Galilee, the Galileans received Him, having seen all the things He did in Jerusalem at the feast; for they also had gone to the feast. John 4:45.

When Jesus sat down to rest at Jacob's well, He had come from Judea, where His ministry had produced little fruit. He had been rejected by the priests and rabbis, and even the people who professed to be His disciples had failed of perceiving His divine character."[24] The two-day stay in the Samaritan village greatly tested the disciples. They found it difficult to associate with the enemies of their own nation and could not understand their Master's behavior. Only supreme trust in Him kept them from stating their contempt for "these people" whom Jesus appeared to love.

No good deed goes unrewarded. After Christ's crucifixion persecution struck the church at Jerusalem. "And when His disciples were driven from Jerusalem, some found in Samaria a safe asylum. The Samaritans welcomed these messengers of the gospel, and the Jewish converts gathered a precious harvest from among those who had once been their bitterest enemies."[25]

A different reception awaited Jesus as He returned home to Galilee than what He had experienced in Judah. With its fertile valleys and mountainous regions stretching from the southern slopes of Mount Hermon in the north to the Plain of Esdraelon in the south, Galilee was not just the home of Jesus but also His disciples. Eyewitnesses had reported His cleansing of the Temple. Many in Galilee thought Jesus to be the Messiah.

Bypassing Nazareth, Jesus went farther north to Cana, site of His first miracle. News of His arrival created a stir. The despondent and sick rejoiced in His return. A crowd soon surrounded the Master. "But the people of Nazareth did not believe on Him. For this reason, Jesus did not visit Nazareth on His way to Cana. The Saviour declared to His disciples that a prophet has no honor in his own country. Men estimate character by that which they themselves are capable of appreciating. The narrow and worldly-minded judged of Christ by His humble birth, His lowly garb, and daily toil. They could not appreciate the purity of that spirit upon which was no stain of sin."[26]

The worldly still find little in religion to attract them.

SIGNS AND WONDERS

Unless you people see signs and wonders, you will by no means believe.

John 4:48.

News of Jesus' arrival spread throughout Galilee. In Capernaum, on the shore of the Sea of Galilee, the news reached an officer in the king's service. (Capernaum boasted a customhouse and a Roman garrison, suggesting it was a border town between the territories of Herod Antipas and his brother Philip.) The best physicians in the land could not heal the official's son. Considering his case hopeless, everyone had given the boy up for death.

Thinking Jesus might be the last hope for his son, the nobleman traveled the 16 miles to Cana to petition for healing in person. Arriving in the small town, he found a large multitude surrounding the Master. As he pushed through the crowd, "his faith faltered when he saw only a plainly dressed man, dusty and worn with travel. He doubted that this Person could do what he had come to ask of Him; yet he secured an interview with Jesus, told his errand, and besought the Saviour to accompany him to his home." [27] Jesus had known his request before he left his home in Capernaum.

The nobleman had set conditions for belief. As with others of his people, he was interested in receiving special help from Jesus for purely selfish reasons. The fact saddened Christ. The Samaritans asked no miracle, yet the Jews, God's chosen people, continued to request proof of divinity. True, the nobleman had faith enough to climb the steep trail to Cana to seek the Saviour's help. Jesus wished to heal the child, but in a larger sense He wanted the nobleman to understand his own need.

"Then Jesus said to him, 'Unless you people see signs and wonders, you will by no means believe'" (John 4:48). Immediately the nobleman glimpsed his own true character. His doubt might cost the life of his son. Knowing Jesus could read his very thoughts, in desperation he cried out, "Sir, come down before my child dies!" (verse 49). Instantly the needed transformation took place. Now Jesus did not delay in granting the petition. Unconditional, unhesitating, unquestioning faith was the key. "The Saviour cannot withdraw from the soul that clings to Him, pleading its great need." [28] Jesus simply told the father, "Go your way; your son lives" (verse 50). Initially the nobleman had sought Jesus to accompany him to Capernaum, but now he must return with no evidence that He had granted his request. It tested his new faith, but the gift required trust.

Do you trust Him?

Believe That We Receive

"Go your way; your son lives." So the man believed the word that Jesus spoke to him, and he went his way. John 4:50.

Jesus told the nobleman to return home, that his son was healed. Now "he must act in faith, believing that he had received what he came to ask for."[29] "Jesus always required unquestioning and unconditional faith *before* divine power could be exercised. The nobleman planned to *believe* if he could first *see*; Jesus required him to *believe* before he should *see*. Faith that is conditional upon the granting of certain requests rests on a weak foundation, and will fail under circumstances when God sees best not to grant what is desired."[30]

At home in Capernaum the family saw the child revive. The fever left him in the heat of the day and he settled into a quiet sleep. "Cana was not so far from Capernaum but that the officer might have reached his home on the evening after his interview with Jesus; but he did not hasten on the homeward journey. It was not until the next morning that he reached Capernaum. What a homecoming was that!"[31]

As he approached home, his servants rushed out to greet him with the news "Your son lives!" (John 4:51). Interestingly, his servants echoed the words Jesus used the day before. It puzzled them when the nobleman showed no surprise at their news. Instead, he asked what time the child had rallied. "And they said to him, 'Yesterday at the seventh hour the fever left him'" (verse 52). It had been the very moment his faith seized the Great Physician's promise! Had it been before or after, there might have been some question as to whether the recovery had resulted from some cause other than the words of Jesus. The healing of the nobleman's son resulted in the conversion of his entire household, preparing the way for Christ's future work in Capernaum and His ministry in Galilee.

"He who blessed the nobleman of Capernaum is just as desirous of blessing us. . . . Not because we see or feel that God hears us are we to believe. We are to trust in His promises. When we come to Him in faith, every petition enters the heart of God. When we have asked for His blessing, we should believe that we receive it, and thank Him that we *have* received it. Then we are to go about our duties, assured that the blessing will be realized when we need it most."[32]

"When we have learned to do this, we shall know that our prayers are answered."[33]

A PRISONER

But Herod the tetrarch, being rebuked by him concerning Herodias, his brother Philip's wife, . . . shut John up in prison.

Luke 3:19, 20.

On his way to visit Rome, Herod Antipas fell in love with Herodias, his niece and wife of his half-brother Herod Philip. Soon Herodias left her husband and Antipas his wife, the daughter of Aretas, king of the Nabataeans. Antipas's first marriage had been a political one to unite the eastern and southern borders of his kingdom against attack by the Nabataeans who lived south of the Dead Sea. The father of the discarded wife was so offended he subsequently waged war and occupied much of Antipas's Transjordanian territory.

John the Baptist publicly rebuked Antipas for his adultery with Herodias. John had been preaching on the Perean side of the Jordan, in Herod Antipas's territory, when arrested. The imprisonment resulted from the undying hatred Herodias held for John. He had exposed her adulterous marriage before the people and caused her great mental anguish; for the Jewish people, as a whole, disapproved of their king's marriage to his half-brother's wife.

Josephus suggested that Herod probably confined John in the fortress of Machaerus, east of the Dead Sea. Others locate the dungeon in Tiberias. Wherever the location, John had spent much of his life outdoors, and the gloomy prison and inactivity weighed upon him. "Despondency and doubt crept over him. His disciples did not forsake him. They were allowed access to the prison, and they brought him tidings of the works of Jesus, and told how the people were flocking to Him. But they questioned why, if this new teacher was the Messiah, He did nothing to effect John's release. How could He permit His faithful herald to be deprived of liberty and perhaps of life?"[34]

Often those who should be friends are the most dangerous of foes! John's disciples did not strengthen his resolve or bring courage to their master. Instead they planted seeds of doubt and discouragement. "Satan rejoiced to hear the words of these disciples, and to see how they bruised the soul of the Lord's messenger."[35] If the Baptist's own disciples questioned the Messiahship of Jesus, how effective had John's ministry been? It troubled him, "but the Baptist did not surrender his faith in Christ."[36] Satan now determined to bring sorrow to Jesus by destroying John. "Jesus did not interpose to deliver His servant. He knew that John would bear the test."[37]

Our words may comfort or bruise. We must guard that we cause no one to falter over the doubts we might voice.

76

Bethesda —House of Grace

When Jesus saw him lying there, . . . He said to him, "Do you want to be made well?"

John 5:6.

Leaving Capernaum, Jesus traveled to Jerusalem for the Passover. No place in the city so plainly spoke of misery and suffering as did the pool of Bethesda near the Sheep Gate. The Sheep Gate (Neh. 3:1) was at the northeast corner of the Temple wall, so the pool was in the northern quarter of the city. Wide porches surrounded the pool on four sides, and a fifth portico over the middle divided it into two halves. Popular superstition held that supernatural powers would periodically disturb the water of the pool. The sufferer who could enter the water first would then be healed. Hundreds packed the porches and eagerly watched the waters for the slightest hint of movement. Should something agitate the water, such a rush of humanity headed for the pool that the weakest and sickest faced a real danger of being crushed. Many despaired of ever reaching the water without assistance. Others succeeded in sliding into the waters, only to drown. Everywhere one looked stood crude shelters erected to provide shade by day and cover by night. Day after suffering day passed until hope finally faded.

At the pool the most selfish, the strongest, and the most determined usually reached the water first. "The most needy were least likely to benefit, whereas Jesus chose the worst case. . . . The gifts of God are for all alike who qualify to receive them."[38] The streets were crowded for Passover and no one noticed the Man from Galilee walking alone, deep in thought and prayer. Looking up, He found Himself before the pool. His gaze took in the multitude of suffering. Jesus plainly saw the evidence of Satan's dominion on earth in the tide of human woe and misery congregated together at the pool. "He saw the wretched sufferers watching for that which they supposed to be their only chance of cure. He longed to exercise His healing power and make every sufferer whole. But it was the Sabbath day. Multitudes were going to the temple for worship, and He knew that such an act of healing would so excite the prejudice of the Jews as to cut short His work."[39]

Jesus finds us lying beside our own Pool of Bethesda and longs to heal our suffering and guilt. Sufferer, wilt thou be made whole?

"WILT THOU BE MADE WHOLE?"

Jesus said to him, "Rise, take up your bed and walk." John 5:8.

Jesus noticed a man crippled for 38 years. Since the pious shunned him because of his past sinful life, he had no one to help him to the water when it moved. From time to time the paralytic lifted his head, gazed longingly at the water, then in disappointment lowered it again as strength faded. Suddenly a face filled with compassion leaned over his small pallet. "Do you wish to be healed?" Jesus asked. Hope flared and faded as he recalled the many times he had tried unsuccessfully to reach the pool's edge. With quiet despair he answered, "Sir, I have no man to put me into the pool when the water is stirred up; but while I am coming, another steps down before me" (John 5:7). Deprived of friends and without hope, he saw no future but death. His focus was still upon the healing miracle of the pool, and he had no thought that Jesus might be capable of helping him.

Jesus commanded, "Rise, take up your bed and walk." Immediately his faith took hold, and he sprang to his feet. "Jesus had given him no assurance of divine help. The man might have stopped to doubt, and lost his one chance of healing. But he believed Christ's word, and in acting upon it he received strength."[40] Retrieving his mat, he straightened for the second time in 38 years and looked about to thank his benefactor, but Jesus had disappeared into the Passover crowd.

As he hurried toward the Temple, several Pharisees stopped the healed man. Joyfully he recounted the miracle of his healing and was surprised they did not share his joy. Piously they stopped his account and coldly demanded to know why he was carrying his bed mat on the Sabbath. The man made no attempt to justify his supposed transgression. Instead he replied, "He who made me well said to me, 'Take up your bed and walk'" (verse 11). The Pharisees knew only one person had the power to perform such a miracle. They wanted proof so they might accuse Him of Sabbathbreaking. But the man could not identify Christ.

Later, in the crowded Temple courtyard, Jesus met the man and explained the relationship between his physical healing and the forgiveness of his sins. "See, you have been made well. Sin no more, lest a worse thing come upon you" (verse 14).

Every miracle Jesus performed served a definite purpose. "His wonderful works were all for the good of others."[41]

SABBATH LEGALISM

For this reason the Jews persecuted Jesus, and sought to kill Him, because He had done these things on the Sabbath. John 5:16.

The Jews had placed so many restrictions upon Sabbath observance that it was no longer a delight. "A Jew was not allowed to kindle a fire nor even to light a candle on the Sabbath. As a consequence the people were dependent upon Gentiles for many services which their rules forbade them to do for themselves. They did not reflect that if these acts were sinful, those who employed others to perform them were as guilty as if they had done the work themselves. They thought that salvation was restricted to the Jews, and that the condition of all others, being already hopeless, could be made no worse. But God has given no commandments which cannot be obeyed by all. His laws sanction no unreasonable or selfish restrictions."[42]

As a result of His miracle at Bethesda, the divine Creator who instituted the Sabbath found Himself brought before the Sanhedrin to answer the charge of Sabbathbreaking. It was only because capital punishment rested with the Roman procurators that the Jewish leaders did not instantly put Him to death. Jesus was slowly, after a year, gaining a following in Jerusalem and Judea. People "could understand His words, and their hearts were warmed and comforted."[43] The prophecy was being fulfilled: "and unto him shall the gathering of the people be" (Gen. 49:10, KJV). The priests and rulers feared Jesus and needed to regain control of the people. A devout Jew dared not disregard the findings of the Sanhedrin. If the assembly denounced Jesus' teachings, the rabbis felt that it would lessen His influence.

Satan took the lead in causing the leaders of Israel to oppose Jesus. The originator of sin, who had declared God's law unjust, he directly opposed Jesus who came to "exalt the law and make it honorable" (Isa. 42:21). Jesus now sought to expose the corrupting and burdensome requirements placed upon His Sabbath. It was to this end that He had chosen to heal the paralytic man upon the Sabbath rather than any other day of the week. And for the same reason He had instructed the man to carry his bed. The opportunity was now His to define what was lawful to do on the Sabbath.

"A wise purpose underlay every act of Christ's life on earth. Everything He did was important in itself and in its teaching."[44] We would do well to study His life with that principle in mind.

79

A WORK OF GOD

But Jesus answered them, "My Father has been working until now, and I have been working." John 5:17.

The Jewish leaders had ample opportunity to know that Jesus was the Messiah. The vision of Zacharias, the announcement of the shepherds, the coming of the Magi, Christ's visit to the Temple at age 12, the witness of John the Baptist—they ignored them all. In addition, they had the Messianic prophecies that all pointed to Jesus, yet they still sought to slay Him for healing a man and commanding him to carry his bed on the Sabbath. Jewish law allowed treatment of the acutely ill but not the chronically sick. "Is a person allowed to heal on the Sabbath? . . . Mortal danger overrides the Sabbath; but if it is doubtful whether he [a sick man] will regain health or not, one should not override the Sabbath." [45] The fact that Jesus chose a man who had been ill for 38 years would seem a clear test of this legal restriction.

Appearing before the Sanhedrin, Jesus pointed out that God worked every day and the demands upon Him were greater upon the Sabbath than upon any other day. "God could not for a moment stay His hand, or man would faint and die. And man also has a work to perform on this day. The necessities of life must be attended to, the sick must be cared for, the wants of the needy must be supplied. He will not be held guiltless who neglects to relieve suffering on the Sabbath. God's holy rest day was made for man, and acts of mercy are in perfect harmony with its intent. God does not desire His creatures to suffer an hour's pain that may be relieved upon the Sabbath or any other day." [46]

"The law forbids secular labor on the rest day of the Lord; the toil that gains a livelihood must cease; no labor for worldly pleasure or profit is lawful upon that day; but as God ceased His labor of creating, and rested upon the Sabbath and blessed it, so man is to leave the occupations of his daily life, and devote those sacred hours to healthful rest, to worship, and to holy deeds. The work of Christ in healing the sick was in perfect accord with the law. It honored the Sabbath." [47] The rabbis could not answer the logic Jesus drew from the Scriptures and nature. Jesus had plainly shown their defense to rest solely upon custom and tradition.

How do you honor the Sabbath day? We are admonished to devote those hours to healthful rest, to worship, and to holy deeds.

FOUR WITNESSES

You search the Scriptures, for in them you think you have eternal life; and these are they which testify of Me. But you are not willing to come to Me that you may have life.

John 5:39, 40.

Standing in the midst of the Sanhedrin, Jesus declared His relationship to His Father in heaven. He chastised His accusers for their ignorance of Scripture. They held the sacred writings that told of the coming Son of God, and yet they rejected that knowledge. Many placed more importance on memorizing the texts than upon understanding them. Jewish law stated: "No one may testify concerning himself."[48] Jesus explained that the rabbis already possessed four great witnesses to His divinity, all of which they consistently had refused to accept. His four arguments were conclusive:

1. "You have sent to John, and he has bore witness to the truth. Yet I do not receive testimony from man, but I say these things that you may be saved" (John 5:33, 34). Although Jesus did not have to rely upon the testimony of common humanity, He nevertheless reminded the leadership that many of them had seen and heard the Baptist.

2. "But I have a greater witness than John's; for the works which the Father has given Me to finish—the very works that I do—bear witness of Me, that the Father has sent Me" (verse 36). The miracles of Christ offered overwhelming evidence of His divinity. "The highest evidence that He came from God is that His life revealed the character of God."[49]

3. "And the Father Himself, who sent Me, has testified of Me. You have neither heard His voice at any time, nor seen His form" (verse 37). Of this speaking to their hearts by the Father, the rabbis knew nothing.

4. "You search the Scriptures, for in them you think you have eternal life; and these are they which testify of Me. But you are not willing to come to Me that you may have life. I do not receive honor from men" (verses 39-41). "Having rejected Christ in His word, they rejected Him in person."[50]

They realized that Jesus was from God, a knowledge that both frightened and emboldened them. Their guilt made them more determined to slay Him. Jesus now departed from Jerusalem and Judea and turned to Galilee and another class of people.

It is not enough to know about Him. You must personally accept Him as your Saviour.

JESUS

MINISTRY IN GALILEE
Christ Our Teacher

Spring A.D. 29 to Spring A.D. 30

Matthew 4:12-15:20

Mark 1:14-7:23

Luke 4:14-9:17

John 6:1-7:1

The Desire of Ages, pp. 231-394

INTO GALILEE

Now after John was put in prison, Jesus came to Galilee, preaching the gospel of the kingdom of God. Mark 1:14.

The first year of Jesus' ministry He devoted to the inhabitants of Jerusalem, the people of Judea, and the leaders of Israel. From the cleansing of the Temple during Passover A.D. 28 to the summons by the Sanhedrin to answer the charge of Sabbathbreaking during Passover A.D. 29, Jesus sought to reach the leadership with His message. "God was seeking to direct their minds to Isaiah's prophecy of the suffering Saviour, but they would not hear. Had the teachers and leaders in Israel yielded to His transforming grace, Jesus would have made them His ambassadors among men."[51] "The jealousy and distrust of the Jewish leaders had ripened into open hatred, and the hearts of the people were turned away from Jesus."[52]

The attraction of tradition and position was strong among the religious leaders. To them, strict tradition determined a person's worth before God, and this took precedence over the standard of God's character as displayed by His own Son. "He came to His own, and His own did not receive Him" (John 1:11). "They sent messengers all over the country to warn the people against Jesus as an impostor. Spies were sent to watch Him, and report what He said and did. The precious Saviour was now most surely standing under the shadow of the cross."[53]

Northeast of Jerusalem, the province of Galilee was a melting pot of citizens from every nation. "The people of Galilee were despised by the rabbis of Jerusalem as rude and unlearned, yet they presented a more favorable field for the Saviour's work."[54] Jesus now traveled home to Galilee and found the people to be sincere and open-minded. They were receptive to what He presented and less biased by the influence of their religious leaders. The public denouncement by the Jerusalem Sanhedrin had sought to frighten Jesus into discontinuing His public ministry, but now, distant from Jerusalem and those who plotted His death, He continued to preach the gospel. Except for the ever-present spies, the reception He received in Galilee was so overwhelming that at times He had to withdraw from the crowds and move from place to place. "The enthusiasm ran so high that it was necessary to take precautions lest the Roman authorities should be aroused to fear an insurrection. Never before had there been such a period as this for the world. Heaven was brought down to men."[55]

Come to Galilee and listen.

HE STOOD UP TO READ

So He came to Nazareth, where He had been brought up. And as His custom was, He went into the synagogue on the Sabbath day, and stood up to read. Luke 4:16.

News of Jesus' miracles and teachings in distant Judea had reached Nazareth. One Sabbath He entered their synagogue to worship. "Here were the familiar forms and faces of those whom He had known from infancy. Here were His mother, His brothers and sisters, and all eyes were turned upon Him."[56] Priests might control the Temple in Jerusalem, but the local synagogue was under the direction of laity. A board of elders supervised the religious and cultural consciousness of the community. At their head a chief officer or "ruler" chose worshipers to read, pray, and exhort. The *chazzan* or deacon removed the sacred scrolls from the ark, a special storage chamber, and replaced them after each reading.

Services were long, and though we do not know their exact contents, they may have consisted of: (1) the *shema*, a recitation of a confession of faith; (2) the *parashah*, a reading from the appointed section of the three-year cycle of the Pentateuch; (3) the *haphtarah*, a reading from the Prophets; (4) the *derashah* or "study" (a sermon, given from a special seat near the lectern called the "chair of Moses" and dealing with the topic of the *haphtarah*); and (5) the benediction, pronounced by a priest if present, otherwise a closing prayer. This particular Saturday the leadership invited Jesus to participate in the service. The *chazzan* delivered Him the scroll of the prophet Isaiah as requested, and He stood. Reverence for the Word required the one reading in public to remain standing.

The passage He selected referred to the coming Messiah. "The Spirit of the Lord God is upon Me, because the Lord has anointed Me to preach the good tidings to the poor; He has sent Me to heal the brokenhearted, to proclaim liberty to the captives, and the opening of the prison to those who are bound; to proclaim the acceptable year of the Lord" (Isa. 61:1, 2). Jesus stopped, handed back the scroll, and sat down. He omitted the favorite portion of the reading, that section which every nationalistic Jew loved, the scriptural passage foretelling "the day of vengeance of our God" (verse 2). Many patriotic Jews believed they alone merited salvation and Gentiles ultimately would receive retribution. "The Jewish idea that salvation was a matter of nationality rather than a personal submission to God blinded the people to the true nature of Christ's mission and led them to reject Him."[57]

We are saved individually, not collectively.

84

PASSING THROUGH THEM

Then He said, "Assuredly, I say to you, no prophet is accepted in his own country." Luke 4:24.

Jesus had just given the *haphtarah*. Handing the scroll back to the deacon, He seated Himself. Every eye focused on Him. The reports of His preaching had not been exaggerated. His former neighbors had now witnessed His manner and thrilled to His gracious words! "The tide of divine influence broke every barrier down; like Moses, they beheld the Invisible. As their hearts were moved upon by the Holy Spirit, they responded with fervent amens and praises to the Lord."[58] Jesus then spoke. "Today this Scripture is fulfilled in your hearing" (Luke 4:21). The meaning of Isaiah became plain as the Holy Spirit enlightened their minds. They saw for the first time that they were the captives in darkness who had departed from God, and they realized their self-righteous attitude threatened their salvation.

The people realized that Jesus was the rumored Messiah, yet what Messiah would speak of His own people in such terms? Reading their self-righteous thoughts, He reminded them of the many widows in Israel during the time of Elijah but that God had sent him to the widow of Zarephath in the land of Sidon. Israel had many lepers during the time of Elisha, but only Naaman the Syrian received cleansing. "Our standing before God depends, not upon the amount of light we have received, but upon the use we make of what we have. Thus even the heathen who choose the right as far as they can distinguish it are in a more favorable condition than are those who have had great light, and profess to serve God, but who disregard the light, and by their daily life contradict their profession."[59]

Jesus' comments aroused national pride, and the people forgot the benediction. Surging forward with angry shouts, they grabbed Him and hurried Him out of the city to a nearby limestone cliff. "Some were casting stones at Him, when suddenly He disappeared from among them. The heavenly messengers who had been by His side in the synagogue were with Him in the midst of that maddened throng. They shut Him in from His enemies, and conducted Him to a place of safety."[60]

"From what dangers, seen and unseen, we have been preserved through the interposition of the angels, we shall never know, until in the light of eternity we see the providences of God. Then we shall know that the whole family of heaven was interested in the family here below, and that messengers from the throne of God attended our steps from day to day."[61]

His Own City

And leaving Naza-
reth, He came and
dwelt in Capernaum,
which is by the sea, in
the regions of
Zebulun and
Naphtali. Matt. 4:13.

Jesus centered His Galilean ministry in the town of Capernaum that He might fulfill what Isaiah had said: "The land of Zebulun and the land of Naphtali, . . . by the way of the sea, beyond the Jordan, in Galilee of the Gentiles. The people who walked in darkness have seen a great light; those who dwelt in the land of the shadow of death, upon them a Light has shined" (Isa. 9:1, 2).

Capernaum, a border town between the states of Herod Antipas and Philip, had a customhouse and Roman garrison. The captain of that garrison built the Jews a synagogue. The generally accepted location for the city placed it two and a half miles from the mouth of the Jordan, on the northwestern shore of the Sea of Galilee where it touched the edge of the Plain of Gennesaret. "The deep depression of the lake gives to the plain that skirts its shores the genial climate of the south. Here in the days of Christ flourished the palm tree and the olive, here were orchards and vineyards, green fields, and brightly blooming flowers in rich luxuriance, all watered by living streams bursting from the cliffs."[62] Stretching back from the shore were clusters of small villages. Fishing boats dotted the lake, and people engaged in common trades.

Capernaum was well situated to become the center of Christ's work. It was on the direct route from Damascus to Egypt, so citizens of many countries passed through on their way to the Mediterranean. Here Jesus had an opportunity to "meet the nations." "At Capernaum Jesus dwelt in the intervals of His journeys to and fro, and it came to be known as 'His own city.'"[63] Here lived the nobleman's son whom Jesus had healed. We know more details of Jesus' Galilean ministry than any other segment of His life. During three separate Galilean tours He taught, healed, and blessed all who came to Him. Initially multitudes flocked to Him and yet, at the end of the year, they would forsake Him.

*"The Sun of Righteousness did not burst upon the world in splendor, to dazzle the senses with His glory. It is written of Christ, 'His going forth is prepared as the morning' (Hosea 6:3, KJV). Quietly and gently the daylight breaks upon the earth, dispelling the shadow of darkness, and waking the world to life. So did the Sun of Righteousness arise, 'with healing in His wings' (Mal. 4:2, KJV)."[64]

HOW HE TAUGHT

Then He went down to Capernaum, a city of Galilee, and was teaching them on the Sabbaths. And they were astonished at His teaching, for His word was with authority.

Luke 4:31, 32.

All who heard the Saviour 'were astonished at His doctrine: for His word was with power.' 'He taught them as one having authority, and not as the scribes' (Luke 4:32; Matt. 7:29)."[65] The priests instructed by rote memorization in a cold and formal monotone. They laced their interpretations of Scripture with rigid requirements, and often gave more than one meaning, which confused the people. Jesus spoke with strong and unquestionable authority. Many understood the deeper truths of God's Word for the first time.

"Christ came to preach the gospel to the poor. He reached the people where they were. He brought plain, simple truth to their comprehension. How simple His language! Even the poorest, the unlearned and ignorant, could understand Him. Not one needed go to a dictionary to obtain the meaning of the high-sounding titles or words that fell from the lips of the greatest Teacher the world ever knew."[66] He knew "how to speak a word in season to him that is weary" (Isa. 50:4, KJV).

Jesus appealed to His listeners' imagination. "The birds of the air, the lilies of the field, the seed, the shepherd and the sheep—with these objects Christ illustrated immortal truth; and ever afterward, when His hearers chanced to see these things of nature, they recalled His words."[67] His message was one of hope and compassion. He was "surrounded with an atmosphere of peace. The beauty of His countenance, the loveliness of His character, above all, the love expressed in look and tone, drew to Him all who were not hardened in unbelief. Had it not been for the sweet, sympathetic spirit that shone out in every look and word, He would not have attracted the large congregations that He did."[68]

Constantly He watched for the glimmer of acceptance His message brought. He rejoiced as he saw familiar faces returning to learn more. But He saw registered on some hardened faces that truth had hit upon a cherished sin they refused to surrender. "Jesus met the people on their own ground, as one who was acquainted with their perplexities. . . . His voice was as music to those who had listened to the monotonous tones of the rabbis. But while His teaching was simple, He spoke as one having authority. This characteristic set His teaching in contrast with that of all others."[69]

The Bible tells us to go and teach (Matt. 28:19, 20).

TEACHING BESIDE THE SEA

And He sat down and taught the multitudes from the boat. Luke 5:3.

The news spread that Jesus was back in Capernaum. Crowds of people sought Him out and brought their sick to be healed. Their constant needs gave Him little chance to rest. As day dawned over the Sea of Galilee, Jesus made His way to the shore in search of quiet time to commune with His Father. The waters of the sea were very clear, so net fishing worked best at night. The disciples had fished all night with little to show for hours of backbreaking labor. Spotting them, Jesus headed for the shore as they approached.

The people had again located Jesus and pressed upon Him. As the disciples landed, Jesus stepped from the rocks along the shore into Peter's boat and asked them to pull out into the water. The people crowding the water's edge now had the opportunity to both see and hear the Saviour. "What a scene was this for angels to contemplate; their glorious Commander, sitting in a fisherman's boat, swayed to and fro by the restless waves, and proclaiming the good news of salvation to the listening throng that were pressing down to the water's edge!"[70]

The wonders of nature surrounded the Creator. "The lake, the mountains, the spreading fields, the sunlight flooding the earth, all furnished objects to illustrate His lessons and impress them upon the mind."[71] Those who heard the good news of salvation thrilled that God loved them. Each time He spoke someone grasped truth and eternal life. "Aged men leaning upon their staffs, hardy peasants from the hills, fishermen from their toil on the lake, merchants and rabbis, the rich and learned, old and young, bringing their sick and suffering ones, pressed to hear the words of the divine Teacher."[72]

Day after day during His Galilean ministry He taught the people. "By the sea, on the mountainside, in the streets of the city, in the synagogue, His voice was heard explaining the Scriptures. Often He taught in the outer court of the temple, that the Gentiles might hear His words."[73] He repeatedly asked, "What saith the Scripture?" "How readest thou?"

"In the Word the Saviour is revealed in all His beauty and loveliness. Every soul will find comfort and consolation in the Bible, which is full of promises concerning what God will do for the one who comes into right relation to Him."[74]

"LET DOWN YOUR NETS"

When He had stopped speaking, He said to Simon, "Launch out into the deep and let down your nets for a catch." Luke 5:4.

The disciples may have followed Jesus for a year, but they still practiced their trade as fishers on Galilee. "The abundance of its fish made fishing a lucrative trade in the time of Jesus." [75] After a night of toil in which they had cast their deep drag nets again and again with no success, the disciples were tired and discouraged. Perhaps they had discussed the recent arrest of John the Baptist. "If such were to be the outcome of John's mission, they could have little hope for their Master, with all the religious leaders combined against Him." [76]

Recent research has shown that fish in Galilee stay below the steep eastern shore at night or in the depths where mineral springs bubble up. As morning approaches, the fish move to shallower places near the mouth of the Jordan River where the current has swept much food into the lake, or near Capernaum and the Seven Springs. Since fish congregate near shore during daylight hours, the fishers consider it foolish to use deep nets after daybreak. But Jesus told them, "Launch out into the deep and let down your nets for a catch." "Love for their Master moved the disciples to obey." [77]

Peter, the master fisher, knew that netting the deep waters in daylight was useless. Discouraged by John's imprisonment, the lack of success in Judea, the hatred of the priests and rulers, and his own lack of success during the night; he questioned Jesus. "Master, we have toiled all night and caught nothing; nevertheless at Your word I will let down the net" (Luke 5:5). The boat made the circuit and closed the loop. Slowly they pulled the net up, but so great was the catch that it began to break. James and John, in their boat nearby, came to aid Peter and Andrew. Both boats were so full they were in danger of sinking. "This miracle, above any other he [Peter] had ever witnessed, was to him a manifestation of divine power. In Jesus he saw One who held all nature under His control." [78] Ashamed for his unbelief, Peter fell at Jesus' feet saying, "Depart from me, for I am a sinful man, O Lord!" (verse 8).

"The deeper lesson which the miracle conveyed for the disciples is a lesson for us also—that He whose word could gather the fishes from the sea could also impress human hearts, and draw them by the cords of His love, so that His servants might become 'fishers of men.'" [79]

FISHERS OF MEN

For he and all who were with him were astonished at the catch of fish which they had taken. . . . And Jesus said to Simon, "Do not be afraid. From now on you will catch men." So when they had brought their boats to land, they forsook all and followed Him. Luke 5:9-11.

Peter was foreman of the fishing enterprise conducted by two sets of brothers and their hired helpers. Peter, Andrew, James, and John centered their fishing business in the small town of Bethsaida Julias, located on the northeastern shore of Galilee and opposite Capernaum. These same disciples had followed Christ off and on since the autumn of A.D. 27. Now in the spring of A.D. 29 Christ asked them to forsake their occupation completely and unite with Him in His ministry.

Here was an opportunity to offer life to those they should meet. At this particular moment, with their huge catch, they were at the pinnacle of business success as fishers. It took no small amount of faith to leave all they knew and enter into an "uncertain livelihood as followers of an itinerant teacher who, up to this time, had apparently had small success."[80] But the men never hesitated. They didn't need time to decide how they would provide for their families. "The decision to dissolve their successful partnership as fishermen for a higher partnership with Jesus as fishers of men was made instantly and intelligently."[81]

Two autumns had passed since they had first learned about the Lamb of God. Though unlearned and humble men, they had the requisite traits necessary for discipleship—they were teachable and devoted to Christ and His mission. Jesus was calling them for their open minds, their loving hearts, and their willing hands. They had native abilities and would graduate from the School of the Master ignorant and uncultured no longer. "God takes men as they are, and educates them for His service, if they will yield themselves to Him. . . . Continual devotion establishes so close a relation between Jesus and His disciple that the Christian becomes like Him in mind and character."[82]

"Our heavenly Father has a thousand ways to provide for us of which we know nothing. Those who accept the one principle of making the service of God supreme, will find perplexities vanish and a plain path before their feet."[83]

God summons us, like Peter, Andrew, James, and John, to enter the School of the Master. "Follow after Me, and I will make you become fishers of men" (Mark 1:17).

HEALING AGAIN ON THE SABBATH DAY

Then they were all amazed, so that they questioned among themselves, saying, "What is this? What new doctrine is this? For with authority He commands even the unclean spirits, and they obey Him."

Mark 1:27.

Jesus' custom of private devotions did not prevent Him from gathering with others on the Sabbath to worship in the synagogue. During the week the synagogue often served as a local court of law or a school, but on the Sabbath it became the center of worship for the entire community. Jesus taught in the synagogues, speaking of the kingdom He had come to establish. While the scribes referred to certain rabbis who said such and such, Jesus spoke with authority. Often He would declare, "I say to you" (Matt. 5:21, 22). His authority came directly from God.

On this particular day a shriek of terror interrupted Him at the exact moment He spoke of His mission to free those who were slaves of sin and Satan. A man rushed forward, screaming, "Let us alone! What have we to do with You, Jesus of Nazareth? Did You come to destroy us? I know who You are—the Holy One of God!" (Mark 1:24). Realizing that Jesus could set him free, the demon-possessed man longed for freedom, but Satan held him back. The battle was violent, throwing the man about in the midst of the congregation. Everything was in turmoil, and people forgot Christ's words in the confusion—as was Satan's plan.

"When the man tried to appeal to Jesus for help, the evil spirit put words into his mouth, and he cried out in an agony of fear."[84] Rebuking the demon, Jesus said, "Be quiet, and come out of him!" (verse 25). Immediately the demon left. The man now stood in total freedom and possession of himself once again. "He who had conquered Satan in the wilderness of temptation was again brought face to face with His enemy."[85] "The healing of the nobleman's son had stirred the city of Capernaum. . . . Now its people witnessed an even greater manifestation of the power of God."[86] Demons recognized in Jesus the Son of God. "Even the demons believe—and tremble!" (James 2:19).

Our condition is no more hopeless than that of the trapped demoniac. Jesus has the power to set us free no matter what chains of sin or addiction bind us!

A Healing Ministry

At evening, when the sun had set, they brought to Him all who were sick and those who were demon-possessed. And the whole city was gathered together at the door.
Mark 1:32, 33.

Leaving the synagogue, Jesus went to Peter's house and discovered that the disciple's mother-in-law was ill with a fever. Luke, ever the physician, tells us that it was a "high fever" (Luke 4:38). "The presence of marshlands not far from Capernaum, whose climate was subtropical, suggests that it may have been malaria." [87] Jesus, entering the house, merely took hold of her hand and assisted her in standing, "and immediately the fever left her. And she served them" (Mark 1:31). This miracle likewise occurred on the Sabbath. Fear of the rabbis kept the inhabitants of Capernaum from coming to Jesus until after the Sabbath had ended, but news of the second miracle spread rapidly.

After sunset, "from the homes, the shops, the market places, the inhabitants of the city pressed toward the humble dwelling that sheltered Jesus. The sick were brought upon litters, they came leaning upon staffs, or, supported by friends, they tottered feebly into the Saviour's presence. Hour after hour they came and went; for none could know whether tomorrow would find the Healer still among them. Never before had Capernaum witnessed a day like this. The air was filled with the voice of triumph and shouts of deliverance." [88] Matthew, Mark, and Luke recorded the memorable occasion. Until then Jesus' ministry in Jerusalem, Judea, and even Nazareth had not seen much success. This outpouring of popular confidence in Him must have encouraged the disappointed men. Mark no doubt exaggerated when he said the "whole city" gathered outside the door; but far into the night Jesus worked, and it was not until the last sufferer had received healing that silence rested once more upon the home of Simon Peter's relative.

"Never was there such an evangelist as Christ. . . . His fame as the Great Healer spread throughout Palestine. The sick came to the places through which He would pass, that they might call on Him for help." [89] "During His ministry, Jesus devoted more time to healing the sick than to preaching. . . . His voice was the first sound that many had ever heard, His name the first word they had ever spoken, His face the first they had ever looked upon. Why should they not love Jesus and sound His praise?" [90]

We should also sound His praise! Gilead does have a balm (Jer. 8:22) to heal the sin-sick soul.

LONG BEFORE DAYLIGHT

Now in the morning, having risen a long while before daylight, He went out and departed to a solitary place; and there He prayed. Mark 1:35.

Far into the night crowds sought the Master Physician. Finally Jesus lay down to rest, sleeping but a few hours. "It being early summer, the sun would rise about 5:00 and the first light of dawn would be visible about 3:30, at the latitude of Capernaum."[91] While still dark, Jesus slipped from town to commune with His Father. "When Jesus took human nature, and became in fashion as a man, He possessed all the human organism. His necessities were the necessities of a man. He had bodily wants to be supplied, bodily weariness to be relieved. By prayer to the Father He was braced for duty and for trial."[92] "Often He passed the entire night in prayer and meditation, returning at daybreak to His work among the people."[93] His communion with His Father provided a continuing source of strength and renewal. "He accepted God's plans for Him, and day by day the Father unfolded His plans. So should we depend upon God, that our lives may be the simple outworking of His will."[94]

From an early age, often prior to a great trial or important event, He would withdraw to speak with His Father. His time alone with God was crucial and valued because of the crowds clamoring for Him. "One of the outstanding and significant characteristics of Christ was that He prayed, often and effectively."[95] Spiritual renewal and refreshment are vital for us too. "We do not value the power and efficacy of prayer as we should."[96]

The disciples awoke with the sun. The people had returned and were asking for Jesus. Searching for and finding Him, the disciples pleaded with Him to return. The people of Capernaum were the first to acclaim Jesus. After so many bitter disappointments, the people's response encouraged the disciples. Perhaps among the fiercely independent Galileans they would find a political base for proclaiming the Messiah. But Jesus surprised them, saying, "Let us go into the next towns, that I may preach there also, because for this purpose I have come forth" (Mark 1:38). Jesus wished the people to recognize their need of spiritual healing. The excitement surrounding His miracles of physical healing was jeopardizing His ability to reach them with spiritual things. His popularity as a great Healer endangered His true mission.

Just as Jesus never lost sight of God's plan for His life, we must focus on His plan for ours.

The Time Is Fulfilled

And Jesus went about all Galilee, teaching in their synagogues, preaching the gospel of the kingdom, and healing all kinds of sickness and all kinds of disease among the people.

Matthew 4:23.

The first Galilean tour took place from early spring to midsummer A.D. 29. It is unclear whether Jesus' companions accompanied Him through Galilee as He proclaimed to the towns and villages that "the time is fulfilled, and the kingdom of God is at hand. Repent, and believe in the gospel" (Mark 1:15). The "time fulfilled" to which He referred was the period Gabriel revealed to Daniel: "Seventy weeks are determined for your people and for your holy city, to finish the transgression, to make an end of sins, to make reconciliation for iniquity, to bring in everlasting righteousness, to seal up vision and prophecy, and to anoint the Most Holy" (Dan. 9:24). Given in symbolism, the prophecy was to be interpreted in prophetic time. A day stands for a year in prophecy (Eze. 4:6; Num. 14:34).

Seventy prophetic weeks equals 490 days or years. The starting period for the prophecy was also known. "Know therefore and understand, that from the going forth of the command to restore and build Jerusalem until Messiah the Prince, there shall be seven weeks and sixty-two weeks" (Dan. 9:25). Sixty-nine weeks equal 483 days or years. The command to restore and build Jerusalem had come from Artaxerxes I Longimanus (Ezra 6:14; 7:1, 9) in the autumn of 457 B.C. Artaxerxes in his seventh regnal year gave Ezra far-reaching powers to reorganize the Jewish state with a great deal of autonomy within the Persian Empire. Later he appointed Nehemiah, his Jewish cupbearer, to be governor of Judea and to complete Jerusalem's city walls.

From 457 B.C., 483 years stretch to the autumn of A.D. 27 (457/456 B.C. to B.C. 1 [no 0 year], A.D. 1 to A.D. 27 [456 + 27 = 483]). Exactly on time Jesus was baptized, received the anointing of the Holy Spirit, and began His ministry. Time was truly fulfilled! Jesus came forth to confirm the covenant with many for one week (seven years), but in the middle of the week (three and a half years) the Messiah was cut off. In the spring of A.D. 31 Christ the supreme sacrifice, which all types pointed to, was offered up on Calvary.

"But like the stars in the vast circuit of their appointed path, God's purposes know no haste and no delay. . . . 'When the fullness of the time was come, God sent forth His Son.'" [97]

THE FINGER OF GOD

Now a leper came to Him, imploring Him, kneeling down to Him and saying to Him, "If You are willing, You can make me clean."

Mark 1:40. •

Lepers were outcasts. Banished from human contact, they warned others as they approached with the mournful cry of "Unclean! Unclean!" No known cure existed, and sufferers were ostracized because of the contagious nature of the disease. Patches of dead and decaying tissue struck fear in the heart of the bravest individual. People considered such a severe disease to be divine retribution for sin. No one could care for a leper, for that would interfere with God's will. Lepers felt abandoned by both society and God Himself.

Jesus' ministry in Galilee had not gone unnoticed by the numerous lepers inhabiting the countryside. Many felt Jesus could not possibly reach them, but one thought, despite the great obstacles, he should make the attempt to contact the Master. There was no record of a leper being healed since Elisha cured Naaman eight centuries before. Could Jesus—would Jesus—attempt to intervene against the supposed direct curse of God? How could he get near enough even to ask for healing?

"Jesus is teaching beside the lake, and the people are gathered about Him. Standing afar off, the leper catches a few words from the Saviour's lips. He sees Him laying His hands upon the sick. . . . He draws nearer and yet nearer to the gathered throng. The restrictions laid upon him, the safety of the people, and the fear with which all men regard him are forgotten. He thinks only of the blessed hope of healing."[98] The crowd, spotting him at last, shrank back in terror. Falling at the feet of Jesus, he uttered his plea. He had great faith and single-mindedness of purpose and total surrender to the ultimate will of the Master!

Jesus reached out His hand and touched the leper. Immediately the man was healed. "His flesh became healthy, the nerves sensitive, the muscles firm. The rough, scaly surface peculiar to leprosy disappeared, and a soft glow, like that upon the skin of a healthy child, took its place."[99] The healing of the leper illustrates Jesus' specific work in cleansing the sinner of sin.

"When we pray for earthly blessings, the answer to our prayer may be delayed, or God may give us something other than we ask, but not so when we ask for deliverance from sin. It is His will to cleanse us from sin, to make us His children, and to enable us to live a holy life."[100]

"SHOW YOURSELF TO THE PRIEST"

See that you say nothing to anyone; but go your way, show yourself to the priest. Mark 1:44.

Jesus charged the leper with silence for several reasons: 1. The priests were the public health officials of their time. They diagnosed leprosy and ordered the segregation of its victims. Only they could lift such a ban and issue a certificate of cleansing. If the priests found out who had healed the man, because of their prejudice against Jesus they might not certify the healing. Silence was necessary for an impartial verdict. Their certification placed official recognition on the miracle.

2. Jesus knew if the leper announced his healing, others with the same disease would rush to Him. His acts of healing would overshadow His message. His miracles were to be secondary to His primary objective of saving humanity from sin.

3. The miracle might play into the hands of those who sought to hinder His work. "The Pharisees had asserted that Christ's teaching was opposed to the law which God had given through Moses; but His direction to the cleansed leper to present an offering according to the law disproved this charge. It was sufficient testimony for all who were willing to be convinced." [101]

The Saviour "longed to reach the priests and teachers who were shut in by prejudice and tradition. He left untried no means by which they might be reached. In sending the healed leper to the priests, He gave them a testimony calculated to disarm their prejudices." [102] Many rejected it, but many others hid the truth away. "During the Saviour's life, His mission seemed to call forth little response of love from the priests and teachers; but after His ascension 'a great company of the priests were obedient to the faith' (Acts 6:7, KJV)." [103]

The miracle took place before a large audience, yet the man, disregarding Jesus' stern warning and thinking Jesus only modest, told everyone about his healing. After the manner of the helpless cripple at the Pool of Bethesda, he glorified the name of Jesus to all who would listen. As a result, people flocked in such numbers to the Master that He had to cease His labors for a time and withdraw into seclusion.

If we exercise the faith, determination, and singleness of purpose the leper showed in seeking healing from Jesus, we may rest assured for "this is the confidence that we have in Him, that if we ask anything according to His will, He hears us" (1 John 5:14).

POWER ON EARTH TO FORGIVE SIN

Which is easier, to say to the paralytic, "Your sins are forgiven you," or to say, "Arise, take up your bed and walk"? Mark 2:9.

Jesus returned from His first Galilean tour to Capernaum after "some days." Matthew tells us He traveled by boat. No sooner had He arrived than people flocked again to Peter's house. The crowd was so dense inside that no one could get through the door. "According to their custom, His disciples sat close about Him, and 'there were Pharisees and doctors of the law sitting by, which were come out of every town of Galilee, and Judea, and Jerusalem.'"[104]

Four friends brought a helpless paralytic to the house, but the crowd outside blocked them. Push though they might, his bearers could make no headway. In desperation, the sick man pleaded with his friends to take him up onto the roof and lower his pallet down. According to Luke, the roof consisted of beams covered with tiles. Removing the tiles, his friends lowered the paralytic to the feet of the Saviour.

Jesus gazed down into the eyes of a man whose faith had overcome every obstacle to gain admittance to the presence of the One who could heal and save. "Son, your sins are forgiven you," Jesus told him (Mark 2:5). Instantly the man's pain ceased, and he felt at peace. The healing stunned the priests, for they had earlier refused to help this very man. "These dignitaries did not exchange words together, but looking into one another's faces they read the same thought in each, that something must be done to arrest the tide of feeling. Jesus had declared that the sins of the paralytic were forgiven. The Pharisees caught at these words as blasphemy."[105] The Levitical penalty for blasphemy, although prohibited by Rome, was death by stoning.

Jesus, reading the priests' thoughts, rebuked them and ordered the man to "arise, take up your bed and walk." The cured man immediately jumped up and walked boldly to the door. As the crowd parted they whispered, "We never saw anything like this!" (verse 12). "This man and his family were ready to lay down their lives for Jesus. No doubt dimmed their faith, no unbelief marred their fealty to Him who had brought light into their darkened home."[106]

"The spirit in which men approach Jesus determines whether they find in Him a steppingstone to heaven or a stumbling block to destruction."[107]

LEVI-MATTHEW

And as He passed by, He saw Levi the son of Alphaeus sitting at the tax office, and said to him, "Follow Me." So he arose and followed Him.
Mark 2:14.

The Roman government auctioned off the privilege of collecting taxes to any citizen who could purchase the franchise. Since the Romans did not pay the *publicanus* a salary, each had to collect enough money through the taxation of his neighbors to earn a living. Naturally the people uniformly despised tax collectors. No self-respecting Jew would sell themselves into usury to a foreign power, betraying their own people and taxing God's free gifts—the land and its bounty—but Matthew was such a "publican." Stationed in Capernaum, he probably collected and split revenues with Herod Antipas. He had heard the Saviour's teachings, and the Holy Spirit was working to show Matthew his sinfulness. Now he longed to speak with Jesus about his needs, but felt that the Teacher would probably condemn him as all the other religious teachers had.

Each day Matthew collected tribute from the caravans and travelers passing along the road from Damascus to Jerusalem. This day he noticed that the Teacher seemed to be moving closer than usual to the tollbooth beside the sea. Stopping, Jesus spoke directly to Levi-Matthew: "Follow Me." Immediately Matthew left his lucrative business and followed Him. To each disciple came the same call. Each had to decide whether to unite with the Master in poverty and hardship or to remain in familiar and comfortable surroundings. "So every soul is tested as to whether the desire for temporal good or for fellowship with Christ is strongest."[108]

The act of calling Matthew outraged the Pharisees. Jesus had selected a publican as a disciple! Such was a high offense not just against social and national custom but also against religious tradition. Jesus had placed Himself outside the behavior expected of a pious religious teacher. The Pharisees now sought to turn the people against Him because He associated with traitors. They failed to see the joy that filled the heart of Matthew the tax-gatherer. "It was enough for him that he was to be with Jesus, that he might listen to His words, and unite with Him in His work."[109]

"Principle is always exacting. No man can succeed in the service of God unless his whole heart is in the work and he counts all things but loss for the excellency of the knowledge of Christ. No man who makes any reserve can be the disciple of Christ, much less can he be His colaborer."[110]

HARVESTING ON THE SABBATH

The Sabbath was made for man, and not man for the Sabbath. Therefore the Son of Man is also Lord of the Sabbath.

Mark 2:27, 28.

One Sabbath Jesus and His disciples walked along a path bordering a field of ripe grain. They had come from the synagogue where Jesus had remained "to a late hour." Hungry and seeing the heads of grain, the disciples plucked and rubbed them together in their hands to extract the kernels. "On any other day this act would have excited no comment, for one passing through a field of grain, an orchard, or a vineyard, was at liberty to gather what he desired to eat. . . . But to do this on the Sabbath was held to be an act of desecration."[1]

Spies, sent by the Pharisees to find fault, recoiled in shock at the double offense. The disciples were plucking, or reaping, as well as rubbing the grain together in their hands which was, after a fashion, threshing. The Pharisees accosted Jesus, "Look, why do they do what is not lawful on the Sabbath?" (Mark 2:24). Jesus defended His disciples by referring "to examples from the Old Testament, acts performed on the Sabbath by those who were in the service of God."[2]

The Jewish leaders knew these passages well. David had entered the house of God and eaten the shewbread that only priests might eat. The religious authorities recognized that the priests worked harder on Sabbath than any other day, for their work was in service to God. How could the disciples, who were working with Christ Himself, be any less engaged in God's service? The Pharisees' blindness had turned Sabbath observance into an endless round of human requirements that misrepresented God as a tyrant.

God created the Sabbath for humanity. It remains the Lord's day, for it belongs to Christ. He set it apart as a memorial of His creation and of His power to sanctify. "Moreover I also gave them My Sabbaths, to be a sign between them and Me, that they might know that I am the Lord who sanctifies them" (Eze. 20:12). "Jesus personally adhered to the requirements of the law of Moses and the Decalogue in every respect and taught His followers to do the same. . . . But throughout His ministry on earth Christ was in conflict with the Jewish leaders over the validity of man-made laws and traditions."[3]

No human may change the sacredness of God's day to a different day or load the Sabbath day down with burdensome restrictions. The seventh-day Sabbath, as ordained by God, is a blessing He gave to the human race to study God's character as revealed by revelation and nature.

GNATS AND CAMELS

Then He said to them, "Is it lawful on the Sabbath to do good or to do evil, to save life or to kill?" Mark 3:4.

The fame of the new Teacher had spread beyond the limits of Palestine, and, notwithstanding the attitude of the hierarchy, the feeling was widespread that this might be the hoped-for Deliverer. Great multitudes thronged the steps of Jesus, and the popular enthusiasm ran high"[4] One Sabbath, as Jesus entered the synagogue, He saw a man with a withered hand. The Pharisees hoped to accuse Jesus of Sabbathbreaking should He heal the man. Jesus motioned the man forward. Turning to the Pharisees, He asked, "Is it lawful on the Sabbath to do good or to do evil?" "What man is there among you who has one sheep, and if it falls into a pit on the Sabbath, will not lay hold of it and lift it out? Of how much more value then is a man than a sheep? Therefore it is lawful to do good on the Sabbath" (Matt. 12:11, 12). They remained silent. The spies could not answer Jesus, for to do so would show they regarded finances above a person's welfare.

Rabbinical tradition prohibited 39 major types of labor on the Sabbath. "The first 11 of these were steps leading to the production and preparation of bread."[5] Twelve more dealt with sewing and seven with preparing deer carcasses for leather or food. The remaining prohibitions concerned writing, building, transporting items, and starting or extinguishing fires. A Sabbath day's journey must not exceed two thirds of a mile. One must not look into a mirror or light a candle. The list seemed endless and hypocrisy existed. "The same regulations permitted an egg laid on the Sabbath to be sold to a Gentile, and a Gentile to be hired to light a candle or a fire."[6] Their attempts to "strain out a gnat and swallow a camel" (Matt. 23:24) made a mockery of the Sabbath. Jesus' commonsense approach was a welcome respite.

Stepping outside before the service concluded, the Pharisees—now extremely distraught—sought to join with their avowed enemies the Herodians. Perhaps Herod would arrest Jesus as he had the Baptist and solve their problem for them. Since early spring they had decided to kill Jesus. By asking them if they thought it right to do good on the Sabbath, Jesus held before them their own wickedness. Was it better to contemplate murdering the Son of God or to bring happiness and healing to the afflicted?

Does your Christian life contain any gnats or camels?

SPLITTING LEGAL HAIRS

But He knew their thoughts, and said to the man who had the withered hand, "Arise and stand here." And he arose and stood. Luke 6:8.

On the day Jesus healed the man with the withered hand, the men sent to observe Jesus "watched Him closely" (Luke 6:7). The religious lawyers sought to find a case against Him that would hold up in a Jewish court. If they could produce such a case, then they could stop His ministry from siphoning off their followers. Jesus would not escape such enemies during the remainder of His sojourn on earth.

The man with the withered hand was probably seated in the rear of the synagogue. Jesus was near the front either sitting or standing near the Moses Seat, for He had just given the sermon. When He invited the man to "arise and stand here" (verse 8), Jesus no doubt placed him in the center of the congregation where everyone present could see him, in contrast to the spies skulking in the shadows and whispering behind the pillars.

Jesus now raised a legal question for the religious experts: "Is it lawful . . . ?" (verse 9). Rabbinical law forbade the relief of pain and suffering on the Sabbath for those who had chronic conditions or illnesses. Further amplification of a different Jewish regulation held that if one refused to do good when they were able, then that was the same as inflicting further injury. To neglect to care for life was to take life. Which took precedence, the sixth commandment or the fourth? Rabbinical law loved to split legal hairs. However, there is no conflict between the two commandments according to the One who wrote God's Law. Their hatred and desire to murder Jesus made the scribes and Pharisees the real Sabbathbreakers. To perform acts of mercy and healing on the Sabbath was wholly in keeping with God's love for His created beings.

Jesus paused for the meaning of His words to register with His hearers. "And when He had looked around at them all, He said to the man, 'Stretch out your hand'" (verse 10). It took great faith for the man to raise an arm that could not move. As with most of His miracles, Jesus required the recipient to cooperate with Him for the healing to take place.

"Do not wait to feel that you are made whole, but say, 'I believe it; it is so, not because I feel it, but because God has promised.'" [7]

AND THEY CAME TO HIM

And He went up on the mountain and called to Him those He Himself wanted. And they came to Him. Mark 3:13.

In the hills west of the Sea of Galilee Jesus spent another night in prayer under the trees. "At times the bright beams of the moon shone upon His bowed form. And then again the clouds and darkness shut away all light. The dew and frost of night rested upon His head and beard while in the attitude of a supplicant. He frequently continued His petitions through the entire night. He is our example."[8] Descending the hill, He summoned 12 from among His followers to meet with Him at first light on the slope overlooking the lake. Jesus called "and they came to Him." Once again people responded without delay when He made the invitation.

Why just 12 disciples? No one knows, but we are told it was not because these particular individuals had anything to recommend them. "All the disciples had serious faults when Jesus called them to His service."[9] Five had been with Jesus from the very beginning. Most of the others had associated for some time with Him in His ministry. Though poor and for the most part illiterate, these Galileans were undergoing daily transformation through the working of the Holy Spirit. Their Master's lessons were slowly developing a harmony and unity of purpose within the little band. The love of and for their Master was the glue binding them to Him and to each other. They had come as "disciples" to learn and now He appointed them as "apostles" to teach. Jesus instructed them in their duties, and when finished He gathered them close around Him. "Kneeling in the midst of them, and laying His hands upon their heads, He offered a prayer dedicating them to His sacred work. Thus the Lord's disciples were ordained to the gospel ministry."[10] It was yet another example of divinity linking with humanity to save the world.

"God takes men as they are, with the human elements in their character, and trains them for His service, if they will be disciplined and learn of Him. They are not chosen because they are perfect, but notwithstanding their imperfections, that through the knowledge and practice of the truth, through the grace of Christ, they may become transformed into His image."[11]

The One who called the fishers to leave their nets is still summoning men and women to His service in the last days of earth's history.

Seek, Find, Follow

Then He appointed twelve, that they might be with Him and that He might send them out to preach. Mark 3:14.

Peter, Andrew, James, and John sought Him, found Him, and followed Him.

Peter, the self-appointed spokesman for the group, was a man of extremes. "In him, diverse and contradictory traits of character existed side by side. He seems always to have been eager, ardent, warmhearted, generous, bold, daring, and courageous, but too often impulsive, inconsistent, unstable, rash, undependable, boastful, overconfident, and even reckless." [12]

Andrew, Peter's brother, was the only one of the fishing partners never to enter the inner circle around Jesus. We know little of Andrew. Being the brother of such an outgoing individual as Peter would tend to make one less noticeable by comparison. "Andrew appears to have been a diligent worker, though perhaps not so gifted in qualities of leadership as his brother." [13]

James was a son of Zebedee and probably older than his brother John, since all biblical accounts mention him first. "The New Testament record presents James as at first a somewhat selfish, ambitious, and outspoken man (Mark 10:35-41), but later as a quiet and capable leader." [14] He would be one of the first martyred, while his brother John would be the last of the 12 to die.

John, the brother of James, was "by nature proud, self-assertive, ambitious of honor, impetuous, resentful under injury, and eager to take revenge. . . . John yielded himself more completely than any of the others to the transforming power of the perfect life of Jesus, and came to reflect the Saviour's likeness more fully than did his fellow disciples." [15] He became the "disciple that Jesus loved."

Of these four, Peter, James, and John drew closer still, and John was the closest of all to Jesus. People noticed that they had been with Christ. "When we see men firm in principle, fearless in duty, zealous in the cause of God, yet humble and lowly, gentle and tender, patient toward all, ready to forgive, manifesting love for souls for whom Christ died, we do not need to inquire: Are they Christians? They give unmistakable evidence that they have been with Jesus and learned of Him." [16]

Christians themselves may not notice the change, but those around them will recognize that all pride and exaltation have been brought low and Christ exalted.

THE FOXES HAVE HOLES

And Jesus said to him, "Foxes have holes and birds of the air have nests, but the Son of Man has nowhere to lay His head."

Matt. 8:20.

Judas Iscariot was unique among the disciples. If Judas was from Kerioth, a small town between the Dead Sea and Beersheba, he was the only disciple who was not Galilean. Jesus didn't summon Judas to join Him on the mountainside. He forced himself into the group in hope that he might gain some high position in the coming new kingdom. Jesus understood Judas's real motivation. Christ made His statement of poverty to show Judas there would be no glory or wealth along the path to the cross.

The man impressed the other disciples because "he was of commanding appearance, a man of keen discernment and executive ability, and they commended him to Jesus as one who would greatly assist Him in His work. They were surprised that Jesus received him so coolly." [17] Each disciple felt the coming Messiah would establish an earthly kingdom. That Jesus did not attempt to secure the favor of those in positions to support such a political movement seemed incomprehensible to them. At the very least, with the assistance of a person such as Judas, they might greatly advance the ministry and approach the necessary leaders.

Christ neither welcomed nor rebuked Judas, but did entrust him with the meager funds that came to the ministry from the contributions of believers. Judas exalted his position, leading everyone to believe the treasurer's guidance was paramount to directing future labors. The disciples reacted in awe to the talented, ambitious, handsome, articulate Judean with all the right political connections. Only Jesus looked upon his heart. "He knew the depths of iniquity to which, unless delivered by the grace of God, Judas would sink. In connecting this man with Himself, He placed him where he might, day by day, be brought in contact with the outflowing of His own unselfish love." [18]

The same opportunities existed for Judas as for the others, yet Judas clung to his own selfish idea of how to promote a Messiah. "The principles that should govern the heart made new were constantly the theme of the teachings of Christ. But they were not received by Judas." [19]

We must be on guard lest we judge by outward appearances alone. "For the Lord does not see as man sees; for man looks at the outward appearance, but the Lord looks at the heart" (1 Sam. 16:7).

THE UNNAMED MOUNTAIN

And seeing the multitudes, He went up on a mountain, and when He was seated His disciples came to Him. Matt. 5:1.

After the ordination, Jesus walked down the hillside to the nearby shore. Although it was yet early, people had started to gather on the beach. Since He had begun His work in Galilee some months before, the Teacher's fame had spread rapidly. "Besides the usual crowds from the Galilean towns, there were people from Judea, and even from Jerusalem itself; from Perea, from Decapolis, from Idumea, away to the south of Judea; and from Tyre and Sidon, the Phoenician cities on the shore of the Mediterranean."[20]

Many in the throng, including His disciples, harbored hope that He was the promised Deliverer. The disciples were perplexed when Jesus did not seek to align Himself with those who might further a political revolt. Yet this day somehow seemed special. Perhaps Jesus would finally announce His intention of establishing the universal kingdom they so desperately sought. They followed Him eagerly now and waited for His long-anticipated announcement.

"Then, as the narrow beach did not afford even standing room within reach of His voice for all who desired to hear Him, Jesus led the way back to the mountainside. Reaching a level space that afforded a pleasant gathering place for the vast assembly, He seated Himself upon the grass, and His disciples and the multitude followed His example."[21] As was the ancient custom for teachers, Jesus sat to teach. The majority of His audience were fishers and the poor. The spies from Jerusalem were present, as were a multitude of curious foreigners. His disciples pressed in close, forming a circle at His feet. All anticipated some great announcement. But the sermon they received was not what they expected. Yet this longest of all documented sermons that the Messiah gave was clearly special.

"The mountain on which Christ delivered the Sermon on the Mount has been called the 'Sinai of the New Testament,' inasmuch as it holds the same relationship to the Christian church as Mount Sinai did to the Jewish nation. It was on Sinai that God proclaimed the divine law. It was on the unknown mountain of Galilee that Jesus reaffirmed the divine law, explaining its meaning in greater detail and applying its precepts to the problems of daily life."[22]

"The truths He taught are no less important to us than to the multitude that followed Him. We no less than they need to learn the foundation principles of the kingdom of God."[23]

THE NATURE OF THE KINGDOM

Blessed are the poor in spirit, for theirs is the kingdom of heaven. Blessed are those who mourn, for they shall be comforted. Matt. 5:3, 4.

Jesus turned the human idea of happiness completely upside down. The disciples couldn't believe what they were hearing. Could it be that the Man they had chosen to give up their fishing enterprise for was not going to form an earthly kingdom? The thrilling anticipation that Israel would soon be honored among nations Christ now shattered in one sentence. "Such teaching is contrary to all they have ever heard from priest or rabbi." [24] Jesus was seeking to give the people a right concept of His kingdom and therefore of His character. Happy are those who know their spiritual poverty and feel their need. "At the commencement of His inaugural address as King of the kingdom of divine grace Christ proclaims that the main objective of the kingdom is to restore the lost happiness of Eden to the hearts of men." [25]

The first requirement for citizenship in His kingdom was to sense one's need of divine help. The haughty priest, the self-righteous Pharisee, the learned Sadducee, those who feel no need of heaven's gift—they are in the worst of all possible spiritual danger. "The proud heart strives to earn salvation; but both our title to heaven and our fitness for it are found in the righteousness of Christ." [26] The poor in spirit see their sinfulness and, like the publican, they can only cry, "God, be merciful to me a sinner" (Luke 18:13).

The second requirement follows closely upon the first. Those who sense their need will naturally sorrow for their sins. Conviction of sin and sorrow for sin are twin workings of the Holy Spirit. When we realize that each sin wounds our Saviour anew, we mourn for those sinful tendencies that cause Him anguish. But mourning alone has no power to remove sin's guilt. The comfort of forgiveness and reconciliation with God and the precious gift of His grace replace our mourning with ultimate rejoicing. "The tears of the penitent are only the raindrops that precede the sunshine of holiness." [27] "The Lord will work for all who put their trust in Him. Precious victories will be gained by the faithful. Precious lessons will be learned. Precious experiences will be realized." [28]

Sorrowing for the sins of the world and an intense longing for the new and heavenly kingdom indicate that Christians have linked themselves with the Man of sorrows.

EVIDENCE OF NOBILITY

Blessed are the meek, for they shall inherit the earth. Matt. 5:5.

One of the beautiful aspects of the "blessings" is that they trace, step by step, the progression of the Christian experience. Meekness is an attitude. "The highest evidence of nobility in a Christian is self-control."[29] Many professed Christians need to master self! The proud and haughty inherit this earth, but the meek *shall* inherit the kingdom of grace. "And whoever exalts himself will be humbled, and he who humbles himself will be exalted" (Matt. 23:12). Those whose highest goal is to learn and do God's will gain entrance into the kingdom.

God regards with great tenderness those who are meek and lowly. "He [God] has shown you, O man, what is good; and what does the Lord require of you but to do justly, to love mercy, and *to walk humbly* with your God?" (Micah 6:8). "Though the Lord is on high, yet He regards the lowly; but the proud He knows from afar" (Ps. 138:6). Our Saviour set the example for us to follow during His life on earth. "Jesus emptied Himself, and in all that He did, self did not appear. He subordinated all things to the will of His Father."[30] "The Saviour's life on earth, though lived in the midst of conflict, was a life of peace. While angry enemies were constantly pursuing Him, He said, 'He that sent me is with me: the Father hath not left me alone; for I do always those things that please him' (John 8:29, KJV)."[31]

The one constantly on guard to protect self is never at peace. The slightest insult or word of condemnation often arouses a swift reply. Instead those words meant to cut and wound us should fall upon deaf ears. Revenge and hatred originated with Satan and are perpetuated by those who feel they must protect self from every perceived slight. "It was through the desire for self-exaltation that sin entered into the world, and our first parents lost the dominion over this fair earth, their kingdom. It is through self-abnegation that Christ redeems what was lost. And He says we are to overcome as He did."[32] Christ was "gentle and lowly in heart" (Matt. 11:29).

Christians should embrace the attributes Jesus set forth that day upon the mountain: "The fruit of the Spirit is love, joy, peace, longsuffering, kindness, goodness, faithfulness, gentleness, self-control. Against such there is no law" (Gal. 5:22, 23).

"But you, O man of God, flee these things and pursue righteousness, godliness, faith, love, patience, gentleness" (1 Tim. 6:11).

LOVE AND MERCY

Blessed are those who hunger and thirst for righteous-ness, for they shall be filled. Blessed are the merciful, for they shall obtain mercy. Matt. 5:6, 7.

God is love. Righteousness is holiness or God's likeness. Most of all, it is love. "The more we know of God, the higher will be our ideal of character and the more earnest our longing to reflect His likeness."[33] It is not enough to believe that Jesus was not some imposter and that Bible religion is not a clever story. Nor is it enough to hold that Jesus can save. The theory of truth will not be enough to get you into the kingdom. Just because your name is on the church rolls is no guarantee of salvation. "Righteousness is right doing, and it is by their deeds that all will be judged. Our characters are revealed by what we do. The works show whether the faith is genuine."[34] The Holy Spirit constantly assists the dedicated believer in attaining the perfection of character that is the fine linen that clothes the saints (Rev. 19:8).

In close approximation to hungering and thirsting for righteousness are mercy and purity of heart. The individual who exhibits compassion for the poor, the downtrodden, the oppressed, is showing mercy to one of the least of Christ's brethren. Micah shows us the way: "He [God] has shown you, O man, what is good; and what does the Lord require of you but to do justly, *to love mercy,* and to walk humbly with your God?" (Micah 6:8). The golden rule is the principle of mercy to others. It is not enough to speak the words; one must do the deeds of mercy (Matt. 25:31-46).

"Kind words, looks of sympathy, expressions of appreciation, would be to many a struggling and lonely one as the cup of cold water to a thirsty soul. A word of sympathy, an act of kindness, would lift burdens that rest heavily upon weary shoulders. And every word or deed of unselfish kindness is an expression of the love of Christ for lost humanity."[35] All those who show mercy will ultimately receive mercy from the compassionate Saviour. The character of the Christian must develop in this life.

"It should be written upon the conscience as with a pen of iron upon a rock, that he who disregards mercy, compassion, and righteousness, he who neglects the poor, who ignores the needs of suffering humanity, who is not kind and courteous, is so conducting himself that God cannot cooperate with him in the development of character."[36]

THEY SHALL SEE GOD

Blessed are the pure in heart, for they shall see God.

Matt. 5:8.

The citizen of the new kingdom will be pure in heart. But Jesus did not have in mind the ceremonial purity that obsessed Pharisee and Sadducee. His reference involved more than sexual purity. Jesus was speaking of the inward cleanliness of the heart and its desires. "In one who is learning of Jesus, there will be manifest a growing distaste for careless manners, unseemly language, and coarse thought. When Christ abides in the heart, there will be purity and refinement of thought and manner."[37]

Jeremiah said: "The heart is deceitful above all things, and desperately wicked; who can know it?" (Jer. 17:9). Those who are pure in heart are not sinless, but Christians who place their trust in Christ and let His grace motivate them to live a better life. Renouncing the sins of the past and pressing on toward the goal of the high calling of God in Christ Jesus (Phil. 3:14), the Christian aims for perfection *in* Him.

We may, through the eyes of faith, see God *now.* Ultimately, in the heavenly kingdom, we will have the privilege of seeing Him face-to-face (1 John 3:2; Rev. 22:4), but "only those who develop the heavenly vision in this present world will have the privilege of seeing God in the world to come."[38] "For now we see in a mirror, dimly, but then face to face" (1 Cor. 13:12). Sin clouds our judgment and fogs our vision, making it harder to see God. If we cherish sin, we will lose any accurate picture of Christ. Self takes the place of Christ and superimposes upon Him the attributes that the sinner wishes. The crystal-clear vision of the character of God, who is: "merciful and gracious, long-suffering, and abounding in goodness and truth" (Ex. 34:6) vanishes. On the other hand, "the pure in heart see God in a new and enduring relation, as their Redeemer; and while they discern the purity and loveliness of His character, they long to reflect His image."[39]

Those who heard His message were amazed. The disciples could not fathom the depths of Christ's words. Their own selfishness blinded them to the Father's love. Even in the midst of people, Jesus walked alone. The far-reaching principles He set forth on the mount were difficult for His listeners to comprehend. "He was understood fully in heaven alone."[40]

We should pray for crystal-clear vision to see God as our Redeemer.

Shalom

Blessed are the peacemakers, for they shall be called sons of God.

Matt. 5:9.

As Jesus spoke these truths, the people looked at each other. How could this be? His teachings were so different from those of the rabbis. The Pharisees regarded wealth highly, yet Jesus had said wealth, power, and status meant nothing. Now, to be a real "son of God," they must be peacemakers!

Those guided by the Spirit of Christ will love their God and their fellow human beings. Jesus is the original "Prince of Peace" (Isa. 9:6). The angels at His birth proclaimed: "Glory to God in the highest, and on earth *peace*, goodwill toward men" (Luke 2:14). Christ came to earth to reunite humanity with God, to restore peace with God through harmony to His law. "Great peace have those who love Your law, and nothing causes them to stumble" (Ps. 119:165).

Being justified by faith in the merits of Jesus, we may achieve peace with God (Rom. 5:1). The feeling of being reconciled and at peace with God fills the heart with joy and gladness. Once again we find ourselves fashioned in God's image, resembling His character, and worthy to be called "children of God." "Beloved, now we are children of God; and it has not yet been revealed what we shall be, but we know that when He is revealed, we shall be like Him, for we shall see Him as He is" (1 John 3:2).

"Shalom" also signifies complete and full peace. Christians are to be at peace with each other. "Pursue peace with all people, and holiness, without which no one will see the Lord" (Heb. 12:14). Maintaining a quiet peaceful attitude toward fellow human beings is difficult. The human heart is ever ready to repay unkindness and slander with equal ferocity. But to turn the other cheek and return love for hatred is the mark of a Christian. The world may deem such action as cowardly, but the Christian is a "child of God." "For as many as are led by the Spirit of God, these are sons of God" (Rom. 8:14). Heaven pulses with perfect peace. The harmony found in the heavenly courts will appear in the life of the true follower of the Prince of Peace.

In the everyday actions of the professed Christian we see the spirit that truly activates the character. "Let nothing but kind, loving words fall from your lips concerning the members of your family or of the church." [41]

PERSECUTION

Blessed are those who are persecuted for righteousness' sake, for theirs is the kingdom of heaven. Matt. 5:10.

Jesus never said the life of the righteous would have no trials or tribulations. The Christian constantly, through a life of devotion to God, stands as a rebuke to the sinner. Such a mirror plainly reveals the sinner's defects. Satan and his followers seek with unabated furor to overcome and destroy the "children of God." Persecution has taken many forms through the ages, but its underlying principle is hatred by the wicked for all those obedient to the God of heaven.

"Rejoice and be exceedingly glad, for great is your reward in heaven" (Matt. 5:12). Persecution should bring joy to the Christian, for it shows that he or she is following Christ. No matter the temptation or trial, the suffering builds character. The stone must be pressed against the lathe, cut, and polished to come forth a jewel. Trials are the Lord's refining process. Rejoice, for you do not suffer by yourself. He said: "My grace is sufficient for you, for My strength is made perfect in weakness" (2 Cor. 12:9).

Those who trust in the Lord realize He is by their side and will never leave them. Their trial may be fierce, but "we know that all things work together for good to those who love God, to those who are the called according to His purpose" (Rom. 8:28). The sacrifice may be great, but the reward is exceedingly greater. "And behold, I am coming quickly, and My reward is with Me, to give to every one according to his work" (Rev. 22:12). James 1:2-4 tells us to be joyful, for trial tests our faith. Faith produces patience, and waiting upon the Lord develops trust. Christ warned His disciples that others would hate them because of Him, "but he who endures to the end will be saved" (Matt. 10:22). Difficulties might cause some to surrender their faith because they might feel the cost too great, "but God is faithful, who will not allow you to be tempted beyond what you are able, but with the temptation will also make the way of escape, that you may be able to bear it" (1 Cor. 10:13). Each follower of Christ must shoulder his or her cross and follow Him.

Those who consider themselves repositories of "truth" are often the first to persecute others and show that they themselves have not the genuine article. Genuine Christianity reveals love.

SALT

You are the salt of the earth; but if the salt loses its flavor, how shall it be seasoned? It is then good for nothing but to be thrown out and trampled underfoot by men. Matt. 5:13.

Jesus used the symbol of salt to direct the people's minds to the influence of the Christian life. By mingling with others, the Christian reaches them with the gospel of Christ. "They are not saved in masses, but as individuals. Personal influence is a power." [42] The salvation of others is the primary goal and responsibility of the disciple of Christ. "The savor of the salt represents the vital power of the Christian—the love of Jesus in the heart, the righteousness of Christ pervading the life." [43] Salt must be in contact with food in order to be an effective preservative. Just so, Christians are not to draw back from humanity and refuse to be channels for God's grace. We are to remain in close contact with our fellow citizens and exert an influence for good in our world. "Though the wicked know it not, they owe even the blessings of this life to the presence, in the world, of God's people whom they despise and oppress." [44]

The priests added salt to every Jewish Temple sacrifice, thus making it acceptable. It represented the righteousness of Christ. "In order that our lives may be 'a living sacrifice, holy, acceptable unto God' (Rom. 12:1, KJV), they must be preserved and seasoned by the perfect righteousness of Jesus Christ." [45]

But what of salt that has lost its savor? Those "having a form of godliness but denying its power" (2 Tim. 3:5) are Christians in name only. Their lives no longer reflect Christ's love for others. Without His power and love, the Christian becomes "good for nothing." Woe to that professed Christian who becomes a detriment to the cause of the kingdom by misrepresenting the principles of Christ. Such a Christian is worse than an unbeliever. The Christian who does not have a living personal relationship with the Saviour cannot depict Him to the world. "We cannot give to others that which we do not ourselves possess." [46]

"As they listened to the words of Christ, the people could see the white salt glistening in the pathways where it had been cast out because it had lost its savor and was therefore useless. It well represented the condition of the Pharisees and the effect of their religion upon society." [47]

Remember, you are a channel for God's grace to the world, the real spice of life.

THE LIGHT OF THE WORLD

*You are the light
of the world.*

Matt. 5:14.

As the Sermon on the Mount started, the morning sun had appeared. Now the sun had risen high enough to chase away the lingering shadows in the valleys and ravines. "The placid surface of the lake reflected the golden light and mirrored the rosy clouds of morning."[48] The towns and villages, situated on surrounding hills for protection, were clearly visible in the bright morning light. Jesus, pointing to them, explained that a Christian is to reflect the light of his or her Master's love. "No other light ever has shone or ever will shine upon fallen man save that which emanates from Christ."[49] As Jesus came to show us the Father, we are to reveal Christ to others.

Those who lived in small one-room dwellings often had only a single lamp to illuminate their home. The small bowls were filled with oil. One end of a wick floated in the oil and the other end was lit and held against the side of the lamp. The lamp then rested upon a stand or a shelf on the wooden or stone center post that supported the roof. Each of Jesus' hearers could visualize the small lamp in their home.

Salvation is for all. The true Christian's profession of faith is light to those in darkness. The oil of the Holy Spirit may not be physically detectable in the life, but the effect of its presence is manifest in the light that shines forth through the disciple who glorifies the Father. "True character is not shaped from without, and put on; it radiates from within. . . . The consistent life, the holy conversation, the unswerving integrity, the active, benevolent spirit, the godly example—these are the mediums through which light is conveyed to the world."[50]

God had blessed the Jews as a nation with great light, but too many had effectively hidden their light under a bushel basket. The church of Christ must reflect the glory of the Father to the world. Rather than cover the gospel message and hide within the walls of the church, Christ's disciples are to scatter abroad and let the light of Christ permeate their world.

"The words of Christ through the gospel prophet, which are reechoed in the Sermon on the Mount, are for us in this last generation: 'Arise, shine; for thy light is come, and the glory of the Lord is risen upon thee' (Isaiah 60:1, KJV)."[51]

THE SPIRIT OF THE LAW

Do not think that I came to destroy the Law or the Prophets. I did not come to destroy but to fulfill. Matt. 5:17.

Jesus' words sounded like heresy. The pious Pharisees whispered to those around them that He was making light of the law. But their narrow objections and misconceptions of truth had buried God's law under ceremonial rubbish. Jesus spoke directly to their accusation: "Do not think that I came to destroy the Law or the Prophets. I did not come to destroy but to fulfill." How ironic that they were questioning the motives of the lawgiver Himself. "It is the Creator of men, the Giver of the law, who declares that it is not His purpose to set aside its precepts. Everything in nature, from the mote in the sunbeam to the worlds on high, is under law." [52] Jesus' favorite questions to His audiences were: "Have ye not read?" and "What is written in the law?" Ever seeking to impart truth to His listeners, Jesus sought to vindicate His law and refute the charge that He was breaking His own sacred principles.

"For assuredly, I say to you, till heaven and earth pass away, one jot or one tittle will by no means pass from the law till all is fulfilled" (Matt. 5:18). The jot, or iota, is the ninth letter of the Greek alphabet. Since Jesus was most likely teaching in Aramaic when He spoke these words, the iota is the Aramaic y, the smallest letter of the Aramaic alphabet. The tittle is but the smallest hook extending from a letter as a serif. His concern for even a small projection from a letter clearly shows the law's immutability.

If anything could have changed the divine law, then Jesus need not have come to earth to ransom fallen humanity from the effects of its own transgression. Jesus' life showed that the law could be kept, and in the process He fulfilled the law in us. His sacrifice did not abrogate the law but established it as being God's expressed will. "For what the law could not do in that it was weak through the flesh, God did by sending His own Son in the likeness of sinful flesh, on account of sin" (Rom. 8:3, 4).

"The law was given to convict [men and women] of sin, and reveal their need of a Saviour. It would do this as its principles were applied to the heart by the Holy Spirit. This work it is still to do." [53]

A PASSPORT TO HEAVEN

Whoever therefore breaks one of the least of these commandments, and teaches men so, shall be called least in the kingdom of heaven; but whoever does and teaches them, he shall be called great in the kingdom of heaven. Matt. 5:19.

Many of the rabbis felt that their own righteousness was their passport to heaven. Through ritualistic ceremonies, their theoretical knowledge of the law, and their professed piety they sought to show others they were holy. Jesus stated their efforts were ineffectual and totally without merit. The scribes ranked the laws and regulations in order of presumed importance so that in the event of a conflict they would observe even the lesser requirement so as to protect the presumed greater one. "From childhood Jesus had acted independently of these rabbinical laws, which were without foundation in the Old Testament."[54]

It troubled the disciples when their religious leaders accused them of being sinners for failing to keep the rites of a "just" Jew. Jesus explained that an external display of religion was but a shallow pretense when the inner motives were corrupt. Rigid observance of ritualistic religion does not change the heart. Many religious leaders thought one might earn merit by performing suitable works. If enough good works accumulated on the ledger to offset the individual's sins, and the general tendency of the sinner was toward the positive, then "God will adjudge him righteous."[55] But to make allowance for sin because humanity is weak and prone to sinful tendencies minimizes its seriousness.

"The greatest deception of the human mind in Christ's day was that a mere assent to the truth constitutes righteousness. In all human experience a theoretical knowledge of the truth has been proved to be insufficient for the saving of the soul. It does not bring forth the fruits of righteousness."[56] "The most fatal delusion of the Christian world in this generation is that in pouring contempt on the law of God they think they are exalting Christ. What a position! It was Christ who spoke the law from Sinai. It was Christ who gave the law to Moses, engraven on tables of stone. It was His Father's law; and Christ says, 'I and my Father are one.' The Pharisees held the reverse of the modern position, but were in just as great an error. They rejected Christ, but exalted the law. And it makes little difference which position is taken, so long as we ignore the true one—that *faith in Christ must be accompanied by obedience to the law of God.*"[57]

The Law Examined

You have heard that it was said to those of old, "You shall not murder," and whoever murders will be in danger of the judgment. But I say to you that whoever is angry with his brother without cause shall be in danger of the judgment.
Matt. 5:21, 22.

Jesus now speaks in an astonishing manner. Numerous times He employs the phrase "I say to you." In direct contrast to the rabbis, who used tradition to interpret scriptural observance, Jesus' authority was noted by those who had never had opportunity to read the law. Recognizing this, Jesus prefaced His remarks with the statement "You have heard that it was said to those of old." He explained that the Ten Commandments had broader principles within them than the rabbis practiced. Many of those present hated the Romans who occupied their country. Since they regarded themselves as God's chosen nation, they felt free to despise and hate all other nationalities and peoples. A general spirit of discontent and a lack of love even affected their attitude toward their own people.

Inner motives prompting any observance of the law, and not outward acts, determine true religion. This is the golden thread running throughout the Sermon on the Mount. Jesus said that they should not be angry with their brother. Most of them immediately related His words to fellow Jews, but Jesus later clearly showed in the parable of the good Samaritan that all human beings are brothers and sisters (Luke 10:29-37). Likewise, "we shall see faults and weaknesses in those about us, but God claims every soul as His property—His by creation, and doubly His as purchased by the precious blood of Christ. All were created in His image, and even the most degraded are to be treated with respect and tenderness. God will hold us accountable for even a word spoken in contempt of one soul for whom Christ laid down His life."[58] The spirit of hatred originated with Satan. The culmination of that hatred led to the death of Christ on the cross. "Bitterness and animosity must be banished from the soul if we would be in harmony with heaven."[59]

The seeds of sin first germinate in the mind. Before we ever act upon evil, the mind has already transgressed God's law by contemplating the idea. We have already injured our moral character before we have committed the deed. What the mind dwells upon forms the character.

David realized the struggle for the heart and mind when He said: "Your word I have hidden in my heart, that I might not sin against You" (Ps. 119:11).

THE SECOND MILE

And whoever compels you to go one mile, go with him two. Matt. 5:41.

Jesus presented things that were hard for His listeners to accept. He told them they must turn the other cheek and not seek revenge, choosing rather to submit to an injury than fight for what they considered their rights. They must not perjure themselves by taking the name of God as a witness and then lying. Instead of resorting to divorce for the most trivial causes, they must work through the problems of their marriages. And they must guard their hearts against lusting after another, for as a person "thinks in his heart, so is he" (Prov. 23:7). Outward actions exhibit the inner character. Jesus revealed the hidden motives His audience cherished as they clung to misguided opinions of self-righteousness.

The Jews thought themselves better than their Roman masters. They looked with disdain upon the pagan practices of the foreigners who occupied their land. "In Capernaum, Roman officials with their gay paramours haunted the parades and promenades, and often the sound of revelry broke upon the stillness of the lake as their pleasure boats glided over the quiet waters."[60] Rather than rebuke the Roman administrators as the Jews hoped, Jesus indicted the evil His hearers cherished in their own hearts. "Capernaum, being a border town, was the seat of a Roman garrison, and even while Jesus was teaching, the sight of a company of soldiers recalled to His hearers the bitter thought of Israel's humiliation."[61] Jesus knew their desire for revenge, and His words were a blow to their pride.

"And whoever compels you to go one mile, go with him two." Roman officials nearly always traveled with detachments of soldiers. Often the officials would seize Jews and force them to carry the military baggage. The occupation forces used violence to get their way, and often the individual who resisted lost his livestock to the task anyway. Roman law and custom allowed such forced service for a distance of one mile. The mile usually went up a mountainside or across rough terrain. The humiliation to the proud Galileans seemed almost beyond endurance. Jesus shocked them when He counseled that a citizen of His kingdom should cheerfully give double the required service. "Jesus bade His disciples, instead of resisting the demands of those in authority, to do even more than was required of them."[62]

To give more than asked under trying conditions is difficult. To do so cheerfully is the mark of a real Christian. "The test of love for God is love for our fellow men (1 John 4:20, KJV)."[63]

Acceptable Worship

Take heed that you do not do your charitable deeds before men, to be seen by them. Otherwise you have no reward from your Father in heaven. Matt. 6:1.

Jesus now changed the direction of His sermon from His previous discussion of true righteousness to the more practical day-to-day duties of a citizen of His kingdom. He contrasted the Jewish requirements of charity, prayer, and fasting with the model of His kingdom.

The Pharisees were a small sect, comprising at most 6,000 individuals during the time of Christ, yet they strongly influenced the national religion. Jesus did not fault what they did but rather the motive prompting them. Some of the Pharisees proclaimed their charitable acts loudly so that all could praise them for their sanctimonious lives. Self-glorification lurked at the root of their charitable deeds, and they would not have bothered with such gifts at all were it not for the adoration and honor others bestowed upon them. Too many selfishly coveted such praise.

Assessments levied upon the community provided for the poor and reflected the giver's ability to donate. In addition to these "taxes" the community expected "freewill" gifts. Leaders often made appeals during special services at the synagogue or during open-air street meetings or general gatherings of the community. "On these occasions men were tempted to pledge large sums in order to win the praise of those assembled. There was also a practice of permitting the one who contributed an unusually large gift to sit in a place of honor by the side of the rabbis. Love of praise was thus all too frequently the motive in these gifts. It was also the case that many pledged large sums but later failed to make good their promises."[64]

Jesus told the crowd that human praise was all such hypocrites would ever receive. Such a donor was concerned not with the needy, but only with public admiration. Jesus referred to the Middle Eastern belief that "the right and left hands are close friends." Even close friends do not need to know what the other is giving or doing for the needy. Such a "chamber of secret gifts" existed within the Temple, where donors could give and the needy could come secretly to obtain assistance. God sees each gift, but more important, He discerns the heart and motive behind it.

"Sincerity of purpose, real kindness of heart, is the motive that Heaven values. . . . We are not to think of reward, but of service."[65]

THE MODEL PRAYER

In this manner, therefore, pray: Our Father in heaven, hallowed be Your name. Matt. 6:9.

Prayer of itself has no merit. The high language and the lengthy petitions spoken for the ears of those assembled represent idle words if they do not express any heartfelt need. "But the prayer that comes from an earnest heart, when the simple wants of the soul are expressed, as we would ask an earthly friend for a favor, expecting it to be granted—this is the prayer of faith."[66]

Twice Jesus gave His disciples instruction on how to pray. He told them not to stand in the synagogue where others could see and hear, but to find a secret spot to commune with their Father in heaven. "Therefore do not be like [the religious leaders]. For your Father knows the things you have need of before you ask Him. In this manner, therefore, pray: 'Our Father . . .'" (Matt. 6:8, 9). Brief and yet expressive, comprehensive, and all-inclusive, the Lord's Prayer has much to teach us, and much still remains hidden from our meager understanding. Jesus encourages us to study the prayer and to be careful not to pronounce it repetitiously without understanding. "Christ has given the prayer, and we should individually study its meaning, and be careful not to pervert its childlike simplicity. In the Lord's prayer, solidity, strength, and earnestness are united with meekness and reverence. It is an expression of the divine character of its Author."[67]

Christ's model prayer offered a marked contrast to the long-winded prayers of the supposed pious ones. Prayers repeated from rote memory and those that are a part of ritual and ceremony are a mockery to God. "He who would pray should enter into the meaning of his prayer, putting heart and soul into his request."[68] The angels who serve before God's throne approach with veiled face, yet many a sinful person rushes into His presence without humility or reverence. The boldness that we are to claim reflects the confidence we have in God to answer our petitions and not an attitude we take with our Father. The self-righteous prayer of the rabbi and Pharisee receives no reward, but God always acknowledges one coming from a contrite spirit. God longs to give every good thing to those He loves. "He watches for some return of gratitude from us, as the mother watches for the smile of recognition from her beloved child. He would have us understand how earnestly and tenderly His heart yearns over us."[69]

He is truly "our Father."

THE SPECK AND THE PLANK

Judge not, that you be not judged.

Matt. 7:1.

Many of the Pharisees cultivated an environment filled with criticism. They became self-absorbed and self-centered. Their haughty impression of self blinded them to their true condition in God's sight. Wrapped in pious robes of self-righteousness, they quickly pronounced judgment upon others. They sent spies to trap those they wished to destroy. Jesus knew those hearing His words were cut from the same cloth. The smallest infraction that they spotted in their neighbors and trumpeted to everyone else they also secretly practiced in their own lives.

No one on earth is qualified to judge another, for human standards are not God's. "Do not set yourself up as a standard. Do not make your opinions, your views of duty, your interpretations of Scripture, a criterion for others and in your heart condemn them if they do not come up to your ideal. Do not criticize others, conjecturing as to their motives and passing judgment upon them."[70] Only God can know us. "O Lord, You have searched me and known me" (Ps. 139:1). We need to examine our own spiritual condition to determine if Christ is really in us (2 Cor. 13:5). Such an evaluation should certainly humble us before our Creator and Father.

When we realize our own position, we should hesitate to judge the motives of anyone else. "For if we would judge ourselves, we would not be judged" (1 Cor. 11:31). Those who judge others assume the spirit of Satan, "the accuser of the brethren" (Rev. 12:10). We may condemn the offense but must be ever ready to forgive the offender. The illustration Jesus gave was that of a mote or splinter of wood or chaff seen in the eye of another. Those who live to criticize and judge their fellow believers will readily see such a small thing, but they will be blind to the beam or plank in their own life. And those driven to criticize are always hypocrites, for they commit the greater sin and add to it conceit and censorship. "Christ is the only true standard of character, and he who sets himself up as a standard for others is putting himself in the place of Christ."[71]

"No one has ever been reclaimed from a wrong position by censure and reproach; but many have thus been driven from Christ and led to seal their hearts against conviction. A tender spirit, a gentle, winning deportment, may save the erring and hide a multitude of sins."[72]

THE NARROW WAY

Enter by the narrow gate; for wide is the gate and broad is the way that leads to destruction, and there are many who go in by it. Matt. 7:13.

Jesus had reached the culmination of His longest recorded sermon. After outlining the characteristics identifying a citizen of His kingdom, He refuted the claim that He had come to destroy the law. In fact, He gave examples from Scripture explaining in greater detail that motives underlie actions. He outlined what constitutes acceptable worship in charity, prayer, and fasting. Now He invited His hearers to accept the way of life He offered—the path of self-denial.

Many of those present lived in walled cities perched upon hills for safety. The town officials opened the gates during the day to allow farmers and shepherds to reach their fields, but at sunset they closed them. Steep uneven pathways often led up to the gates, and "the traveler journeying homeward at the close of the day often had to press his way in eager haste up the difficult ascent in order to reach the gate before nightfall. The loiterer was left without."[73] Travelers must fix their minds upon the one goal of entering the gate in time.

Jesus used this familiar example to impress upon His hearers the progress of the Christian life. The path is narrow and the gate is difficult to reach. The follower of Christ must strive to reach the gate and enter it. Few want to put forth the effort required to squeeze through the narrow rocky defile, since the other path is broad and wide and has an easy grade. Christians must empty their backpacks of self to get through the "narrow" way.

Satan's path may appear easy, but it is strewn with sorrow and disappointment. Thus neither path is easy. "The Christian life is a battle and a march. But the victory to be gained is not won by human power. The field of conflict is the domain of the heart. The battle which we have to fight—the greatest battle that was ever fought by man—is the surrender of self to the will of God, the yielding of the heart to the sovereignty of love."[74]

"Strive to enter through the narrow gate, for many, I say to you, will seek to enter and will not be able" (Luke 13:24).

FOUNDED ON THE ROCK

And the rain descended, the floods came, and the winds blew and beat on that house; and it did not fall, for it was founded on the rock.
Matt. 7:25.

Many listening to Jesus had spent their entire lives beside the Sea of Galilee. They knew the history of the steep ravines and gorges through which mountain streams flowed to the lake. Most dried up in summer, but during wet winters they could become raging torrents, overflowing their banks and flooding surrounding valleys. The floods frequently swept away homes built upon the slopes. Further up the hillside stood homes built upon solid bedrock. They survived the rains because "they were founded upon the rock, and wind and flood and tempest beat upon them in vain."[75]

Jesus repeated the parable of the two houses twice for emphasis. The only difference between the two accounts is the foundation. The foolish man realized he should do more to secure a firm foundation, but he followed his own conscience. Resting upon his own efforts, he was safe while the sun shone, but let the raging torrent caused by the heavy winter rains descend upon his house, and it collapsed. Building in high or rocky areas is difficult work and requires much toil. Simply to erect a hovel on a level sandy spot is a far simpler matter. Luke tells us the builder of the house founded upon the rock "dug deep" (Luke 6:48). It requires effort and time. "Self is but shifting sand. If you build upon human theories and inventions, your house will fall. By the winds of temptation, the tempests of trial, it will be swept away. But these principles that I have given will endure. Receive Me; build upon My words."[76]

Jesus' words must be the foundation stones of our lives and characters. "The word of our God stands forever" (Isa. 40:8). Through the ages His principles have stood and will stand. "Heaven and earth will pass away, but My words will by no means pass away" (Matt. 24:35). The immutability of the law, which reflects God's very nature, stands revealed in the words of Christ. Jesus is indeed the Rock of Ages, and he or she who would build a life in safety must construct it upon that Rock.

"As you receive the word in faith, it will give you power to obey. As you give heed to the light you have, greater light will come. You are building on God's word, and your character will be builded after the similitude of the character of Christ."[77]

"He Loves Our Nation"

And when they came to Jesus, they begged Him earnestly, saying that the one for whom He should do this was deserving, "for he loves our nation, and has built us a synagogue." Luke 7:4, 5.

Perhaps the same day He delivered the Sermon on the Mount, Jesus in late afternoon entered Capernaum. Approaching the city, He encountered a deputation of Jewish elders bearing a strange request. A certain centurion ("commander of a hundred men") had a paralyzed servant near death. Although he had never met Jesus, the officer had heard reports about the new Teacher. His faith was strong, for he believed Jesus could heal his servant.

Attached to the local garrison, the centurion had charge of a "century" of Roman soldiers (between 50 and 100) on loan to Herod Antipas. The officer was unique for several reasons. His desire to see a slave healed was especially noteworthy. Normally masters treated slaves with indifference and often abused them, yet this one was a favorite, and the centurion wished him to recover. The centurion was also a friend to the Jewish community, for he had, from his own resources, funded the construction of a synagogue for them. Although not a convert, he was convinced the Jewish religion was superior.

Feeling unworthy as a Gentile to enter Jesus' presence, he petitioned the elders to approach the Master. According to custom, the correct way to reach an individual for a favor that might be refused was to use an intermediary who might secure the favor more easily. While the Jewish elders saw the Roman as "worthy," he himself felt "unworthy" to contact Christ. He didn't want to embarrass the Saviour by having Him enter a Gentile home. "Jesus immediately set out for the officer's home; but, pressed by the multitude, He advanced slowly."[78] The incident is one of the few times Jesus and some Jewish elders ever agreed on anything. The Jews approved of the centurion's works, while Jesus approved of his faith!

"The centurion, born in heathenism, educated in the idolatry of imperial Rome, trained as a soldier, seemingly cut off from spiritual life by his education and surroundings, and still further shut out by the bigotry of the Jews, and by the contempt of his own countrymen for the people of Israel—this man perceived the truth to which the children of Abraham were blinded. He did not wait to see whether the Jews themselves would receive the One who claimed to be their Messiah."[79]

The decision to reach out to Christ is a personal one. No one comes to Jesus at the point of a sword or gun.

NOR EVEN IN ISRAEL

When Jesus heard these things, He marveled at him, and turned around and said to the crowd that followed Him, "I say to you, I have not found such great faith, not even in Israel." Luke 7:9.

News of Jesus' approach reached the centurion, and he immediately sent a message to Christ. "Lord, do not trouble Yourself, for I am not worthy that You should enter under my roof" (Luke 7:6). Finally the man delivered the message in person: "Therefore I did not even think myself worthy to come to You. But say the word, and my servant will be healed. For I also am a man placed under authority, having soldiers under me. And I say to one, 'Go,' and he goes; and to another, 'Come,' and he comes; and to my servant, 'Do this,' and he does it" (verses 7, 8). The centurion realized that Jesus represented the power and authority of heaven just as he himself symbolized that of Rome. Jesus marveled at the Roman citizen's faith. Unlike the Jewish nobleman from Capernaum who a year before had asked for a sign, this man did not even expect one. The only question worrying the centurion was not whether Jesus could heal his servant, but whether He would condescend to do such an act for a Gentile.

Faith is the key to the story, and it caused Jesus to marvel for several reasons. Belief that a word spoken by Jesus was sufficient to heal was impressive, yet the fact that the centurion had never seen Jesus or heard Him made it even more remarkable. The centurion was not afraid to ask for help. His desire did not rest upon any good thing he had done, but upon his great need for the Master. The Jewish elders were impressed because of what the centurion had accomplished for them. "Not by works of righteousness we have done, but according to His mercy He saved us" (Titus 3:5). With joy Jesus looked upon this Gentile as an example of the many who would come seeking Him. Turning back from the crowd, He spoke directly to him. "Go your way; and as you have believed, so let it be done for you" (Matt. 8:13). The servant recovered the same hour.

"It is faith that connects us with heaven and brings us strength for coping with the powers of darkness." [80]

ACCORDING TO YOUR FAITH

And when He had come into the house, the blind men came to Him. And Jesus said to them, "Do you believe that I am able to do this?" They said to Him, "Yes, Lord."

Matt. 9:28.

The miracle of the two blind men probably occurred in Capernaum. The two men followed and hailed Him, crying out, "Son of David, have mercy on us!" (Matt. 9:27). They realized that Jesus was the Messiah and addressed Him as such by using the expression "Son of David." The Lord performed many of His miracles in the presence of crowds, but He did not heal these two men in public. As with most miracles He performed, Jesus required the recipient to participate in the event. Unless those who sought healing exercised their faith, Jesus would not be able to use His power. "But without faith it is impossible to please Him, for he who comes to God must believe that He is, and that He is a rewarder of those who diligently seek Him" (Heb. 11:6).

"Jesus said to them, 'Do you believe that I am able to do this?' They said to Him, 'Yes, Lord.'" Jesus reached out and touched them. The contact of His hand was personal and powerful. Jesus often touched those He healed, a personal act conveying both the healing and the sympathy of the Healer. Both men immediately regained their sight. Jesus now strongly commanded them not to tell others of the miracle. As with the healing of the leper, Jesus did not want to impede His mission by gaining a reputation as a mere miracle worker. Miracles were of secondary importance to His real mission, humanity's salvation.

As often happened, the two men ignored His directions. "Jesus was not satisfied to attract attention to Himself merely as a wonder-worker or as a healer of physical disease. He was seeking to draw men to Him as their Saviour. While the people were eager to believe that He had come as a king to establish an earthly reign, He desired to turn their minds from the earthly to the spiritual. Mere worldly success would interfere with His work."[81]

Many feel that they are deficient in faith and therefore not able to approach Christ. But "'him that cometh to me I will in no wise cast out' (John 6:37, KJV). As you come to Him, believe that He accepts you, because He has promised. You can never perish while you do this—never."[82]

RULER OF DEMONS

But the Pharisees said, "He casts out demons by the ruler of the demons."

Matt. 9:34.

The friends of a demon-possessed man brought him to Jesus, since he could not speak for himself, being mute. He was indeed fortunate to have friends who could take his case to Jesus, who cast the demon out, enabling the man to speak. "And the multitudes marveled, saying, 'It was never seen like this in Israel!'" (Matt. 9:33). The fame of the Healer had spread and had attracted more and more sick to Capernaum. The crush of the crowds made it harder to preach the message of salvation. The priests watched with growing dissatisfaction Jesus' increasing popularity. As His influence grew, theirs decreased. Desperate to silence Jesus, they would stop at nothing.

Asserting Christ's miracles were nothing more than the working of evil spirits, they claimed that Jesus and Satan were in league and that Jesus' mission was evil. Scripture does not record any reply Jesus made to the charges. Perhaps His enemies never voiced them within His hearing. The spies and Pharisees had learned their lesson about confronting Jesus before the people. Undoubtedly they now worked behind His back to discredit His work. The charges spread widely, for even in Nazareth, "His [Jesus'] brothers heard of this, and also of the charge brought by the Pharisees that He cast out devils through the power of Satan. They felt keenly the reproach that came upon them through their relation to Jesus. They knew what a tumult His words and works created, and were not only alarmed at His bold statements, but indignant at His denunciation of the scribes and Pharisees."[83]

Such accusations and condemnations were difficult trials for Jesus to bear. At such times Christ found strength only through communing with His Father. He understands what we face. "Those who accept Christ as their personal Saviour are not left as orphans, to bear the trials of life alone. He receives them as members of the heavenly family; He bids them call His Father their Father. They are His 'little ones,' dear to the heart of God, bound to Him by the most tender and abiding ties. He has toward them an exceeding tenderness, as far surpassing what our father or mother has felt toward us in our helplessness as the divine is above the human."[84]

When you endure false accusations and condemnation for His sake, rejoice! You are dear to His heart.

OVERVIEW: HIS FIRST TOUR

And Jesus went about all Galilee, teaching in their synagogues, preaching the gospel of the kingdom, and healing all kinds of sickness and all kinds of disease among the people. Matt. 4:23.

After His baptism and ministry in Judea and Samaria, Jesus returned after one year to an unpleasant homecoming in Nazareth. He therefore centered His ministry in Capernaum. Between the Passovers of A.D. 29 and A.D. 30 Jesus made three distinct circuits of Galilee. Accounts of these trips form the largest portion of the Gospels.

Calling Peter, Andrew, James, and John from their nets, Jesus proceeded to the synagogue, where He healed a demoniac. Later, after the Sabbath ended, He healed Peter's mother-in-law. Subsequent healing proceeded far into the night. Seeking solitude, He retired to pray. Returning to the people, Jesus healed the leper by touching him and then called Levi-Matthew to be a disciple. Watching closely, spies accused His disciples of reaping and threshing on the Sabbath. Jesus chose the Sabbath to heal the man with the withered hand.

Christ ordained the twelve and presented His inaugural address as King of the kingdom of grace (the Sermon on the Mount) near the Sea of Galilee. He then set forth the constitution of the kingdom and gave examples of the character necessary to become a citizen of heaven. The sermon closed with an admonition to apply His words and build upon the Rock of Ages. Jesus returned to Capernaum, where the elders presented the case of the centurion. The healing of the demon-possessed mute culminated in the accusation that Jesus was working in concert with Satan. The tour had six recorded miracles.

Most important, Jesus' disciples were training to becoming apostles. "It was by personal contact and association that Jesus trained His disciples. Sometimes He taught them, sitting among them on the mountainside; sometimes beside the sea, or walking with them by the way. He revealed the mysteries of the kingdom of God. He did not sermonize as men do today. Wherever hearts were open to receive the divine message, He unfolded the truths of the way of salvation. He did not command His disciples to do this or that, but said, 'Follow Me.' On His journeys through country and cities He took them with Him, that they might see how He taught the people. He linked their interest with His, and they united with Him in the work."[85]

We must link our teaching by personal contact as He did and not by preaching sermons alone.

ARISE

When the Lord saw her, He had compassion on her and said to her, "Do not weep." Luke 7:13.

The small town of Nain sits on a plateau just on the edge of the wide Plain of Esdraelon. As Jesus began His second circuit of Galilee a large group of people followed His footsteps from Capernaum. It was probably early autumn A.D. 29. Then, as now, the small village of Nain had only one approach, up a narrow and rocky path entering from the east. "About half a mile east of the village is a rock-hewn burial ground still in use today."[86]

As the group neared the village gate, a funeral procession emerged from the town with great wailing and keening. The body was not embalmed, merely washed, anointed with sweet-smelling spices, and wrapped in linen cloth. Normally the casket remained open for all to see the body. "The deceased was the only son of this mother, and she a widow. The lonely mourner was following to the grave her sole earthly support and comfort. 'When the Lord saw her, He had compassion on her.' As she moved on blindly, weeping, noting not His presence, He came close beside her, and gently said, 'Weep not.' Jesus was about to change her grief to joy, yet He could not forbear this expression of tender sympathy."[87]

Jesus had no spoken request from the woman. "But in His sympathy for suffering humanity Jesus answered the unuttered prayer, as He does so often for us today."[88] Jesus reached up and touched the bier, a signal for the pallbearers to halt. "In clear, authoritative voice the words are spoken, 'Young man, I say unto thee, Arise.' That voice pierces the ears of the dead. The young man opens his eyes. Jesus takes him by the hand, and lifts him up. His gaze falls upon her who has been weeping beside him, and mother and son unite in a long, clinging, joyous embrace. The multitude look on in silence, as if spellbound."[89]

Jesus tells us today, "Weep not." He holds the keys to death and the grave (Rev. 1:18) and will soon throw open those earthen bonds and release forever those who love Him. "Then we who are alive and remain shall be caught up together with them in the clouds to meet the Lord in the air. And thus we shall always be with the Lord. Therefore comfort one another with these words" (1 Thess. 4:17, 18).

A KINGDOM DIVIDED

Every kingdom divided against itself is brought to desolation, and every city or house divided against itself will not stand.

Matt. 12:25.

As Jesus' popularity increased, so too did the resentment and opposition. People saw in Him a great rabbi, possibly even a prophet, but the majority did not consider Him to be the Messiah. Judging Him against their own ideal, they failed to recognize Him as the Son of David. It especially enraged the Pharisees that Jesus healed the demon-possessed man, for they could not deny that a miracle had taken place. They were even more upset that at least some of the people considered Jesus to be the Messiah. Refusing to even mention His name, they referred to Him as "this fellow" (Matt. 12:24), accusing Him of controlling demons by being in league with them. Jesus met their logic. How could Satan cast out Satan? If He fought against himself, how could His kingdom stand?

Pressing them further, Jesus asked, "And if I cast out demons by Beelzebub, by whom do your sons cast them out?" (verse 27). The Pharisees claimed they also could cast out demons. If true, did they exorcise demons in concert with Satan also? When confronted, they affirmed that they worked through the Spirit of God. Likewise, Jesus said, He utilized the power of God to work His miracles. "The miracles of Christ for the afflicted and suffering were wrought by the power of God through the ministration of the angels."[1] "Every miracle that Christ performed was a sign of His divinity. He was doing the very work that had been foretold of the Messiah; but to the Pharisees these works of mercy were a positive offense. . . . That which led the Jews to reject the Saviour's work was the highest evidence of His divine character. The greatest significance of His miracles is seen in the fact that they were for the blessing of humanity. The highest evidence that He came from God is that His life revealed the character of God."[2]

Jesus now stated: "He who is not with Me is against Me, and he who does not gather with Me scatters abroad" (verse 30). Every person takes a position either for or against Christ. No middle ground can exist. Many feel comfortable sitting upon the fence, but such a position is also a rejection of the Saviour. The changed life of a Christian tells the world on which side of the conflict the soul stands, "for a tree is known by its fruit" (verse 33).

Choose this day whom you will serve. Do not delay another hour.

A Personal Saviour

For whoever does the will of My Father in heaven is My brother and sister and mother. Matt. 12:50.

Negative reports about Jesus had reached His brothers. They had heard that He didn't have much time to eat and that He was constantly surrounded by multitudes of people. His continuous labors were wearying Him, yet instead of sleeping, He often devoted whole nights to prayer. They had difficulty understanding the charges leveled at Him by the Pharisees, who said He was in league with the devil. Jesus' attitude toward the Pharisees and His outspoken reproof of their actions continually embarrassed them. Through their relationship to Jesus they felt their neighbors' disapproval and criticism. Something had to be done to control the actions of their younger Brother. Jesus' brothers "induced Mary to unite with them, thinking that through His love for her they might prevail upon Him to be more prudent."[3] Together, the family traveled down the mountain path to Capernaum.

When Jesus was a child in Nazareth, His brothers had tried to intimidate and control Him. When trials came, He had accepted setbacks with serenity. His dignity had angered His brothers. "Jesus loved His brothers, and treated them with unfailing kindness; but they were jealous of Him, and manifested the most decided unbelief and contempt. They could not understand His conduct."[4] Once again they thought they knew what was best for their little Brother and sought to control Him. Jesus had just healed the man possessed, blind, and mute. "While He was still talking to the multitudes, behold, His mother and brothers stood outside, seeking to speak with Him" (Matt. 12:46).

The disciples may have brought Jesus the message, but He already knew of His family's mission. Turning to the messenger, He answered, "Who is My mother and who are My brothers?" (verse 48). Stretching out His hand, He pointed to His disciples. "Here are My mother and My brothers! For whoever does the will of My Father in heaven is My brother and sister and mother" (verses 49, 50). Jesus loved His family, but clearly they had no right to interfere with His ministry or try to control it. As at the Temple in Jerusalem when just a lad, Jesus again affirmed that He must be about His Father's business.

Each one who accepts God as their Father is a member of the family of God (Eph. 3:14, 15). "The ties that bind Christians to their heavenly Father and to one another are stronger and truer even than blood ties, and more enduring."[5]

THE PURPOSE OF PARABLES

Then His disciples asked Him, saying, "What does this parable mean?" Luke 8:9.

Somewhere along the shore of Galilee between Capernaum and Magdala, where the Plain of Gennesaret meets the lake, Jesus delivered a sermon by the sea. He crafted numerous wonderfully compact examples of everyday life into beautiful illustrations of spiritual things. Jesus spoke of a sower and his seed, the process of growing, and one of the smallest of all seeds—the mustard. His sermon told of wheat and tares, and fish caught in a net, of new things and old, hidden treasure found, and a pearl of great price. The wisdom of the ages skillfully blended common objects to forever link them with powerful spiritual truths. "In all His teaching, Christ brought the mind of man in contact with the Infinite Mind. He did not direct the people to study men's theories about God, His Word, or His works. He taught them to behold Him as manifested in His works, in His Word, and by His providences."[6]

Those seeking truth understood the deeper meanings of the parables, while others left with but interesting stories. Jesus said, "To you it has been given to know the mysteries of the kingdom of God, but to the rest it is given in parables, that 'Seeing they may not see, and hearing they may not understand [Isa. 6:9]'" (Luke 8:10). The truths contained in the parables of Christ were often understood but not accepted. The Holy Spirit illuminated the hearts and minds of the hearers and pressed home the divine meaning so that it revealed long-cherished sins. "But the natural man does not receive the things of the Spirit of God, for they are foolishness to him; nor can he know them, because they are spiritually discerned" (1 Cor. 2:14). Many sinners simply refuse to see or hear straight truth.

The Pharisees tried continually to silence Him, so Jesus crafted His stories so that they might not use His words against Him. "But while He evaded the spies, He made truth so clear that error was manifested, and the honest in heart were profited by His lessons."[7] "Light comes to the soul through God's Word, through His servants, or by the direct agency of His Spirit; but when one ray of light is disregarded, there is a partial benumbing of the spiritual perceptions, and the second revealing of light is less clearly discerned. So the darkness increases, until it is night in the soul."[8]

Walking in the light is our only safeguard.

THE SOWER

Behold, a sower
went out to sow.

Matt. 13:3.

As the people pressed close, Jesus soon had no room to minister to them. Stepping into a fishing boat, He told the disciples to push off a little into the lake. Seating Himself, He began to teach. "Beside the sea lay the beautiful plain of Gennesaret, beyond rose the hills, and upon hillside and plain both sowers and reapers were busy, the one casting seed and the other harvesting the early grain. Looking upon the scene, Christ said, 'Behold, the sower went forth to sow . . .'"[9] As the parable ended, the disciples came and asked Him His meaning. Jesus explained that as the sower, He had left heaven and gone "out to sow." The seed sown is the Word of God. The Scriptures are the only sure word of authority. "The education to be secured by searching the Scriptures is an experimental knowledge of the plan of salvation."[10]

Some pay little attention to the vital truths they hear. The parable depicts them as *seed sown by the wayside.* Absorbed by the world's cares and pleasures, they do not try to understand spiritual things. Many become critical of the message or the messenger, and the Word has no effect. They make themselves susceptible to false teachers who preach half-truths and theories that come like crows and devour them.

Others have a superficial conviction, but either they cannot handle the slightest reproach or they refuse to surrender cherished sin. The seed falls upon the *stony ground* of their unconverted hearts. Such transitory Christians do not have a personal relationship with Jesus and put forth no effort to gain one. Persecution or difficulties cause them to surrender their conviction easily, for it had never taken root. They are Christians in name only. Others profess belief, but the *thorns* of our world choke out any personal commitment they have to remain attached to Christ on a daily basis. They place self and their own important agenda before any effort to secure greater knowledge of the Saviour. The seed and sower are always the same, only the soils differ. "Merely to hear or to read the word is not enough. He who desires to be profited by the Scriptures must meditate upon the truth that has been presented to him."[11] The Spirit breaks up the soil of the heart, and the seed takes root and grows. Good soil brings forth a change in character and a flowering of good works.

"Because of its simplicity the parable of the sower has not been valued as it should be."[12]

A GROWING SEED

The kingdom of God is as if a man should scatter seed on the ground, and should sleep by night and rise by day, and the seed should sprout and grow, he himself does not know how. Mark 4:26, 27.

Any disciple who spreads the good news is a sower. Given a chance, the seed will sprout in the hearer's life without the sower fully understanding the process taking place. The working of the Holy Spirit within the heart of an individual is as the wind that blows the grass and rustles the leaves upon the trees. "Every seed grows, every plant develops, by the power of God."[13] Jesus sought to impress upon His disciples that they of themselves had nothing that would guarantee the successful outcome of their witnessing. Only the power of God working through the Holy Spirit could cause the hearer to respond. Just as a seed takes hold and starts to develop, so spiritual life begins. Almost imperceptibly the individual develops into the likeness of his or her Creator. God's plan is for each soul to grow to full stature and advance from stage to stage in spiritual development until complete in the Lord. "Sanctification is the work of a lifetime."[14]

Christian growth depends upon the spiritual nourishment received. Such nourishment comes through study of His Word, prayer, the influence of the Spirit, and the assurance of a personal relationship with God. They can develop only over time through trust. "The object of the Christian life is fruit bearing—the reproduction of Christ's character in the believer, that it may be reproduced in others."[15] The Christian witnesses to the world of Christ's power to save. The mature Christian displays the fruit of the Spirit—love, joy, peace, longsuffering, kindness, goodness, faithfulness, gentleness, and self-control (Gal. 5:22, 23).

Each Christian has an opportunity to sow seed for the Master. We may not see any results from our actions, but the response is not always for us to know. The process of growth goes on in the lives of those we touch whether we remain with them or move on to other places. The sower may tend the seed and water it, may weed the area and fertilize it, but the eventual germination of the seed requires the spark of life from the Holy Spirit. That spark increases faith and deepens the love felt for the Saviour.

We must be willing to spread the seed and leave the result in God's hands.

THE MUSTARD SEED

The kingdom of heaven is like a mustard seed, . . . which indeed is the least of all the seeds; but when it is grown it is greater than the herbs and becomes a tree.

Matt. 13:31, 32.

Jesus continued to speak to the multitude gathered to hear Him. The crowd contained many Pharisees. They smugly recognized that few among those who surrounded the Teacher from Galilee actually acknowledged Him as the Messiah. How, then, could such a lowly teacher ever attain the world domination their Messianic vision required? Christ had no power base, no fame, no finances, no large political following or honor that would boost Him toward a kingdom. They dismissed Him as someone insignificant and who would never amount to much of anything. Jesus read their thoughts and answered them in yet another parable.

Nearby swayed the mustard plant in the surrounding fields. "As Jesus spoke this parable, the mustard plant could be seen far and near, lifting itself above the grass and grain, and waving its branches lightly in the air. Birds flitted from twig to twig, and sang amid the leafy foliage. Yet the seed from which sprang this giant plant was among the least of all seeds."[16] The kingdom of Christ was to have small and insignificant beginnings. Worldly kingdoms hold sway by force of arms and often maintain themselves through threat and intimidation. The Prince of Peace founds and rules the kingdom of Christ.

"When Christ spoke this parable, there were only a few Galilean peasants to represent the new kingdom. Their poverty, the fewness of their numbers, were urged over and over again as a reason why men should not connect themselves with these simple-minded fishermen who followed Jesus."[17] From such humble beginnings the message of the kingdom of grace spread to encircle the globe. Crossing nationalities and continents it has spanned the oceans to reach all those who would hear its theme of hope. Into each heart the Holy Spirit plants a tiny seed, and when it has grown, who can measure the height or depth of its influence? "The kingdom and its subjects might appear insignificant now, but, says Christ, this will not always be the case."[18]

The little seed of the gospel message has indeed triumphed and become a mighty tree that spreads its message to "every nation, tribe, tongue, and people" (Rev. 14:6).

THE LEAVEN

Another parable He spoke to them: "The kingdom of heaven is like leaven."

Matt. 13:33.

In the "great throng all classes of society were represented. There were the poor, the illiterate, the ragged beggar, the robber with the seal of guilt upon his face, the maimed, the dissipated, the merchant and the man of leisure, high and low, rich and poor, all crowding upon one another for a place to stand and hear the words of Christ."[19] How could such people possibly be material for the kingdom? The Pharisees saw only an audience of unlearned peasants, but Christ perceived potential in His hearers. Not one individual was so hopeless or evil as to be beyond hope of salvation.

As with the mustard seed, the effect of leaven is small in the beginning. "As leaven permeates every part of the dough in which it is placed, so the teachings of Christ would penetrate the lives of those who received them and were willing to be transformed thereby."[20] Quietly the truth enters the soul. Slowly and steadily its transforming power changes the individual. Old habits die as new thoughts take the place of former evil ones. The person feels new motivation, and a desire to be like Christ arises. Conscience reawakens, and refined and awakened traits that glorify God replace old ones.

Conversion transforms the soul as leaven changes the loaf. Many claim conversion yet cling to old habits. They are quick to anger, to take offense, to judge, to protect self, to speak harshly, to dictate. But those who exhibit such traits are not converted. True conversion shows love. "Love is manifested in kindness, gentleness, forbearance, and long-suffering. The countenance is changed. Christ abiding in the heart shines out in the faces of those who love Him and keep His commandments."[21]

The great change that humanity seeks it will find in God's Word. Bible study strengthens the conversion of the soul through faith. "So then faith comes by hearing, and hearing by the word of God" (Rom. 10:17). Prayer and careful reading of the Scriptures, coupled with a conviction of sin awakened through the workings of the Holy Spirit, create a need for Jesus. This need awakens faith and love for Christ that transforms lives. Once changed and "leavened," we are ready to do His will.

Sanctification is our life's work. "Sanctify them by Your truth. Your word is truth" (John 17:17).

WHEAT AND TARES

The kingdom of heaven is like a man who sowed good seed in his field; but while men slept, his enemy came and sowed tares among the wheat and went his way.

Matt. 13:24, 25.

This parable offers a striking example of fair-weather Christians. Bearing Christ's name while denying His character, they discredit the church and endanger those new to the faith or still weak in their belief. The field is Christ's church, and the seed is the gospel. It is not uncommon in the Middle East for people to take revenge by sowing tares or weeds in the fields of their enemies. The weeds injure the crop, reduce the yield, and bring trouble and financial loss to the owner. Satan sows his evil seed among Christ's followers. If the devil can point to professed followers bringing disrepute upon the church, and trumpet their evil deeds to the world as examples of what "Christians" are capable of doing, then he can misrepresent the truth and sow discontent and distrust within the church itself.

"Christ has plainly taught that those who persist in open sin must be separated from the church, but He has not committed to us the work of judging character and motive." [22] Too often people in their zeal to purify the church become guilty of destroying some of the wheat as they attempt to uproot the tares. Christ tells us to let the tares grow alongside the wheat until the end of probation. It is clear from this parable that both classes will be in the church to the very end. "Many who think themselves Christians will at last be found wanting. Many will be in heaven who their neighbors supposed would never enter there. Man judges from appearance, but God judges the heart." [23] We are to humbly distrust our motivations and look to our own cases. Simply because our name is on the church roll is no proof that we are Christians or heaven-bound.

As they grow together during the spring both wheat and tares are alike green, but come summer the wheat turns golden and the tare reveals itself as the worthless weed it is. The farmer burns the tares, and they have no second probation to change their character and become wheat.

"Christ Himself will decide who are worthy to dwell with the family of heaven. He will judge every man according to his words and his works. Profession is as nothing in the scale. It is character that decides destiny." [24]

THE DRAGNET

Again, the kingdom of heaven is like a dragnet that was cast into the sea and gathered some of every kind, which, when it was full, they drew to shore; and they sat down and gathered the good into vessels, but threw the bad away.

Matt. 13:47, 48.

Beside the Sea of Galilee fishers mended their nets. These "sagene" were long weighted nets strung out from the fishing boats as they made a slow circuit in the water. The net's heavy edge sank as the boat moved to close the opening. The crew hauled up the catch, then transported it to shore and sorted it. "Fishers of men" (see Luke 5:10) spread the gospel net over the whole world. Many come into the church as the folds of the gospel net encircle men and women with differing attitudes, desires, motives, personalities, and characters. Not every fish is caught. Many willfully swim away from the net. "Both the parable of the tares and that of the net plainly teach that there is no time when all the wicked will turn to God. The wheat and the tares grow together until the harvest. The good and the bad fish are together drawn ashore for a final separation. Again, these parables teach that there is to be no probation after the judgment. When the work of the gospel is completed, there immediately follows the separation between the good and the evil, and the destiny of each class is forever fixed." [25]

Character decides destiny (Micah 6:8). Neither status nor position has anything to do with fitness for heaven. "God measures character in terms of whether a man has lived in harmony with all the light that has shone upon his pathway, whether, to the best of his knowledge and ability, he has cooperated with heavenly agencies in perfecting a character patterned after the perfect example of Jesus." [26] "Let us hear the conclusion of the whole matter: Fear [love] God and keep His commandments, for this is man's all. For God will bring every work into judgment, including every secret thing, whether good or evil" (Eccl. 12:13, 14).

God wishes all to repent and be saved. "'As I live,' says the Lord God, 'I have no pleasure in the death of the wicked, but that the wicked turn from his way and live'" (Eze. 33:11). A superficial change will not be sufficient for salvation. The shallow individual won't put forth the effort needed to know God.

We must study His character, commune with Him, and then we will trust Him.

HIDDEN TREASURE

Again, the kingdom of heaven is like treasure hidden in a field, which a man found and hid; and for joy over it he goes and sells all that he has and buys that field.

Matt. 13:44.

Because of the political turmoil and unrest of New Testament times, many kept their valuables buried in the soil of their fields as protection against sudden invasion or loss. Theft and robbery were frequent, and whenever the ruling power changed hands those with wealth often had to pay a heavy tribute to the new government. The owner of buried wealth might die, be imprisoned, or be exiled, and knowledge of the hiding place might easily get lost. Should the owner come to a tragic end without divulging the location of his treasure to his family members, the valuables might pass to the one who next purchased the land. Christ used this common event to teach a powerful lesson.

The laws of Leviticus required the finder of anything lost to return the item to its rightful owner (Lev. 6:3, 4). The finder of this treasure could not follow the Mosaic law, for the original owner was, in all likelihood, long dead and the money couldn't be returned. As such, "the finder had as much right to it as anyone, and title to the treasure legally went along with title to the land." [27]

Perhaps a hired man, walking behind the oxen as they tilled the soil, unearthed a buried treasure of gold and silver ornaments or coins. Quickly he purchased the ground, knowing that it was worth much more than its asking price. Jesus explained that the Holy Scriptures represent just such a treasure. The gospel is the true treasure, and our salvation depends upon the knowledge we may gain from the Bible. God wills that we search for the revelation that He has given us.

As the Spirit enlightens us, we better understand God's Word and appreciate its worth. The gospel treasure is ours, but we must seek diligently and give all to obtain the knowledge of God. "And this is eternal life, that they may know You, the only true God, and Jesus Christ whom You have sent" (John 17:3).

Prayer unlocks the power of the Spirit and helps you discern the hidden depths of Christ's sayings. "Yes, if you cry out for discernment, and lift up your voice for understanding, if you seek her as silver, and search for her as for hidden treasures; then you will understand the fear of the Lord, and find the knowledge of God" (Prov. 2:3-5).

THE PRICELESS PEARL

Again, the kingdom of heaven is like a merchant seeking beautiful pearls, who, when he had found one pearl of great price, went and sold all that he had and bought it. Matt. 13:45, 46.

The parable of the hidden treasure represents those who find truth without actually searching for it. Once found, however, they realize its value and sell all to purchase it. The merchant in the parable is intent on searching for truth. The narrative does not present the pearl as a gift. The merchant must purchase it with all he possesses. "Christ Himself is the pearl of great price."[28] "Salvation is a free gift, and yet it is to be bought and sold. In the market of which divine mercy has the management, the precious pearl is represented as being bought without money and without price. In this market all may obtain the goods of heaven. The treasury of the jewels of truth is open to all."[29]

Life eternal requires that we know God and Jesus Christ whom He sent (John 17:3). The price for such knowledge, though, is total surrender. "Peace with God costs all that a man has, but it is worth infinitely more. Man purchases salvation at the cost of things that, of themselves, have no permanent value anyway, and thus loses nothing worthwhile in the transaction."[30] One cannot earn salvation, but one must seek for it as if it were the only thing that matters in life, as indeed it is. Some seek for the pearl their entire lives but don't quite make the transaction. "Almost Christians" do not surrender the world, take up their cross, and follow Christ. "By comparing the kingdom of heaven to a pearl, Christ desired to lead every soul to appreciate that pearl, above all else. The possession of the pearl, which means the possession of a personal Saviour, is the symbol of true riches. It is a treasure above every earthly treasure."[31]

The parable also teaches that while humanity seeks Christ, Christ is also searching for humanity. Christ is the heavenly merchant who sees in lost humanity the pearl He is willing to sacrifice all to obtain. God did not count us worthless, but sent His Son to redeem us and pay sin's penalty.

God placed all the riches of the universe upon the cross to purchase the fallen pearl of great price. "'They shall be Mine,' says the Lord of hosts, 'on the day that I make them My jewels'" (Mal. 3:17).

The Old and the New

Then He said to them, "Therefore every scribe instructed concerning the kingdom of heaven is like a householder who brings out of his treasure things new and old."

Matt. 13:52.

The truths God has shared with each believer the disciples of every age must communicate to the world. "The great storehouse of truth is the Word of God—the written word, the book of nature, and the book of experience in God's dealing with human life. Here are the treasures from which Christ's workers are to draw."[32] The treasures of the gospel are ours, and in a special sense each of us typifies the "householder." Both the Old and New Testaments contain the Word of God. "Christ as manifested to the patriarchs, as symbolized in the sacrificial service, as portrayed in the law, and as revealed by the prophets, is the riches of the Old Testament. Christ in His life, His death, and His resurrection, Christ as He is manifested by the Holy Spirit, is the treasure of the New Testament. Our Saviour, the outshining of the Father's glory, is both the Old and the New."[33]

Many today accept only the gospel and refuse to preach the Old Testament, yet Jesus taught that "these are they which testify of Me" (John 5:39). Others believe only the Old Testament and reject the New. They place no belief in the teachings of Jesus and in doing so show their disbelief in the patriarchs of the Old Testament. "For if you believed Moses, you would believe Me; for he wrote about Me" (verse 46). The whole of the Word of God is tied together. "No man can rightly present the law of God without the gospel, or the gospel without the law. The law is the gospel embodied, and the gospel is the law unfolded. The law is the root, the gospel is the fragrant blossom and fruit which it bears."[34] The Old Testament pointed to the Christ to come, while the New Testament revealed the Christ who had come.

Here at the close of His sermon by the sea, Jesus urged His disciples to share with others the old and new treasures in their possession. Christianity and the household of God rest upon "the foundation of the apostles and prophets, Jesus Christ Himself being the chief cornerstone, in whom the whole building, being fitted together, grows into a holy temple in the Lord" (Eph. 2:20, 21).

"In giving us His word, God has put us in possession of every truth essential for our salvation."[35]

A DIFFERENT STANDARD

Come to Me, all you who labor and are heavy laden, and I will give you rest. Matt. 11:28.

Jesus took pity on the people. The scribes prescribed strict ritualistic practices and ceremonies as the only way to please God. Many followed the rites, only to find themselves further troubled by inadequacy. Jesus knew the burden of sin would cause the strongest to fall if shouldered alone. The rules and regulations of the rabbis were such that the people might study a lifetime and never learn them all. Jesus offered a new way, a new discipline—yet one that sounded familiar. The rabbis often referred to the Torah as a "yoke" or way of life, and the people understood this imagery. Jesus' "yoke" designates more than a way of life—it represents service. "By this illustration Christ teaches us that we are called to service as long as life shall last. We are to take upon us His yoke, that we may be coworkers with Him." [36]

The yoke worn by the oxen is not an additional burden placed upon their backs to make their work harder but rather a unifying influence to make the work easier to bear through sharing and teamwork. Jesus says: "For My yoke is easy and My burden is light" (Matt. 11:30). The steps to take He plainly outlines, and they do not consist of endless tasks to gain salvation. "Learn from Me, for I am gentle and lowly in heart, and you will find rest for your souls" (verse 29). If we seek the kingdom of God first, He will add everything else. "Our heavenly Father has a thousand ways to provide for us, of which we know nothing. Those who accept the one principle of making the service and honor of God supreme will find perplexities vanish, and a plain path before their feet." [37]

Many professed followers of Jesus fear the idea of total surrender. The cares and anxiousness they carry, while a burden, still strangely comfort them. Total surrender requires giving up self. Whatever the trial or difficulty, bring it to Jesus. Learn of Him and find rest. "You will keep him in perfect peace, whose mind is stayed on You, because he trusts in You" (Isa. 26:3).

"Redemption is that process by which the soul is trained for heaven. This training means a knowledge of Christ." [38] Trust in Him, and He will give you the perfect peace you seek and lighten your burden of care under His yoke of service.

A DISTANT SHORE

Then He arose and rebuked the wind, and said to the sea, "Peace, be still!" And the wind ceased and there was a great calm.

Mark 4:39.

Jesus needed to escape the crowds. "Day after day He had ministered to them, scarcely pausing for food or rest. The malicious criticism and misrepresentation with which the Pharisees constantly pursued Him made His labors much more severe and harassing; and now the close of the day found Him so utterly wearied that He determined to seek retirement in some solitary place across the lake."[39] Dismissing the crowd, Jesus and the disciples set off. Refusing to disperse, the people climbed into boats to follow Him across the lake. Lying down in the stern of the boat, rocked gently by the motion of the waves, Jesus soon fell asleep. The Sea of Galilee is 13 miles long and seven miles across at its greatest width. Ringed about by hills, it sits in the deep trough that forms the Jordan rift valley. Blowing over these hills and funneled down steep canyons, the wind can reach terrific speeds before swirling out onto the lake. Then racing across the lake, the wind whips the surface into a seething white-capped storm with little warning. The calm evening suddenly shattered. It was now past sunset and the inky blackness of night had settled. No light pierced the gloom.

"The waves, lashed into fury by the howling winds, dashed fiercely over the disciples' boat, and threatened to engulf it. Those hardy fishermen had spent their lives upon the lake, and had guided their craft safely through many a storm; but now their strength and skill availed nothing."[40] The boat filled with water, and in the terror of the moment, as they realized that they were sinking, the disciples forgot that Jesus was with them. Absorbed in trying to save themselves, they had forgotten the One with power to save them all. Another quick flash of lightning and they saw Jesus peacefully sleeping and undisturbed. "Lord, save us! We are perishing!" (Matt. 8:25) they exclaimed. Jesus awakened. "Never did a soul utter that cry unheeded. As the disciples grasp their oars to make a last effort, Jesus rises. He stands in the midst of His disciples, while the tempest rages, the waves break over them, and the lightning illuminates His countenance. He lifts His hand, so often employed in deeds of mercy, and says to the angry sea, 'Peace, be still.'"[41]

Any helpless soul who in despair turns to Christ and cries "Save me, Lord, I perish" will find deliverance.

142

"PEACE, BE STILL"

But He said to them, "Why are you fearful, O you of little faith?" Then He arose and rebuked the winds and the sea, and there was a great calm.
Matt. 8:26.

The storm died away as quickly as it had come. The clouds rolled back, and stars appeared. The waves subsided and lapped gently against the sides of the boat. The disciples were in awe. Peter, the master fisher, sat stunned. Never had he seen such a demonstration of power. Those in the other boats accompanying the disciples had been in the same danger. The vessels had drifted close together, and those aboard the other craft had witnessed the miracle. They and the disciples whispered, "Who can this be, that even the wind and the sea obey Him!" (Mark 4:41).

Jesus was at peace. He had trusted the Father to care for Him in all situations. But it was not the case with the disciples. Had they trusted in Christ, they also would not have felt any terror of the tempest. We often find ourselves in the same identical position as the disciples. Struggling to manage the winds of strife and the temptations that assail us, we see difficulties as insurmountable. Striving by our own efforts to overcome, we tend to forget the One ready to help us in any difficulty. "We trust to our own strength till our hope is lost, and we are ready to perish. Then we remember Jesus, and if we call upon Him to save us, we shall not cry in vain. Though He sorrowfully reproves our unbelief and self-confidence, He never fails to give us the help we need." [42]

Too often we accept needless cares and burdens that God does not intend for us to bear. They make life difficult, especially when we neglect prayer. Christ fortified Himself through daily prayer. It allowed Him to sleep through the tempest. "The path of sincerity and integrity is not a path free from obstruction; but in every difficulty we are to see a call to prayer. There is no one living who has any power that he has not received from God, and the source whence it comes is open to the weakest human being." [43] "Every sincere prayer is heard in heaven. It may not be fluently expressed; but if the heart is in it, it will ascend to the sanctuary where Jesus ministers, and He will present it to the Father without one awkward, stammering word, beautiful and fragrant with the incense of His own perfection." [44]

"Lord, save us! We are perishing!" (Matt. 8:25).

THE OTHER SIDE OF THE SEA

Then they came to the other side of the sea, to the country of the Gadarenes.

Mark 5:1.

As morning dawned, the boats made landfall. The peaceful feeling of once more being on firm ground after a terrifying night upon the sea would be very short-lived. From among the caverns dug in the soft limestone cliffs two demon-possessed men had seen the approaching boats and rushed to intercept them. Once again forgetting they were in the presence of the Son of God, the disciples scattered in panic. Although chained hand and foot by the citizens of the area, the demon-possessed individuals had managed to free themselves repeatedly. In their fury they had cut themselves with sharp stones. Their hair was long and matted, their eyes glared in fury, and they had screamed as they hurtled toward the visitors.

Suddenly the disciples noticed Jesus calmly standing on the shore where they had left Him. Raising the same hand that stilled the tempest, Jesus signaled the madmen to come no closer. Possessed with fury, they helplessly raged at their inability to approach their prey. Jesus ordered the evil spirits to release the men. Vaguely the two men realized that here was One who could help them. They fell at His feet in worship, but in the intense internal struggle the demons would not let them go. Loudly they protested, "What have I to do with You, Jesus, Son of the Most High God? I implore You by God that You do not torment me" (Mark 5:7). Jesus asked the name of the speaker. "My name is Legion; for we are many" (verse 9), a voice replied. A Roman legion consisted of 6,000 footmen and 700 horsemen when at full strength. We understand we have no way of determining the exact number of demons, but suffice it to say they were numerous.

The defiant spokesperson for the demons pleaded for mercy, begging Jesus not to send them out of the district but rather into a nearby swineherd grazing on a hillside. Panic seized the animals as the demons seized them. Madly the animals rushed over a cliff and plunged into the sea, where they drowned. The swineherders, who had witnessed the event, rushed to town to tell what they had seen. Meanwhile the two men, now clothed, sat quietly at Jesus' feet. He who had the power to change demon-possessed men into missionaries can surely transform us.

"The gospel is to be presented, not as a lifeless theory, but as a living force to change the life." [45]

SAVED TO SERVE

Go home to your friends, and tell them what great things the Lord has done for you, and how He has had compassion on you. Mark 5:19.

After the swineherders made their report the entire population hurried out to meet the Man who could do such a thing. To their amazement, they saw seated upon the ground at the feet of the Saviour the two men whom all had feared. A calm filled their faces as they listened with rapt attention to the Master's words. The loss of the herd was, however, of more importance to the villagers than the salvation of the two men. Even though the disciples related their tale of the night upon the sea and the wonderful things they had seen, the people begged Jesus to leave. "They were so fearful of endangering their earthly interests that He who had vanquished the prince of darkness before their eyes was treated as an intruder, and the Gift of heaven was turned from their doors. We have not the opportunity of turning from the person of Christ as had the Gergesenes; but still there are many who refuse to obey His word, because obedience would involve the sacrifice of some worldly interest. Lest His presence shall cause them pecuniary loss, many reject His grace, and drive His Spirit from them."[46]

As Jesus started to step into the boat, the two men pleaded with Him not to leave them. Perhaps for a moment they feared that if He departed, the demons would return. Jesus gently told them they could not follow Him back to the western shore. The fact that they were Gentiles might hinder His work among the Jews. As few scribes and Pharisees visited the primarily Gentile area, Jesus instructed them to proclaim what had happened to them, something He rarely permitted those healed within the boundaries of the Jewish nation to do. During the following months they would tell everyone in Decapolis how Jesus had saved them. Sharing their testimony drew them nearer to Christ than if they had stepped into the boat and accompanied Him.

"Not one sermon from His lips had ever fallen upon their ears. . . . But they bore in their own persons the evidence that Jesus was the Messiah. They could tell what they knew; what they themselves had seen, and heard, and felt of the power of Christ. This is what everyone can do whose heart has been touched by the grace of God."[47]

145

SINNERS NEED REPENTANCE

I did not come to call the righteous, but sinners, to repentance.

Mark 2:17.

Upon His return to the western shore, Jesus went to the home of Levi-Matthew, the site of a feast held with Jesus as guest of honor. He had not hesitated to accept the invitation. The call of Levi-Matthew aroused great rancor among Christ's followers. The choice seemed an affront to religious and social custom. The Pharisees quickly used it as a wedge to separate His followers from Him. The publicans, however, reacted with interest. Perhaps there was hope for them after all. "He well knew that this would give offense to the Pharisaic party, and would also compromise Him in the eyes of the people. But no question of policy could influence His movements. With Him external distinctions weighed nothing. That which appealed to His heart was a soul thirsting for the water of life." [48]

The guests ate at a set of tables arranged in a square with three sides enclosed and the fourth left open for servants to come and go with food. Around the outside, couches sloped away from the table. Diners rested upon their left arms facing inward. Jesus took advantage of the occasion to present lessons that met the needs of His listeners. "By His own example He taught them that, when attending any public gathering, their conversation need not be of the same character as that usually indulged in on such occasions." [49] Some of those present took their stand for Jesus, while others would do so following His resurrection.

The banquet made the Pharisees livid. Approaching the disciples, they complained to them, hoping to alienate them from Jesus. "This is the way in which Satan has worked ever since the disaffection in heaven; and all who try to cause discord and alienation are actuated by his spirit." [50] To eat or drink with a Gentile violated ritual law, causing ceremonial uncleanness. The Jews classified publicans with Gentiles, considering them outcasts. The Pharisees thought themselves more worthy than those they despised, and yet the publicans were less bigoted, less self-absorbed. They were more open to receive and appreciate the gift of salvation than the Pharisees, who saw no need for mercy. Those who feel spiritually whole don't need a doctor, but those who feel the disease of sin know their deficiency.

"The test of His mission as the Saviour of men turned on the point of what He could do for sinners." [51]

FRIENDS OF THE BRIDEGROOM

And Jesus said to them, "Can the friends of the bridegroom fast while the bridegroom is with them?" Mark 2:19.

The Pharisees weren't content to separate Jesus from His own disciples. They sought out the disciples of John the Baptist and attempted to alienate them, too. John's disciples were sorrowing for their imprisoned master. Although John languished in Herod Antipas' dungeon, public sentiment was still with him. The fact that Jesus made no effort to follow their leader's lifestyle confused John's disciples. Jesus and His disciples feasted with publicans and sinners, yet John led a life of solitude and fasting. The Pharisees pointed out the differences between the two men. To them, Jesus was setting aside the ancient traditions of the people. How could He be the one whom John had heralded? If God had sent Him, why did Jesus and His disciples' behavior differ from that of John? Such questions found fertile ground with the disciples of John the Baptist. They observed the law and fasted regularly. Fasting was a sign of merit, and the more orthodox of them practiced it twice a week. John's disciples, supported by the Pharisees, came to Jesus, asking, "Why do the disciples of John and of the Pharisees fast, but Your disciples do not fast?" (Mark 2:18).

Jesus knew the men were fasting to gain favor. Such righteousness by works availed them nothing, however. Jesus didn't try to correct their misconceptions regarding fasting, but rather tried to show His own mission. Using the same figure of speech the Baptist had employed when he settled the dispute between his disciples and Christ's, Jesus now spoke of John as the "friend of the bridegroom." John's disciples couldn't fail to link the words with their teacher. Jesus wished to show them that their forms of religion had replaced its true spirit.

Jesus would ask His disciples not to fast but rather to rejoice while He was in their presence. Soon enough He would leave them for the cross and the tomb. At that time their hearts would break, and they would weep. When He should arise, they would once again rejoice. Christ's fast was of a different type. He had chosen "to loose the bonds of wickedness, to undo the heavy burdens, to let the oppressed go free, and [to] break every yoke" (Isa. 58:6).

"Not in idle mourning, in mere bodily humiliation and multitudinous sacrifices, is the true spirit of devotion manifested, but it is shown in the surrender of self in willing service to God and man." [52]

LEGALISM

And no one puts new wine into old wineskins; or else the new wine bursts the wineskins, the wine is spilled, and the wineskins are ruined. But new wine must be put into new wineskins. Mark 2:22.

Jesus explained to John's disciples that differences existed between His and the Pharisees' teachings. Any attempt to blend the two would reveal the contrast. The legalistic religion of many of the scribes, priests, and Pharisees had caused their hearts to wither like old brittle wineskins. Seeking human praise, they fasted and prayed repetitious prayers. And extolling their piety and virtue, they felt they needed no instruction. The teachings of Jesus were fresh and new and therefore disturbing and a threat to their self-righteousness.

As a result Jesus looked elsewhere for new vessels to fill with His message. "In the untutored fishermen, in the publican at the market place, in the woman of Samaria, in the common people who heard Him gladly, He found His new bottles for the new wine."[53] He took unlearned fishers from humble surroundings and educated them for His use. Jesus' teachings were not new doctrine. His was the message preached from the beginning of time. The Pharisees had simply lost sight of it. Customs, traditions, and practices of the past now blocked access to their hearts and minds.

"It was this that proved the ruin of the Jews, and it will prove the ruin of many souls in our own day. Thousands are making the same mistake as did the Pharisees whom Christ reproved at Matthew's feast. Rather than give up some cherished idea, or discard some idol of opinion, many refuse the truth which comes down from the Father of light. They trust in self, and depend upon their own wisdom, and do not realize their spiritual poverty. They insist on being saved in some way by which they may perform some important work. When they see that there is no way of weaving self into the work, they reject the salvation provided."[54] We can never purchase salvation by our own efforts. "A legal religion can never lead souls to Christ; for it is a loveless Christless religion."[55] New bottles are open to the love of Christ, and He reproduces His character in their lives.

"The sacrifices of God are a broken spirit, a broken and a contrite heart—these, O God, You will not despise" (Ps. 51:17).

"TALITHA, CUMI"

Then He took the child by the hand, and said to her, "Talitha, cumi," which is translated, "Little girl, I say to you, arise."

Mark 5:41.

As He returned from Gergesa, a multitude immediately greeted Jesus. After healing and teaching for some time, He had pressed on to Levi-Matthew's home. There a distraught Jairus found Him and humbly prostrated himself at His feet. Each Jewish synagogue had a "ruler" with the responsibility of conducting public worship. Jairus held such a respected position. While most of his class vocally opposed Jesus, Jairus recognized that Jesus alone could help him. "My little daughter lies at the point of death. Come and lay Your hands on her, that she may be healed, and she will live" (Mark 5:23). Immediately Jesus got up to accompany him.

As the crowd multiplied, it became more difficult to get through. The father was understandably anxious for the Master to hurry. "Jesus, pitying the people, stopped now and then to relieve some suffering one, or to comfort a troubled heart."[56] Then a messenger pressed through the crowd and whispered to Jairus, "Do not trouble the Master further, for your daughter is dead." Overhearing, Jesus turned in the midst of the throng and said, "Do not be afraid; only believe" (verse 36). Only believe! Jairus would do anything for his little daughter, but this? Now the Master had asked him to exercise greater faith!

The clamoring and wailing of the paid mourners jarred Jesus. Seeking quiet, He told them the child was asleep, but they laughed at Him. They had seen death before and knew the child was dead. How little they understood that to Him death was but a sleep (1 Cor. 15:51-55; 1 Thess. 4:13-17). Taking only the father and mother, Peter, James, and John with Him, Jesus entered the room where the girl lay. Approaching the bedside, He took the child's hand and softly spoke in Aramaic, "Little girl, I say to you, arise." "Instantly a tremor passed through the unconscious form. The pulses of life beat again. The lips unclosed with a smile. The eyes opened widely as if from sleep, and the maiden gazed with wonder on the group beside her. She arose, and her parents clasped her in their arms, and wept for joy."[57]

Death is but a sleep from which the Giver of all life will awaken all who rest in His care. He has the keys to the grave and will one day forever banish all the weeping and sorrow (John 3:16; Rom. 6:23; Rev. 1:18). "Do not be afraid; only believe" (Mark 5:36).

"Who Touched Me?"

*And He said to her,
"Daughter, your
faith has made you
well. Go in peace,
and be healed of
your affliction."
Mark 5:34.*

The narrow streets of Capernaum had slowed Jesus' progress toward the home of Jairus. The crowd included a woman who had suffered for 12 years from a medical condition that had burdened her life. She had long since used up her money in the search for a physician who could cure her. But hope sprang up when she heard that Jesus had returned once again to Capernaum. "In weakness and suffering she came to the seaside where He was teaching, and tried to press through the crowd, but in vain. Again she followed Him from the house of Levi-Matthew, but was still unable to reach Him. She had begun to despair, when, in making His way through the multitude, He came near where she was." [58] Weak from constant loss of blood and also embarrassed by being ceremonially unclean, the woman was reluctant to mention her problem. Rather she was sure that if she could simply touch the hem of His garment, she would be healed. She put great faith in that one trembling touch of His garment. Instantly the pain and weakness left her and in their place came the glow of health. The healing that flowed out from the Great Physician was "wrought by the power of God through the ministration of the angels." [59]

Jesus stopped. Trying to melt into the crowd unnoticed, the woman was aghast as, turning, He asked above the tumult, "Who touched My clothes?" (Mark 5:30). Peter, never at a loss for words, replied, "Master, the multitude throng thee and press thee, and sayest thou, Who touched me?" (Luke 8:45, KJV). But Jesus knew the difference between the jostling of the crowd and the determined touch of faith. Looking directly at the woman, Jesus again insisted on knowing who had touched Him. No longer able to hide the fact, the woman fearfully came forward. Had she gotten herself in trouble? Would He take back the gift of healing that she had received? Falling down at His feet, she confessed all. Gently Jesus said to her, "Daughter, your faith has made you well. Go in peace, and be healed of your affliction." "It is not enough to believe *about* Christ; we must believe *in* Him. The only faith that will benefit us is that which embraces Him as a personal Saviour; which appropriates His merits to ourselves." [60]

Reach out in faith and grasp Him as your personal Saviour.

OVERVIEW: HIS SECOND TOUR

Then Jesus went about all the cities and villages, teaching in their synagogues, preaching the gospel of the kingdom, and healing every sickness and every disease among the people. Matt. 9:35.

It is no surprise that Matthew 4:23 closely resembles Matthew 9:35. Each passage describes the end of a tour through the countryside of Galilee. Beginning and ending in Capernaum, the second tour of Galilee occupied most of early autumn A.D. 29. We witness only the highlights of a ministry increasingly noted for its parables and miracles. The second tour visited the small village of Nain, where a widow was burying her only son. After His miracle over the power of death we find Jesus casting out demons and facing accusations from the Pharisees of being in league with the devil. Jesus' mother and brothers attempted to convince Him to moderate His censure of the priests and Pharisees, but He reaffirmed that He must be about His Father's business.

We next find Him beside the western shore of the Sea of Galilee, where He sought to shed more light upon the kingdom described in the Sermon on the Mount. His lakeside parables illustrated more fully the principles of the gospel through the symbolism of a sower, a mustard seed, leaven, a man planting good seed, a dragnet, a treasure hidden in a field, a merchant and a pearl, and a householder with new and old treasures. That evening Jesus and His disciples sailed across the lake and found themselves caught in a violent storm that the Creator of all nature calmed with a word. The following morning in Gaderene, the disciples again witnessed the power of their Master to summon evil spirits from demoniacs. Still later that same busy day, Jesus returned to Capernaum and attended a feast at the home of Levi-Matthew. Following another confrontation with the Pharisees, who tried to stir up trouble among the twelve and also John the Baptist's disciples, He answered the summons of Jairus and raised his daughter from the dead. Along the way Jesus healed the woman who with supreme faith had touched the hem of His garment.

Throughout the second Galilean tour Jesus repeatedly had revealed His power over death, evil spirits, and the elements of nature. The twelve continued to receive training in evangelism. During the third tour they would find themselves having to put it into practice as Christ sent them out as His ambassadors.

"All who receive the gospel message into the heart will long to proclaim it. The heaven-born love of Christ must find expression." [61]

EVANGELISTS

Then He said to His disciples, "The harvest truly is plentiful, but the laborers are few. Therefore pray the Lord of the harvest to send out laborers into His harvest."

Matt. 9:37, 38.

The third Galilean tour began with these words. Matthew 10 follows with instructions the Master gave to His disciples. During the winter of A.D. 29-30 He sent them out two by two to the surrounding countryside to preach the gospel. Scripture says little of their successes or failures. The Bible records only the rejection of Jesus at Nazareth during this time. As the twelve started their missionary circuit, Jesus and His other disciples likewise continued to teach and reach the multitudes. Jesus felt with increasing urgency the need to reach the people. Up till now only He and His group of disciples had been active, but separating into a number of groups made more efficient progress. The scattered sheep of the house of Israel were the Good Shepherd's main concern. Those appointed to watch over the sheep had neglected them. The people were so demoralized by the religious leaders of the day that they no longer even attempted to improve their religious situation.

The third tour started a new and exciting phase of Christ's ministry. The next step in advancing the gospel involved branching out to reach more people and further training of the 12 disciples to become active evangelists. Up to then the disciples had just aided Jesus as He proclaimed the good news. "They assisted in arranging the people, bringing the afflicted ones to the Saviour, and promoting the comfort of all. They watched for interested hearers, explained the Scriptures to them, and in various ways worked for their spiritual benefit. They taught what they had learned of Jesus, and were every day obtaining a rich experience. But they needed also an experience in laboring alone." [62]

For the first time Scripture mentions the twelve as a group assigned a specific responsibility. "Christ sent out His disciples two and two, to go to places to which He would afterward follow." [63] "The work of the disciples needed molding and correcting by tenderest discipline, and by opening to others a knowledge of the Word they themselves had received." [64]

We may also obtain a rich experience in Christ by teaching others what we have learned of Him.

"PEACE TO THIS HOUSE"

But whatever house you enter, first say, "Peace to this house." Luke 10:5.

Because of Jewish prejudice, Jesus directed the disciples first to fellow Jews. "If they had now preached the gospel to the Gentiles or the Samaritans, they would have lost their influence with the Jews."[65] Each apostle, literally "one sent forth," complemented the other in some character trait. Simon Peter and his brother Andrew, James and his brother John, Philip and Bartholomew, Thomas and Matthew, James the son of Alphaeus and Thaddaeus, and lastly Simon the Canaanite and Judas Iscariot, made up the six groups.

Jesus' instructions were explicit. They were to go only to those places He had previously visited. Instead of entering synagogues or calling people together in large groups, they were rather to meet others one-on-one in house-to-house labor. Taking no money, provisions, or clothing, they were to rely upon the generosity of those they visited. When a house received them, the disciples were to proclaim "Peace" upon its hospitality, but to shake the dust from their feet and move on when they encountered those who refused to hear what they had to say.

Jesus gave additional instruction to those who would follow these first apostles. They were to exhibit gentleness, being as harmless as doves yet quick and alert for opportunities to spread the gospel. Each was to be as wise as serpents in the conduct of their affairs and aware of dangers constantly surrounding them. The disciples would face persecution and have to appear before councils and tribunals to answer for their faith. Each would have to be prepared to answer anyone for their faith (1 Peter 3:15). Christ's representatives must not worry about the future (Matt. 6:34), but trust God to care for them.

The life of His witnesses might be difficult, yet He promised assistance. "A daily, earnest striving to know God, and Jesus Christ whom He has sent, would bring power and efficiency to the soul. The knowledge obtained by diligent searching of the Scriptures would be flashed into the memory at the right time. But if any had neglected to acquaint themselves with the words of Christ, if they had never tested the power of His grace in trial, they could not expect that the Holy Spirit would bring His words to their remembrance. They were to serve God daily with undivided affection, and then trust Him."[66]

We still obtain preparation to serve through daily prayer and study.

"Art Thou He That Should Come?"

And when John had heard in prison about the works of Christ, he sent two of his disciples and said to Him, "Are You the Coming One, or do we look for another?"

Matt. 11:2, 3.

John the Baptist, accustomed to the wilderness, was now imprisoned in a small cell within the dungeon of Herod Antipas. As the prison's gloom weighed heavily upon him doubt crept over him. His disciples had free access to his cell, however, and brought him news of Christ's ministry. They also sowed seeds of doubt. "Oh, how often those who think themselves the friends of a good man, and who are eager to show their fidelity to him, prove to be his most dangerous enemies! How often, instead of strengthening his faith, their words depress and dishearten!" [67]

John still expected Jesus to claim the throne of David and rule as an earthly king, yet Jesus gathered to Himself disciples but no army. The futility of his own mission as Jesus' herald disappointed the Baptist's disciples. "If John, the faithful forerunner, failed to discern Christ's mission, what could be expected from the self-seeking multitude?" [68] The Baptist, however, refused to share their doubts. The sight of the dove and the voice of God at the Jordan still convinced him that Jesus was the Messiah. He sent two of them to the Messiah to strengthen their belief. The disciples approached Jesus and asked, "Are You the Coming One, or do we look for another?" (Luke 7:20).

Rather than answer directly, Jesus allowed them to observe His ministry. Finally He told them, "Go and tell John the things you have seen and heard: that the blind see, the lame walk, the lepers are cleansed, the deaf hear, the dead are raised, the poor have the gospel preached to them. And blessed is he who is not offended because of Me" (verses 22, 23).

"The disciples bore the message, and it was enough. John recalled the prophecy concerning the Messiah: 'The Lord hath anointed me to preach good tidings unto the meek; he hath sent me to bind up the brokenhearted, to proclaim liberty to the captives, and the opening of the prison to them that are bound; to proclaim the acceptable year of the Lord' (Isa. 61:1, 2). The works of Christ not only declared Him to be the Messiah, but showed in what manner His kingdom was to be established." [69]

No life that directs others to Christ is spent in vain.

154

A REED SHAKEN BY THE WIND

As they departed, Jesus began to say to the multitudes concerning John: "What did you go out into the wilderness to see? A reed shaken by the wind?" Matt. 11:7.

As John's messengers departed, Jesus presented a eulogy of the Baptist. Six months later John the Baptist would seal his message with his life. "The Saviour's heart went out in sympathy to the faithful witness now buried in Herod's dungeon. He would not leave the people to conclude that God had forsaken John, or that his faith had failed in the day of trial."[70] Many of those present had gone to hear John. The largest portion of his ministry took place in the Jordan Valley, where reeds grew in abundance. An allusion to the reeds recalled the forceful message the people had heard in that river setting. John was no vacillating reed. "In his faithfulness to principle he was as firm as a rock."[71]

Jesus asked, "But what did you go out to see? A prophet? Yes, I say to you, and more than a prophet" (Matt. 11:9). John was the forerunner of the Messiah. He introduced the world to the Son of God and connected the Testaments. The Old closed with the promise of his coming (Mal. 3:1; 4:5, 6; Isa. 40:3-5) and the New opened with the fulfillment of that prophecy (Matt. 3:1-3; Mark 1:1-3).

From spring of A.D. 27 to spring of A.D. 29 "so faithfully did he fulfill his mission, that as the people recalled what he had taught them of Jesus, they could say, 'All things that John spake of this Man were true.'"[72] The Baptist had received the opportunity to behold Christ, yet Jesus said, "He who is least in the kingdom of heaven is greater than he" (Matt. 11:11).

"Aside from the joy that John found in his mission, his life had been one of sorrow. . . . It was not his privilege to be with Christ and witness the manifestation of divine power attending the greater light. It was not for him to see the blind restored to sight, the sick healed, and the dead raised to life. He did not behold the light that shone through every word of Christ, shedding glory upon the promises of prophecy. The least disciple who saw Christ's mighty works and heard His words was in this sense more highly privileged than John the Baptist, and therefore is said to have been greater than he."[73]

Unlike John, we can rejoice in the words and assurance of Christ when He promises, "Lo, I am with you always, even to the end of the age" (Matt. 28:20).

IS THIS NOT THE CARPENTER?

Now He could do no mighty work there, except that He laid His hands on a few sick people and healed them. And He marveled because of their unbelief. Mark 6:5, 6.

While Galileans flocked to Jesus, His own neighbors refused to believe. They followed the news regarding their native Son with interest but doubted that He actually was the Messiah. "Since His rejection there, the fame of His preaching and His miracles had filled the land. None now could deny that He possessed more than human power. The people of Nazareth knew that He went about doing good, and healing all that were oppressed by Satan."[74]

Now the spring of A.D. 30, and nearing the end of His Galilean ministry, Jesus again wound His way up the familiar mountain road to Nazareth. He arrived before the Sabbath, and on the Sabbath day He went to the synagogue and stood to teach. As His words fell upon their ears the Holy Spirit touched the Nazarenes, but it seemed simply too incredible to believe their neighbor could be the Son of God. "'Where did this Man get these things? And what wisdom is this which is given to Him, that such mighty works are performed by His hands! Is this not the carpenter, the Son of Mary, and brother of James, Joses, Judas, and Simon? And are not His sisters here with us?' So they were offended at Him" (Mark 6:2, 3). Because Joseph was now dead, the people referred to Jesus as "the Son of Mary." How must she have felt about her Son? His brothers and sisters did not believe at this time that He was the Messiah (John 7:5). Those who grew up around Him and witnessed His character and acts of compassion did not find themselves attracted to Him because His exemplary life presented theirs in an unfavorable light.

The pride of the Jewish leaders would not allow them to accept Jesus, for "they loved the highest seats in the synagogue. They loved greetings in the market places, and were gratified with the sound of their titles on the lips of men. As real piety declined, they became more jealous for their traditions and ceremonies."[75] His purity of character exposed their own false piety and pretension. Jesus could do nothing as long as such unbelief existed. He forever departed Nazareth and those blinded by their desire to see a Messiah who fit their own conceptions.

"Truth was unpopular in Christ's day. It is unpopular in our day."[76]

COME APART AND REST

And He said to them, "Come aside by yourselves to a deserted place and rest a while."

Mark 6:30, 31.

For a number of weeks the apostles labored separately from their Master. Now, not long before Passover, they gathered to relate their experiences and report on their winter journeys. "They had committed errors in their first work as evangelists, and as they frankly told Christ of their experiences, He saw that they needed much instruction. He saw, too, that they had become weary in their labors, and that they needed to rest."[77] Far from the highways of Galilee on the northern end of the Sea of Galilee lay the plain of *El Batiha*. Nearby was the city of Bethsaida Julias. Seeking to reach the area without attracting attention was no easy task, but they did their best to leave Capernaum unnoticed. Despite their best plans, people followed them on foot as they set out in their boat.

Jesus had been visiting other villages while the disciples were away. The rest that the disciples and Jesus now took was not devoted to pleasure but to the work itself. "They talked together regarding the work of God, and the possibility of bringing greater efficiency to the work."[78] Jesus corrected their mistakes and gave them greater insights into methods of evangelism. He clarified the message and gave them courage and hope for future successes. The rabbis of the day felt the sum of religion was zealous and constant activity, but Jesus knew that when the cares of the work overcome people they forget to pray. The disciple who failed to pray was in danger of losing sight of God and his or her dependence upon Him.

"No other life was ever so crowded with labor and responsibility as was that of Jesus; yet how often He was found in prayer! How constant was His communion with God!"[79] Jesus recognized the need to seek frequent communion with His Father. Such times of prayer brought Him comfort and joy.

We find and know God's will as we listen to Him speak to our hearts. "When every other voice is hushed, and in quietness we wait before Him, the silence of the soul makes more distinct the voice of God. He bids us, 'Be still, and know that I am God' (Ps. 46:10, KJV). Here alone can true rest be found. And this is the effectual preparation for all who labor for God."[80]

HIDDEN REVENGE

For Herod himself had sent and laid hold of John, and bound him in prison for the sake of Herodias, his brother Philip's wife; for he had married her.

Mark 6:17.

Herod was convinced that John was a prophet of God, but his fear of Herodias was stronger than his desire to free the prophet. Time and again he delayed releasing John. His wife tried every wile to get Herod to slay him, but to no avail. The spirit of revenge burned deeply within her, and she could not forgive the shame and embarrassment his denunciation had brought her before the people. She carefully concealed her anger and waited. "On the king's birthday an entertainment was to be given to the officers of state and the nobles of the court. There would be feasting and drunkenness. Herod would thus be thrown off his guard, and might then be influenced according to her will."[81] Herodias sent her daughter Salome into the banquet room to dance for the king and his guests. Decorated with flowers, sparkling jewels, and bracelets, and with little regard for modesty, she danced for the amusement of the king just as her mother wished. The sight of the nearly nude young girl captivated the guests in their drunken stupors. As it was not customary for women to participate in such parties, those present complimented the king on his selection of entertainment.

Herod, in a rash moment, promised Salome with an oath that she might have anything she wished, even to half of his kingdom. Rushing to her mother, she breathlessly asked what she should request. At first horrified by her mother's ghastly suggestion, Salome refused to make it. But the mother prevailed and urged haste. Upon returning to the banquet, Salome pronounced the death sentence upon John. "I will that thou give me by and by in a charger the head of John the Baptist" (Mark 6:25, KJV).

"Herod was astonished and confounded. His riotous mirth ceased, and his guests were thrilled with horror at this inhuman request."[82] All present knew John was an innocent servant of God. Had one guest spoken in John's behalf and relieved Herod of his oath, the ruler would have spared the prophet. But they were all so drunk that "no voice was raised to save the life of Heaven's messenger."[83]

"Oh, how often has the life of the innocent been sacrificed through the intemperance of those who should have been guardians of justice!"[84]

THE AFTERMATH OF THE CRIME

When his disciples heard of it, they came and took away his corpse and laid it in a tomb.

Mark 6:29.

While John lived, Herodias was sure Herod's sympathies for the prophet kept him in mental turmoil. She thought she would find release for her husband's conscience by slaying John. The aftermath of the hideous crime was not so easy as Herodias had hoped. Once she received the prophet's bloody head, she exalted in her revenge. "But this inhuman act on her part made her name notorious and abhorred.... Her corrupt life, and her satanic revenge, stand upon the page of sacred history, making her name infamous." [85] Filled with remorse, Herod could find no release for his guilty conscience. "While engaged in the affairs of the nation, receiving honors from men, he bore a smiling face and dignified mien, while he concealed an anxious, aching heart, and was constantly terrified with fearful forebodings that the curse of God was upon him." [86]

In a moment of drunken stupor, Herod committed a crime that would haunt him for the rest of his troubled life. "The very act which he thought, while his reason and judgment were perverted, was maintaining his honor and dignity, made his name detestable." [87] Herod Antipas, ruler of Galilee and Perea, the man whom Jesus called "that fox" (Luke 13:32), for his cunning, his ambition, and his love of luxury, was a ruined man. When he heard the teachings of Jesus he became convinced that the Baptist had come back from the dead to torment him further.

The disciples wondered among themselves why Jesus did not rescue John. Had he not been a cousin to the Master? "John was but a sharer in the sufferings of Christ. All who follow Christ will wear the crown of sacrifice." [88] "Jesus did not interpose to deliver His servant. He knew that John would bear the test.... But for the sake of thousands who in after years must pass from prison to death, John was to drink the cup of martyrdom." [89]

"God never leads His children otherwise than they would choose to be led, if they could see the end from the beginning, and discern the glory of the purpose which they are fulfilling as coworkers with Him. Not Enoch, who was translated to heaven, not Elijah, who ascended in a chariot of fire, was greater or more honored than John the Baptist, who perished alone in the dungeon. 'Unto you it is given in the behalf of Christ, not only to believe on him, but also to suffer for his sake' (Phil. 1:29, KJV)." [90]

A CROWD OF 5,000

And Jesus went up on the mountain, and there He sat with His disciples. Now the Passover, a feast of the Jews, was near.

John 6:3, 4.

John's death cast a shadow over Jesus, and He longed to be with His disciples in solitude. Seeking to escape the crowds, they sailed east from Capernaum. But they didn't leave unnoticed. People followed, hoping they would land so that Jesus might speak with them. Pilgrims on their way to Passover swelled the throng. Arriving ahead of them, Jesus spent but a brief period encouraging His disciples. Then seeing the crowd, Jesus "'was moved with compassion toward them, because they were as sheep not having a shepherd.' Leaving His retreat, He found a convenient place where He could minister to them." [1]

The crowd had traveled east of Bethsaida Julias more than four miles overland while the disciples had come three miles by sea. The men numbered 5,000, and many had brought wives and little children with them.

Eager to hear about salvation, the people forgot they had not eaten. Jesus was also weary and hungry. "But He could not withdraw Himself from the multitude that pressed upon Him." [2] The disciples urged their Master to send the people into the surrounding towns and villages to purchase food.

Philip, a resident of Bethsaida, knew the local merchants. Turning to him, Jesus said, "Where shall we buy bread, that *these* may eat?" (John 6:5). Jesus was testing him. Surveying the crowd, Philip estimated that it would take more than 200 Roman denarii of bread to feed such a multitude. The silver coin, or denarii, was a working man's daily wage. Six months' wages would minimally give everyone a small morsel. Jesus challenged Philip's faith, and the disciple hesitated. Turning to the others, Jesus asked, "How many loaves do you have? Go and see." Andrew returned and reported, "There is a lad here who has five barley loaves and two small fish, but what are they among so many?" (verse 9).

Philip did the math and spent time figuring the odds of success. Andrew, stepping out in faith, took Jesus at His word and sought food from among the crowd. Two disciples—two different reactions! "The means in our possession may not seem to be sufficient for the work; but if we will move forward in faith, believing in the all-sufficient power of God, abundant resources will open before us. If the work be of God, He Himself will provide the means for its accomplishment." [3]

Are you a Philip or an Andrew?

"Gather Up the Fragments"

So when they were filled, He said to His disciples, "Gather up the fragments that remain, so that nothing is lost."

John 6:12.

The five loaves had been made of barley flour, the fish probably dried and used as a spicy relish to accompany the bread. "It was humble fare that had been provided; the fishes and barley loaves were the daily food of the fisher folk about the Sea of Galilee."[4] Jesus did not seek to feed the people upon rich and lavish food. He promises those who follow in His footsteps to meet only their basic needs. But "never did people enjoy the luxurious feasts prepared for the gratification of perverted taste as this people enjoyed the rest and the simple food which Christ provided so far from human habitations."[5]

Jesus directed the disciples to organize the people. The groups formed semicircles with one side open for the disciples to enter and serve. This early in the spring the rainfall had turned the meadow into a soft green table. Mothers with small children welcomed the opportunity to finally rest upon the soft grass. All could see the Saviour. Jesus took the bread in His hands and in His own special way gave thanks to the Father for the gift of food. The food multiplied within His hands as He broke it and passed the pieces to the disciples. Each time a disciple returned with an empty basket, Jesus waited there with more. "The miracle of the loaves teaches a lesson of dependence upon God."[6] Each time we return to Him for spiritual food, He is there with an abundant supply to fill our need.

After the people had eaten, Jesus ordered the disciples to waste nothing. "Gather up the fragments that remain, so that nothing is lost." After filling 12 small wicker baskets, the disciples and Jesus then together ate the heaven-sent food. The crowd carried some of the "miracle bread" with them and shared with their friends the "bread of life" preached that day. "Christ received from the Father; He imparted to the disciples; they imparted to the multitude; and the people to one another. So all who are united to Christ will receive from Him the bread of life, the heavenly food, and impart it to others."[7]

Christ continues to work today through human agencies. We are privileged to be coworkers with the Master in carrying heaven's blessings to others.

THEY DARED NOT DISOBEY

Immediately Jesus made His disciples get into the boat and go before Him to the other side, while He sent the multitudes away. Matt. 14:22.

The miracle they had just witnessed greatly impressed the people. Hadn't God fed Israel with manna in the Sinai? And hadn't Moses foretold a future prophet would do likewise? All day grew the people's belief that "this is He who will make Judea an earthly paradise, a land flowing with milk and honey. He can satisfy every desire. He can break the power of the hated Romans. He can deliver Judah and Jerusalem. He can heal the soldiers who are wounded in battle. He can supply whole armies with food. He can conquer the nations, and give to Israel the long-sought dominion."[8]

Since Jesus did not seek to crown Himself King of Israel, they would do it for Him. The disciples thought that only Christ's modesty prevented Him from accepting the honor. The throne of David was rightfully His to claim. "Judas was first to take advantage of the enthusiasm excited by the miracle of the loaves. It was he who set on foot the project to take Christ by force and make Him king. His hopes were high. His disappointment was bitter."[9] Violence and insurrection with Rome would have resulted if anyone had acted on the hastily thought-out plan. It would have cut Jesus' ministry short. One year remained to spread the news of salvation. "Prompt and decisive action on the part of Jesus was necessary in order to quell the popular sentiment of the people and to control His own disciples."[10] Jesus firmly ordered the disciples to return to the boat and immediately cast off. Reluctantly, they obeyed.

Then Jesus commanded the crowd to disperse. "His manner is so decisive that they dare not disobey. The words of praise and exaltation die on their lips. In the very act of advancing to seize Him their steps are stayed, and the glad, eager look fades from their countenances. . . . The kingly bearing of Jesus, and His few quiet words of command, quell the tumult, and frustrate their designs. They recognize in Him a power above all earthly authority, and without a question they submit."[11] When finally alone, Jesus climbed the mountainside to seek His Father in prayer, feeling hurt that His disciples' vision limited itself to worldly honor and power.

Jesus prayed that all might catch His vision of another kingdom where one might store treasure. Catch His vision!

THE FOURTH WATCH OF THE NIGHT

Now in the fourth watch of the night Jesus went to them, walking on the sea.

Matt. 14:25.

When Jesus ordered His disciples to return at once to Capernaum, they refused to leave. Didn't He understand the moment had come to rise up against Rome? Jesus now spoke with authority. Never had He raised His voice in such a way to them. "They knew that further opposition on their part would be useless, and in silence they turned toward the sea."[12] The disciples might not have wanted to leave their Master, but their thoughts were already far from Him and His message. The wonder of the loaves and fishes had gone, replaced by disappointment and growing unbelief.

They tarried, hoping Jesus would soon join them. But as darkness descended they reluctantly pushed off from shore and raised sail for Capernaum. Meanwhile, a sudden violent storm, so common to Galilee, had arisen. The sea rose rapidly before the wind, threatening to sink the boat. Bailing water and dropping sail, the disciples rowed to keep the bow facing the rising waves. The short journey from Bethsaida to Capernaum was suddenly beyond reach as wind drove them south into open water. They rowed 25 to 30 furlongs (three to three and a half miles) into the strong head wind. For eight hours they labored. "Until the fourth watch of the night they toiled at the oars. Then the weary men gave themselves up for lost. In storm and darkness the sea had taught them their own helplessness, and they longed for the presence of their Master."[13]

Jesus was watching over His disciples. "At the moment when they believe themselves lost, a gleam of light reveals a mysterious figure approaching them upon the water. But they know not that it is Jesus. The One who has come for their help they count as an enemy. Terror overpowers them. The hands that have grasped the oars with muscles like iron let go their hold. The boat rocks at the will of the waves; all eyes are riveted on this vision of a man walking upon the white-capped billows of the foaming sea."[14] The disciples fear it is a harbinger of destruction. "Jesus advances as if He would pass them; but they recognize Him, and cry out, entreating His help. Their beloved Master turns, His voice silences their fear, 'Be of good cheer: it is I; be not afraid.'"[15]

Jesus watches over us today in our own stormy trials, admonishing us likewise, "Be not afraid."

"LORD, SAVE ME!"

But when he saw that the wind was boisterous, he was afraid; and beginning to sink he cried out, saying, "Lord, save me!"

Matt. 14:30.

When the disciples set sail they "were more impatient and dissatisfied with Christ than they had ever been since they acknowledged Him as their Lord."[16] In the midst of the angry storm, with waves so high the disciples feared that at any moment they would capsize, they recognized their need of a Saviour. "At last the disciples saw that their efforts were in vain, that they were unable to help themselves. With feelings of remorse they remembered their impatience with Jesus, and called upon God for pardon. And now the time had come for Jesus to help them. Placing His feet upon the waters, He stepped from one white-capped wave to another, as if walking upon dry land."[17]

Once the disciples felt assured the figure was Jesus, Peter exclaimed, "Lord, if it is You, command me to come to You on the water" (Matt. 14:28). Jesus answered, "Come." Springing over the side of the boat with great confidence, Peter walked toward Jesus upon the windswept waves. As long as his eyes remained fixed upon his Master, he was safe. Just a darting glance down at the deep waters beneath his feet and then back to his companions in the boat, and he started to sink in a trough between two huge waves. Looking back to where Jesus was standing, he could no longer see Him, since the towering waves had hidden Christ from view. Peter's faith now failed as he felt himself sinking into a watery grave. Frantically he searched for Jesus. Finally fixing his eyes upon Him, he begged, "Lord, save me!" (verse 30). "Immediately Jesus grasped the outstretched hand, saying, 'O thou of little faith, wherefore didst thou doubt?' Walking side by side, Peter's hand in that of his Master, they stepped into the boat together."[18] Without delay Jesus immediately saved Peter and then gently rebuked his lack of faith. "A fisherman all his life, Peter knew how to swim (see John 21:7). But a sea like this, in which a boat was not safe, was even less safe for a swimmer."[19]

"When trouble comes upon us, how often we are like Peter! We look upon the waves, instead of keeping our eyes fixed upon the Saviour. . . . Those who fail to realize their constant dependence upon God will be overcome by temptation. . . . Only through realizing our own weakness and looking steadfastly unto Jesus can we walk securely."[20]

GENNESARET

When they had crossed over, they came to the land of Gennesaret.

Matt. 14:34.

As soon as Jesus took His place in the boat, the sea became calm and the vessel made landfall along the fertile plain of Gennesaret, west of Capernaum. "The night of horror was succeeded by the light of dawn. The disciples, and others who also were on board, bowed at the feet of Jesus with thankful hearts, saying, 'Of a truth Thou art the Son of God!'"[21] Meanwhile, people flocked from Bethsaida to the site of the miracle of the loaves and fishes, expecting to find Jesus, only to discover He had landed west of Capernaum. "As soon as it was known that He had landed, the people 'ran through that whole region round about, and began to carry about in beds those that were sick, where they heard he was' (Mark 6:55, KJV)."[22] Jesus healed those brought while moving slowly toward the synagogue of Capernaum. Here the multitudes coming west from Bethsaida finally found Him.

The disciples related the story of their stormy night crossing, faithfully recounting the stilling of the wind and waves. The people questioned Jesus, hoping for details. "Rabbi, when did You come here?" (John 6:25). Realizing that they desired sensational news, He addressed instead their motivation in seeking Him. Sadly He commented, "Most assuredly, I say to you, you seek Me, not because you saw the signs, but because you ate of the loaves and were filled" (verse 26). "His laying bare of their materialistic motives applied not only to the satisfaction of their physical appetites but also to the whole range of their ambitious expectations that He would assert Himself as a military conqueror and political ruler."[23] Jesus wished them to seek those things that endured. "Do not labor for the food which perishes, but for the food which endures to everlasting life, which the Son of Man will give you, because God the Father has set His seal on Him" (verse 27).

All their lives the people had attempted to gain heaven through good works. Knowing that they desired additional duties to do to merit heaven, He corrected their mistaken belief about heaven's price tag. "This is the work of God, that you believe in Him whom He sent" (verse 29).

"The price of heaven is Jesus. The way to heaven is through faith in 'the Lamb of God, which taketh away the sin of the world' (John 1:29, KJV)."[24] Salvation is by faith alone!

THE BREAD OF LIFE

I am the living bread which came down from heaven.
John 6:51.

The crowd could not understand how Jesus could claim to be the Messiah and yet refuse to be Israel's king. The rabbis instantly saw an opening. "What sign will You perform then, that we may see it and believe You?" one of them asked. "What work will You do? Our fathers ate the manna in the desert; as it is written, 'He gave them bread from heaven to eat'" (John 6:30, 31). The Jews mistakenly attributed to Moses the sending of the manna. Jesus, the real giver of the manna, now stood before them, and they did not recognize that fact. "Most assuredly, I say to you," Jesus replied, "Moses did not give you the bread from heaven, but My Father gives you the true bread from heaven. For the bread of God is He who comes down from heaven and gives life to the world" (verses 32, 33).

The people, thinking Jesus referred to temporal food, asked Him to supply the bread of God forever. "Much as the Samaritan woman had requested water that would forever quench her thirst that she might not need to draw water again, so now the Jews asked for a continual supply of bread. Moses, as they thought, had provided Israel with heavenly bread for 40 years; if Jesus were truly the Messiah, surely He could work a yet greater miracle and supply them forever."[25] Jesus now replied plainly, "I am the bread of life. He who comes to Me shall never hunger, and he who believes in Me shall never thirst" (verse 35). Three times He had announced that He was the bread of life (verses 41, 48, 51) and that those who received Him gained eternal life.

The Jews knew the deep spiritual implications of and references to bread. Jeremiah had said: "Your words were found, and I ate them, and Your word was to me the joy and rejoicing of my heart" (Jer. 15:16). Every word the Saviour said was life to those that heard the message of salvation and believed. Day after day Jesus performed miracles and signs before the unbelieving multitudes. They had so prejudiced their minds against Him that no amount of evidence would sway their perverse hearts.

Just as we take temporal food into the physical body to preserve and strengthen it, we must also take the bread of life into our spiritual lives that we may grow in grace and in the knowledge of our Lord and Saviour, Jesus Christ.

THIS IS A HARD SAYING

From that time many of His disciples went back and walked with Him no more. John 6:66.

Tradition records that Jesus gave His "Bread of Life" sermon in the synagogue of Capernaum. The disciples He spoke to included more than the twelve, who routinely accompanied Him. Since He had refused to let the multitude crown Him king, those "other" disciples had become more and more unhappy with Jesus and His ministry. They had now come hoping for the food that would enable them to never hunger again. Expecting food similar to the miracle loaves and fishes, they instead received spiritual food. The crowd neither appreciated nor understood the gift. Jesus called upon them all to receive Him and partake of His character. They had to give up their cherished idea of an earthly kingdom and become more like Jesus. His followers needed to become self-sacrificing and humble. Many of His disciples said, "This is a hard saying; who can understand it?" (John 6:60).

"The test was too great. The enthusiasm of those who had sought to take Him by force and make Him king grew cold. This discourse in the synagogue, they declared, had opened their eyes. Now they were undeceived. In their minds His words were a direct confession that He was not the Messiah, and that no earthly rewards were to be realized from connection with Him. They had welcomed His miracle-working power; they were eager to be freed from disease and suffering; but they would not come into sympathy with His self-sacrificing life. They cared not for the mysterious spiritual kingdom of which He spoke. The insincere, the selfish, who had sought Him, no longer desired Him. If He would not devote His power and influence to obtaining their freedom from the Romans, they would have nothing to do with Him." [26]

"They rejected their Saviour, because they longed for a conqueror who would give them temporal power." [27] "Souls are tested today as were those disciples in the synagogue at Capernaum. When truth is brought home to the heart, they see that their lives are not in accordance with the will of God. They see the need of an entire change in themselves; but they are not willing to take up the self-denying work. Therefore they are angry when their sins are discovered. They go away offended, even as the disciples left Jesus. [28]

Do you claim the title without the cross? Are you willing to change your behavior to meet Christ's self-sacrificing example, or is it a hard saying for you to hear?

YOU ARE THE CHRIST

Then Jesus said to the twelve, "Do you also want to go away?" John 6:67.

Those who had once professed belief now abandoned Jesus. The larger multitude rejected His mission. Seeking out His enemies, these previous believers united with priest and Pharisee to twist the words of Christ and misrepresent His miracles and teachings. Popular feeling turned against His ministry, and He stood more surely in the cross's shadow than ever before. Jesus had reached a crossroad in Galilee just as He had the year before in Judea. By reaching for temporal needs, the people had lost eternal glory. Approaching His disciples, Jesus asked, "Do you also want to go away?" Peter, ever the spokesman for the twelve, quickly answered, "Lord, to whom shall we go? You have the words of eternal life. Also we have come to believe and know that You are the Christ, the Son of the living God" (John 6:68, 69).

The disciples longed to stay with their Master. Jesus brought the test to His disciples at this point in His ministry so He could personally encourage their faith. He knew that His death would fill them with grief and sorrow. It would shatter their hopes for a temporal kingdom and strongly test their faith. The crowd had heard the lessons and witnessed the miracles of Christ, yet they had turned from Him in disbelief when He would not give them the temporal prizes they desired. The twelve accepted the same words and works by faith. "When men submit entirely to God, eating the bread of life and drinking the water of salvation, they will grow up into Christ. Their characters are composed of that which the mind eats and drinks. Through the Word of life, which they receive and obey, they become partakers of the divine nature. Then their entire service is after the divine similitude, and Christ, not man, is exalted."[29]

Jesus had seen those leaving Him but made no attempt to stop them. "The consciousness that His compassion was unappreciated, His love unrequited, His mercy slighted, His salvation rejected, filled Him with sorrow that was inexpressible. It was such developments as these that made Him a man of sorrows, and acquainted with grief."[30] Rejected in Judea and now in Galilee, hounded by scribes and Pharisees, shadowed by spies seeking evidence with which to put Him to death, Jesus knew His life was in danger. He was "despised and rejected by men" (Isa. 53:3).

"Do you also want to go away?" (John 6:67).

Traditions of the Elders

Why do Your disciples not walk according to the tradition of the elders, but eat bread with unwashed hands? Mark 7:5.

The Galilean ministry now entered a less visible phase as Jesus quietly tended His followers in Capernaum. Jesus' popularity following the third Galilean tour had alarmed Jewish leaders. His enemies had expected Him in Jerusalem for Passover, but Jesus, aware of their scheming, did not attend. But a deputation brought their scheme to Him. "The leaders in Jerusalem looked upon the illiterate and simple people of Galilee with contempt, and commonly referred to them as 'amme ha'ares, literally, 'people of the soil.'"[31] Rudely disrupting Him as He spoke with the people, they lodged a complaint calculated to alienate the simple peasants from Jesus.

Ceremonial purification required "pouring a small quantity of water [the minimum prescribed was that which could be contained in one and a half eggshells] upon the fingers and palm of first one hand and then the other with the hand tilted so that the water ran from the palm to the wrist, but no farther . . . , then alternately rubbing one hand with the palm of the other hand."[32] The pious considered neglecting the rite a terrible sin. Such precepts, in many cases, had evolved to become more highly regarded than the biblical law itself. By the time of Christ, if they found a conflict between the commandments of Sinai and the rabbinical precepts, the leaders leaned toward the latter. "Christ and His disciples did not observe these ceremonial washings, and the spies made this neglect the ground of their accusation."[33]

Jesus made no attempt to defend His disciples. Instead He illustrated the duplicity of rabbinical precepts by pointing to the system of "Corban." By simply saying the word "Corban," or "an offering," over an item, it became dedicated to God. One was free to use the item until such time as he wished to donate it to the Temple. His parents might live in poverty while he benefited from the object, yet he did not have to come to their aid. A man might thus defraud his parents, refusing to support them in the name of religion, and all with the full support of the priests. Such was clearly never the intent of the injunction to "honor your father and your mother" (Ex. 20:12). The priests had obviously invalidated the fifth commandment by tradition. Christ's words indicted the whole system.

Do you worship Him in vain today? Do you keep human traditions or the law of God?

169

GREAT PRECEPTS/ PETTY RULES

He said to them, "All too well you reject the command- ment of God, that you may keep your tradition." Mark 7:9.

Jesus said, "Hear Me, everyone, and understand: There is nothing that enters a man from outside which can defile him; but the things which come out of him, those are the things that defile a man. If any- one has ears to hear, let him hear!" (Mark 7:14-16). He chose to answer their hand washing question as pre- sented. It directly related to the manner in which one might eat food (i.e., with unclean hands) and whether the lack of that ceremonial act could cause moral defile- ment. His answer had nothing to do with the *kind* of food that a person could or could not consume. Many in the multitude seized upon His statement as justifica- tion for eating unclean foods. But they ignored the dis- cussion's context. Jesus did not do away with the distinction between clean and unclean flesh foods.

When Jesus entered a house, His disciples came to Him with questions. They did not understand the meaning of "things entering and things coming out of a man." "So He said to them, 'Are you thus without understanding also? Do you not perceive that whatever enters a man from outside cannot defile him, because it does not enter his heart. . . . What comes out of a man, *that* defiles a man. For from within, out of the heart of men, proceed evil thoughts, adul- teries, fornications, murders, thefts, covetousness, wickedness, deceit, lewd- ness, an evil eye, blasphemy, pride, foolishness. All these evil things come from within and defile a man' " (verses 18-23). Though often people hide such cherished sins within the heart, they are as destructive as if acted out upon one's neighbor. "Now the works of the flesh are evident, which are: adultery, fornication, uncleanness, lewdness, idolatry, sorcery, hatred, contentions, jealousies, outbursts of wrath, selfish ambitions, dissensions, heresies, envy, murders, drunkenness, revelries, and the like" (Gal. 5:19-21). Jesus wanted His disciples to replace sinful soul-defiling traits with the fruit of the Spirit: "love, joy, peace, longsuffering, kindness, goodness, faithfulness, gentleness, self-control. Against such there is no law" (Gal. 5:22, 23).

When they observe human precepts over those of God, then His disciples must beware! The hatred and anger of the spies were more defiling to their souls than neglecting the ritual of hand washing they held in such high esteem. "For God will bring every work into judgment, including every secret thing, whether good or evil" (Eccl. 12:14).

JESUS

MINISTRY IN RETIREMENT
Christ Our Shepherd

Spring A.D. to Autumn A.D. 30

Matthew 15:21-17:27

Mark 7:24-9:29

Luke 9:18-43

The Desire of Ages, pp. 395-442

ABSENT FROM JERUSALEM

Then Jesus went out from there and departed to the region of Tyre and Sidon. Matt. 15:21.

The third Galilean tour had caused great consternation among Jewish leaders. Jealousy consumed them as the people seemed to be flocking to the new Teacher. The disciples' missionary tour spread the gospel to areas where it came into direct conflict with local rabbis who complained bitterly to Jerusalem. Following the silencing of their latest deputation, the threats and anger of the Jewish leaders made it evident that Jesus' life was in danger. During His two and one-half years of ministry, Jesus had been almost uniformly "despised and rejected by men" (Isa. 53:3). Now He shifted His outreach to areas outside of Galilee and Judea. Although the confrontation with the deputation sent out from Jerusalem prompted the departure from Galilee, at the same time Jesus sought an opportunity to expand the disciples' vision toward non-Jews. It was evident the "chosen" had rejected the offer of salvation, yet the disciples clung to the belief that Israel alone would receive God's blessings.

"After the encounter with the Pharisees, Jesus withdrew from Capernaum, and crossing Galilee, repaired to the hill country on the borders of Phoenicia. Looking westward, He could see, spread out upon the plain below, the ancient cities of Tyre and Sidon, with their heathen temples, their magnificent palaces and marts of trade, and the harbors filled with shipping. Beyond was the blue expanse of the Mediterranean, over which the messengers of the gospel were to bear its glad tidings to the centers of the world's great empire. But the time was not yet. The work before Him now was to prepare His disciples for their mission."[34] Jesus wanted seclusion and a chance to teach His disciples without interference from the rabbis and their spies. "And He entered a house and wanted no one to know it, but He could not be hidden" (Mark 7:24).

His disciples still did not fully understand His mission. He now followed His own admonition: "And whoever will not receive you nor hear your words, when you depart from that house or city, shake off the dust from your feet" (Matt. 10:14). The crowds of Galilee would never again be so large. The political urge to place Him on the throne would die down. People now had a chance to hear the gospel without the noise of popular tumult.

The gospel is for everyone, not a "chosen" few.

BREAD CRUMBS

Then she came and worshiped Him, saying, "Lord, help me!" Matt. 15:25.

The Canaanites were an ancient people numbered among those nations God ordered the Israelites to destroy upon entering the Promised Land (Deut. 20:17). That any survived resulted from Israel's only partial obedience. Skilled merchants, they lived along the north coast between the hills of Galilee and the Mediterranean. News of Jesus's ministry had penetrated even to there. A Canaanite woman had heard of the miracles. "Inspired by a mother's love, she determined to present her daughter's case to Him." [35] Would Jesus condescend to hear her plea? Knowing the situation, He placed Himself where He would encounter her. Crying out to the Master, she said, "Have mercy on me, O Lord, Son of David! My daughter is severely demon-possessed" (Matt. 15:22). Jesus did not reply. The disciples felt His behavior entirely appropriate. Most Jews treated Gentiles in just such a cold manner. Jesus had ministered before to non-Jews, and in each instance one might argue that circumstances had thrust the situation upon Him. The Samaritans, the centurion of Capernaum, the demoniacs at Gergesa—the disciples saw no inconsistencies in Jesus' behavior or in the prejudices the Jews held against the Gentiles. Annoyed, they urged Jesus to send the woman away.

"I was not sent except to the lost sheep of the house of Israel," Jesus replied. "It is not good to take the children's bread and throw it to the little dogs" (verses 24-26). The disciples didn't grasp their own rebuke. "This answer would have utterly discouraged a less earnest seeker. But the woman saw that her opportunity had come. Beneath the apparent refusal of Jesus, she saw a compassion that He could not hide." [36] Falling at His feet, she pleaded, "Yes, Lord, yet even the little dogs eat the crumbs which fall from their masters' table" (verse 27). No nationalistic barrier would prevent her from pressing her request. "The Saviour is satisfied. He has tested her faith in Him. . . . Christ now grants her request, and finishes the lesson to the disciples." [37] From that very hour her daughter recovered.

"The spirit which built up the partition wall between Jew and Gentile is still active. Pride and prejudice have built strong walls of separation between different classes of men. . . . There are no barriers which man or Satan can erect but that faith can penetrate. . . . The blessings of salvation are for every soul." [38]

Ephphatha, "Be Opened"

Then they brought to Him one who was deaf and had an impediment in his speech, and they begged Him to put His hand on him.

Mark 7:32.

Continuing north toward the port city of Sidon, Jesus spent valuable time with His disciples. In the area lived many who had traveled to Galilee to hear His message (Mark 3:7, 8). The pressure from the Pharisees was negligible here, and the time He spent with the disciples had no interruption or controversy. Turning again southward toward the Sea of Galilee, Jesus and His disciples passed beyond the scene of His Galilean ministry to the area of the 10 Cities (the Decapolis). Nine of the 10 cities lay east of the Jordan River and south of the Sea of Galilee. The lone exception to those in the Transjordan Region was the town of Scythopolis (Beth-shean from Old Testament times). The people of the 10 cities region were now ready to listen to Jesus. Immediately after the destruction of their swineherd they had begged Him to depart. Now they had heard the messengers left behind, and they longed to see Him again (Mark 5:20).

Crowds gathered, and friends brought a deaf, stammering man to Jesus. Taking the man aside, He "put His fingers in his ears, and He spat and touched his tongue. Then, looking up to heaven, He sighed, and said to him, 'Ephphatha,' that is, 'Be opened.' Immediately his ears were opened, and the impediment of his tongue was loosed, and he spoke plainly" (Mark 7:33-35). This miracle differed from most. The man did not seek out the Master, but rather friends had brought him. Their faith sought out the Messiah. The man could speak, but not plainly (verse 35). Perhaps his deafness gave no feedback to correct the sounds created by his own voice. Jesus took the man aside and through accentuated movements He placed His fingers in the man's ears. By this action He showed him that He was interested in his affliction. Jesus touched the man's tongue. Both organs in need of healing received His attention. It was the only occasion during which Jesus looked heavenward during a miracle. "Apparently upon this occasion the purpose of the gesture was to direct the deaf-mute's thoughts to God and heaven, in order to make clear to him that healing would come only through divine power."[39]

How like our Saviour to tailor His actions to the special needs of the one who sought Him. Bring your special need to the Great Physician today.

A MIRACLE FOR GENTILES

And He took the seven loaves and the fish and gave thanks, broke them and gave them to His disciples; and the disciples gave to the multitude.

Matt. 15:36.

The Gentiles now crowded the Great Healer so He led them up a mountainside above the beach. It was summer A.D. 30, perhaps late June or early July. "For three days they continued to throng about the Saviour, sleeping at night in the open air, and through the day pressing eagerly to hear the words of Christ, and to see His works."[40] By ancient reckoning, three days constituted one full day and any parts of those preceding or following. Apparently the people had provided food for the first two days but had insufficient supplies to get through a third. Jesus called upon His disciples for a solution to the food shortage. Again they showed a lack of faith. "Then His disciples said to Him, 'Where could we get enough bread in the wilderness to fill such a great multitude?'" (Matt. 15:33). He had already fed the 5,000 with five loaves and two small fishes, the lunch of a small lad. On this occasion the disciples found seven loaves and a few little fish, certainly not sufficient food to feed a crowd numbering 4,000 men alone.

The disciples had witnessed the miracle of the feeding of the 5,000, but it had benefited Jews, not Gentiles. Jesus had repeatedly shown His disciples that Gentile faith was often greater than that of the "house of Israel," but so ingrained was the prejudice taught by synagogue elder, scribe, and Pharisee, that the disciples only slowly overcame their nationalistic pride. They believed that God had entrusted the "bread" of salvation (John 6:32, 33) only to Jews! Thus they couldn't accept that a miracle performed for 5,000 Jews just a few months before could or would be visited upon Gentiles. But Jesus, concerned for the people's well being and not wishing to send them away hungry, sought to meet their physical need. Commanding them to sit down upon the ground, He took the loaves and fishes, gave thanks to His Father in heaven, broke them into pieces, and handed them to the disciples to distribute to the people.

The sequence is important. All good things come from the Father. Jesus multiples everything we surrender to Him and fully meets every one of our needs. Christ calls His disciples, both then and now, to be active participants in reaching out to help others. His hands to our hands to their hands!

KOPHINOI OR SPURIDES?

So they all ate and were filled, and they took up seven large baskets full of the fragments that were left. Matt. 15:37.

Many believe the feeding of the 4,000 and the 5,000 to be the same event. Christ performed both events far from cities for large groups of people gathered near the shore of Galilee. Both specifically mention Jesus' sympathy for the people and His use of His disciples. And both times the food consisted of bread and fishes. The blessing, breaking, and distribution of food are identical. Each account mentions leftover food.

Can we trust the Bible that they were separate miracles? The stories differ in detail. In one instance Jesus arrives by boat, in the second He and the disciples reach the region on foot. He fed the 5,000 Jews near Bethsaida Julias (near the northeastern shore) at Passover and the 4,000 Gentiles near Gergesa on the eastern shore later in the year. The 5,000 ate after one day, the 4,000 after three days of teaching. Jesus sought seclusion with His disciples prior to the first miracle. During the second He journeyed the region healing. The 5,000 brought no supplies, but the 4,000 had enough for two days. The disciples, looking out for the welfare of 5,000 fellow Jews, brought their problem to Jesus' attention. Jesus pointed out the same problem among the Gentiles, telling the disciples to do something for them as well. Jesus instructed the 5,000 to seat themselves upon the grass. During Passover the grass would have been green. The 4,000 were told to sit upon the ground. By late summer all grass would have withered.

The baskets used to collect remnants for the 5,000 were 12 *kophinoi,* or small hand baskets carried by Jews on small journeys. The baskets used for the 4,000 were seven *spurides,* or large "hamperlike" baskets (Matt. 16:9, 10). Jews carried larger baskets on journeys deep into Gentile country so they wouldn't have to purchase food from Gentiles. Jesus sent the disciples ahead by boat to Capernaum and a storm arose in the first story, while during the second He accompanied them to Magdala.

Why should we care whether the 5,000 are the same as the 4,000? Because "to the disciples the amazing and unexpected thing was not that Jesus could *supply the bread, but rather that He would* do *so for Gentiles."* [41] *By our standards, many "sinners" will be saved in His kingdom, while many "saints" having great light will be lost because they disregard it.*

A RENEWED ATTACK

Then the Pharisees and Sadducees came, and testing Him asked that He would show them a sign from heaven.

Matt. 16:1.

Jesus and His disciples left the southeastern shores of Decapolis and crossed the Sea of Galilee. They made landfall near Magdala (Magadan), a town situated at the southern end of the Plain of Gennesaret. The sermons on the mount and by the sea had taken place near there. Here Jesus had ordained the twelve. "Now as He landed once more in Galilee, where His power had been most strikingly manifested, where most of His works of mercy had been performed, and His teaching given, He was met with contemptuous unbelief."[42] The Gennesaret valley would once again witness confrontation between Jesus and the enemies who awaited His return to Galilee.

As we mentioned earlier, the Pharisees seem to have been the successors of the Hasidim, or "pious ones," who had fought the Syrians for Jewish independence. Now they fostered passive resistance against the Roman invader at every turn. The Sadducees, on the other hand, were liberals. "Finding themselves 'in the world,' they were quite ready and willing to be 'of' it as well."[43] This practical party collaborated with Romans and Herodians to accomplish what they could for the nation during the occupation. They flocked to public office and formed the aristocracy of the land. The Pharisees, then, were middle class, pious, strictly orthodox, self-appointed religious leaders of the common person, while the Sadducees were upper-class, practical, political, and government office holders. The two classes did not see eye-to-eye. John the Baptist had called both Sadducees and Pharisees a "brood of vipers" (Matt. 3:7).

Jesus and the Pharisees had clashed previously when they had tried to cause contention between the disciples of John and Jesus (Matt. 9:11, 14). They accused Jesus of exorcising demons by the power of Satan (verse 34; 12:24) and they had bitterly opposed Christ's teachings concerning the uselessness of tradition (Matt. 15:1, 2, 12). Jesus denounced their displays of piety, for their legalism hid a multitude of sins. For this reason Jesus branded them hypocrites (Matt. 23). Thus the Pharisees dogged each step of Jesus' ministry, ready to accuse and challenge. And the Sadducees would join them.

"How often our service to Christ, our communion with one another, is marred by the secret desire to exalt self! . . . It is the love of self, the desire for an easier way than God has appointed that leads to the substitution of human theories and traditions for the divine precepts."[44]

SIGNS OF THE TIMES

"Hypocrites! You know how to discern the face of the sky, but you cannot discern the signs of the times."

Matt. 16:3.

The minute Jesus set foot again in Galilee His enemies confronted Him. In an unusual confederation, Sadducee and Pharisee united. Together, they asked for a sign to prove Christ's divinity. A sign beyond human power to control: thunder or lightning on command, fire from heaven, the sun standing still, manna falling from the sky—any would do. In their ignorance they had already refused the signs given their nation. "The song of the angels to the shepherds, the star that guided the wise men, the dove and the voice from heaven at His baptism, were witnesses for Him."[45] Jesus sighed. The religious leaders had closed their eyes to the light that had been shining upon them from the moment Jesus' ministry began. "My people are destroyed for lack of knowledge. Because you have rejected knowledge, I also will reject you from being priest for Me; because you have forgotten the law of your God, I also will forget your children" (Hosea 4:6). They had substituted human tradition for God's law.

Many Jewish leaders looked upon human suffering as always the direct result of individual sin, scorning such individuals as accursed of God. "That which led the Jews to reject the Saviour's work was the highest evidence of His divine character. The greatest significance of His miracles is seen in the fact that they were for the blessing of humanity. The highest evidence that He came from God is that His life revealed the character of God."[46] The chosen of Israel refused to hear Him and spurned Christ's teachings.

Jesus refused to debate, but called their attention to the weather. An east wind from the Arabian Desert meant hot, dry weather. If the wind came from the west, forming over the Mediterranean, the weather would be rainy. They could accurately predict the weather because they watched for its signs. But they paid no attention to the signs of their times.

Many today seek a sign, some miracle attesting to God's power. "The change in human hearts, the transformation of human characters, is a miracle that reveals an ever-living Saviour, working to rescue souls. A consistent life in Christ is a great miracle."[47]

LEAVEN OF THE PHARISEES

Then Jesus said to them, "Take heed and beware of the leaven of the Pharisees and the Sadducees. . . ." Then they understood that He did not tell them to beware of the leaven of bread, but of the doctrine of the Pharisees and Sadducees.

Matt. 16:6-12.

Jesus turned away from those who continued to oppose Him. Reentering the boat, the disciples and Jesus crossed to the shore near Bethsaida Julias. Close by was the site where He had fed the 5,000— Gentile country. In their haste to leave Magdala, the disciples failed to bring sufficient food. Purchasing food from non-Jews was not an option. Jesus said to them, "Take heed and beware of the leaven of the Pharisees and the Sadducees" (Matt. 16:6). Misunderstanding His comment, the disciples concluded that Jesus was concerned because they had brought insufficient bread with them for their journey into Gentile territory. "Their lack of faith and spiritual insight had often led them to similar misconception of His words. Now Jesus reproved them for thinking that He who had fed thousands with a few fishes and barley loaves could in that solemn warning have referred merely to temporal food. There was danger that the crafty reasoning of the Pharisees and the Sadducees would leaven His disciples with unbelief, causing them to think lightly of the works of Christ." [48]

Jews since the time of the Exodus had removed leaven from their homes during the Passover celebration. They regarded leaven as a type, or symbol, of sin. Any good Jew should have instantly understood what Jesus was saying. Jesus was talking about doctrine. As leaven transformed the entire loaf of bread, so the false teachings of a Pharisee or Sadducee would affect any of their followers. The mask of false piety still fooled Christ's disciples into thinking such individuals were godly and spiritually wise. But their refusal to accept plain truth should have opened the disciples' eyes to the hypocrisy of the national religious leaders. The disciples were vulnerable, because they still wanted to seek great things. They still desired to be foremost among their people. The underlying motive of the Pharisees and Sadducees consisted of a craving to glorify self. That same hypocrisy, practiced nearly 2,000 years ago, is still at work today.

"It is the love of self, the desire for an easier way than God has appointed that leads to the substitution of human theories and traditions for the divine precepts. . . . Only the power of God can banish self-seeking and hypocrisy. This change is the sign of His working." [49]

PILATE'S MASSACRE

There were present at that season some who told Him about the Galileans whose blood Pilate had mingled with their sacrifices.

Luke 13:1.

Herod the Great "passed away in his 34th regnal year at the age of 69, in 4/3 B.C., most probably in the spring of 4 B.C."[50] His last will and testament left the kingdom to his sons. Augustus honored the dying wishes of Herod. Herod Archelaus received the areas of Judea, Samaria, and Idumea. He was a cruel tyrant. "Archelaus' choice of high priests, his private life, and his cruelties annoyed the Jews, who, joined by the Samaritans, sent deputations to Rome, and finally persuaded Augustus to recall Archelaus. . . . His territory was placed under a Roman procurator, who served as a direct representative of the Roman provincial administration."[51] Caponius, the first Roman governor, assumed the post in A.D. 6. Tiberius continued the policy of Augustus, appointing Pontius Pilate as the fifth governor to Palestine in A.D. 26-36.

Pilate's bungling actions enraged the Jews and set them against him almost immediately. Soldiers carried Roman standards with the emperor's image upon them into Jerusalem, a practice the Jews considered a sacrilege. Placing shields with the emperor's name engraved upon them in the former palace of Herod was an additional affront. Pilate removed the offensive items only after Jewish nobles petitioned Tiberius. Also, Pilate tapped Temple treasury money to pay for an aqueduct to carry water into Jerusalem. When the Jews complained about the misappropriation of sacred money, he reacted ruthlessly.

"Some of the measures of Pontius Pilate, the governor of Judea, had given offense to the people. There had been a popular tumult in Jerusalem, and Pilate had attempted to quell this by violence. On one occasion his soldiers had even invaded the precincts of the temple, and had cut down some Galilean pilgrims in the very act of slaying their sacrifices."[52] The slaughter of Herod Antipas' innocent Galileans may have been the initial reason for his dislike of Pontius Pilate. The intrigue between the two rulers appears in the jurisdictional dispute they held over Jesus during His trial. The stage was being set for Christ's crucifixion even before His arrest.

"Blessed be the name of God forever and ever, for wisdom and might are His, and He changes the times and the seasons; He removes kings and raises up kings; He gives wisdom to the wise and knowledge to those who have understanding" (Dan. 2:20, 21).

Men Walking Like Trees

So He took the blind man by the hand and led him out of the town. And when He had spit on his eyes and put His hands on him, He asked him if he saw anything. And he looked up and said, "I see men like trees, walking." Then He put His hands on his eyes again and made him look up. And he was restored and saw everyone clearly. Mark 8:23-25.

Jesus and the disciples made landfall near Bethsaida Julius. Perhaps the need to purchase supplies prompted them to go to the town itself. There the friends of a blind man brought him to Jesus. The incident is nearly identical to that of the blind man just healed in the Decapolis. Jesus led the man into the countryside, where he could focus on what Christ was about to do for him. Also, the people of the town might have misunderstood the healing and attributed it to magic. Thus Christ took the blind man away from distracting influences.

The account is the only recorded instance in which Jesus asked someone to describe his condition prior to the miracle. Perhaps Jesus did it to strengthen the man's faith. Ancient physicians and miracle workers thought that saliva channeled certain healing properties. Jesus now spit on the man's eyes and touched them, partially healing him. It is the only instance of a healing occurring in two stages.

Jesus placed His hands directly upon the eyes. When He lifted them, the man could see clearly. Jesus then told him to go home and not to return to Bethsaida or tell anyone of the event. Knowledge of the miracle would prevent the privacy Jesus needed with His disciples. Once again Jesus had fulfilled a Messianic prophecy: "I, the Lord, have called You in righteousness, and will hold Your hand; I will keep You and give You as a covenant to the people, as a light to the Gentiles, *to open blind eyes,* to bring out prisoners from the prison, those who sit in darkness from the prison house" (Isa. 42:6, 7).

"In Him was life, and the life was the light of men. And the light shines in the darkness, and the darkness did not comprehend it" (John 1:4, 5). Without Him we see only dimly. Pray that He will open your eyes to His love for you.

INTO CAESAREA PHILIPPI

When Jesus came into the region of Caesarea Philippi, He asked His disciples, saying, "Who do men say that I, the Son of Man, am?" Matt. 16:13.

The work of Christ on earth was hastening to a close. Before Him, in vivid outline, lay the scenes whither His feet were tending. Even before He took humanity upon Him, He saw the whole length of the path He must travel in order to save that which was lost. . . . The path from the manger to Calvary was all before His eyes."[53] Such scenes still mercifully remained hidden from His disciples, though. Soon, however, they would witness His betrayal and death upon the cross. Jesus now led the disciples 25 miles north of Galilee to a small town near the city of Caesarea Philippi. Situated on the southern slope of Mount Hermon, the city was located near one of the main springs of the Jordan River. Here, Philip the tetrarch had built the largest city in the province of Ituraea and named it "Caesarea" in honor of Tiberius Caesar. As Palestine had two cities named Caesarea, people commonly referred to this one as Caesarea Philippi to differentiate it from Caesarea on the Mediterranean coast. The Gentile area isolated the disciples from the influence of the Jewish leaders. From now until the fall Feast of Tabernacles the time Jesus spent with the disciples would be special.

Leaving them, Jesus sought solace in prayer. "He was about to tell them of the suffering that awaited Him. But first He went away alone, and prayed that their hearts might be prepared to receive His words."[54] It would be difficult for the disciples to accept that their beloved Master would die. They still dreamed of cabinet positions around the reclaimed throne of King David. "The influence of their early training, the teaching of the rabbis, the power of tradition, still intercepted their view of truth. From time to time precious rays of light from Jesus shone upon them, yet often they were like men groping among shadows."[55]

Today many widely espouse the teaching of popular ministers in large churches as truth but make little effort to prove or disprove their positions. Tradition clings strongly to those blinded by self-serving doctrine. They need rays of light to point the way to truth. "Your righteousness is an everlasting righteousness, and Your law is truth" (Ps. 119:142).

FOUR OPINIONS

He said to them, "But who do you say that I am?" Matt. 16:15.

Before Jesus spoke with the disciples, He tested their faith. "Who do men say that I, the Son of Man, am?" he asked (Matt. 16:13). Unless they accepted Jesus as the Messiah, His sacrifice would be meaningless to them. "He who would find salvation in the cross of Calvary must first recognize that the One who hung upon the cross was none other than the Son of God, the Saviour of the world, the Messiah, the Christ."[56] To believe otherwise negates the atoning power of His sacrifice. The Jewish majority believed Jesus to be a good man, a rabbi perhaps with a powerful gift, but not the long-awaited Messiah. Few were willing to accept His kingdom of spiritual grace. The disciples answered Christ with the four most widely held opinions. "So they said, 'Some say John the Baptist, some Elijah, and others Jeremiah or one of the prophets'" (verse 14).

1. John the Baptist, a prophet of great dimensions, had touched the nation's conscience. Herod Antipas was convinced, as were others, that Jesus was John reincarnated (Mark 6:14). It was a tribute to John's short ministry! Jesus indeed taught with the power of John. 2. Elijah was the prophet of prayer and miracles. His prayers had rained fire from heaven, raised the dead, caused drought, then brought rain. Many thought Elijah would return to earth to herald the Messiah (Mal. 4:5, 6). Indeed, Jesus' miracles were every bit as astounding as any Elijah had performed. 3. Jeremiah was the prophet of compassion, shedding tears over the children of Israel in Babylonian captivity. Indeed, Jesus had Jeremiah-like compassion for the people in their captivity to sin. 4. Many Israelites thought Jesus was the prophet that would precede the Messiah. "The Lord your God will raise up for you a Prophet like me from your midst, from your brethren. Him you shall hear" (Deut. 18:15). "The fiction that Jesus was merely a great and good man, perhaps the best man who ever lived, but nothing more, is as absurd as it is incredible. . . . Jesus of Nazareth was either the Christ, the Son of the living God, or He was the most colossal imposter of all time."[57]

Four excellent choices—but four wrong ones! Jesus embodied the powerful teaching of John, the miracles of Elijah, the compassion of Jeremiah, the greatness of the prophet Moses—but He was also the Son of God.

The question is relevant today: "But who do you say that I am?"

THE KEYS TO THE KINGDOM

Jesus answered and said to him, "Blessed are you, Simon Bar-Jonah. . . . You are Peter, and on this rock I will build My church, and the gates of Hades shall not prevail against it." Matt. 16:17, 18.

Peter, ever willing to be spokesperson, answered Jesus' question regarding His identity. "You are the Christ, the Son of the living God" (Matt. 16:16). "The truth which Peter had confessed is the foundation of the believer's faith."[58] "Blessed are you, Simon Bar-Jonah," Jesus answered, "for flesh and blood has not revealed this to you, but My Father who is in heaven" (verse 17). Needless controversy has surrounded Matthew 16:18. Many believe Peter to be "this rock" upon which Jesus intended to start His church. Others hold that Peter's faith in Christ was the rock upon which the Christian church would be founded, while still others suggest Christ Himself is the "rock." Fortunately Scripture does not leave us in doubt as to Christ's meaning.

The name Peter means "rolling stone," from the Greek *Petros.* But the disciple was not the pebble upon which Christ established His church. There is only One against whom the gates of hell cannot prevail. Peter referred to Jesus as "a living stone, rejected indeed by men, but chosen by God and precious. . . . A chief cornerstone, elect, precious. . . . The stone which the builders rejected has become the chief cornerstone" (1 Peter 2:4-8). Matthew recorded Christ's own testimony (Matt. 21:42), wherein He refers to Himself by that same term.

"Had Christ made Peter chief among the disciples, they would not thereafter have been involved in repeated arguments about which of them 'should be accounted the greatest' (Luke 22:24, KJV)."[59] Jesus alone is the Rock *(petra)* of our salvation. "For no other foundation can anyone lay than that which is laid, which is Jesus Christ" (1 Cor. 3:11). "Nor is there salvation in any other, for there is no other name under heaven given among men by which we must be saved" (Acts 4:12). The Bible repeatedly refers to God as "the Rock." "He is the Rock, His work is perfect; for all His ways are justice" (Deut. 32:4). "The Lord is my rock and my fortress and my deliverer; my God, my strength, in whom I will trust" (Ps. 18:2). He is "the shadow of a great rock in a weary land" (Isa. 32:2). Jesus spoke of building upon His Word as erecting a "house on the rock" (Matt. 7:24).

"Christ founded His church upon the living Rock. That Rock is Himself—His own body, for us broken and bruised. Against the church built upon this foundation, the gates of hell shall not prevail."[60]

SELF SPEAKS UP

From that time Jesus began to show to His disciples that He must go to Jerusalem, and suffer many things from the elders and chief priests and scribes, and be killed, and be raised the third day. Matt. 16:21.

Jesus had not discussed His impending death with His disciples until now. Only to Nicodemus had He mentioned the symbolism of the cross (John 3:14, 15). The disciples had not been present during the night encounter. Following their profession of faith in Christ as the Messiah, the way was now clear for Him to show them the road that lay ahead. "Speechless with grief and amazement, the disciples listened."[61] In plain language Jesus announced His coming death and resurrection. Disbelief clouded their minds, and they heard only what they wished to hear. Their upbringing had hidden the message of the prophecies. "The people, in their darkness and oppression, and the rulers, thirsting for power, longed for the coming of One who would vanquish their enemies and restore the kingdom of Israel. They had studied the prophecies, but without spiritual insight. Thus they overlooked those scriptures that point to the humiliation of Christ's first advent, and misapplied those that speak of the glory of His second coming. Pride obscured their vision. They interpreted prophecy in accordance with their selfish desires."[62]

Taking Jesus off to one side, Peter started to rebuke Him. "Far be it from You, Lord; this shall not happen to You!" (Matt. 16:22). His Master stopped him before he could say more, making one of the sternest rebukes recorded in Scripture. Turning His back on Peter, Christ said, "Get behind Me, Satan! You are an offense to Me, for you are not mindful of the things of God, but the things of men" (verse 23). Peter, who had expressed such faith in Christ as the Son of the living God, now attempted to prevent Him from fulfilling the mission He had come to earth to perform. Satan had planted the thought in Peter's mind. Jesus recognized His old nemesis from the wilderness. Uttering the same words then, "Get behind Me, Satan!" (Luke 4:8), Jesus again answered Satan's temptation to find an easy way around the cross.

"The words of Christ were spoken, not to Peter, but to the one who was trying to separate him from his Redeemer."[63] Peter had much to learn. Christ's disciples must not place any stumbling blocks in the way of their Lord or His mission.

We too must accept Christ's mission as our own without attempting to change it to fit our goals and aspirations.

TAKE UP YOUR CROSS

Then Jesus said to His disciples, "If anyone desires to come after Me, let him deny himself, and take up his cross, and follow Me." Matt. 16:24.

Crucifixion was a characteristic Roman mode of execution. However, Roman citizens were never crucified, this form of punishment being reserved for persons held in utter contempt. . . . The lingering death upon a cross was horrible indeed, for victims commonly lived for many hours, sometimes several days."[64] The Jewish method of punishment, stoning the condemned to death, could in certain instances be mercifully short by comparison. Jesus here used graphic language to describe the voluntary submission to humiliation that would be the lot of those who followed Him. The disclosure saddened the disciples. Jesus seemed set in His path to the cross, and they could think of nothing they could do to swerve Him from His choice. "No more complete self-surrender could the Saviour's words have pictured."[65]

While God does not call all of us to give our lives, He does expect a willingness to give up all for Him. A disciple must be ready to bear any cross placed upon him for the sake of the gospel. Not only must we endure the cross patiently; we must walk in Jesus' footsteps. "For to this you were called, because Christ also suffered for us, leaving us an example, that you should follow His steps" (1 Peter 2:21). Each disciple of Christ has to make a clear choice. We choose to accept either the selfish plan of "saving" our own life or Christ's plan of "renouncing" our own life. Luke 9:23 suggests daily surrender to the will of God. It is strange indeed that in the process of giving our life up, we gain eternal life. "For what profit is it to a man if he gains the whole world, and loses his own soul? Or what will a man give in exchange for his soul?" (Matt. 16:26). Christ's followers should focus on the salvation of lost humanity. For this reason, Jesus came to our world and gave His life. "He who says he abides in Him ought himself also to walk just as He walked" (1 John 2:6). There is no crown without a cross.

"The Christian is ever to realize that he has consecrated himself to God, and that in character he is to reveal Christ to the world. The self-sacrifice, the sympathy, the love, manifested in the life of Christ are to reappear in the life of the worker for God." [66]

THREE SELECT WITNESSES

Now after six days Jesus took Peter, James, and John his brother, brought them up on a high mountain by themselves, and He was transfigured before them. Matt. 17:1, 2.

For six days Jesus and the disciples had traveled south from Caesarea Philippi. Evening approached as Jesus called Peter, James, and John to Him and led them up a steep mountain path. "The light of the setting sun still lingers on the mountain top, and gilds with its fading glory the path they are traveling. But soon the light dies out from hill as well as valley, the sun disappears behind the western horizon, and the solitary travelers are wrapped in the darkness of night. The gloom of their surroundings seems in harmony with their sorrowful lives, around which the clouds are gathering and thickening."[67] Silently the three followed until Jesus told them they need go no farther. Slipping off to one side, He began to pray. How could He help them understand His mission? How could He prepare them for His death? The three disciples with Him would face extra severe trials. They would witness His agony in Gethsemane and would need encouragement.

"The dew is heavy upon His bowed form, but He heeds it not. The shadows of night gather thickly about Him, but He regards not their gloom. So the hours pass slowly by."[68] Jesus wished His disciples might behold the glory that was His before He came to earth, for it would comfort them during the experiences ahead. He longed to provide them with strong proof that He was the Messiah. Also, He prayed for strength to bear the coming test, enduring until the end and ransoming fallen humanity. Peter, James, and John possessed greater spiritual insight than the other nine disciples, yet Jesus knew even they needed strengthening. For a brief time the three continued in prayer with their Master, but fatigue and sleep overtook them. In Gethsemane their Master would again ask them to pray with Him. But once more they would succumb to sleep. On this mountainside they failed to gain all that God desired to give them. They would not understand Christ's suffering and the glory that would follow. The simple act of remaining awake and in prayer would have explained much and been an enormous blessing in their time of despair.

They lost the blessing because they failed to share in His self-sacrifice. The choice was theirs and is ours. Asleep or in prayer, His treasures are there.

COLABORERS WITH CHRIST

And behold, Moses and Elijah appeared to them, talking with Him.

Matt. 17:3 .

God responded to Jesus' prayer. "While He is bowed in lowliness upon the stony ground, suddenly the heavens open, the golden gates of the city of God are thrown wide, and holy radiance descends upon the mount, enshrouding the Saviour's form. Divinity from within flashes through humanity, and meets the glory coming from above. Arising from His prostrate position, Christ stands in godlike majesty. The soul agony is gone. His countenance now shines 'as the sun,' and His garments are 'white as the light.' "[69]

The disciples awakened to a blinding light. Gradually as their eyes adjusted to the brilliance they noticed their Master was not alone. Two beings that the disciples sensed were Moses and Elijah were involved in intimate conversation with Him. "Instead of choosing angels to converse with His Son, God chose those who had themselves experienced the trials of earth."[70] Moses, through the tribulations of leading the children of Israel through the wilderness, knew what it took to deal with a rebellious people. He had pleaded with God to spare His wayward children (Ex. 32: 32). Elijah had known the enmity of his nation for three and one half years of famine. Alone he had stood firm for God on Mount Carmel against the priests of Baal.

"Moses was present to represent those who will be raised from the dead at the second appearing of Jesus. And Elijah, who was translated without seeing death, represented those who will be changed to immortality at Christ's second coming and will be translated to heaven without seeing death."[71] They had come to convey to Christ all heaven's intense interest in His mission. "The hope of the world, the salvation of every human being, was the burden of their interview."[72] Heaven sent human beings to comfort Christ. The two had longed for the salvation of their fellow humanity. They had faced Satan's trials and temptations. Now they acknowledged Christ as the Messiah.

A bright cloud descended, and the disciples heard the voice of God proclaim His Son. Although they did not hear all that transpired, they later testified that they "were eyewitnesses of His majesty" (2 Peter 1:16). Facedown upon the earth, they hid their faces as the mountain trembled before God. Finally Jesus touched them, saying, "Arise, and do not be afraid" (Matt. 17:7).

They were alone with the One they now knew without a doubt was the Son of God. Arise, and be not afraid. He is the Son of God. Have faith!

"WHAT ARE YOU DISCUSSING WITH THEM?"

And when He came to the disciples, He saw a great multitude around them, and scribes disputing with them.
Mark 9:14.

Returning to the plain below, Jesus, Peter, James, and John met the other disciples and a large group of people. Something was not quite right. The disciples seem agitated. Jesus knew that some had just brought a lad with an evil spirit to them for healing. In the name of Jesus Christ the disciples had commanded the spirit to leave, but it had mocked them. The scribes had seized upon their failure and humiliated the nine. Jesus, "fixing His gaze upon the scribes inquired, 'What question ye with them?' "[73] A hush fell upon the multitude as the father of the boy pushed forward. Falling at Jesus' feet, he explained, "Teacher, I brought You my son, who has a mute spirit. And wherever it seizes him, it throws him down; he foams at the mouth, gnashes his teeth, and becomes rigid. So I spoke to Your disciples, that they should cast it out, but they could not" (Mark 9:17, 18). Jesus immediately said, "Bring him to Me" (verse 19).

"The boy was brought, and as the Saviour's eyes fell upon him, the evil spirit cast him to the ground in convulsions of agony. He lay wallowing and foaming, rending the air with unearthly shrieks."[74] "How long has this been happening to him?" Jesus asked (verse 21). "From childhood," the father answered. "And often he has thrown him both into the fire and into the water to destroy him. But if You can do anything, have compassion on us and help us" (verses 21, 22). Jesus noted the hint of disbelief, "If You can . . ." Christ had the power to help, but it would require the father's faith. "If you can believe, all things are possible to him who believes," Jesus told him (verse 23).

That instant the man realized his son's fate rested in his hands. With tears in his eyes, he pleaded, "Lord, I believe; help my unbelief!" (verse 24). Jesus commanded the spirit to leave and immediately it convulsed the lad and departed. The boy became so still that the crowd feared he was dead. Taking him by the hand, Jesus presented him whole to his father. The crowd was stunned, the scribes defeated, and the disciples amazed.

Many feel they lack enough faith to approach Jesus. "Grasp His promise, 'Him that cometh to Me I will in no wise cast out' (John 6:37, KJV). Cast yourself at His feet with the cry, 'Lord, I believe; help thou mine unbelief.' You can never perish while you do this—never."[75]

FAITH AS A MUSTARD SEED

So Jesus said to them, . . . "If you have faith as a mustard seed, . . . nothing will be impossible for you."

Matt. 17:20.

After the crowd dispersed, the disciples came to Jesus and asked, "Why could we not cast it out?" (Mark 9:28). Why had the power granted them to expel demons during their missionary tour departed? The scribes had led them to believe the demon had superior power. "The real trouble, however, lay not in the power of the demon, but in the spiritual impotence of the disciples."[76] The disciples hadn't spent their time profitably during Jesus' absence. Focusing on discouragement and personal grievance, they had harbored jealousy, feeling that they also should have been included in the group accompanying Jesus up the mountainside. They had relied upon their own strength to accomplish a miracle. But no one can expect to triumph over the forces of evil unless God is on their side.

Nor can one receive the ability to perform such a miracle in a moment. It takes daily prayer, meditation, and faith to prevail against the forces of darkness. Even so small a faith as that of the mustard seed, the smallest of all seeds, might do mighty things for the Lord. "With God all things are possible" (Mark 10:27). No difficulty will be too great for the disciple to accomplish when he or she believes. "Earnest, persevering supplication to God in faith—faith that leads to entire dependence upon God, and unreserved consecration to His work—can alone avail to bring men the Holy Spirit's aid in the battle against principalities and powers, the rulers of the darkness of this world, and wicked spirits in high places."[77]

Simple, trusting faith in the Word of God and in Jesus is sufficient to accomplish miracles in this life. Even small faith grows as it feeds upon the nourishment found in the Word. Daily study and prayer are the life-giving agents that cause it to mature and grow. When difficulties arise, as they will in the life of any Christian, a strong faith perseveres. "The agency by which God protects His people is presented in the words of the psalmist: 'The angel of the Lord encampeth round about them that fear Him, and delivereth them' (Ps. 34:7, KJV)."[78]

"The fact that Christ has conquered should inspire His followers with courage to fight manfully the battle against sin and Satan."[79]

"GO TO THE SEA"

Does your Teacher not pay the temple tax? Matt. 17:24.

Jesus quietly took up residence in Capernaum. Hearing He had returned, the tax collector paid a visit. When Peter answered the door, the man asked, "Does your Teacher not pay the temple tax?" Peter recognized the question as a Pharisee trap. Every Jewish male over 20 annually donated a half-shekel tribute to support the Temple. A public notice went out in the month of Adar and each community set up tables to collect the tribute. Adar had long ago passed. The tribute was months late. Levites, priests, and prophets did not have to pay it, and therein lay the trap. "To refuse to pay the tax would imply disloyalty to the Temple, but to pay it would imply that Jesus did not consider Himself a prophet, and thus exempt from it."[1]

When Peter returned to where Jesus was, Christ asked him a question. "'What do you think, Simon? From whom do the kings of the earth take customs or taxes, from their sons or from strangers?' Peter said to Him, 'From strangers.' Jesus said to him, 'Then the sons are free. Nevertheless, lest we offend them, go to the sea, cast in a hook, and take the fish that comes up first. And when you have opened its mouth, you will find a piece of money; take that and give it to them for Me and you'" (Matt. 17:25-27). Jesus was not just a prophet but the Son of God. Surely the Son did not have to pay tribute to His Father. While Peter had quickly protected his Master's honor before the priests and scribes, he had forgotten the larger principle that Christ need not pay the tribute at all.

Only here does the New Testament mention fishing with a hook and line. As predicted, the first fish pulled from Galilee contained a silver coin worth four drachmas! The double drachma equaled one shekel and would just pay the tribute for two. Here was a fishing miracle. Jesus didn't tell Peter to cast a net, then gather and sort many fish until one might have a coin in its mouth. No, he was to let down a single line and take not the second or third but the first fish caught.

"The miracle was designed to teach Peter a lesson, and to silence the critical taxgatherers, who had sought to place Christ in the category of an ordinary Israelite, and thereby challenge His right to teach."[2]

Jesus has the power to shape our lives miraculously if we will let Him.

WHO IS THE GREATEST IN HEAVEN?

Assuredly, I say to you, unless you are converted and become as little children, you will by no means enter the kingdom of heaven. Matt. 18:3.

Peter had gone fishing when Jesus called His disciples. "What was it you disputed among yourselves on the road?" (Mark 9:33). To their great embarrassment they had been arguing about who should be greatest in the coming kingdom. Even though Jesus had told them He would soon die, His mention that He would be going up to Jerusalem had stirred hopes that He might instead set up His kingdom. The supremacy dispute raged during their entire journey through Galilee and finally climaxed upon entering Capernaum.

"On Peter's return from the sea, the disciples told him of the Saviour's question, and at last one ventured to ask Jesus, 'Who is the greatest in the kingdom of heaven?'"[3] The disciples manifested the same striving for supremacy that had led Lucifer to state: "I will be like the Most High" (Isa. 14:14). His spirit directly opposed Christ's, for Jesus "made Himself of no reputation, taking the form of a bondservant, and coming in the likeness of men. And being found in appearance as a man, He humbled Himself and became obedient to the point of death, even the death of the cross" (Phil. 2:7, 8). The disciples didn't value humility. But to fill the humblest position in the Lord's work is to be crowned with glory and honor.

Jesus sought to teach them a lesson. "If anyone desires to be first, he shall be last of all and servant of all" (Mark 9:35). Gathering a little child into His arms, He said "Whoever receives one of these little children in My name receives Me; and whoever receives Me, receives not Me but Him who sent Me" (verse 37). Ridicule, censure, rebuke, and harsh dealing too often characterize those who have been Christian for some time. Jesus was concerned that the overbearing behavior of His disciples would injure new disciples. "The simplicity, the self-forgetfulness, and the confiding love of a little child are the attributes that Heaven values. These are the characteristics of real greatness."[4] Worldly pride and position are worth nothing in heaven's ledgers.

All must partake of Christ's humble nature to effectively herald His soon second coming.

HOW OFTEN SHOULD I FORGIVE?

Then Peter came to Him and said, "Lord, how often shall my brother sin against me, and I forgive him? Up to seven times?" Matt. 18:21.

Peter asked what was no doubt on the minds of the other disciples, "Isn't there some limit to how many times I must forgive my brother?" Forgiveness must have been difficult for Peter and the others. He was always ready to protect self, seek revenge, or push for advantage. Peter now questioned how far his patience must stretch before he would be justified in exacting retribution. The rabbinical limit for forgiveness was three times. Peter doubled it and added one for good measure. Surely seven times should be sufficient to please a Lord who interpreted the law in its broadest sense. But the disciple learned to his surprise that numbering forgiveness misses the whole point.

Tracking forgiveness causes it to become mechanical. Forgiveness is an attitude not an act! True forgiveness does not operate as if down the road at some distant time forgiveness runs out. Peter had already forgotten the sermon on the mount. "For if you forgive men their trespasses, your heavenly Father will also forgive you," Christ had said. "But if you do not forgive men their trespasses, neither will your Father forgive your trespasses" (Matt. 6:14, 15). The unmerciful cannot expect the Lord's pardoning grace to cover their shortcomings. When is it right to cease forgiving? When may a Christian rightly say "I will never forgive you what you have done"? If an individual confesses their sin against you, when are you justified in exacting more humility?

Jesus' answer of "up to seventy times seven" is symbolic. The question of whether the Greek means 490 or 77 misses the point. "If the spirit of forgiveness actuates the heart, a person will be as ready to forgive a repentant soul the eighth time as the first time, or the 491st time as the eighth. True forgiveness is not limited by numbers; furthermore, it is not the act that counts, but the spirit that prompts the act." [5]

We must not perform forgiveness "by the numbers." No true Christian will exhibit an unforgiving spirit. "Nothing can justify an unforgiving spirit." [6] The greatest example of forgiveness that the world has witnessed occurred when Jesus pleaded, "Father, forgive them, for they do not know what they do" (Luke 23:34).

SHOWING MERCY TOWARD OTHERS

Therefore the kingdom of heaven is like a certain king who wanted to settle accounts with his servants.

Matt. 18:23.

Peter's question about forgiveness prompted a parable. A king had many officials administering his affairs. One had gotten himself into serious financial difficulty with the king's money. His debt amounted to nearly 10,000 talents. Talents were a unit of measurement equaling 965 troy ounces. The man owed a staggering amount. Debtors often went to jail, where they stayed until their families could discharge their debt. The creditor might also sell the debtor and his family into slavery to recover the amount owed. This official couldn't possibly repay his debt, so the king ordered him cast into prison.

The servant pleaded, "'Master, have patience with me, and I will pay you all.' Then the master of that servant was moved with compassion, released him, and forgave him the debt" (Matt. 18:26, 27). The same official then happened upon an individual who owed him 100 denarii. The denarii resembled a dime-sized silver coin. The high official "took him by the throat, saying, 'Pay me what you owe!' So his fellow servant . . . begged him, saying, 'Have patience with me, and I will pay you all.' And he would not, but . . . threw him into prison till he should pay the debt" (verses 28-30).

Others observed the shabby treatment, and reported the first official to the king, who became furious. "You wicked servant! I forgave you all that debt because you begged me. Should you not also have had compassion on your fellow servant, just as I had pity on you?" (verses 32, 33). The ruler threw the man into prison until he should pay his debt. The king could tolerate injustice against himself but not against one of his subjects. The monarch in the parable is Christ. The forgiveness offered is the divine pardon for sin. We cannot possibly pay the price to ransom our souls (although some religions would have you believe that you can work off your debt to God). "Here is the ground upon which we should exercise compassion toward our fellow sinners. 'If God so loved us, we ought also to love one another' (1 John 4:11, KJV)."[7]

"Here is the great lesson of the parable—the infinite contrast between the heartlessness and cruelty of man toward his fellow men and the long-suffering and mercy of God toward us. . . . In view of God's infinite mercy toward us, we should likewise show mercy toward others."[8]

WE HINDERED HIM

But Jesus said to him, "Do not forbid him, for he who is not against us is on our side."

Luke 9:50.

Jesus had just stated a truth that troubled John. Previously, he and his brother James had rebuked someone for casting out demons in the name of their Master. Now John was not so sure he and James had done the proper thing. Jesus' sojourns in Judea and Galilee had led to a few new disciples. Many of those who heard His words had not taken a stand either for or against the Master. If this individual wouldn't outwardly show that he was a "true" follower of Christ, the disciples decided, then he shouldn't use Christ's name to heal. The brothers had judged the man by their narrow standard, and he hadn't measured up. "He was not one of the regular, acknowledged disciples of Jesus." [9]

James and John jealously guarded what they believed to be their exclusive prerogative to cast out demons. Failing to understand that their duty was to promote the kingdom of heaven, they took instead the responsibility of dictating what others might do for Christ. "The fact that one does not in all things conform to our personal ideas or opinions will not justify us in forbidding him to labor for God." [10] The character and ministry of the worker for Christ are always the true test of discipleship. "Our Lord is put to shame by those who claim to serve Him, but who misrepresent His character; and multitudes are deceived, and led into false paths." [11]

The Christian walks a fine line. We must preserve truth while not judging the efforts of others to spread the gospel. Nor should we restrict those with less education, experience, eloquence, or discernment than we might have. The meek and lowly exert the greatest witness for Christ. The world needs to hear, from the lips of those God has blessed, an account of His love in their redeemed life. A sermon observed is more powerful than an eloquent one preached from a pulpit.

What harmony the church might have if members would remember the words of Christ: "Do not forbid him, for he who is not against us is on our side." Many cause others to stumble by rebuking their efforts for Jesus.

JESUS

MINISTRY IN SAMARIA AND PEREA
Christ Our Anointed

Autumn A.D. 30 to Spring A.D. 31

Matthew 18:12-14; 19:1-20:34; 26:1-16

Mark 10; 14:1-11

Luke 7:36-50; 9:51-19:27; 22:1-6

John 7:1-12:11

The Desire of Ages, pp. 447-568

FEAST OF TABERNACLES

After these things Jesus walked in Galilee; for He did not want to walk in Judea, because the Jews sought to kill Him. Now the Jews' Feast of Tabernacles was at hand.

John 7:1, 2.

Autumn A.D. 30 now approached. Jesus had avoided Jerusalem since His arraignment before the Sanhedrin and the healing of the paralytic at the Pool of Bethesda in the spring of A.D. 29. His brothers now wondered if He was going to attend the Feast of Tabernacles, which closed the yearly required festival attendance. The seven-day feast was a pageant that not only commemorated the harvest and God's bounties but also memorialized God's protection during the Exodus from Egypt and the wanderings in the wilderness. "In commemoration of their tent life, the Israelites during the feast dwelt in booths or tabernacles of green boughs. These were erected in the streets, in the courts of the temple, or on the housetops. The hills and valleys surrounding Jerusalem were also dotted with these leafy dwellings, and seemed to be alive with people."[12] The people erected the booths in response to the Lord's command: "You shall dwell in booths for seven days" (Lev. 23:42).

The people went up to the morning sacrifice at the Temple with willow branches in their hands. Once within the confines of the courtyard, they "marched joyfully around the altar of burnt offering once each day and seven times on the seventh day."[13] At dawn the priests sounded a blast on their trumpets, and the answering trumpets and glad shouts of the people from their booths echoed over hill and valley, welcoming the festal day. Then the priest dipped from the flowing waters of the Kidron a flagon of water. He bore the flagon to the altar in the court of the priests. Here stood two silver basins. "The flagon of water was poured into one, and a flagon of wine into the other; and the contents of both flowed into a pipe which communicated with the Kedron, and was conducted to the Dead Sea. This display of the consecrated water represented the fountain that at the command of God had gushed from the rock to quench the thirst of the children of Israel."[14] Levites sang psalms, and the Temple became the center of vocal praise. The festival was a splendid pageant, causing the worshipers to sing, "Oh, give thanks to the Lord, for He is good! For His mercy endures forever" (Ps. 106:1).

Shouldn't we give thanks and praise to our Lord for His daily goodness and mercy?

"My Time Has Not Yet Fully Come"

Now the Jews' Feast of Tabernacles was at hand. His brothers therefore said to Him, "Depart from here and go into Judea, that Your disciples also may see the works that You are doing." John 7:2, 3.

Jesus, a true nonconformist, mingled with publicans, set aside tradition, and had little regard for rabbinical observances. He questioned religious authorities about their policies and they in turn scorned and criticized Him. "To avoid useless conflict with the leaders at Jerusalem, He had restricted His labors to Galilee. His apparent neglect of the great religious assemblies, and the enmity manifested toward Him by the priests and rabbis, were a cause of perplexity to the people about Him, and even to His own disciples and His kindred."[15]

His teachings impressed many, but traditions died hard. Why wasn't Jesus more respectful of the priests? Why didn't He pay homage to those who might further His kingdom? Why didn't He capitalize on His popularity with the common people? Jesus' brothers felt He should go up to the Feast of Tabernacles. "If He really possessed such power, why not go boldly to Jerusalem, and assert His claims? Why not perform in Jerusalem the wonderful works reported of Him in Galilee? Do not hide in secluded provinces, they said, and perform your mighty works for the benefit of ignorant peasants and fishermen. Present yourself at the capital, win the support of the priests and rulers, and unite the nation in establishing the new kingdom."[16]

His brothers felt the sting of rejection when Jesus' Galilean disciples abandoned Him. They didn't believe Him to be the Messiah, but they hoped He might set up a temporal kingdom. Jesus knew ambition drove their desire for Him to attend the feast in Jerusalem. As a result, He told them, "You go up to this feast. I am not yet going up to this feast, for My time has not yet fully come" (John 7:8). Having tried to control His ministry in Capernaum when they had convinced Mary to persuade Him to be more careful in His denunciation of the scribes and Pharisees, they again felt they knew what was best for their little Brother. Mary herself had tried to push Jesus to the front at the wedding feast (John 2:3, 4). Jesus' answer then and now showed His adherence to the divine timetable: "My hour has not yet come."

Often we mistakenly try to coerce another to do what we think they should do when perhaps they have a clearer concept of God's calling in their lives than we do.

SPELLBOUND

Now about the middle of the feast Jesus went up into the temple and taught. John 7:14.

Jesus' fame had spread throughout the Roman Empire. Some came to the Feast of Tabernacles with hopes of seeing Him. Everywhere people spoke about Jesus of Nazareth. Few were bold enough to voice the opinion in public that He might be the Messiah, yet many frankly discussed the possibility among themselves. The crowd divided in their opinion of Him. Many felt He was "a good man" while others thought Him a deceiver. Into their debate came the object of their curiosity.

Jesus arrived in Jerusalem at midfeast. Journeying by Himself, He had quietly selected a route not often traveled. He wished nothing to interfere with His mission. Slipping into the city just as the excitement about Him reached a peak, He entered the court of the Temple. "Because of His absence from the feast, it had been urged that He dared not place Himself in the power of the priests and rulers. All were surprised at His presence. Every voice was hushed. All wondered at the dignity and courage of His bearing in the midst of powerful enemies who were thirsting for His life."[17] Jesus spoke with such power that it held the multitude spellbound. Captivated by His depth of understanding and breadth of scriptural knowledge, they could say nothing but "How does this Man know letters, having never studied?" (John 7:15). "Self-education in the Scriptures was not unheard of, but such an education was looked upon as vastly inferior to the recognized training in the rabbinical schools."[18] True, Jesus had never studied in the rabbinical schools, but God was His teacher.

Jesus taught the people daily as they came to the Temple. By mocking Jesus' birth the rabbis sought to deflect any consideration of Him as the Messiah, but He refused to be drawn into a debate about His parentage. "You both know Me, and you know where I am from; and I have not come of Myself, but He who sent Me is true, whom you do not know. But I know Him, for I am from Him, and He sent Me" (verses 28, 29). The Jewish leaders didn't recognize Christ as the Son of God because their false concept of God saw Him as a cruel taskmaster, not a loving, merciful Father. In failing to recognize Jesus as God, the Jews ignored God's revelation to them of His character.

Does your concept of God the Father allow you to recognize Jesus as the Son of God?

THE TEMPLE POLICE

The Pharisees heard the crowd murmuring these things concerning Him, and the Pharisees and the chief priests sent officers to take Him. John 7:32.

The Pharisees, more than any other segment of Palestinian society, sought to quiet Jesus. Being the keepers of the "traditions of the elders" that governed every minute detail of an individual's life, they especially reacted to Jesus' teachings regarding the spirit of the law and His rebuke of legalism. Now they took the lead in calling the Sanhedrin together to condemn Him. As the chief Jewish religious body, the Sanhedrin's jurisdiction extended only to Judea, but the effect of its rulings rippled throughout the Jewish world. The Sanhedrin limited its scope to religious ordinances. By narrowing authority to the religious arena, the Sanhedrin maintained some control over the nation despite the fact that Rome controlled civil authority in Palestine. The Sanhedrin had no leverage with Rome other than dealing with specific violations that profaned the Temple. In this one area the Sanhedrin could put to death even a Roman citizen. The body employed its own police force and zealously suppressed false prophets and sects that might mislead the people.

The Sanhedrin now dispatched their Temple police to arrest Jesus and bring Him before them. The Feast of Tabernacles was winding down. The people had seen the water libation ceremony performed each of the seven days of the feast and it had done nothing to satisfy their great thirst for salvation. Then Jesus suddenly lifted His voice. "If anyone thirsts, let him come to Me and drink. He who believes in Me, as the Scripture has said, out of his heart will flow rivers of living water" (John 7:37, 38).

Those sent to arrest Jesus soon returned empty-handed. "Why have you not brought Him?" the chief priests asked. "With solemn countenance they answered, 'Never man spake like this Man.' Hardened as were their hearts, they were melted by His words. While He was speaking in the temple court, they had lingered near, to catch something that might be turned against Him. But as they listened, the purpose for which they had been sent was forgotten. They stood as men entranced."[19]

"'If any man thirst, let him come unto me.' . . . The cry of Christ to the thirsty soul is still going forth, and it appeals to us with even greater power than to those who heard it in the temple on that last day of the feast. The fountain is open for all."[20]

MIGHT MAKES RIGHT?

Are you also deceived? Have any of the rulers or the Pharisees believed in Him? But this crowd that does not know the law is accursed.

John 7:47-49.

The failure of the Temple police to seize Jesus enraged the Pharisees. They asked, "Are you also deceived? Have any of the rulers or the Pharisees believed in Him? But this crowd that does not know the law is accursed." They regarded the people as too ignorant to know what constituted truth and felt that they alone could accurately judge what the people ought to hear. The leadership had had Jesus shadowed since His arrival in Jerusalem. "The priests and rulers were watching to entrap Him. They were planning to stop Him by violence. But this was not all. They wanted to humble this Galilean rabbi before the people."[21] If they could show He had not obtained their permission to teach, they might discredit Him. Jesus answered their charge by clearly stating, "My doctrine [teaching] is not Mine, but His who sent Me" (John 7:16).

They tried to discredit Him by saying that He was paranoid. "You have a demon. Who is seeking to kill You?" they demanded (verse 20). Jesus pointed out that they stood ready to break the sixth commandment. Exposed, they next claimed His works had come from the devil. It was not a new claim. Jesus silenced His every accuser, yet they refused to recognize Him as Messiah. "You both know Me, and you know where I am from; and I have not come of Myself, but He who sent Me is true, whom you do not know. But I know Him, for I am from Him, and He sent Me" (verses 28, 29). It was a clear assertion that He was the Son of God.

The rulers, now furious, tried to arrest Him, but an unseen power restrained them. Quite a number of those in the Temple listening to Jesus had allowed the rabbis to sway their attitude toward Him. "Many are deceived today in the same way as were the Jews. Religious teachers read the Bible in the light of their own understanding and traditions; and the people do not search the Scriptures for themselves, and judge for themselves as to what is truth; but they yield up their judgment, and commit their souls to their leaders."[22]

"Lacking scriptural support, men seek to supply the deficiency by employing force and the power of authority. Men who resist often seal their testimony with their blood. The future will see a similar attempt by the civil authorities to suppress truth (Rev. 13)."[23]

A FRIEND IN COURT

Nicodemus (he who came to Jesus by night, being one of them) said to them, "Does our law judge a man before it hears him and knows what he is doing?"

John 7:50, 51.

Failing in two attempts, the priests and rulers now let their desire to arrest Christ and stop His message become an all-consuming obsession. He had undermined their authority as established religious leaders, and His teaching was different than theirs. "Action and voice, delivery and articulation, are things that must be seen and heard to be appreciated. That our Lord's manner was peculiarly solemn, arresting, and impressive, we need not doubt. It was probably something very unlike the Jewish intonations at the readings of the Law, and quite different from what officers and people were accustomed to hearing."[24] Christ's words captivated the crowd, and even those sent to arrest Him became so enthralled with His message that they forgot their errand.

As the Sanhedrin discussed methods for silencing Christ, Nicodemus, one of its members, suddenly spoke for Jesus before the assembly. "Does our law judge a man before it hears him and knows what he is doing?"

"The lesson that Christ had given to Nicodemus had not been in vain. Conviction had fastened upon his mind, and in his heart he had accepted Jesus. Since his interview with the Saviour, he had earnestly searched the Old Testament Scriptures, and he had seen truth placed in the true setting of the gospel."[25] Moses had stated, "You shall not be afraid in any man's presence, for the judgment is God's" (Deut. 1:17). The accused must receive a hearing and have a chance to confront accusers. Nicodemus, in a simple but eloquent defense, simply reminded them that they must exercise justice and fair play.

"Silence fell on the assembly. The words of Nicodemus came home to their consciences. They could not condemn a man unheard. But it was not for this reason alone that the haughty rulers remained silent, gazing at him who had dared to speak in favor of justice. They were startled and chagrined that one of their own number had been so far impressed by the character of Jesus as to speak a word in His defense."[26] Rather than heed him, they mocked Nicodemus, saying, "Are you also from Galilee? Search and look, for no prophet has arisen out of Galilee" (John 7:52). Nicodemus knew otherwise. The council came to a halt. No hearing—no condemnation.

When Christians listen to one side of a story and believe—that is condemnation, not justice.

CAST THE FIRST STONE

He who is without sin among you, let him throw a stone at her first. John 8:7.

Early the next morning Jesus returned to the Temple. Seating Himself, He began to teach. Suddenly He heard an interruption. A group of scribes and Pharisees, dragging a terror-stricken woman between them, now approached Him. Rudely shoving her in front of Him, they announced, "Teacher, this woman was caught in adultery, in the very act. Now Moses, in the law, commanded us that such should be stoned. But what do You say?" (John 8:4, 5). "The Law of Moses prescribed death for adultery when a married woman was involved, but did not specify the manner of death. According to the Mishnah death in these cases was inflicted by strangulation. . . . The law prescribed death by stoning when a betrothed woman was involved (Deut. 22:23, 24). . . . It seems likely, therefore, that the case in question was one of a betrothed woman." [27]

Many thought Jesus would pity the woman, for they knew His capacity to forgive. If He sought leniency, they could charge that He despised the law. But if He agreed to a death sentence, He usurped Rome's exclusive prerogative to pass a death sentence. As with most plots, this one seemed to present Jesus no options. "Jesus looked upon the scene—the trembling victim in her shame, the hard-faced dignitaries, devoid of even human pity. His spirit of stainless purity shrank from the spectacle. Giving no sign that He had heard the question, He stooped and, fixing His eyes upon the ground, began to write in the dust." [28] The very men present had been responsible for luring the woman into sin. To trap Jesus they had positioned her so she would succumb to adultery. They selectively overlooked the provision of the law that stated both the man and woman taken in adultery must suffer the same penalty. Where was the other guilty party?

Moments stretched into minutes. As the accusers' "eyes, following those of Jesus, fell upon the pavement at His feet, their voices were silenced. There, traced before them, were the guilty secrets of their own lives. Rising, and fixing His eyes upon the plotting elders, Jesus said, 'He that is without sin among *you,* let him first cast a stone at her.' . . . And stooping down, He continued writing." [29] Before the judgment bar of heaven the men stood more guilty than the woman and they knew it.

Those who accuse others must think themselves without sin. If they only knew! Christians build up while accusers tear down.

"NEITHER DO I CONDEMN YOU"

And Jesus said to her, "Neither do I condemn you; go and sin no more."

John 8:11.

As the last of the self-righteous accusers left Jesus' presence, His eyes fell upon the trembling victim. "His words, 'He that is without sin among you, let him first cast a stone,' had come to her as a death sentence. She dared not lift her eyes to the Saviour's face, but silently awaited her doom."[30] Jesus had not set aside the law of Moses nor presumed upon Rome's authority. He had stymied His enemies, but there remained the victim of the plot. It was true she had committed adultery and broken the law. Jesus did not excuse—He abhorred the sin (Matt. 5:27-32), just as He did the sin of self-righteous judging (Matt. 7:1-5).

What would become of the woman? She continued to cower before Jesus while furtively glancing around her. Those who had so recently hauled her from a bed of sin and thrust her into the midst of the Temple square crowd had vanished. Suddenly the most beautiful words she had ever heard came to her as Jesus said, "Neither do I condemn you; go and sin no more." "Her heart was melted, and she cast herself at the feet of Jesus, sobbing out her grateful love, and with bitter tears confessing her sins. This was to her the beginning of a new life, a life of purity and peace, devoted to the service of God. . . . This penitent woman became one of His most steadfast followers. With self-sacrificing love and devotion she repaid His forgiving mercy."[31]

Jesus came to the world to save rather than accuse and punish. "For God did not send His Son into the world to condemn the world, but that the world through Him might be saved" (John 3:17). Christ realizes the circumstances surrounding each sinner. The more guilt we possess, the more we need His divine love, sympathy, and forgiveness.

"Those who are forward in accusing others, and zealous in bringing them to justice, are often in their own lives more guilty than they. Men hate the sinner, while they love the sin. Christ hates the sin, but loves the sinner. This will be the spirit of all who follow Him. Christian love is slow to censure, quick to discern penitence, ready to forgive, to encourage, to set the wanderer in the path of holiness, and to stay his feet therein."[32]

THE LIGHT OF THE WORLD

I am the light of the world. He who follows Me shall not walk in darkness, but have the light of life. John 8:12.

Jesus stood at daybreak in the Court of the Women on the last day of the Feast of Tabernacles. Special lamps had burned each evening of the festival to commemorate the pillar of light that guided Israel from Egypt and also the hope of a Messiah who would light the nation with His glory.

"The sun had just risen above the Mount of Olives, and its rays fell with dazzling brightness on the marble palaces, and lighted up the gold of the temple walls, when Jesus, pointing to it, said, 'I am the light of the world.'"[33] The people understood Jesus to have just said that He was the Messiah, the Promised One! "In the manifestation of God to His people, light had ever been a symbol of His presence. At the creative word in the beginning, light had shone out of darkness. Light had been enshrouded in the pillar of cloud by day and the pillar of fire by night, leading the vast armies of Israel. Light blazed with awful grandeur about the Lord on Mount Sinai. Light rested over the mercy seat in the tabernacle. Light filled the temple of Solomon at its dedication. Light shone on the hills of Bethlehem when the angels brought the message of redemption to the watching shepherds. God is light; and in the words, 'I am the light of the world,' Christ declared His oneness with God, and His relation to the whole human family."[34]

The Pharisees and rulers immediately seized upon His statement as that of an arrogant itinerant Teacher. "You bear witness of Yourself; Your witness is not true," they said (John 8:13). According to the Mishnah, a man needed others to bear witness to his sanctification. It was something one might not claim for self. John, the disciple of Christ, would later give just such a witness: "In Him was life, and the life was the light of men. And the light shines in the darkness, and the darkness did not comprehend it" (John 1:4, 5). Peter also testified when he wrote: "And so we have the prophetic word confirmed, which you do well to heed as a light that shines in a dark place, until the day dawns and the morning star rises in your hearts" (2 Peter 1:19).

The Light still shines in the darkness, and some comprehend it not, choosing to hide their deeds in shadow. Some things never change.

"BEFORE ABRAHAM WAS, I AM"

Jesus said to them, "Most assuredly, I say to you, before Abraham was, I AM." John 8:58.

Jesus had just stated He was the light of the world, the Messiah. He chose not to debate His assertion, but it did touch a nerve when He said, "If you abide in My word, you are My disciples indeed. And you shall know the truth, and the truth shall make you free" (John 8:31, 32). What they perceived to be a reference to their continued slavery under Rome rankled the Jewish leaders. "We are Abraham's descendants, and have never been in bondage to anyone," they indignantly responded. "How can you say, 'You will be made free?'" (verse 33). What they failed to understand was that they were in bondage to sin. "A mere lineal descent from Abraham was of no value. Without a spiritual connection with him, which would be manifested in possessing the same spirit, and doing the same works, they were not his children. . . . Descent from Abraham was proved, not by name and lineage, but by likeness of character."[35] The scribes and priests plotted to murder Him whose ministry had only served to bless others. The priests would rather have turned their backs upon Jesus and closed their eyes to truth than humbled themselves by admitting they harbored ill will in their hearts.

Jesus now referred to Abraham. "'Your father Abraham rejoiced to see My day, and he saw it and was glad.' Then the Jews said to Him, 'You are not yet fifty years old, and have You seen Abraham?' Jesus said to them, 'Most assuredly, I say to you, before Abraham, I AM'" (verses 56-58). "Silence fell upon the vast assembly. The name of God, given to Moses to express the idea of the eternal presence, had been claimed as His own by this Galilean Rabbi. He had announced Himself to be the self-existent One."[36] It shocked the priests and rulers that Jesus had claimed divinity. Because in their opinion He had presumed to take upon Himself the name of God, they sought to stone Him for blasphemy. Stones were no doubt handy, for the Temple was still under construction. "Now many of the people, siding with the priests and rabbis, took up stones to cast at Him. 'But Jesus hid Himself, and went out of the temple, going through the midst of them, and so passed by.'"[37]

Evil men still hate to hear truth spoken and will do anything to silence it.

BLIND FROM BIRTH

And His disciples asked Him, saying, "Rabbi, who sinned, this man or his parents, that he was born blind?"

John 9:2.

It is likely that on the Sabbath following the Feast of Tabernacles (John 9:14) Jesus passed the blind man. He had been blind from birth. Some Jews thought of God as an exacting deity of vengeance and judgment who punished sin by inflicting physical suffering. The question posed by Christ's disciples reflected a common thinking of their day. This particular ailment presented a difficulty, however, since the man had been born blind and could not have sinned in the womb. The question was a favorite with the scribes, for they loved to sit in the Temple and debate such perplexing trivia by the hour.

The book of Job clearly points out that Satan brings suffering upon the innocent. God in His mercy usually overrules Satan and intervenes to save His children. While all suffering ultimately comes as a consequence of breaking God's law, God does not bring the disease and death that naturally follow sin. "Satan, the author of sin and all its results, had led men to look upon disease and death as proceeding from God—as punishment arbitrarily inflicted on account of sin. Hence one upon whom some great affliction or calamity had fallen had the additional burden of being regarded as a great sinner."[38] Based on that reasoning many Jews later saw Christ's suffering and death as proof He wasn't the Messiah, thus explaining the text: "We esteemed [judged] Him stricken, smitten by God, and afflicted" (Isa. 53:4).

Jesus gave no explanation for the man's condition. Instead He answered, "Neither this man nor his parents sinned, but that the works of God should be revealed in him" (John 9:3). Spitting upon the ground, He mixed clay with saliva and anointed the blind man's eyes. Then He told him, "Go, wash in the pool of Siloam" (verse 7). The man faithfully went and was healed. As with the man at the Pool of Bethesda, Jesus chose the Sabbath to heal a chronic sufferer. He had kneaded the clay with the spittle to form a paste and anointed the man's eyes, both acts forbidden by rabbinical rules. Thus the Pharisees claimed that Jesus had violated the Sabbath. "The Pharisees could not but be astonished at the cure. Yet they were more than ever filled with hatred; for the miracle had been performed on the Sabbath day."[39]

Even today some believe God causes pain and death. Perhaps we need our eyes opened by the anointing of the Spirit and the revelations of Job to see truth.

THE EYES OF HIS UNDERSTANDING

Since the world began it has been unheard of that anyone opened the eyes of one who was born blind. If this Man were not from God, He could do nothing.

John 9:32, 33.

Friends brought the previously blind man to the council of the Pharisees, where he testified, "He put clay on my eyes, and I washed, and I see" (John 9:15). The Pharisees asked, " 'What do you say about Him because He opened your eyes?' He said, 'He is a prophet' " (verse 17). Rather than accept the miracle, the Pharisees chose instead to doubt the man had ever been blind. Calling his parents, they asked, "Is this your son, who you say was born blind? How then does he now see?" (verse 19).

"The Pharisees had one hope left, and that was to intimidate the man's parents. . . . The parents feared to compromise themselves; for it had been declared that whoever should acknowledge Jesus as the Christ should be 'put out of the synagogue;' that is, should be excluded from the synagogue for thirty days. . . . The sentence was regarded as a great calamity; and if it failed to produce repentance, a far heavier penalty followed." [40] The couple shrank back from religious penalties rather than stand for truth. Excommunication overcame conviction. They stated, "We know that this is our son, and that he was born blind; but by what means he now sees we do not know, or who opened his eyes we do not know. He is of age; ask him. He will speak for himself" (verses 20, 21).

But the blind man remained unafraid. The Pharisees proclaimed, "Give God the glory! We know that this Man is a sinner" (verse 24). The man replied, "Whether He is a sinner or not I do not know. One thing I know: that though I was blind, now I see" (verse 25). Although the Pharisees badgered the man, he stood firm. "The frowning priests and rabbis gathered about them their robes, as though they feared contamination from contact with him; they shook off the dust from their feet, and hurled denunciations against him— 'Thou wast altogether born in sins, and doest thou teach *us*?' And they excommunicated him." [41] Jesus heard of their act and found the man. When told that Jesus was the Son of God, "the man cast himself at the Saviour's feet in worship. Not only had his natural sight been restored, but the eyes of his understanding had been opened." [42]

None are so blind as those who refuse to see. We will stand judged by the light we have received or might have received had we put forth effort to obtain it.

THEY KNOW HIS VOICE

And when he brings out his own sheep, he goes before them; and the sheep follow him, for they know his voice. John 10:4.

Sheep in Palestine remain in an enclosed courtyard when not in the fields. A night porter watches several flocks within it, and at daybreak the shepherds come to claim their sheep. The sheep know their shepherd. He calls and they follow. "Through the prophet, Jesus declares, 'I have loved thee with an everlasting love: therefore with loving-kindness have I drawn thee.' He compels none to follow Him. 'I drew them,' He says, 'with cords of a man, with bands of love' (Ps. 77:20, KJV; Jer. 31:3, KJV; Hosea 11:4, KJV. . . . As the shepherd goes before his sheep, himself first encountering the perils of the way, so does Jesus with His people. 'When he putteth forth his own sheep, he goeth before them.' The way to heaven is consecrated by the Saviour's footprints. The path may be steep and rugged, but Jesus has traveled that way; His feet have pressed down the cruel thorns, to make the pathway easier for us. Every burden that we are called to bear He Himself has borne."[43]

Christ states plainly, "I am the door. If anyone enters by Me, he will be saved, and will go in and out and find pasture" (John 10:9). Humanity can obtain access to heaven through Jesus Christ only. Some have always sought to lead God's sheep astray by offering other means of salvation. The Pharisees did not see themselves in the parable of the shepherd. They maintained that one gained heaven only by scrupulously keeping the Torah and religious tradition. The recognized shepherds of Israel had just cast from the sheepfold one who professed belief in the Messiah.

Certain religions today teach alternatives to Christ. Those who do not agree they excommunicate and expel from the flock. Such was not Christ's practice. "'What a lesson for pastors who seek to drive the church like cattle and fail. The true pastor leads in love, in words, in deeds' (A. T. Robertson, *Word Pictures on the New Testament,* on John 10:4)."[44] "Many have been cast out of the church whose names were registered upon the book of life."[45] In the last days some will rely upon religious leaders to determine their eternal destiny. They have not learned to recognize the voice of the true Shepherd. Christ warns, "Beware of false prophets, who come to you in sheep's clothing, but inwardly they are ravenous wolves" (Matt. 7:15).

Woe to false shepherds and those who listen to a false voice and follow it blindly!

The Door of the Sheep

I am the good shepherd. The good shepherd gives His life for the sheep. John 10:11.

The Mishnah mentions four types of shepherds, each having a different stake in the flock. The borrower must personally pay for every loss to the flock. The paid bailee must pay for each loss, but the owner deducts it from his final pay. The gratuitous bailee must swear to how the loss occurred before he is free from liability, unless the loss resulted from his negligence. The hireling, should thieves or predators appear, forsakes his charges and flees, for he has no stake in the flock. Four guardians, each with a decreasing personal commitment to the sheep!

"Of all creatures the sheep is one of the most timid and helpless, and in the East the shepherd's care for his flock is untiring and incessant. Anciently as now there was little security outside of the walled towns. Marauders from the roving border tribes, or beasts of prey from their hiding places in the rocks, lay in wait to plunder the flocks."[46] Good shepherds protected their charges with their own life. Jesus knows our infirmities, our names, our needs, our joys, and our sorrows. " 'You are My flock, the flock of My pasture; you are men, and I am your God,' says the Lord God." (Eze. 34:31).

"In the parable of the shepherd Jesus puts His own interpretation on His work and mission, and represents Himself as the good shepherd, feeding and taking charge of the sheep. He said, 'He that entereth not by the door [by himself] into the sheepfold, but climbeth up some other way, the same is a thief and a robber.' Christ said that all who came before Him claiming to be the Messiah were deceivers. . . . The deceivers did not come in the way in which it was prophesied that the world's Redeemer should come; but Christ came, answering every specification. Types and symbols had represented Him, and in him type met antitype. In the life, mission, and death of Jesus every specification was fulfilled."[47] Jesus willingly surrendered His life for His flock. How can we say that He does not care for us? "I have called you by your name; you are Mine" (Isa. 43:1). "See, I have inscribed you on the palms of My hands" (Isa. 49:16).

"He will never abandon one for whom He has died. Unless His followers choose to leave Him, He will hold them fast."[48] Learn to recognize His voice so false shepherds will not mislead you.

BEYOND JORDAN

Now it came to pass, when Jesus had finished these sayings, that He departed from Galilee and came to the region of Judea beyond the Jordan. Matt. 19:1.

A year and a half had passed since the healing by the Pool of Bethesda, and nothing had changed in the City of David. Again the priests accused Jesus of Sabbathbreaking and tried to arrest Him. His mission in Judea now drew to a close. Only six months remained. Now He began a slow circuit that would eventually end on Calvary. He would spend little time in Judea or Jerusalem, for His presence would only hasten His sacrifice. For the first time Jesus entered Perea, a district across the Jordan from Judea under Herod Antipas' jurisdiction. "The region contained a fairly large proportion of Jews, and was at this time rather densely populated."[49] During the time Jesus had made His third Galilean tour and sent out the Twelve, many followers had remained with Him. Now He appointed 70 from among them and sent them out two by two to every city and place He was about to visit (Luke 10:1).

The advance teams were to go to the cities of Samaria first, since many believed in Him in that region. Jesus still had a burden for Samaria, even though a recent event had upset His disciples. A certain village had rejected Jesus because the Samaritans perceived Him to be traveling to Jerusalem to worship. Their response rose out of their belief that one could worship just as well upon their own sacred Mount Gerizim. It greatly annoyed James and his brother John. "Coming to Christ, they reported to Him the words of the people, telling Him that they had even refused to give Him a night's lodging. They thought that a grievous wrong had been done Him, and seeing Mount Carmel in the distance, where Elijah had slain the false prophets, they said, 'Wilt thou that we command fire to come down from heaven, and consume them, even as Elias did?'"[50] Jesus wanted His disciples to understand that He still loved the Samaritans. He had come to save, not destroy, and now sent the 70 to those who had rejected the Saviour. "The Saviour's own visit to Samaria, and later, the commendation of the good Samaritan, and the grateful joy of that leper, a Samaritan, who alone of the ten returned to give thanks to Christ, were full of significance to the disciples. The lesson sank deep into their hearts."[51]

"Love your enemies" (Matt. 5:44).

FOXES AND BIRDS

Now it happened as they journeyed on the road, that someone said to Him, "Lord, I will follow You wherever You go." Luke 9:57.

Individuals often came to Jesus seeking to become disciples. Judas volunteered in the summer of A.D. 29. "With great earnestness and apparent sincerity he declared, 'Master, I will follow thee whithersoever thou goest.' Jesus neither repulsed nor welcomed him, but uttered only the mournful words: 'The foxes have holes, and the birds of the air have nests; but the Son of man hath not where to lay his head' (Matt. 8:19, 20, KJV). Judas believed Jesus to be the Messiah; and by joining the apostles, he hoped to secure a high position in the new kingdom. This hope Jesus designed to cut off by the statement of His poverty."[52] The lot of a disciple was not one of luxury.

The second recorded volunteer appeared weeks later, the third in late autumn of A.D. 30. A scribe approached as Jesus entered a boat to cross the Sea of Galilee, stating, "Teacher, I will follow You wherever You go." Jesus said, "Follow Me." The man replied, "Lord, let me first go and bury my father" (Luke 9:59). Such a request was not as simple as it appeared, for in all probability the man's father still enjoyed good health. Jesus would not have told the man to delay burial, for it neglected the sacred duty of a son. More likely the man wanted to procrastinate until a better time came to forsake all and follow Him. Christ knew this and said, "Let the dead bury their own dead, but you go and preach the kingdom of God" (verse 60). Do not wait. Go now and preach. Let those who are spiritually dead and do not feel the call of God bury the physically dead.

"And another also said, 'Lord, I will follow You, but let me first go and bid them farewell who are at my house'" (verse 61). Jesus had but six months left to live. It might well take more than that for the man to arrange his affairs. If he wanted to be a disciple of Christ, he should not delay. "The claims of God take precedence over those of men, even of close relatives."[53] Jesus now paraphrased a well-known proverb. "No one, having put his hand to the plow, and looking back, is fit for the kingdom of God" (verse 62). The original proverb of Hesiod, a Greek poet of the eighth century B.C., read: "He who would plow straight furrows must not look about him."[54]

True discipleship requires undivided and total devotion to God's cause.

MISSION OF THE 70

The harvest truly is great, but the laborers are few.

Luke 10:2.

The directions to the seventy were similar to those that had been given to the twelve; but the command to the twelve, not to enter into any city of the Gentiles or of the Samaritans, was not given to the seventy."[55] Jesus had met with success during His early ministry in Samaria (John 4:5-42). "And many of the Samaritans of that city [Sychar] believed in Him" (verse 39). Christ had mentioned to His disciples at Jacob's well the rich harvest ready to be reaped. He was of course speaking of the harvest of souls among the Samaritan people. Now He repeated His dramatic portrayal of evangelism. "The harvest truly is great, but the laborers are few; therefore pray the Lord of the harvest to send out laborers into His harvest" (Luke 10:2).

The Pharisees were plotting the destruction of Christ and His message so Jesus warned the 70 to be careful. "Go your way; behold, I send you out as lambs among wolves" (verse 3). The missionaries were to take no provisions, but should eat what people offered them and be thankful for the gift of hospitality. For the time being they would enter only the homes of Jews and Samaritans and not Gentiles. It would place them in homes that provided food consistent with the laws of Moses. The 70 received no permission to eat unclean foods as some would today imply from the text: "Eat such things as are set before you" (verse 8).

"Jesus' great heart of love was filled with longing to proclaim the words of life to all nationalities, and he did this in a large measure. He placed Himself in the great thoroughfares of travel, where the crowds passed to and fro, and preached to large concourses of different peoples. But he saw numerous fields opening up for missionary labor. There was abundant opportunity for the twelve disciples to work, and not only for them, but for a very large number of workers."[56] The 70 returned with joy after a highly successful mission.

Abundant opportunity still exists for the true disciple to work for Jesus and to find joy in sharing the gospel.

LEGAL RIGH-TEOUSNESS

And behold, a certain lawyer stood up and tested Him, saying, "Teacher, what shall I do to inherit eternal life?"
Luke 10:25.

The religious leaders recruited a Jericho religious expert (lawyer) to ask Jesus a test question calculated to trap Him. The rabbis spent many hours in debate about eternal life, and the crowd anxiously awaited Jesus' response to the question, "What shall I do to inherit eternal life?" Jesus turned it back on the lawyer. "What is written in the law? What is your reading of it?" (Luke 10:26). Christ linked salvation to the keeping of the commandments. Many priests and rabbis felt Jesus was soft on the law because He often broke with human custom. Here He showed His firm support for the Ten Commandments. The lawyer's question revealed that he agreed with the predominant Jewish way of thinking about salvation. Human endeavor gained salvation. Thus a starting place for working one's way to heaven must certainly be doing those things the scribes and rabbis valued.

The Sermon on the Mount spoke to the spirit of the law and not the letter. The lawyer might have been a keen student of the letter of the law, but he didn't understand its spirit. He answered Jesus, "You shall love the Lord your God with all your heart, with all your soul, with all your strength, and with all your mind, and your neighbor as yourself" (verse 27). Every devout Jew recited the scripture passage twice daily. Jesus confirmed the man's response. "You have answered rightly; do this and you will live" (verse 28). "Man's destiny will be determined by his obedience to the whole law. Supreme love to God and impartial love to man are the principles to be wrought out in the life." [57] If you love God you will keep the first four commandments. And if you love your neighbor you will obey the last six.

The lawyer felt he had kept the commandments rather well and yet suspected there was more to gaining salvation than observing the "letter of the law." He knew he had not practiced true love toward humanity. "Partly as a means of evading his inner conviction, he proceeded to 'justify himself' by making it appear that there were major difficulties in actually loving one's fellow men." [58]

"Christ knew that no one could obey the law in his own strength." [59] *Only by accepting the virtue and grace of Christ can we observe the law. We keep the ten-commandment law out of loving obedience and not to earn credit for heaven.*

"WHO IS MY NEIGHBOR?"

But he, wanting to justify himself, said to Jesus, "And who is my neighbor?" Luke 10:29.

The lawyer now asked another hotly debated theological question: "And who is my neighbor?" "In the thinking of the lawyer, heathen and Samaritans were excluded from the category of 'neighbour'; the only question lay in the problem as to which of the fellow Israelites he was to consider as 'neighbours.' "[60] Jesus told the Jericho crowd a story. "A certain man went down from Jerusalem to Jericho, and fell among thieves, who stripped him of his clothing, wounded him, and departed, leaving him half dead. Now by chance a certain priest came down that road. And when he saw him, he passed by on the other side. Likewise a Levite, when he arrived at the place, came and looked, and passed by on the other side" (Luke 10:30-32). "This was no imaginary scene, but an actual occurrence, which was known to be exactly as represented. The priest and Levite who had passed by on the other side were in the company that listened to Christ's words."[61]

The trail from Jerusalem to Jericho wandered down the Wadi Qelt through barren uninhabited hills. By coincidence the priest and Levite had been returning from Jerusalem after finishing their terms of service at the Temple. As God's representatives, they should have had "compassion on those who are ignorant and going astray" (Heb. 5:2). Instead, they passed by, since touching the victim would have meant ritual defilement. Such a thing would have been a problem for one obeying the letter and not the spirit of the law. Jesus continued, "But a certain Samaritan, as he journeyed, came where he was. And when he saw him, he had compassion. So he went to him and bandaged his wounds, pouring on oil and wine; and he set him on his own animal, brought him to an inn, and took care of him" (Luke 10:33, 34). The Samaritan was a foreigner in Israel. He knew the Jews despised him, yet he provided for the injured traveler. Supporting the man until they reached an inn, he tended to him all night and in the morning provided money for the man's continued care.

The story over, Jesus, fixing His eyes upon the lawyer, asked, "So which of these three do you think was neighbor to him who fell among the thieves?" (verse 36). "The lawyer would not, even now, take the name Samaritan upon his lips, and he made answer, 'He that showed mercy on him.' Jesus said, 'Go, and do thou likewise.' "[62]

THE GOOD SAMARITAN

But a certain Samaritan, as he journeyed, came where he was. And when he saw him, he had compassion.
Luke 10:33.

Who is my neighbor? It was a seemingly simple question but with profound implications. Both Levite and priest came "near" the injured man, yet had not demonstrated themselves "neighborly." The Samaritan hadn't considered personal danger. His concern was for the injured human being in need of assistance. "Neighborliness is not so much a matter of proximity as it is of willingness to bear another's burdens. Neighborliness is the practical expression of the principle of love for one's fellow man."[63] "Love does no harm to a neighbor; therefore love is the fulfillment of the law" (Rom. 13:10). Christ said, "You have heard that it was said, 'You shall love your *neighbor* and hate your enemy.' But I say to you, love your enemies, bless those who curse you, do good to those who hate you, and pray for those who spitefully use you and persecute you, that you may be sons of your Father in heaven" (Matt. 5:43-45).

The law of God points us back to the supreme love of our Father. God gave His only Son to save fallen humanity and thus uphold the law. Just thinking to do right is of no value. God accepts only the actual deed benefiting another. "Pure and undefiled religion before God and the Father is this: to visit orphans and widows in their trouble, and to keep oneself unspotted from the world" (James 1:27).

"Thus the question, 'Who is my neighbor?' is forever answered. Christ has shown that our neighbor does not mean merely one of the church or faith to which we belong. It has no reference to race, color, or class distinction. Our neighbor is every person who needs our help. Our neighbor is every soul who is wounded and bruised by the adversary. Our neighbor is everyone who is the property of God."[64] We must be "doers" of the Word. "He who says he abides in Him ought himself also to walk just as He walked" (1 John 2:6). The spirit we show to others reveals our true attitude toward God.

"Many who profess His name have lost sight of the fact that Christians are to represent Christ. Unless there is practical self-sacrifice for the good of others, in the family circle, in the neighborhood, in the church, and wherever we may be, then whatever our profession, we are not Christians."[65] "The law of the Lord is perfect, converting the soul" (Ps. 19:7).

"MARTHA, MARTHA"

Now it happened as they went that He entered a certain village; and a certain woman named Martha welcomed Him into her house. Luke 10:38.

Entering Bethany after hiking the steep and dusty trail from Jericho, Jesus and His disciples were tired. Bethany sat upon the eastern slope of the Mount of Olives about a mile and a half east of Jerusalem. On this occasion the group first entered the home of Lazarus and his two sisters, Mary and Martha. Martha was apparently the eldest, and she "welcomed" Jesus into their home.

Jesus' life had not been easy. The rejection of His message in Jerusalem, Judea, Galilee, and lately Samaria had been difficult. He had aptly stated that "the Son of Man has nowhere to lay His head" (Luke 9:58). "Our Saviour appreciated a quiet home and interested listeners. He longed for human tenderness, courtesy, and affection."[66] On this particular occasion Martha busied herself in seeing to her visitors. Mary chose to sit at Jesus' feet and just listen. "But Martha was distracted with much serving, and she approached Him and said, 'Lord, do You not care that my sister has left me to serve alone? Therefore tell her to help me'" (Luke 10:40). Martha needed inward composure and to forget the immediate and concentrate on the future. Jesus required no special preparations to make Him content. Mary's concern was for things spiritual, Martha's for things practical.

Martha's duties "distracted" her. Feeling the pressure of so many guests in her home, she realized that a direct appeal to Mary for help would fall upon deaf ears, and turned to Christ. Deeply concerned for her, Jesus replied, "Martha, Martha [a double Martha!], you are worried and troubled about many things. But one thing is needed, and Mary has chosen that good part, which will not be taken away from her'" (verses 41, 42). "The 'one thing' that Martha needed was a calm, devotional spirit, a deeper anxiety for knowledge concerning the future, immortal life, and the graces necessary for spiritual advancement. She needed less anxiety for the things which pass away, and more for those things which endure forever."[67] "But seek first the kingdom of God and His righteousness, and all these things shall be added to you" (Matt. 6:33).

While God has room in His service for such people as Martha, who have a strong sense of duty, they must order their priorities and first sit at the feet of the Master.

THE FEAST OF DEDICATION

Now it was the Feast of Dedication in Jerusalem, and it was winter. And Jesus walked in the temple, in Solomon's porch.

John 10:22, 23.

Judas Maccabaeus instituted the Feast of Dedication to celebrate the cleansing and restoration of the Temple following its defilement by Antiochus Ephiphanes (168-165 B.C.). Most Jews still celebrate it as Hanukkah or "the festival of lights." It was now winter. "According to the Talmud . . . winter extended from about the middle of Kislev to the middle of Shebat (about the middle of December to the middle of February). The word for winter *(cheimon)* may refer either to the season or simply to wet, stormy weather. John may have introduced the remark simply to show that Jesus was in Solomon's porch (v. 23) because the weather was inclement at that season."[68] Solomon's porch lay east of the Temple.

Remarkably, Jesus had returned to the spot where the crowd had recently tried to stone Him. A large multitude asked, "How long do You keep us in doubt? If You are the Christ, tell us plainly" (John 10:24). Jesus, during His ministry, rarely referred to Himself as "the Christ." To answer yes would have confused the Jews looking for a political "Christ." But to have said no would have been to deny His mission. Instead He rebuked them. "I told you, and you do not believe. The works that I do in My Father's name, they bear witness of Me. But you do not believe, because you are not of My sheep, as I said to you. My sheep hear My voice, and I know them, and they follow Me. And I give them eternal life, and they shall never perish; neither shall anyone snatch them out of My hand. My Father, who has given them to Me, is greater than all; and no one is able to snatch them out of My Father's hand. I and My Father are one" (verses 25-30).

Jesus did not claim that His sheep were "once saved, always saved." Satan may lure, but we leave of our own volition. The Jews realized Jesus had just claimed equality with Jehovah. His statement "I and My Father are One" enraged them. Once again, as they had done just two months earlier, they seized stones to kill Him, but "He escaped out of their hand" (verse 39).

A sheep might still wander away from the shepherd. Through personal choice we may depart from our Lord just as did the Pharisees.

218

Teach Us to Pray

Now it came to pass, as He was praying in a certain place, when He ceased, that one of His disciples said to Him, "Lord, teach us to pray, as John also taught his disciples." Luke 11:1.

The disciples had often seen their Master go off alone and spend the whole night in prayer. "One day after a short absence from their Lord, they found Him absorbed in supplication. Seeming unconscious of their presence, He continued praying aloud. The hearts of the disciples were deeply moved. As He ceased praying, they exclaimed, 'Lord, teach us to pray.'"[69] His prayers were most certainly different from those the disciples heard the rabbis and priests of the Temple offer. Their prayers were repetitive and contained no heartfelt emotion. In contrast, Jesus' prayers were sincere and personal. Jesus now gave His disciples a prayer. We call it the Lord's Prayer, but perhaps we should term it the "Disciples' Prayer," for Jesus certainly had no need to pray for forgiveness of sin.

The prayer teaches us to recognize God as our Father. The fact that He resides in heaven should cause us to realize our position before Him. We are to reverence God's name, for it is "hallowed" or honored. "God's name stands for his character (see Ex. 34:5-7). The significance the Jews attached to the divine name is reflected in the reverence with which they uttered it, or, more commonly, left it unarticulated."[70] Jesus taught His disciples to look for the kingdom of glory to come. Sin will cease to exist when God has finally accomplished His will on earth. Christ sums up our desire to see God's will supreme in the first part of the prayer. The second half of the prayer deals with our spiritual and temporal needs and our relationship to our neighbors. Our daily bread includes both areas. We may ask forgiveness of our sins, but only if we are willing to forgive others. Also, we must ask for protection when temptation comes—as it will (John 17:15)—and for God to lead us in ways of His choosing and not our own. The doxology or ending found in the Lord's Prayer mirrors David's praise to God as found in 1 Chronicles 29:11-13.

When we pray "Give us this day our daily bread" we need to realize that it is more than simply physical nourishment from wheat flour. Our daily bread is also Jesus, the Bread of Life. We must ask Him to sustain us each day.

THE MIDNIGHT GUEST

Ask, and it will be given to you; seek, and you will find; knock, and it will be opened to you. Luke 11:9.

Jesus expanded His prayer instruction into a parable. In the Middle East individuals traveled in the cool evening to escape the blistering daytime heat. (A midnight guest arrived unexpectedly, and his host had no food in the house, so he ran next door.) We might lack the spiritual food another needs, but we must never turn away one who comes for the bread of the gospel. God will supply what we should set before others. The next-door neighbor had retired for bed and barred his door. "In many parts of the Orient even today all members of the family sleep together in one room, often on 'pallets' on the floor, or, perhaps, on low, raised platform-style beds. For one member of the family to arise would easily awaken all."[71]

It wasn't that the lazy neighbor could not give bread to the neighbor seeking help; he just did not want to be inconvenienced. But the neighbor did not give up easily. "In the parable the petitioner was again and again repulsed, but he did not relinquish his purpose. So our prayers do not always seem to receive an immediate answer; but Christ teaches that we should not cease to pray. Prayer is not to work any change in God; it is to bring us into harmony with God."[72] Central to the parable of the midnight loaves is the need to be persistent. Delay tests our perseverance and genuineness.

Prayer for the benefit of others is equally important. The host sought bread for his friend and not his own household. When it comes to personal needs we should not come to God with selfish desires, trying to change Him. Rather, prayer is to work a change in us and not in God's plan for us. "Christ's lessons in regard to prayer should be carefully considered. There is a divine science in prayer, and His illustration brings to view principles that all need to understand. He shows what is the true spirit of prayer, He teaches the necessity of perseverance in presenting our requests to God, and assures us of His willingness to hear and answer prayer. Our prayers are not to be a selfish asking, merely for our own benefit. We are to ask that we may give."[73]

"Our mission to the world is not to serve or please ourselves; we are to glorify God by cooperating with Him to save sinners."[74]

HYPOCRISY VERSUS SINCERITY

In the meantime, when an innumerable multitude of people had gathered together, so that they trampled one another, He began to say to His disciples first of all, "Beware of the leaven of the Pharisees, which is hypocrisy."
Luke 12:1.

Jesus routinely warned the people to avoid the example of the Pharisees, because their religion had become an insufferable burden to the people. "But woe to you, scribes and Pharisees, hypocrites! For you shut up the kingdom of heaven against men; for you neither go in yourselves, nor do you allow those who are entering to go in" (Matt. 23:13). Such leaders believed the kingdom to be exclusively for them and that the common people could never gain entrance.

Now as Jesus stood before thousands who jostled to get near enough to hear Him, He initially spoke to just His disciples. He warned again of the leaven of the Pharisees. It was a common theme He had often shared with them. In the past Jesus had used the term *leaven* to represent the doctrine of the Pharisees, but now He employed it to symbolize their entire way of life. Through both doctrine and example the Pharisees had led the people away from God. Jesus knew the Sadducees and Pharisees would attempt to nullify His ministry. Once He was gone they would try to persuade the disciples that Jesus was not the Son of God. It put the disciples at risk. They themselves thought Jesus should perhaps show some divine sign to silence His critics. If such hypocrisy continued to fester in the disciples' minds and hearts, they would eventually disbelieve Christ entirely.

The Pharisees misapplied Scripture and harbored self-glorification. Their human theories sought to make their lot in life easier to the detriment of God's law. They misapplied or ignored divine precepts while upholding human traditions. The human authors of the traditions thus received fame and glory. Unfortunately the disciples were not immune to such thinking. "The same influences are working today through those who try to explain the law of God in such a way as to make it conform to their practices. This class do not attack the law openly, but put forward speculative theories that undermine its principles. They explain it so as to destroy its force."[75]

Beware of anything that leads you, either by doctrine or practice, from the Word of God and truth.

221

THE RICH
FOOL

*Then one from the
crowd said to Him,
"Teacher, tell my
brother to divide the
inheritance with
me." Luke 12:13.*

As Jesus spoke with the people at the Feast of Dedication, a young man pushed forward, saying, "Teacher, tell my brother to divide the inheritance with me." According to Old Testament law the eldest son received a double portion of a father's estate. This man felt cheated of his "rightful" share of the inheritance. "He reasoned that if Jesus should speak to his brother with the same bold authority, he would not dare to do otherwise than what Jesus told him to do. He conceived of the gospel of the kingdom as nothing more than a means for furthering his own selfish interests."[76]

Jesus recognized the young man's selfish disposition and spoke sternly to him. "'Man, who made Me a judge or an arbitrator over you?' . . . 'Take heed and beware of covetousness, for one's life does not consist in the abundance of the things he possesses'" (Luke 12:14, 15). Both sons actually exhibited such covetousness. "Materialism is at the root of many of the world's major problems today. It provides the basis for most political and economic philosophies, and is thus responsible for most of the class and national conflicts that plague mankind."[77]

Jesus now delivered a powerful parable. "The ground of a certain rich man yielded plentifully. And he thought within himself, saying, 'What shall I do, since I have no room to store my crops?' So he said, 'I will do this: I will pull down my barns and build greater, and there I will store all my crops and my goods. And I will say to my soul, "Soul, you have many goods laid up for many years; take your ease; eat, drink, and be merry."' But God said to him, 'Fool! This night your soul will be required of you; then whose will those things be which you have provided?'" (verses 16-20). "He heaps up riches, and does not know who will gather them" (Ps. 39:6). The man failed to realize that God had made him a steward so that he might use his goods to benefit others.

Christ counsels, "Do not lay up for yourselves treasures on earth, where moth and rust destroy and where thieves break in and steal; but lay up for yourselves treasures in heaven" (Matt. 6:19, 20). Where is your treasure?

A PUBLIC ANNOUNCE-MENT

Therefore you also be ready, for the Son of Man is coming at an hour you do not expect. Luke 12:40.

On the street outside a Pharisee's home, for the first time Jesus publicly announced that He would come a second time. Wishing to prepare His disciples for His death, resurrection, and ascension, He told them a story. "Let your waist be girded and your lamps burning; and you yourselves be like men who wait for their master, when he will return from the wedding, that when he comes and knocks they may open to him immediately. Blessed are those servants whom the master, when he comes, will find watching" (Luke 12:35-37). The servant does not do his or her duty out of fear the master will return and judge them, but with an expectation that the mission will be completed.

"Those who are watching for the Lord are purifying their souls by obedience to the truth. With vigilant watching they combine earnest working. Because they know that the Lord is at the door, their zeal is quickened to cooperate with the divine intelligences in working for the salvation of souls. . . . They are declaring the truth that is now specially applicable. As Enoch, Noah, Abraham, and Moses each declared the truth for his time, so will Christ's servants now give the special warning for their generation."[1] God will hold us accountable for doing the service He has equipped us to perform. For the right use of our talents the Lord will judge accordingly. It will be a sad commentary on the lives of many as they finally recognize what their unused talents might have meant had they diligently applied them to the Lord's work.

Because no human being knows the hour of the Son of man's appearing, Christ encourages us always to be alert. "And if he should come in the second watch, or come in the third watch, and find them so, blessed are those servants" (verse 38). The second watch extended from 9:00 p.m. to midnight, the third from midnight to 3:00 a.m. The wee hours of the morning will find those who take up the burdens of their Lord still faithfully doing His work. "In the great judgment day those who have not worked for Christ, those who have drifted along, carrying no responsibility, thinking of themselves, pleasing themselves, will be placed by the Judge of all the earth with those who did evil. They receive the same condemnation."[2]

"Then Peter said to Him, 'Lord, do You speak this parable only to us, or to all people?'" (verse 41). What do you think?

"LET IT ALONE THIS YEAR ALSO"

Then he said to the keeper of his vineyard, "Look, for three years I have come seeking fruit on this fig tree and find none. Cut it down; why does it use up the ground?"
Luke 13:7.

Those surrounding Jesus now told Him of the Galilean pilgrims slaughtered in the Temple by order of Pontius Pilate. They expected Him to condemn the slain as great sinners. Certainly those killed were less favored of God than those who had escaped the random act of His vengeance, they reasoned. The disciples were not so quick to judge. They sympathized with the victims, being from Galilee themselves, yet they still expected Jesus to confirm the men as great sinners for having such a calamity befall them. Jesus' answer surprised them. "Do you suppose that these Galileans were worse sinners than all other Galileans, because they suffered such things? I tell you, no; but unless you repent you will *all* likewise perish" (Luke 13:2, 3). Looking down through the ages Jesus foresaw the destruction of the Jewish nation by Roman armies. Many more Jews would succumb to Roman swords within the Temple compound. "In August [A.D. 70], according to Josephus' account, the Temple was conquered and against the command of Titus burned to the ground. The southwestern hill of Jerusalem, called the upper city, fell to the Romans in September. Josephus claims that more than 1 million Jews lost their lives during the siege of Jerusalem, and that 97,000 were made prisoners."[3]

God still extended His mercy toward His nation. "The generation to whom the Saviour had come were represented by the fig tree in the Lord's vineyard—within the circle of His special care and blessing."[4] God through Jesus had been seeking fruit from the Jewish nation for three years and had found none. The gardener begged the owner to allow him to give the tree additional special care. Jesus did not tell His listeners the outcome of the fig tree parable, for it depended upon the nation's response. "Every advantage that Heaven could bestow was given them, but they did not profit by their increased blessings. By Christ's act in cursing the barren fig tree, the result was shown. They had determined their own destruction."[5]

Why when we think of judgment do we want others judged harshly yet desire limitless amounts of mercy for ourselves? Are we producing the fruit of repentance or just fooling ourselves that we are saved?

THE CARE OF THE GARDENER

But he answered and said to him, "Sir, let it alone this year also, until I dig around it and fertilize it. And if it bears fruit, well. But if not, after that you can cut it down." Luke 13:8, 9.

For more than a thousand years the Jewish nation had abused God's mercy and invited His judgments. They had rejected His warnings and slain His prophets. For these sins the people of Christ's day made themselves responsible by following the same course."[6] The Father and Son loved Israel. As a result the nation enjoyed increased opportunities. We also have been planted in His vineyard under the watchful eye of the gardener. God has also given us great opportunities and privileges.

"You have taken the name of Christ, you are outwardly a member of the church which is His body, and yet you are conscious of no living connection with the great heart of love. The tide of His life does not flow through you. The sweet graces of His character, 'the fruits of the Spirit,' are not seen in your life."[7] Such an indictment may stand against many of us, but our merciful God has not seen fit to cut us down. He would spare us this year also even though we have had many years to bear fruit. Not only have many of us not borne fruit, we have taken up space and obstructed others from spreading the gospel. Our negativity and criticism have dampened their zeal and hindered them from developing a Christlike spirit. The hottest fire some Christians show is only sufficient to warm a few inches of a pew.

The parable states the tree should be cut down because it uses up the ground. "In addition to bearing no fruit itself, the tree also took up space that might otherwise be made productive. The Jewish nation had come to the place where it was not merely useless, so far as fulfilling the role God had appointed it; it had become an obstruction to the carrying out of the plan of salvation for others."[8] Christ does not question the right of the Father to cut it down and replace it with a productive tree, yet He longs to lavish still more attention upon it. He seeks to have it respond to His intercession.

Israel refused the extra effort God put forth when He sent His Son to save them. He has sent His Son to you, also. Will you bear fruit?

THE BENT-OVER WOMAN

And behold, there was a woman who had a spirit of infirmity eighteen years, and was bent over and could in no way raise herself up. Luke 13:11.

In Luke 13 we have recorded the last occasion of Jesus' teaching and healing in a synagogue. Jesus' previous Sabbath miracles included: healing the invalid at the Pool of Bethesda (John 5:1-15), the demoniac at the synagogue (Mark 1:21-28), Peter's mother-in-law (Mark 1:29-31), the man with the withered hand (Mark 3:1-6), and the man born blind (John 9:1-41). This particular Sabbath, while in a Peraean synagogue, Jesus saw a woman with chronic curvature of the spine. Calling her over, He said, " 'Woman, you are loosed from your infirmity.' And He laid His hands on her, and immediately she was made straight, and glorified God" (Luke 13:12, 13). After 18 years of gazing at the dust and people's feet, the very first face the woman saw straight on was that of Jesus. Imagine her gratitude. Little wonder she glorified God! Others present, though, were not so happy.

"But the ruler of the synagogue answered with indignation, because Jesus had healed on the Sabbath; and he said to the crowd, 'There are six days on which men ought to work; therefore come and be healed on them, and not on the Sabbath' " (verse 14). Jewish law did not allow treatment of chronic sufferers until after the Sabbath. Jesus repeatedly challenged this rule. His test case at the Pool of Bethesda had been crippled for 38 years, and this woman hardly fit the "acute illness" category.

Jesus now spoke to the synagogue leader. "Hypocrite! Does not each one of you on the Sabbath loose his ox or donkey from the stall, and lead it away to water it? So ought not this woman, being a daughter of Abraham, whom Satan has bound—think of it—for eighteen years, be loosed from this bond on the Sabbath?" (verses 15, 16). "She not only was a human being, and thus infinitely more important than an animal, but was of the favored race."[9] Jesus' compassion rebuked the official for allowing the woman to suffer for 18 years while doing nothing. Many still subscribe to the false doctrine that suffering is retribution from God, and thus think to avoid their responsibility to their neighbor. But anyone in need of our help is our neighbor.

Christianity is more than carrying your Bible to church. It is also carrying your neighbor's burden.

ANOTHER PHARISEE PLOT

On that very day some Pharisees came, saying to Him, "Get out and depart from here, for Herod wants to kill You." Luke 13:31.

Almost a year had passed since Herod Antipas had put John the Baptist to death, but he had not gained any sense of peace. "News of the preaching of the apostles throughout Galilee reached Herod, calling his attention to Jesus and His work. 'This is John the Baptist,' he said; 'he is risen from the dead;' and he expressed a desire to see Jesus."[10] Jesus had left Galilee for the final time and now preached to the multitudes in Peraea. As Herod Antipas ruled both Galilee and Peraea, the Pharisees came to Jesus and warned Him, "Get out and depart from here, for Herod wants to kill You" (Luke 13:31). The incident must have surprised Christ's disciples. The very men who wished their Master dead were now warning Him to flee for His life. "In view of the awe in which Herod held Jesus (see . . . Matt. 14:1, 2), and his desire to see Him (see Luke 23:8), it is most unlikely that he actually sought Jesus' life. Apparently the Pharisees used this device in an attempt to frighten Jesus out of Peraea into Judea, where they could lay hands on Him themselves. For nearly two years the Jewish leaders had been plotting His death . . . and the Jews had recently tried twice to stone Him."[11]

Jesus said, "Go, tell that fox, 'Behold, I cast out demons and perform cures today and tomorrow, and the third day I shall be perfected.' Nevertheless I must journey today, tomorrow, and the day following; for it cannot be that a prophet should perish outside of Jerusalem'" (Luke 13:32, 33). Jesus indicated to the Pharisees that His ministry would soon close. His destiny was to die upon a cross for all humanity. Not until the prayer in Gethsemane would He utter the words, "I have glorified You [God the Father] on the earth. I have finished the work which You have given Me to do" (John 17:4). Then His mission would be "perfected" or complete. Herod would not stop prematurely what Jesus had yet to do. "Jesus [was] not concerned about His safety while laboring in the territory under Herod's jurisdiction. He [knew] full well that He [would] be killed in Jerusalem."[12]

Jesus recognized what the future held for Him, and He knows what destiny is prepared for us. Trust Him, and everything will work out as planned to our ultimate benefit.

THE LOWLY PLACE

Now it happened, as He went into the house of one of the rulers of the Pharisees to eat bread on the Sabbath, that they watched Him closely. Luke 14:1.

While Jesus was dining one Sabbath with a well-respected and highly influential Pharisee, a man with edema presented himself, hoping to be healed. Turning to the "doctors of the law," Jesus asked, "Is it lawful to heal on the Sabbath?" (Luke 14:3). They refused to answer. Jesus healed the man's disease and asked, "Which of you, having a donkey or an ox that has fallen into a pit, will not immediately pull him out on the Sabbath day?" (verse 5). But the lawyers would not admit they cared more for their livestock than for a human being.

When Jesus looked around Him He saw that most of the guests had vied for the more prestigious seats near the guest of honor and the host. He said that it was far better to take a place of lesser honor than to be humiliated in the pursuit for position. If the host asked someone to move because another individual more important had just arrived, it would be embarrassing. But if they took a less honorable place, the host might ask them to move closer to the head of the table. "For whoever exalts himself will be humbled, and he who humbles himself will be exalted" (verse 11). The desire to exalt oneself was Lucifer's sin. Jesus humbled Himself and became obedient to the point of death (Phil. 2:8).

Turning to His host, Jesus said, "When you give a dinner or a supper, do not ask your friends, your brothers, your relatives, nor rich neighbors, lest they also invite you back, and you be repaid. But when you give a feast, invite the poor, the maimed, the lame, the blind. And you will be blessed, because they cannot repay you; for you shall be repaid at the resurrection of the just" (Luke 14:12-14). Hospitality should not arise from selfish motives. Entertaining those truly in need of food or friendship and who cannot repay will gain reward at the resurrection of the "just." The statement would also imply a resurrection of the "unjust." Paul mentioned the two resurrections in Acts 24:15: "I have hope in God, which they themselves also accept, that there will be a resurrection of the dead, both of the just and the unjust."

"Blessed and holy is he who has part in the first resurrection" (Rev. 20:6).

THE GREAT SUPPER

Now when one of those who sat at the table with Him heard these things, he said to Him, "Blessed is he who shall eat bread in the kingdom of God!" Luke 14:15.

The speaker was insincere. Not wanting to contemplate inviting poor and homeless to his table, he decided to emphasize the reward rather than the task. In response Jesus told a story about a great banquet. The host had invited many, and when the meal was ready, a servant went to remind the guests to attend. Everyone had an excuse for not going. The first had bought a piece of ground and wished to go see it. The second had purchased a yoke of oxen and wanted to try them out. The third had taken a wife and could not make it. When the servant reported back that no one was answering the summons, the master became angry and sent him into the streets to invite the poor, the crippled, and the blind. Those who had shunned the first invitation were not included in the second.

It is a Middle Eastern custom to follow up an invitation with a courtesy message to remind guests that the time has arrived to show up as promised. "Among some Arabs, to decline an invitation at the time of the reminder, . . . after having accepted the original invitation, is considered a declaration of hostility."[13] The three excuses Jesus related were poor and based upon selfish interests. The individual who purchased the land had not done so without first surveying it for value. He wanted to have another look to make sure he had gotten a good deal. The second man had likewise not bought the oxen without first trying them out. The first two at least politely asked to be excused, but the third rudely stated that he simply wasn't coming.

"By the great supper, Christ represents the blessings offered through the gospel. The provision is nothing less than Christ Himself."[14] God offered the religious elite of Israel the greatest gift imaginable—His Son—and they spurned it. Today He invites us to come to Christ. "All the resources of heaven have been invested in the work of salvation, and the least men can do is to appreciate and accept what God has provided."[15] But we let our temporal interests, our husbands and wives, and our social relationships interfere. Amazingly enough, people are still using the same excuses as to why they cannot accept the gospel.

"The heart that is absorbed in earthly affections cannot be given up to God."[16] Whatever gets between you and God is a poor and ultimately fatal excuse.

THE HIGHWAYS AND HEDGES

Then the master said to the servant, "Go out into the highways and hedges, and compel them to come in, that my house may be filled." Luke 14:23.

The Jewish leaders had rejected Christ. God had offered them Christ, the Bread of Life, at the feast and they refused to partake of His message or spirit. Now Jesus told them the invitation would go to those they despised: the poor, the maimed, the lame, and the blind. Jesus forever rejected the Jewish way of thinking regarding those afflicted with disease. He denied that they were outcasts from God. While they might be guilty of many sins, yet He still invited them to come to the feast. The highways and hedges represented the world beyond the Jewish nation. The gospel was to go to the Gentiles, to "every nation, tribe, tongue, and people" (Rev. 14:6).

The master told his servant to "compel" others to attend the feast. It doesn't mean that God forces men and women to come to Him against their will. Compel rather implies a sense of urgency in the request. The individuals should not delay in accepting the invitation. The invitation goes to all. "Whoever desires, let him take the water of life freely" (Rev. 22:17). Nowhere does Scripture advocate that we should coerce religion on anyone or that we should persecute people into following Christ. Jesus "leads" His sheep and they follow Him. "The gospel never employs force in bringing men to Christ." [17]

It is a simple equation but one the world has yet to figure out. "Salvation consists of the invitation extended by God, and man's acceptance of it. Neither can be effective without the other." [18] We are now living in the last days of God's merciful call. Humanity is so busy with temporal interests that it does not consider things of a spiritual nature important enough to leave day-to-day cares behind. "Every time you refuse to listen to the message of mercy, you strengthen yourself in unbelief. Every time you fail to open the door of your heart to Christ, you become more and more unwilling to listen to the voice of Him that speaketh. You diminish your chance of responding to the last appeal of mercy." [19]

"Let it not be written of you, as of ancient Israel, 'Ephraim is joined to idols; let him alone' (Hosea 4:17, KJV)." [20]

BUILDING A TOWER

And whoever does not bear his cross and come after Me cannot be My disciple. Luke 14:27.

Jesus plainly tells the multitude that discipleship is not for those who hold back. It consists of four principles. 1. Each of us must bear our crosses, forsaking all and placing total loyalty in Christ and His mission. We cannot take halfhearted measures. 2. Before making that kind of commitment, we should fully understand the cost. 3. The kingdom of heaven is to have our first and foremost allegiance. 4. As disciples we must permanently sacrifice personal ambition and worldly possessions. Those with personal agendas that come before service to God cannot be disciples. Earthly possessions are not the problem. Rather, cherishing them to the exclusion of the Lord's work is. When worldly business takes precedence over the Lord's, then the alleged disciple is not a true disciple after all.

Jesus now gave two parables, that of building a tower and that of a king going to war. Both parables warn that one must calculate the cost of discipleship from the beginning and be prepared to stay the course rather than drop out when the task is only half completed. The story of the feast shows plainly that those guests who had been invited and had agreed to attend, only to back out of the invitation at the last minute, were not serious about the initial invitation. Lukewarm Christians appear in every church. For many, the closest they get to being "on fire" for their Lord is to slightly "warm the pew" each Sabbath. "The 'cost' of discipleship is the complete and permanent renunciation of personal ambitions and of worldly interests. He who is not willing to go all the way may as well not even start."[21] Scripture mentions the church of Laodicea as being "lukewarm." The representation is of a church body neither hot nor cold but simply filling pews.

Jesus' examples cover both business and politics. One wouldn't start a costly building without drawing up plans and obtaining estimates. Likewise one wouldn't underestimate the strength of a military foe without giving serious consideration to suing for peace if necessary to avert annihilation. "Discipleship involves the complete placing on the altar of all that a man has in this life—plans, ambitions, friends, relatives, possessions, riches—anything and everything that might interfere with service for the kingdom of heaven."[22] The disciple who would plow straight furrows must not look about him or her.

Total devotion is the requirement of the true disciple.

THE LOST SHEEP

So He spoke this parable to them, saying: "What man of you, having a hundred sheep, if he loses one of them, does not leave the ninety-nine in the wilderness and go after the one which is lost until he finds it?"

Luke 15:3, 4.

It is now but two short months until the Crucifixion. The haughty rabbis pointed out that prominent among the crowd listening to Jesus were many publicans and sinners. Although the rabbis felt uncomfortable in Jesus' presence, yet sinners and publicans seemed drawn to Him. "It angered these guardians of society that He with whom they were continually in controversy, yet whose purity of life awed and condemned them, should meet, in such apparent sympathy, with social outcasts. They did not approve of His methods. They regarded themselves as educated, refined, and preeminently religious; but Christ's example laid bare their selfishness." [23] The very fact that Jesus accepted sinners was the strength of His appeal to other sinners. He welcomed every one of them.

Looking around Him at the broad pastures east of the Jordan, Jesus presented the parable of the ninety and nine for the shepherds and sheep owners in the crowd. "As a shepherd seeks out his flock on the day he is among his scattered sheep, so will I seek out My sheep and deliver them from all the places where they were on a cloudy and dark day" (Eze. 34:12). "If there had been but one lost soul, Christ would have died for that one." [24] The creator of men and women considered them all of inestimable value.

Patiently Christ searched for His lost lamb. "The sheep that has strayed from the fold is the most helpless of all creatures. It must be sought for by the shepherd, for it cannot find its way back. So with the soul that has wandered away from God; he is as helpless as the lost sheep, and unless divine love had come to his rescue he could never find his way to God." [25] Success crowns the parable's end result. We also have a work to do for those in our families, churches, and communities.

"Those who love Jesus will love those for whom Christ died. If many of the sinners that are around us had received the light which has blessed us, they would have rejoiced in the truth, and have been in advance of many that have had a long experience and great advantages. Take these lost sheep as your special burden, and watch for souls as they that must give an account." [26]

Who Is Looking For Whom?

I say to you that likewise there will be more joy in heaven over one sinner who repents than over ninety-nine just persons who need no repentance.

Luke 15:7.

To lose a sheep financially hurt its owner, but more important to a shepherd, it meant the loss of a member of his trusting flock. For that reason, he left the 99 unguarded in their fold and went looking for his lost sheep. The lost sheep symbolized both the sinner trapped in sin and the smallest speck of a world cut off from God's vast universe. "Desponding soul, take courage, even though you have done wickedly. Do not think that perhaps God will pardon your transgressions and permit you to come into His presence. God has made the first advance. While you were in rebellion against Him, He went forth to seek you." [27]

The Jews liked to state that a sinner must first experience repentance before God would extend acceptance. For this reason the Pharisees could not understand how it was that Jesus could associate with sinners. Jesus used His parable to teach the truth that "salvation does not come through our seeking after God but through God's seeking after us. . . . We do not repent in order that God may love us, but He reveals to us His love in order that we may repent." [28] "But God demonstrates His own love toward us, in that while we were still sinners, Christ died for us" (Rom. 5:8).

The rabbis believed heaven rejoiced when God destroyed a sinner. "Jesus taught that to God the work of destruction is a strange work. That in which all heaven delights is the restoration of God's own image in the souls whom He has made." [29] "All heaven is interested in the work of saving the lost. Angels watch with intense interest to see who will leave the ninety and nine, and go out in tempest and storm and rain into the wild desert to seek the lost sheep. The lost are all around us, perishing and sadly neglected. But they are of value to God, the purchase of the blood of Christ. . . .We are to seek to save those that are lost. We are to search for the one lost sheep, and bring him back to the fold; and this represents personal effort." [30] Many Pharisees, after Christ's ascension, finally "united with His disciples in the very work outlined in the parable of the lost sheep." [31]

Let us seek for the lost sheep and bring joy to heaven.

TEN SILVER COINS MINUS ONE

Or what woman, having ten silver coins, if she loses one coin, does not light a lamp, sweep the house, and search carefully until she finds it? Luke 15:8.

Christ gave the parable of the lost sheep for the men in His audience, and the parable of the lost coin for the listening women. Women, in biblical times, regarded their bridal dowry as their most cherished possession. Sometimes it might be a family heirloom passed to the eldest daughter upon her marriage, thus becoming a perpetual legacy connecting the women of the family. They considered it a calamity to lose any part of it. "In the East the houses of the poor usually consisted of but one room, often windowless and dark. The room was rarely swept, and a piece of money falling on the floor would be speedily covered by the dust and rubbish. In order that it might be found, even in the daytime, a candle must be lighted, and the house must be swept diligently."[32]

"The lost sheep knows that it is lost. It has left the shepherd and the flock, and it cannot recover itself. It represents those who realize that they are separated from God and who are in a cloud of perplexity, in humiliation, and sorely tempted. The lost coin represents those who are lost in trespasses and sins, but who have no sense of their condition. They are estranged from God, but they know it not. Their souls are in peril, but they are unconscious and unconcerned. In this parable Christ teaches that even those who are indifferent to the claims of God are the objects of His pitying love. They are to be sought for that they may be brought back to God."[33]

Carelessness lost the coin. Now, taking great care to cover every inch of the dirt floor, "its owner sought it because it was of value. So every soul, however degraded by sin, is in God's sight accounted precious. As the coin bore the image and superscription of the reigning power, so man at his creation bore the image and superscription of God. Though now marred and dim through the influence of sin, the traces of this inscription remain upon every soul. God desires to recover that soul and to retrace upon it His own image in righteousness and holiness."[34]

The spiritual welfare of our loved ones should guide our behavior toward them. Our children often become lost within our own homes, our members lost within our churches. We should light a lamp and search until we find them!

THE LOST SON

And he arose and came to his father. But when he was still a great way off, his father saw him and had compassion, and ran and fell on his neck and kissed him.

Luke 15:20.

Jesus continues the "lost" parables: a sheep, a coin, and now a boy. The parable of the prodigal son is one of the most beautiful He ever gave. A father loved his two sons, but love was not enough. No matter how understanding, merciful, just, or compassionate the father was, the younger son questioned his intentions, rebelled, and demanded his inheritance. Division of an inheritance would normally occur after the father's death, when the family would divide or sell the land. The young son's request was totally out of line. By law the elder son received a double inheritance and the younger the remaining third. This boy wanted everything liquidated for hard cash while the father still lived. Then, taking his share, he went to a "far country."

Famine arose and the boy soon spent his cash. His fair-weather friends melted away like snow before the sun. Now alone, he became servant to a Gentile and cared for unclean animals. A more degrading line of work for a Jew would be hard to imagine. "And he would gladly have filled his stomach with the pods that the swine ate, and no one gave him anything. But when he came to himself, he said, 'How many of my father's hired servants have bread enough and to spare, and I perish with hunger! I will arise and go to my father'" (Luke 15:16-18). What had changed? Certainly his surroundings had not, but his attitude toward his father had altered! Realizing that his father was a just man now gave him hope that he might receive humane treatment. The boy finally turned homeward.

In the parables of the sheep and the coin God initiated the search. And in the prodigal son we see God wooing those who decided to leave Him. "Never a prayer is offered, however faltering, never a tear is shed, however secret, never a sincere desire after God is cherished, however feeble, but the Spirit of God goes forth to meet it. Even before the prayer is uttered or the yearning of the heart made known, grace from Christ goes forth to meet the grace that is working upon the human soul." [35]

God sees us while we are "still a great way off" and has "compassion" upon us. Forgetting the dignity of old age, this Father runs with eagerness and joy to welcome home His lost child.

THE OTHER SON

But he was angry and would not go in. Therefore his father came out and pleaded with him.

Luke 15:28.

The Parable of the Lost Son emphasizes man's part in responding to the love of God and acting in harmony with it. . . . In the parable the younger son represents the publicans and the sinners, the older son, the scribes and the Pharisees."[36] The father greeted his wayward son, covered his rags with his own robe, slipped the family signet ring on his finger, placed shoes upon his bare feet, and summoned his servants to prepare a feast. "And bring the fatted calf here and kill it, and let us eat and be merry; for this my son was dead and is alive again; he was lost and is found" (Luke 15:23, 24). To this point the parable appeared to have a happy ending. But all was not well in the home.

The elder son, returning from the fields, heard the music and dancing. Discovering that his younger brother had returned and that a feast was in progress, he became sullen and angry, refusing to enter the house. His father came out and pled with him to join the celebration. Instead, the older brother quickly pointed out that he had always been faithful. He hadn't run off to make a fool of himself in a foreign land, nor had he made unreasonable demands upon his father's estate. Always he had dutifully kept the rules of the house. "Son," his father answered, "you are always with me, and all that I have is yours. It was right that we should make merry and be glad, for your brother was dead and is alive again, and was lost and is found" (verses 31, 32).

The elder son hadn't indulged in vice and outwardly he appeared righteous, but inwardly he was jealous for the lifestyle he had seen his sibling pursuing. Buried deep within his heart lurked animosity toward a brother who had lived sinfully while he had been stuck in a "religious" straight jacket. Love for his father did not motivate his behavior. He felt that everyone should appear as obedient and feel as miserable as he did. The older brother took no pleasure in the reinstatement of his younger brother to the family.

Our heavenly Father welcomes each prodigal who returns home, but too often strict "Christians" will not joyfully welcome a backslider back into church fellowship. Sad to say, many of us are hypocrites who love to hate the sinner because we secretly wish we could sin ourselves.

THE PLAN TO SAVE FACE

Then the steward said within himself, "What shall I do? For my master is taking the stewardship away from me." Luke 16:3.

Jesus wished to present a lesson in preparedness. Basing His story upon an actual case that had just happened among the publicans, Jesus recounted the story of a shrewd and crafty man who had formulated a plan of escape from a difficulty that he had brought upon himself. Christ's tale was not a parable that we should apply literally. Dishonesty has no virtue.

A certain rich man had placed his business affairs in the hands of a trusted steward. After a while the master concluded that his servant had been systematically stealing. Believing his estates had not been honestly managed, he ordered an investigation of the accounts. At first his steward saw only three avenues of escape from detection and dismissal. He could labor hard to replace the money before the investigation discovered it missing. Perhaps he could beg for leniency and throw himself on the mercies of his employer; or he could leave the house. Because he had no references, the last option would have resulted in starvation. Rather than surrendering to panic, however, he hit upon a new plan.

Quickly the steward called together all those who had borrowed money from his master. He had kept such poor records that he had to ask exactly how much each debtor really owed (Luke 16:5), then suggested that they pay just a fraction of it. "This unfaithful servant made others sharers with him in his dishonesty. He defrauded his master to advantage them, and by accepting this advantage they placed themselves under obligation to receive him as a friend into their homes."[37] It amazed the master when he found out about it. "The rich man did not condone his steward's dishonesty; it was for dishonesty that he was being relieved of his duties. But the cleverness with which this scheming rascal brought his career of misconduct to a climax was so amazing, and the thoroughness with which he carried out his plan so worthy of more noble objectives, that the rich man could not help admiring his steward's sharpness and diligence."[38] "The servant in the parable had made no provision for the future. The goods entrusted to him for the benefit of others he had used for himself; but he had thought only of the present."[39]

"The lesson of this parable is for all. Everyone will be held responsible for the grace given him through Christ. Life is too solemn to be absorbed in temporal or earthly matters."[40]

DESTINY FIXED

But Abraham said, "Son, remember that in your lifetime you received your good things, and likewise Lazarus evil things; but now he is comforted and you are tormented." Luke 16:25.

Jesus moved on in His discussion of the opportunities of the present life and how they determine destiny. Turning from His disciples, He addressed the Pharisees directly. The parable of the rich man and Lazarus speaks of a man who became "so engrossed . . . in the society of his friends that he lost all sense of his responsibility to cooperate with God in His ministry of mercy."[41] Much controversy involving this parable would not exist if we considered it in context with the parables surrounding it. The poor man Lazarus patiently suffered every day, but he wondered that the rich man would not help him. Finally both died. Here people often misuse the parable to support nonbiblical positions.

"To interpret this parable as teaching that men receive their rewards immediately at death clearly contradicts Jesus' own declaration that 'the Son of man shall . . . reward every man according to his works' when He 'shall come in the glory of his Father with his angels' (see . . . Matthew 16:27; 25:31-41)."[42] (Additional support for the concept that we receive our reward at the Second Coming appears in 1 Corinthians 15:51-55; 1 Thessalonians 4:16, 17; and Revelation 22:12.) "The doctrine of a conscious state of existence between death and the resurrection was held by many of those who were listening to Christ's words. The Saviour knew of their ideas, and He framed His parable so as to inculcate important truths through these preconceived opinions."[43]

The rich man had done nothing wrong against Lazarus, but he had withheld mercy. By doing no positive good, he was guilty of doing wrong. Believing that God vented His wrath upon the poor and afflicted, the Pharisees neglected them also. This in turn caused them to become proud of their own positions and possessions. Jesus wished to show them that "no man is valued for his possessions; for all he has belongs to him only as lent by the Lord. A misuse of these gifts will place him below the poorest and most afflicted man who loves God and trusts in Him. Christ desires His hearers to understand that it is impossible for men to secure the salvation of the soul after death."[44]

"Thus Christ represented the hopelessness of looking for a second probation. This life is the only time given to man in which to prepare for eternity."[45]

A PARABLE CONFIRMING HELL?

For the living know that they will die; but the dead know nothing. Eccl. 9:5.

In His parable Jesus took Lazarus to Paradise and the rich man to hell. Many Jews believed that upon death they would go to the heavenly kingdom where Abraham would welcome them at its gates, a concept remarkably similar to that of many Christians who today have Peter greeting the saints at heaven's gates. The Jews improperly placed their belief and trust in eternal life upon Abraham rather than God. Salvation comes to no person except through Christ. "Nor is there salvation in any other" (Acts 4:12).

Tormented with thirst, the rich man looked up to heaven and saw Lazarus in the bosom of Abraham. Calling to the former beggar, he requested a little mercy, just some water to cool his tongue and ease his torment. Are we to believe that heaven exists within sight of hell? Is this what Jesus taught? "Can it be that heaven and hell are within speaking distance, and that those in heaven witness the suffering of friends and loved ones in hell without being able to alleviate their torment, while those in hell can observe the bliss of the righteous in heaven? Yet this is precisely what this parable teaches *if* it is to be taken literally."[46] The parable is figurative. Jesus compared death to a sleep (John 11:11, 14). We must not link biblical truth selectively, but consider all it has to say on a topic.

The parable should make us realize that death forever fixes our destiny. Even if Lazarus had warned the rich man's brothers to repent of their selfish ways, they would not have heeded the message. If they would not listen to God's Word, they would not heed any warning from someone raised from the dead. "There are many today who are following the same course. Though church members, they are unconverted. . . . They desire to live for themselves, not for God. He is not in their thoughts; therefore they are classed with unbelievers. Were it possible for them to enter the gates of the city of God, they could have no right to the tree of life, for when God's commandments were laid before them with all their binding claims they said, No. They have not served God here; therefore they would not serve Him hereafter. They could not live in His presence, and they would feel that any place was preferable to heaven."[47]

The parable of the rich man is a modern-day warning.

MUSTARD-SEED FAITH

And the apostles said to the Lord, "Increase our faith." Luke 17:5.

The disciples' questions and requests show an interesting aspect of their development into apostles. "Lord, save us!" (Matt. 8:25). "Why do You speak to them in parables?" (Matt. 13:10). "Explain to us the parable of the tares of the field" (verse 36). "Where could we get enough bread in the wilderness to fill such a great multitude?" (Matt. 15:33). "Why could we not cast it out?" (Matt. 17:19). "Who then is the greatest in the kingdom of heaven?" (Matt. 18:1). "Lord, how often shall my brother sin against me, and I forgive him? Up to seven times?" (verse 21). "Who then can be saved?" (Matt. 19:25). "Lord, teach us to pray" (Luke 11:1). Perhaps the most thought-provoking statement appears in Luke 17:5: "Increase our faith." Who wouldn't like to have more faith?

The request concerning faith is faulty. It implies that we must have a certain "amount" of required faith. Jesus points out that the quality of one's faith is the important point. "Either a person has faith or he does not have faith. The very smallest amount of faith is sufficient to accomplish seemingly impossible tasks. It is not so much the amount of faith, as the genuineness of it."[48] Quality, not quantity, determines success. The mustard plant might have small seeds, but hidden within it is the power to grow into a mighty bush. The disciples had too much faith in self and too little in God. How like them we all are! "Now faith is the substance of things hoped for, the evidence of things not seen" (Heb. 11:1).

The miracles of Christ called for faith from those suffering. Healing was conditional upon the exercise of their faith. God enabled the person to grasp the promise of health and salvation, but Jesus asked him or her to believe. "Here is where thousands fail: they do not believe that Jesus pardons them personally, individually. They do not take God at His word. It is the privilege of all who comply with the conditions to know for themselves that pardon is freely extended for every sin."[49]

When we forget that the impossible with God is entirely possible, we limit Him. With God all things are possible. "Let not your heart be troubled; you believe in God, believe also in Me" (John 14:1).

They Have Their Wages

Does he thank that servant because he did the things that were commanded him? I think not.

Luke 17:9.

One day Jesus brought up the topic of wages with His disciples. A man employed servants and sent them out to work. The servants received appropriate wages for the labor performed. "The master has received his due from them, but nothing more worth mentioning. He has not profited by their service to the extent that he should feel obliged to show them special honor. They have their wages, and that is all they should expect. He is under no particular obligation to them. In other words, Jesus had a right to expect much of His disciples, and God has a right to expect much of us today."[50]

"Look at the life of many who claim to be Christians. The Lord has endowed them with capabilities, and power, and influence; He has entrusted them with money, that they may be coworkers with Him in the great redemption. All His gifts are to be used in blessing humanity, in relieving the suffering and the needy. We are to feed the hungry, to clothe the naked, to care for the widow and the fatherless, to minister to the distressed and downtrodden. God never meant that the widespread misery in the world should exist. He never meant that one man should have an abundance of the luxuries of life, while the children of others should cry for bread. The means over and above the actual necessities of life are entrusted to man to do good, to bless humanity."[51] Many see good fortune in business as a sign of approval from God, little realizing that God is under no obligation to them, but rather they are indebted to Him for everything they possess.

"Paul reflects the spirit of true service when he remarks that all he has endured and suffered for Christ's sake is 'nothing to glory of' (1 Cor. 9:16, KJV). His service was motivated by a profound sense of obligation to his Master. In preaching the gospel he was discharging a weighty obligation—'woe is unto me, if I preach not the gospel!' (verse 16, KJV)."[52] Sadly, few Christians recognize that they owe the Master a debt too large to repay. Instead, the majority seem to feel that God owes them eternal life for some small act they performed for Him once or twice a year.

"Every year millions upon millions of human souls are passing into eternity unwarned and unsaved."[53] Why?

"LAZARUS IS DEAD"

"Therefore the sisters sent to Him, saying, "Lord, behold, he whom You love is sick."

John 11:3.

Jesus was still in Perea, about 25 miles distant from Bethany, when the message came. Lazarus, brother to Mary and Martha and beloved friend to the Master, had taken ill. Jesus often rested in his home and found there a haven from the suspicion and hatred surrounding His ministry. Here within this small family Jesus felt free to share with His hearers deeper views of heaven. Among such friends He could speak without resorting to parables. Now sickness had invaded the home of His dear friend, and the two sisters had summoned Him to come to their aid.

The messenger hurried to the Master with a simple message: "Lord, behold, he whom You love is sick." The disciples assumed that Jesus would fly immediately to the bedside of their friend, yet He lingered for two days before making any move toward Bethany. During those days He never mentioned Lazarus, and the disciples could not help thinking of the violent death of John the Baptist. Was it the lot of all who followed the Master? The delay mystified them. "Would He forsake them in trial? Some questioned if they had mistaken His mission. All were deeply troubled."[54] It especially worried the two sisters, who watched and waited as hour by hour their brother's condition worsened until he breathed his last.

After two days Jesus said, "Let us go to Judea again" (John 11:7). By then the disciples had forgotten about Lazarus, but not about the hatred of the Jewish leaders toward them. Returning to Judea seemed the height of folly, and Thomas could see only certain death for them all. Timid and fearful though his character was, he determined loyally to follow his Master back into Judea. Jesus simply said, "Our friend Lazarus sleeps, but I go that I may wake him up" (verse 11). The disciples interpreted Jesus to mean that Lazarus was now calmly sleeping and the crisis had passed. Jesus understood that Lazarus had fallen into the unconscious sleep of death (Eccl. 9:5, 6). His breath had gone, his thoughts had perished (Ps. 146:4). Now, wanting no misunderstanding, Jesus plainly stated, "Lazarus is dead" (John 11:14).

"Christ represents death as a sleep to His believing children. Their life is hid with Christ in God, and until the last trump shall sound those who die will sleep in Him."[55]

THE RESURRECTION AND THE LIFE

Jesus said to her,
"I am the resurrection and the life."
John 11:25.

At last Jesus arrived in Bethany. For Mary and Martha "the moment of greatest discouragement is the time when divine help is nearest."[56] "Among the mourning friends were relatives of the family, some of whom held high positions of responsibility in Jerusalem. Among these were some of Christ's bitterest enemies."[57] Jesus wished to meet with the sisters away from the confusion. Martha quietly received His message and quickly found the Master. "Lord, if You had been here, my brother would not have died (John 11:21)." Jesus replied, "Your brother will rise again" (verse 23). Martha knew Lazarus would rise on the resurrection morn. Jesus tested her immediate faith by stating, "'I am the resurrection and the life. He who believes in Me, though he may die, he shall live. And whoever lives and believes in Me shall never die. Do you believe this?' She said to Him, 'Yes, Lord, I believe that You are the Christ, the Son of God, who is to come into the world'" (verses 25-27).

Secretly Martha sent for Mary, whose greeting to Jesus was identical to Martha's (verse 32). As Jesus beheld the other family members following Mary, their hypocritical sorrow angered Him, yet "in His humanity, Jesus was touched with human sorrow, and wept with the sorrowing."[58] Arriving at the tomb, Jesus ordered that they remove the stone covering. Martha's faith crumbled as she protested. The body had certainly decayed after four days. Tradition said a soul returned for three days with hopes of reentering the body. By the fourth day relatives ceased their vigil for the deceased. Jarius's daughter, the Pharisees claimed, had been simply sleeping. None could argue that here.

Lifting His eyes to heaven, Jesus thanked His Father for the manifestation of His power and then in a calm, loud voice commanded, "Lazarus, come forth!" (verse 43). "His voice, clear and penetrating, pierces the ear of the dead. As He speaks, divinity flashes through humanity. . . . There is a stir in the silent tomb, and he who was dead stands at the door of the sepulcher. His movements are impeded by the graveclothes in which he was laid away, and Christ says to the astonished spectators, 'Loose him, and let him go.'"[59] Lazarus, now in the vigor of health, threw himself at the feet of his Saviour. As sorrow turned to joy, the crowd erupted in thanksgiving. Quietly Jesus withdrew, and when they searched for Him, no one could find him.

One day soon He will call from the grave those who sleep in Him. "Do you believe this?"

A Common Foe

*And one of them,
Caiaphas, being
high priest that year,
said to them, "You
know nothing at all,
nor do you consider
that it is expedient
for us that one man
should die for the
people, and not that
the whole nation
should perish."
John 11:49, 50.*

It took no time at all for the news of Lazarus' resurrection to reach the Jewish rulers in Jerusalem. They called a hasty meeting of the Sanhedrin to decide what they should do. The bulk of the chief priests were Sadducees, a faction that refused to believe that resurrection of the dead was possible at all. Now Jesus had proved their theory false! The Pharisees, who believed in a resurrection, were none the less eager to halt Jesus' influence. His miracle of raising Lazarus from the dead now united both Pharisee and Sadducee in mutual hatred of Him.

"Nicodemus and Joseph had, in former councils, prevented the condemnation of Jesus, and for this reason they were not now summoned. There were present at the council other influential men who believed on Jesus, but their influence prevailed nothing against that of the malignant Pharisees."[60] The council could not agree on everything. Many, as they recalled events from Christ's life, were fearful and troubled. "Under the impression of the Holy Spirit, the priests and rulers could not banish the conviction that they were fighting against God. While the council was at the height of its perplexity, Caiaphas the high priest arose. Caiaphas was a proud and cruel man, overbearing and intolerant. Among his family connections were Sadducees, proud, bold, reckless, full of ambition and cruelty, which they hid under a cloak of pretended righteousness."[61] Even if Jesus were innocent of all charges, he argued, it was necessary to put Him away for the good of the people. His words rang through the hall, "You know nothing at all, nor do you consider that it is expedient for us that one man should die for the people, and not that the whole nation should perish" (John 11:49, 50). Caiaphas was concerned with retaining power and preserving the national state. Unknowingly, he had just spelled out exactly Jesus' true mission.

By His death Christ would gather from all nations of the earth all who should believe in Him. "Then, from that day on, they plotted to put Him to death" (verse 53).

UNDER SENTENCE OF DEATH

Then, from that day on, they plotted to put Him to death. Therefore Jesus no longer walked openly among the Jews, but went from there into the country near the wilderness, to a city called Ephraim, and there remained with His disciples.

John 11:53, 54.

As the Sanhedrin debated the problem of Christ, Satan quickly brought to the minds of its members the indignities they had suffered. "How little He had honored their righteousness. He presented a righteousness far greater, which all who would be children of God must possess. Taking no notice of their forms and ceremonies, He had encouraged sinners to go directly to God as a merciful Father, and make known their wants. Thus, in their opinion, He had set aside the priesthood. He had refused to acknowledge the theology of the rabbinical schools. He had exposed the evil practices of the priests, and had irreparably hurt their influence. He had injured the effect of their maxims and traditions, declaring that though they strictly enforced the ritual law, they made void the law of God."[62]

Wishing to put Jesus to death yet fearing to seize Him in broad daylight, the Sanhedrin decided to bide their time and take Jesus quietly. "Jesus had now given three years of public labor to the world. His example of self-denial and disinterested benevolence was before them. His life of purity, of suffering and devotion, was known to all. Yet this short period of three years was as long as the world could endure the presence of its Redeemer. His life had been one of persecution and insult. Driven from Bethlehem by a jealous king, rejected by His own people at Nazareth, condemned to death without a cause at Jerusalem, Jesus, with His few faithful followers, found temporary asylum in a strange city. He who was ever touched by human woe, who healed the sick, restored sight to the blind, hearing to the deaf, and speech to the dumb, who fed the hungry and comforted the sorrowful, was driven from the people He had labored to save. He who walked upon the heaving billows, and by a word silenced their angry roaring, who cast out devils that in departing acknowledged Him to be the Son of God, who broke the slumbers of the dead, who held thousands entranced by His words of wisdom, was unable to reach the hearts of those who were blinded by prejudice and hatred, and who stubbornly rejected the light."[63]

Is His life attractive to you? By this you will know if you are His disciple.

A SAMARITAN SAYS THANK YOU

Then as He entered a certain village, there met Him ten men who were lepers, who stood afar off. Luke 17:12.

Leaving the vicinity of Bethany because of the hostility directed toward Him, Jesus made one last circuit over the countryside where He had labored for three years. As He started to enter a village, 10 lepers living in the fields called to Him. Society did not allow lepers to mingle with the residents of any city or those who traveled along the roads. Standing far off, they begged, "Jesus, Master, have mercy on us!" (Luke 17:13).

Jesus did pity them and, in keeping with the Mosaic law, He encouraged them, "Go, show yourselves to the priests" (verse 14). It was the duty of the priests to act as public health officers. They alone diagnosed leprosy and ordered segregation, and only they might lift the quarantine order and issue a certificate of cleansing. The 10 men immediately started for the Temple to show themselves to the priests. As they went they received healing. It had been "conditional upon an act of faith. They were not healed so long as they lingered in Jesus' presence, but only as they proceeded to carry out His instructions. When they left Jesus they were still leprous."[64] Once they started their journey to Jerusalem all evidence of the disease left their bodies. Now a curious thing happened. One of the 10 returned to Jesus and fell down on his face at His feet. He praised God for His generous blessing. "Possibly the other nine felt that, as sons of Abraham, they deserved to be healed. But this Samaritan, who may have considered that he did not deserve the blessing of health that had come to him suddenly and unexpectedly, appreciated the gift Heaven now bestowed upon him."[65]

Jesus, looking down at the man, asked, "Were there not ten cleansed? But where are the nine? Were there not any found who returned to give glory to God except this foreigner?" (verses 17, 18). The other nine should have also been grateful for their healing. "Arise, go your way," he said to the healed leper. "Your faith has made you well" (verse 19). It matters to God that we thank Him for His gifts.

"Those who forget to thank God for blessings received, and truly to appreciate what God does for them, are in grave danger of forgetting Him altogether (see Rom. 1:21, 22)."[66]

SECRET LIGHTNING?

For as the lightning that flashes out of one part under heaven shines to the other part under heaven, so also the Son of Man will be in His day.
Luke 17:24.

The Pharisees met Jesus again only weeks before Passover. Again they raised the familiar question, "When will the kingdom of God come?" John the Baptist had declared four years earlier, "Repent, for the kingdom of heaven is at hand!" (Matt. 3:2). Jesus had said the same thing. "The time is fulfilled, and the kingdom of God is at hand. Repent, and believe in the gospel" (Mark 1:15). The Pharisees now wished to know when it would in fact appear. In making such a demand they refused to accept Jesus as the long-awaited Messiah. They looked for a political kingdom and not one of grace. Jesus patiently explained again that "the kingdom of God begins in the heart. Look not here or there for manifestations of earthly power to mark its coming."[67]

Turning to His disciples, Jesus warned them that the kingdom of glory would arrive at His literal second coming. His return would be as impossible to hide as a stroke of lightning. No man knows during a storm in which quadrant of the sky the next lightning bolt will blaze. Suddenly a bright flash dazzles the eye and shocks the senses. The swiftness and brilliance of the light can cause one to jolt back in surprise. So will be the second coming of the Son of man. But "first He must suffer many things and be rejected by this generation" (Luke 17:25). "It was not until after Christ's ascension to His Father, and the outpouring of the Holy Spirit upon the believers, that the disciples fully appreciated the Saviour's character and mission. After they had received the baptism of the Spirit, they began to realize that they had been in the very presence of the Lord of glory."[68] Gradually shadows would lift and they would long once again to sit at His feet and hear Him speak to them.

"It is as true now as in apostolic days, that without the illumination of the divine Spirit, humanity cannot discern the glory of Christ. The truth and work of God are unappreciated by a world-loving and compromising Christianity. Not in the ways of ease, of earthly honor or worldly conformity, are the followers of the Master found. . . . And now, as in Christ's day, they are misunderstood and reproached and oppressed by the priests and Pharisees of their time."[69]

NO RAPTURE HERE

Two men will be in the field: the one will be taken and the other left.

Luke 17:36.

Jesus lifted the curtain of the future for His disciples and described events just preceding His second coming. Just as the Flood surprised the antediluvians and the inhabitants of Sodom and Gomorrah were unaware of their fate, "even so will it be in the day when the Son of Man is revealed" (Luke 17:30). Luke 17 and Matthew 24 contain dual prophecies. Jesus foretold in Matthew 24 the destruction of Jerusalem by Roman armies in A.D. 70. An estimated 100,000 Jews died within the besieged city in a three-month period. No Christian perished during the siege, however. Jesus had warned them not to return from the field to get personal effects or come down from the housetop to take anything from the home. They must flee to the mountains with the clothes upon their backs and not look back. The similarity to Lot and his family was striking.

What common thread binds Luke 17 and Matthew 24? Time. "When will the kingdom of God come?" The discussion is not about *how* it will happen but about *when* it will happen. *When* it takes place some will be prepared and some will not! We must not become so engrossed in the things of this world that we cannot leave them in an instant. "Remember Lot's wife" (Luke 17:32). On the surface two people may appear identical, but one has his or her heart focused on this world while the other is ready for heaven.

Many denominations use these texts to support their belief that God will rapture Christians from this earth before Christ's literal second coming. The word "rapture" does not appear in the Bible. Remember, Christ was stressing preparation for *when* he comes. We know *how* He will arrive: "Behold, He is coming with clouds, and every eye will see Him" (Rev. 1:7). "For as the lightning comes from the east and flashes to the west, so also will the coming of the Son of Man be" (Matt. 24:27). Scripture does not teach a secret Second Coming and then a glorious Third Coming! The Lord's elect will not sneak off the planet. The message is simply this—"Watch therefore, for you know neither the day nor the hour in which the Son of Man is coming" (Matt. 25:13).

All the saints will go through the tribulation (Rev. 7:14). Be ready!

WILL HE FIND FAITH?

Then He spoke a parable to them, that men always ought to pray and not lose heart, saying: "There was in a certain city a judge who did not fear God nor regard man." Luke 18:1, 2.

Jesus told His disciples the story of a widow who could not get from a hardened and corrupt judge what was already due her. "It would seem that the widow's husband had left her property, perhaps mortgaged to others, which they refused to return at the stipulated time according to the provisions of the law. . . . Evidently having no one to champion her rights, the widow was wholly dependent upon the judge's sense of justice and mercy—but he was neither just nor merciful." [70] God is totally unlike this unjust judge! And therein lies the point. The judge does not represent God! "The appeals of the needy and distressed are considered by Him with infinite compassion." [71]

The widow persisted until finally the judge relented and granted her a settlement. She had simply worn the man down. Jesus wants us to understand that if this kind of persistence could sway even a corrupt person, then how much more readily will God respond to those who ask for deliverance. We are His elect, His chosen ones. Often we as Christians fail to realize that God is answering our prayers. He may already be setting in motion forces that will in the long run bring about a better solution than any rapid response. Perhaps He may delay the answer to cause us to realize and appreciate our true need. Sometimes He may be perfecting our character through adversity and trial. Or He may be working through the suffering of His people to reach those who persecute them.

"While the world is progressing in wickedness, none of us need flatter ourselves that we shall have no difficulties. But it is these very difficulties that bring us into the audience chamber of the Most High. . . . Prayer moves the arm of Omnipotence." [72] "If we surrender our lives to His service, we can never be placed in a position for which God has not made provision." [73] "Not one sincere prayer is lost. Amid the anthems of the celestial choir, God hears the cries of the weakest human being." [74]

"There is no danger that the Lord will neglect the prayers of His people. The danger is that in temptation and trial they will become discouraged, and fail to persevere in prayer." [75]

JUSTIFIED

*Two men went up
to the temple to
pray, one a Pharisee
and the other a
tax collector.*

Luke 18:10.

Two men prayed in the Temple. The Pharisee was at the pinnacle of self-professed piety, educated, self-righteous, and proud, while the publican was humble, distrusting of self. The Pharisee loudly proclaimed, "God, you should be glad that You have someone like me in Your church! I fast, I pay tithe, I attend church faithfully, I serve as a church leader. But do You see that scoundrel of a publican over there? Thanks for not making me like him!" The Pharisee strictly observed the law because he sought righteousness through His own efforts. His conduct allowed little room for love of God and none for his fellow humans. God's promise "Blessed are the poor in spirit" (Matt. 5:3) was lost upon him. "There is nothing so offensive to God or so dangerous to the human soul as pride and self-sufficiency. Of all sins it is the most hopeless, the most incurable." [76]

The publican offered a different prayer. Lowering his eyes, he sobbed, "God, be merciful to me a sinner! You alone have the power to redeem me from my sin." Recognizing that he was a sinner, he could not even lift his head to heaven when he prayed, for he saw nothing in his life to recommend him to God. But that is not something that we discover on our own (Jer. 17:9). Only Christ can enable us to fully understand how far from righteousness we are. Outward show and professed piety count for nothing before the Lord, but He values a humble and contrite spirit. Christ can save only the one who recognizes that he or she is a sinner. The one who quietly does the Lord's work with little fanfare or hope of reward God will finally exalt in heaven. "I tell you," Jesus concluded, "this man went down to his house justified [accepted by God and declared righteous before Him] rather than the other; for everyone who exalts himself will be humbled, and he who humbles himself will be exalted" (Luke 18:14). "The Pharisee thought himself righteous (see verse 11) but God did not think so. The publican knew he was a sinner (see verse 13), and this realization opened the way for God to pronounce him sinless—a sinner justified by divine mercy." [77]

"It was the attitudes of the two men toward themselves and toward God that made the difference." [78]

MARRIAGE AND DIVORCE

The Pharisees also came to Him, testing Him, and saying to Him, "Is it lawful for a man to divorce his wife for just any reason?" Matt. 19:3.

For nearly two years spies had attempted to discredit Jesus and halt His work. They had faulted the disciples for eating bread with ceremonially unwashed hands (Mark 7:2). Another time they had accused Jesus of not paying the Temple tax (Matt. 17:24). Framing a woman, they had tried to get Him to agree that she should be stoned for adultery (John 8:4, 5). Now they confronted Him with a question on marriage. "Is it lawful for a man to divorce his wife for just any reason?"

Jesus answered with Scripture, stating, "What God has joined together, let not man separate" (Matt. 19: 6). "The marriage relationship was instituted by God, sanctified by God. It was an all-wise Creator who provided for the marriage relationship; it is He who made it possible and desirable. All who enter upon the marriage relationship are therefore 'joined,' according to the original plan of God, for life."[79] Except for sexual immorality (verse 9), heaven honors no divorce. The Jews had reduced the sanctity of the relationship to a mere legality that one could break on the simplest of whims.

"According to Oriental custom every woman was attached to some man, either her father or her husband, and to be unattached represented disgrace and brought want. Thus when a man dismissed his wife he cast her adrift to fend for herself in a society that had no place for her and that was unsympathetic and hostile toward her. With a view to ameliorating the lot of the divorced woman, God mercifully ordained that a woman thus divorced be given a certificate identifying her as a divorced woman. Thus, she might legally and properly become the wife of another man without any stigma attaching to her."[80] The Pharisees reasoned that if Jesus said divorce was unlawful, He spoke against Moses and the certificate of divorce granted by the Lord. But if He said divorce was lawful, then He undermined the original law of God. The question seemed to offer Jesus a no-win situation! However, He showed that God had never repealed His original law of marriage and that a callous disregard for the wife's rights indicated a national hardness of heart.

In Christ's day God permitted divorce only because of the hardness of the hearts of those who cast out their wives with nothing. God remains a God of love even if a husband's or wife's love and/or support disappears.

THAT HE MIGHT TOUCH THEM

But Jesus called them to Him and said, "Let the little children come to Me, and do not forbid them; for of such is the kingdom of God." Luke 18:16.

Jesus loved children! "He accepted their childish sympathy and their open, unaffected love. The grateful praise from their pure lips was music in His ears, and refreshed His spirit when oppressed by contact with crafty and hypocritical men. Wherever the Saviour went, the benignity of His countenance, and His gentle, kindly manner won the love and confidence of children."[81] It was common practice for parents to bring their children at age 1 to a rabbi for a blessing. The disciples felt Jesus' work was far too important for Him to stop and pay attention to children. They considered the mothers and their children an intolerable distraction. On this particular day, "one mother with her child had left her home to find Jesus. On the way she told a neighbor her errand, and the neighbor wanted to have Jesus bless her children. Thus several mothers came together, with their little ones. Some of the children had passed beyond the years of infancy to childhood and youth. When the mothers made known their desire, Jesus heard with sympathy the timid, tearful request. But He waited to see how the disciples would treat them."[82] He did not have long to wait. The disciples, seeking to protect Him, rudely told the mothers to take the children away and not bother the Master.

"But when Jesus saw it, He was greatly displeased and said to them, 'Let the little children come to Me, and do not forbid them; for of such is the kingdom of God. Assuredly, I say to you, whoever does not receive the kingdom of God as a little child will by no means enter it'" (Mark 10:14, 15). Jesus placed His hands upon the children and pronounced a blessing. He did not baptize them but rather committed them to the care and love of the Father. His words to their little ones comforted, strengthened, and blessed the mothers. Anyone who should make it difficult for little ones to find Jesus will encounter His displeasure and stern rebuke. "[The grace of Christ in the heart] will lead fathers and mothers to treat their children as intelligent beings, as they themselves would like to be treated."[83]

Lead your children to Jesus and treat them as He did, with kindness, gentleness, and love.

CHECKLIST FOR HEAVEN

Now behold, one came and said to Him, "Good Teacher, what good thing shall I do that I may have eternal life?" Matt. 19:16.

A person in the crowd observed the blessing of the children. "He was so deeply moved that as Christ was going on His way, he ran after Him, and kneeling at His feet, asked with sincerity and earnestness the question so important to his soul and to the soul of every human being, 'Good Master, what shall I do that I may inherit eternal life?'"[84] Jesus referred him to the commandments. Obviously Christ held obedience to them in high regard, since He stated that we must keep them to reach the kingdom. The young lawyer quickly accepted this, because he had obeyed the law from youth. "Which ones must I keep?" he persisted. Jesus gave him a sampling of the last six. Each of them dealt with human relationships. By now the young man felt pretty smug. He had not murdered anyone or committed adultery. "What do I still lack?" he asked (Matt. 19:20). Knowing that the man didn't truly understand the law and that his salvation depended on realizing that fact, Jesus quickly brought him to a test. "If you want to be perfect, go, sell what you have and give to the poor, and you will have treasure in heaven; and come, follow Me" (verse 21).

"True, the letter of the law is negative in form, but its spirit calls for positive action. It is not enough to avoid hating or hurting our fellow men; the gospel calls upon us to love and help them as we love ourselves."[85] The one thing the lawyer lacked was vital. He needed the love of God for others to activate his spirit of charity. Jesus longed for him to respond, and the struggle was intense, but his possessions overwhelmed him and he sorrowfully turned away. "But few realize the strength of their love for riches until the test is brought to bear upon them. Many who profess to be Christ's followers then show that they are unprepared for heaven."[86] We expend God-given talents upon personal gain rather than the work of the Lord. Fear of want causes many to build up assets continually because they distrust God and are selfish.

"Only those who will become coworkers with Christ, only those who will say, Lord, all I have and all I am is Thine, will be acknowledged as sons and daughters of God."[87]

A DENARIUS A DAY

"So the last will be first, and the first last. For many are called, but few chosen." Matt. 20:16.

The rich young ruler discovered, to his dismay, that he wasn't ready to sacrifice for others, and thus disqualified for heaven. Turning to His disciples, Jesus said, "Assuredly, . . . it is hard for a rich man to enter the kingdom of heaven" (Matt. 19:23). His statement shocked them. The rabbis taught that wealth indicated God's favor. They asked, "Who then can be saved?" (verse 25). Peter said, "See, we have left all and followed You. Therefore what shall we have?" (verse 27). In other words, "Lord, we were first to follow You. We expect to be adequately compensated for our time in Your service." "In the light of the Saviour's words, their own secret longing for power and riches was revealed."[1] "While they had been attracted by the love of Jesus, the disciples were not wholly free from Pharisaism. They still worked with the thought of meriting a reward in proportion to their labor. They cherished a spirit of self-exaltation and self-complacency, and made comparisons among themselves."[2]

Jesus told them the parable of the vineyard workers. A householder went to the village to find help. Early in the morning he hired several men, promising a denarius for a full day's work. At 9:00 he brought back additional laborers, then still more at noon and again at 3:00. At the eleventh hour, or 5:00 p.m., he hired those still waiting for work. They had not been in the square earlier. Evening arrived, and the householder summoned his steward. "Call the laborers and give them their wages, beginning with the last to the first" (Matt. 20:8). Those hired at 5:00 received a denarius for the hour they worked until sunset. Those who had started work earlier, seeing the generosity of the householder, expected a much larger remuneration for spending all day in the hot sun. But he also gave them a single denarius. When they complained the householder reminded them they had agreed upon the wage when hired and thus had no right to be upset with him. "Take what is yours and go your way" (verse 14). "Divine favor is not earned, as the rabbis taught."[3] Simply because the disciples followed Christ first gave them no additional merit in heaven. The first and last will share the eternal reward, and the first should gladly welcome the last. All should work with an unselfish heart!

"It is not the length of time we labor but our willingness and fidelity in the work that makes it acceptable to God."[4]

"FOR THE SIXTH TIME I TELL YOU"

Behold, we are going up to Jerusalem, and the Son of Man will be betrayed to the chief priests and to the scribes; and they will condemn Him to death, and deliver Him to the Gentiles to mock and to scourge and to crucify. And the third day He will rise again.

Matt. 20:18, 19.

As Jesus headed His little band toward Jerusalem, the disciples were amazed and not a little afraid for their Master and themselves. When Jesus walked on ahead of the disciples it puzzled them also, for usually He stayed with them. Now it seemed as if He wished to be alone. Finally He paused and waited for them. Taking them aside from the other pilgrims journeying to Passover, He began to tell them what would occur in the coming week. It was at least the sixth attempt on His part to convey to them that He would be betrayed and put to death. His language was definite and graphic (see Mark 10:33, 34).

For two years the Jewish leadership had conspired to put Jesus to death. Since the miracle at the Pool of Bethesda, spies had hounded His every step. As His ministry in Galilee expanded, His opposition had become bolder in their public attacks. On two separate occasions they had sought to stone Him. While in Perea they had tried to scare Him into leaving the area out of a fear of Herod. The raising of Lazarus united His enemies, and their plans took on a more sinister shape. The disciples knew danger waited in Jerusalem, but they couldn't see their Master's enemies ever succeeding in killing Him.

"For the first time Jesus specifically mentions the fact that the Gentiles, the Roman authorities, will be instrumental in His death. . . . Three years before, Jesus had told Nicodemus that He must be 'lifted up,' thus implying crucifixion. . . . Now, for the first time, He clearly foretells the manner of His death."[5] The disciples cannot accept what their preconceptions regarding the nature of the kingdom will not allow. "Had not the prophets foretold the glory of the Messiah's reign? In the light of these thoughts, His words in regard to betrayal, persecution, and death seemed vague and shadowy. Whatever difficulties might intervene, they believed that the kingdom was soon to be established."[6] But we should not rush to judge the disciples' failure to understand Jesus' words.

Who of us live as if we truly believe Him when He repeatedly tells us, "Behold, I am coming quickly!" (Rev. 3:11).

SALOME'S FAVOR

Then the mother of Zebedee's sons came to Him with her sons, kneeling down and asking something from Him. . . . "Grant that these two sons of mine may sit, one on Your right hand and the other on the left, in Your kingdom." Matt. 20:20, 21.

One day Peter asked what the twelve might expect as reward for following Jesus. Jesus answered, "Assuredly I say to you, that in the regeneration, when the Son of Man sits on the throne of His glory, you who have followed Me will also sit on twelve thrones, judging the twelve tribes of Israel" (Matt. 19:28). Perhaps His reply prompted what happened next. "John, the son of Zebedee, had been one of the first two disciples who had followed Jesus. He and his brother James had been among the first group who had left all for His service. . . . Their mother was a follower of Christ, and had ministered to Him freely of her substance. With a mother's love and ambition for her sons, she coveted for them the most honored place in the new kingdom."[7] Thus began another of the simple incidents that showed that the disciples had no idea what was to come.

The mother of James and John was most likely Salome (Matt. 27:56; Mark 15:40; 16:1). Some think that perhaps she was a sister to Mary, the mother of Christ (John 19:25). Whether a relation or not, she asked that her sons should sit on His right and left hand. Jesus didn't rebuke the three for their covetousness. Instead, He asked if they could drink the cup He would drink and be baptized as He would be. Although they didn't understand His mysterious words, they quickly replied that they would consider such a thing an honor. Christ answered, "You will indeed drink My cup, and be baptized with the baptism that I am baptized with; but to sit on My right hand and on My left is not Mine to give, but it is for those whom it is prepared by My Father" (Matt. 20:23). Jesus would drink His cup of suffering in Gethsemane, and His baptism would be His death upon Calvary. James would die by the sword, the first disciple martyred. John would outlive the others but would die in exile on Patmos.

"Position [in heaven] is not awarded on the basis of influence or favoritism, nor can it be earned. It is awarded exclusively on the basis of fitness, and fitness is measured by the spirit of service for others."[8]

GREATNESS IS SERVING

For even the Son of Man did not come to be served, but to serve, and to give His life a ransom for many.

Mark 10:45.

The disciples were furious! Each was upset that two fellow disciples had seemingly stolen the best positions while they themselves had hesitated to ask for them. The strife for supremacy had not ceased. Here, during the last few days of Christ's ministry, we see depicted a sad truth. The disciples still did not esteem others greater than themselves. They could not seem to break free from the belief that the one in charge gets there by virtue of advanced education, influence, wealth, or family position. Religion was for them all about authority!

Jesus had taught that no position was superior to that of a servant. The disciples had already forgotten His Capernaum counsel. Their dispute over greatness then had led Him to say, "If anyone desires to be first, he shall be last of all and servant of all" (Mark 9:35). "Therefore whoever humbles himself as this little child is the greatest in the kingdom of heaven" (Matt. 18:4). Our world recognizes power, but Christ calls the strong to mentor the weak. God grants us power to nurture and serve.

"You know that those who are considered rulers over the Gentiles lord it over them, and their great ones exercise authority over them. Yet it shall not be so among you; but whoever desires to become great among you shall be your servant. And whoever of you desires to be first shall be slave of all. For even the Son of Man did not come to be served, but to serve, and to give His life a ransom for many" (Mark 10:42-45). "Christ was establishing a kingdom on different principles. He called men, not to authority, but to service, the strong to bear the infirmities of the weak. Power, position, talent, education, placed their possessor under the greater obligation to serve his fellow."[9] Unselfish love is the measure of true greatness.

"The life of Jesus was preeminently a life of service. Throughout His ministry He took advantage of none of the privileges commonly claimed by the rabbis, He had no possessions that He might call His own, He never exercised divine power for His own advantage."[10] Jesus is our example. When granted opportunities to share the mission of our Lord, we must look for the true reward.

Remember, true greatness is found in serving others.

BLIND BARTIMAEUS

Then Jesus said to him, "Go your way; your faith has made you well." And immediately he received his sight and followed Jesus on the road.

Mark 10:52.

Jesus and His disciples crossed the Jordan about five miles east of Jericho and accompanied the large Passover crowds toward Jerusalem. Set with palms and a wide variety of flowers and fruits, Jericho beckoned all to stop and spend some time before starting the steep and desolate climb up the Wadi Qelt. Sitting just outside the city gates most every day was a blind man named Bartimaeus, or more correctly, the son of Timaeus. As the throng passed, he heard the people discussing the "Son of David." Hearing that Jesus was nearby, he began to call out, "Jesus, Son of David, have mercy on me!" The people tried to quiet him. If Roman or even Jewish authorities heard him, there would be trouble. But he only pleaded louder, "Son of David, have mercy on me!"

Jesus stopped. Facing those around Him, He commanded that someone bring the man to Him. Those nearest Bartimaeus told him to rejoice. "Be of good cheer. Rise, He is calling you" (Mark 10:49). Casting aside his cloak, Bartimaeus let himself be led to Jesus. So far the story doesn't differ from other miracles performed during Christ's ministry. It is unique, however, for it shows amazing clarity of vision on the part of one without sight and amazing blindness on the part of those claiming superior spiritual vision. "Blind Bartimaeus is waiting by the wayside; he has waited long to meet Christ. Throngs of people who possess their sight are passing to and fro, but they have no desire to see Jesus." [11]

Jesus asked, "What do you want Me to do for you?" (verse 51). "It was obvious that the blind man sought to have his sight restored. As usual, however, Jesus desired that the suppliant make a specific request, as a recognition of need and an evidence of faith. It was not alone for Bartimaeus himself, however, that Jesus put this question to him. He desired that those who witnessed the event should better understand the significance of the miracle." [12] Christ said to him, "Go your way; your faith has made you well" (verse 52).

"All who feel their need of Christ as did blind Bartimaeus, and who will be as earnest and determined as he was, will, like him, receive the blessing which they crave." [13] "A sense of need and of dependence upon Christ must accompany faith." [14]

We must not have "blind faith," but rather blind (Bartimaeus) faith!

MAKE HASTE AND COME DOWN

And when Jesus came to the place, He looked up and saw him, and said to him, "Zacchaeus, make haste and come down, for today I must stay at your house."
Luke 19:5.

Jericho was one of the cities anciently set apart for the priests, and at this time large numbers of priests had their residence there. But the city had also a population of a widely different character. It was a great center of traffic, and Roman officials and soldiers, with strangers from different quarters, were found there, while the collection of customs made it the home of many publicans. 'The chief among the publicans,' Zacchaeus, was a Jew, and detested by his countrymen."[15] Extortion, graft, bribery, and kickbacks might buy a high standard of living, but they couldn't purchase friends.

Zacchaeus had heard the Baptist preach at the river Jordan. He knew his life didn't conform to Scripture, but the Spirit's power was working on his heart. Having heard of Jesus, he longed to meet the Man who had within His own disciples a publican named Matthew. Word reached him, "Jesus is entering Jericho." "The streets were crowded, and Zacchaeus, who was small of stature, could see nothing over the heads of the people. None would give way for him; so, running a little in advance of the multitude, to where a wide-branching fig tree hung over the way, the rich tax collector climbed to a seat among the boughs, whence he could survey the procession as it passed below. The crowd comes near, it is going by, and Zacchaeus scans with eager eyes to discern the one figure he longs to see."[16] Suddenly, just beneath the tree, the group stopped, "and One looks upward whose glance seems to read the soul. Almost doubting his senses, the man in the tree hears the words, 'Zacchaeus, make haste, and come down; for today I must abide at thy house.'"[17] Jesus knew his name and his heart's longing! And He wanted to visit his home even if the man's neighbors wouldn't!

Those present couldn't understand Jesus' actions. Zacchaeus was a thief! Turning to them, Zacchaeus confessed, "'Look, Lord, I give half of my goods to the poor; and if I have taken anything from anyone by false accusation, I restore fourfold.' And Jesus said to him, 'Today salvation has come to this house'" (Luke 19:8, 9). The law of Moses required that one fifth be added to the principal as restitution. Fourfold restoration was extreme, but Zacchaeus was serious about repentance.

"No repentance is genuine that does not work reformation."[18]

259

LAZARUS MUST ALSO DIE

But the chief priests plotted to put Lazarus to death also, because on account of him many of the Jews went away and believed in Jesus. John 12:10, 11.

Jesus entered Bethany six days before Passover, while many of those traveling with Him pressed on to Jerusalem and spread the news of His coming. Jesus spent the Sabbath in the home of Lazarus, Mary, and Martha. "Many flocked to Bethany, some out of sympathy with Jesus, and others from curiosity to see one who had been raised from the dead. Many expected to hear from Lazarus a wonderful account of scenes witnessed after death. They were surprised that he told them nothing. He had nothing of this kind to tell. Inspiration declares, 'The dead know not anything. . . . Their love, and their hatred, and their envy, is now perished' (Eccl. 9:5, 6, KJV). But Lazarus did have a wonderful testimony to bear in regard to the work of Christ. He had been raised from the dead for this purpose. With assurance and power he declared that Jesus was the Son of God."[19]

The chief priests in Jerusalem could charge Lazarus with no crime, and yet they felt that they had to silence him. The man was a living rebuke of their denial of the resurrection. The same night that Jesus attended the feast at Simon's, the assembly of priests and rulers met. They had already decided to have Jesus killed at the earliest opportunity, but the raising of Lazarus filled them with great fear. "Events of the first few days of the crucifixion week served only to intensify the feeling of the people that in Jesus the nation had found the Leader of whom the prophets had spoken, and the Pharisees exclaimed in genuine perplexity, 'Perceive ye how ye prevail nothing? behold, the world is gone after him' (John 12:19, KJV; *The Desire of Ages*, pp. 570, 572, 590, 594). A crisis was imminent, and unless they could dispose of Him, their own fall appeared certain. They felt that they must act swiftly and secretly. Furthermore, a popular uprising in support of Jesus as Messiah-King . . . would certainly bring down the oppressive might of Rome even more firmly upon the nation. On the other hand, to seize Jesus openly might spark a popular uprising in His favor."[20] Many of these same individuals had mourned the death of Lazarus and pretended to pity his sisters. Now they decided that Lazarus and Jesus must both die if they were to retain their position over the people.

The desire to maintain power is a dangerous intoxicant.

Shame Seized Him

Then one of the Pharisees asked Him to eat with him. And He went to the Pharisee's house, and sat down to eat. Luke 7:36.

Simon of Bethany was one of the few Pharisees who openly followed Jesus. "He acknowledged Jesus as a teacher, and hoped that He might be the Messiah, but he had not accepted Him as the Saviour. His character was not transformed; his principles were unchanged."[21] Jesus had cured Simon of leprosy, and now he sought to honor Him with a feast. He invited Mary, Martha, and Lazarus. Mary had heard Jesus describing His imminent death. The resurrection of her beloved brother and the incredible joy Jesus had brought into her life deeply touched her. She had no difficulty acknowledging Christ as her Saviour. "It was He who had lifted her from despair and ruin. Seven times she had heard His rebuke of the demons that controlled her heart and mind."[22]

At great personal expense she had purchased an alabaster box containing spikenard ointment with which she intended to embalm her Lord's body. Now people said He was to be crowned King. Confused and yet joyful her Lord was not to be killed, Mary sought to honor Jesus. Breaking the box, she poured it upon His feet; then, mingling her tears with the ointment, she knelt and wiped His feet with her long hair. As Jesus' feet were away from the table, what she did at first occurred in secret. "The ointment filled the room with its fragrance, and published her act to all present. Judas looked upon this act with great displeasure. Instead of waiting to hear what Christ would say of the matter, he began to whisper his complaints to those near him, throwing reproach upon Christ for suffering such waste."[23]

Judas's criticism swayed Simon the Pharisee. Surprised that Jesus did not rebuke Mary, he could not understand why Christ would allow a woman "whose sins were too great to be forgiven"[24] to approach Him in this manner. He forgot that he himself had led Mary into sin.[25] Jesus kindly pointed out that He had saved Simon from the living death of leprosy, yet he still questioned Christ's divinity. His hardened heart caused him to judge others harshly. Yes, Mary had been forgiven much, yet Jesus had dealt with Simon no less compassionately. Shame seized the man. "He saw the magnitude of the debt which he owed his Lord. His pride was humbled, he repented, and the proud Pharisee became a lowly, self-sacrificing disciple."[26]

How much has been forgiven you?

HER HEART TREMBLED

Then He said to her, "Your sins are forgiven."

Luke 7:48.

Judas was treasurer for the disciples, and from their little store he had secretly drawn for his own use, thus narrowing down their resources to a meager pittance. He was eager to put into the bag all that he could obtain. The treasure in the bag was often drawn upon to relieve the poor; and when something that Judas did not think essential was bought, he would say, Why is this waste?"[27] Thus Judas was the first to complain about Mary. "Why was this fragrant oil not sold for three hundred denarii and given to the poor? This he [Judas] said, not that he cared for the poor, but because he was a thief, and had the money box; and he used to take what was put in it" (John 12:5, 6).

"Mary heard the words of criticism. Her heart trembled within her. She feared that her sister would reproach her for extravagance. The Master, too, might think her improvident. Without apology or excuse she was about to shrink away, when the voice of her Lord was heard, 'Let her alone, why trouble ye her?' He saw that she was embarrassed and distressed. He knew that in this act of service she had expressed her gratitude for the forgiveness of her sins, and He brought relief to her mind. Lifting His voice above the murmur of criticism, He said, 'She hath wrought a good work on me. For ye have the poor with you always, and whensoever ye will ye may do them good; but me ye have not always. She hath done what she could: she is come aforehand to anoint my body to the burying.'"[28]

Mary seized the opportunity to lavish her love upon the Master while He yet lived. Her act of love strengthened him. "And as He went down into the darkness of His great trial, He carried with Him the memory of that deed, an earnest of the love that would be His from His redeemed ones forever."[29] Mary's example is one we all need to emulate. We must speak words of kindness and reconciliation now rather than at the graveside of the one we wish we had honored. Fewer still appreciate what Christ has done for them.

"In the gift of Jesus, God gave all heaven."[30] *Many put off giving Him gifts of devotion until it is too late to offer anything at all. He has given us so much and He asks for so little!*

THE RIGID RULE OF JUSTICE

Then He turned to the woman and said to Simon, "Do you see this woman? . . . Her sins, which are many, are forgiven, for she loved much. But to whom little is forgiven, the same loves little."

Luke 7:44-47.

The gift of the spikenard ignited a controversy. Simon took the side of Judas. Quick to judge, he was slow to show compassion or mercy. In the midst of the murmuring, Jesus turned to Simon and said, "There was a certain creditor who had two debtors. One owed five hundred denarii, and the other fifty. And when they had nothing with which to repay, he freely forgave them both. Tell Me, therefore, which of them will love him more?" (Luke 7:41, 42). Quickly Simon answered, "I suppose the one whom he forgave more" (verse 43). Jesus said, "You have rightly judged" (verse 43). The two debtors represented Simon and Mary. The point of the parable was not to set a degree of obligation upon certain sins, but to teach that each owed much more than they could ever hope to reimburse. Simon needed to understand that he was not more righteous than Mary was. His sins were every bit as serious as hers, yet he saw himself through self-righteous eyes and judged others harshly. Many Christians are like Simon. It is easy to put on robes of sanctimonious judgment but hard to remove them.

The Pharisee understood that Jesus could read motives underlying acts. He had invited Jesus to supper not out of gratitude for healing but as a way to appear important before others. "Simon's coldness and neglect toward the Saviour showed how little he appreciated the mercy he had received. He had thought he honored Jesus by inviting Him to his house. But he now saw himself as he really was."[31] "Tactfully the Saviour led the proud Pharisee to realize that his sin, his seduction of Mary, was greater than hers, as 500 denarii was greater than 50."[32] Though Simon had treated Mary shamefully, it deeply touched him that Jesus did not shame him before his guests. Such an action would have hardened the proud man's heart against Christ. Simon now understood what Jesus meant when he told Mary, "Your faith has saved you. Go in peace" (verse 50). "The hospitality of Simon was insignificant by comparison with the boundless gratitude of Mary."[33]

"Jesus knows the circumstances of every soul. You may say, I am sinful, very sinful. You may be; but the worse you are, the more you need Jesus. He turns no weeping, contrite one away." [34]

REVENGE FOR REPROOF

But Jesus said,

"Let her alone."

John 12:7.

As financier [Judas] thought himself greatly superior to his fellow disciples, and he had led them to regard him in the same light. He had gained their confidence, and had a strong influence over them. His professed sympathy for the poor deceived them, and his artful insinuation caused them to look distrustfully upon Mary's devotion."[35] Jesus understood the motives of the disciple's heart. It would have been easy to expose him for the traitor he was, but "had Christ unmasked Judas, this would have been urged as a reason for the betrayal. And though charged with being a thief, Judas would have gained sympathy, even among the disciples. The Saviour reproached him not, and thus avoided giving him an excuse for his treachery. But the look which Jesus cast upon Judas convinced him that the Saviour penetrated his hypocrisy, and read his base, contemptible character."[36]

Judas had taken a dramatic stand against Mary's actions. Jesus now took a decidedly different stance. The disciple interpreted Jesus' support of Mary as an insult. He felt that he had lost face before the others, and, feeling rebuked, decided to get revenge. "From the supper he went directly to the palace of the high priest, where he found the council assembled, and he offered to betray Jesus into their hands."[37] The sudden turn of events overjoyed the priests. Here was their chance to take Jesus quietly and secretly. Judas had received every opportunity afforded the other disciples, yet he had allowed greed to overcome him. He begrudged the expense showered upon Jesus and wished it for himself. In this sense he duplicated the sin of Satan, who coveted the position of Christ and desired it himself. The fact that the box of ointment cost 300 denarii vanished in the low price he set upon his Lord. For all of his skills as treasurer, Judas made a bad bargain. For one tenth the cost of the ointment, he sold his Master. For 30 pieces of silver, the price of a slave, he betrayed his Lord.

"The loneliness of Christ, separated from the heavenly courts, living the life of humanity, was never understood or appreciated by the disciples as it should have been." [38] *Perhaps we do not understand or appreciate it as we should either.*

A RELIGIOUS FRAUD

Then one of the twelve, called Judas Iscariot, went to the chief priests and said, "What are you willing to give me if I deliver Him to you?" And they counted out to him thirty pieces of silver. Matt. 26:14, 15.

One cannot look at the life of Judas without wondering what went wrong. Here was a man who had joined himself to the Master early in the ministry. He had felt the tugging of the Holy Spirit. Jesus had accepted him into the twelve, sent him out as an evangelist, and given him power to cast out devils and heal the sick. "But Judas did not come to the point of surrendering himself fully to Christ. He did not give up his worldly ambition or his love of money. . . . He felt that he could retain his own judgment and opinions, and he cultivated a disposition to criticize and accuse."[39]

The disciples considered Judas to be the most educated and capable one among them. The respect the disciples showed him, however, wasn't mutual. "Judas summed up all the disciples, and flattered himself that the church would often be brought into perplexity and embarrassment if it were not for his ability as a manager."[40] At the same time he subtly sought to undermine Jesus. Often he confused the disciples by introducing texts having nothing to do with the context of Jesus' words. He stirred up hopes for a temporal kingdom and played down the spiritual tone of conversations. "The dissension as to which of them should be greatest was generally excited by Judas."[41]

In his heart Judas had deserted Jesus after the Bread of Life sermon. He understood then that the kingdom to come was spiritual, not temporal. Still, he sought to advance Jesus as king and planned somehow to save John the Baptist from prison. But none of it happened. Then he thought Jesus should avenge John's death. Again Jesus did nothing. As each step in his plan fell apart, so too did belief. Judas never really imagined that Jesus would permit Himself to be arrested. He would just force Jesus into action and get credit for placing Him on the throne of David. Thus Judas hoped to gain the first position next to Christ in the new kingdom. Invariably Judas asked of everything, "What's in it for me?" True to form, he asked this time, "What are you willing to give me if I deliver Him to you?"

How many of us are religious frauds like Judas?

JESUS

MINISTRY IN DEATH
Christ Our Sacrifice

Passion Week—Spring A.D. 31

Matthew 21:1-27:66

Mark 11:1-15:47

Luke 19:29-23:56

John 12:12-19:42

The Desire of Ages, pp. 569-778

HOSANNA TO THE SON OF DAVID

Rejoice greatly, O daughter of Zion! Shout, O daughter of Jerusalem! Behold, your King is coming to you; He is just and having salvation, lowly and riding on a donkey, a colt, the foal of a donkey. Zech. 9:9.

Early Sunday morning multitudes of people flocked from Jerusalem toward Bethany to catch a glimpse of Jesus. The perfect spring weather made the joy of the people more festive. "All nature seemed to rejoice. The trees were clothed with verdure, and their blossoms shed a delicate fragrance on the air. A new life and joy animated the people. The hope of the new kingdom was again springing up."[42] The disciples were excited as their hope for a temporal kingdom seemed about to come true. They had forgotten their Lord's words about His suffering and death. Today would witness a coronation! The 500-year-old prophecy of Zechariah was about to be fulfilled.

Jesus normally avoided publicity, but now He sent two disciples to borrow an ass and its colt. Always before Jesus had traveled by foot, and it surprised the disciples that He now chose to ride. He was following Jewish custom by riding upon the animal the former kings of Israel had ridden to their coronations. Lazarus led the colt. Also Jesus did something else different that day. He called Himself *"Kurios,"* or "Lord." Normally He referred to Himself as the Son of man.

As the procession left Bethany for Jerusalem, the crowd grew larger. Excited and glad, the people eagerly hailed Jesus as King of the Jews. The title would soon be hurled back at Him and nailed above His head to His cross. "Spectators were constantly mingling with the throng, and asking, Who is this? What does all this commotion signify?"[43] Thousands welcomed Jesus. Waving palm fronds and singing songs of praise, many removed their mantles and spread them before the colt. "The priests at the temple sound the trumpet for evening service, but there are few to respond, and the rulers say to one another in alarm, 'The world is gone after him.'"[44] Never had the world seen such a triumphant procession! The Pharisees tried to quiet the people, but their pleas and threats only increased the adulation. The Romans would not allow such demonstrations, they protested as they pushed through the crowd. "Teacher, rebuke Your disciples," they demanded (Luke 19:39). Jesus replied, "I tell you that if these should keep silent, the stones would immediately cry out" (verse 40).

How many of us find ourselves cowed into silence by those who don't want to hear about Jesus?

"HOW CAN I GIVE YOU UP?"

Now as He drew near, He saw the city and wept over it. Luke 19:41.

The loud Hosannas rang from mountaintop to mountaintop and across the Kidron Valley to Jerusalem. It seemed the whole city was prepared to meet her King. "The blind whom He had restored to sight were leading the way. The dumb whose tongues He had loosed shouted the loudest hosannas. The cripples whom He had healed bounded with joy, and were the most active in breaking the palm branches and waving them before the Saviour. Widows and orphans were exalting the name of Jesus for His works of mercy to them. The lepers whom He had cleansed spread their untainted garments in His path, and hailed Him as the King of glory. Those whom His voice had awakened from the sleep of death were in that throng."[45] The procession reached the crest of the Mount of Olives. Below, the declining sun outlined Jerusalem. The Sheep Gate (to the northeast of the city) and, beyond it, Calvary, were visible. The Temple stood in splendor in the midst of the panorama as Jesus halted.

"Jesus gazes upon the scene, and the vast multitude hush their shouts, spellbound by the sudden vision of beauty. All eyes turn upon the Saviour, expecting to see in His countenance the admiration they themselves feel. But instead of this they behold a cloud of sorrow. They are surprised and disappointed to see His eyes fill with tears, and His body rock to and fro like a tree before the tempest, while a wail of anguish bursts from His quivering lips, as if from the depths of a broken heart."[46] Jesus saw what the multitude could not. Looking down through the years to Roman armies encircling the doomed city, He watched its residents perish. Jerusalem had rejected the prophets and even now was preparing to reject the Son of God. Had it not been for the pride of the Pharisees, their hypocrisy, their hatred, their jealousy, Jesus might have been able to reach Israel with His message of salvation. Now their doom was about to be sealed. Had Jerusalem heeded the messages from God, she might have been the world's crowning city, but the vision was fading away.

Jesus wept. How could He give them up? A whole nation was willing itself to reject truth. How can He give us up? Jesus still weeps.

THEIR DAY OF LIGHT

And Jesus went into Jerusalem and into the temple.

Mark 11:11.

As the procession paused upon the Mount of Olives, Jerusalem's rulers arrived to halt the great crusade. "Jesus knew that this episode in His life mission would inevitably lead to the cross, yet went through with it steadfastly and purposefully. It was necessary that the eyes of all men be turned toward Him in the closing days of His life, that all might understand, if they would, the significance of His mission to earth."[47] "He came to His own, and His own did not receive Him" (John 1:11).

The priests brought no palm branches, the symbol of triumph. No shouts of Hosanna escaped their lips. Instead they asked His disciples, "Who is this?" "The disciples, filled with the spirit of inspiration, answer this question. In eloquent strains they repeat the prophecies concerning Christ: *Adam* will tell you, It is the seed of the woman that shall bruise the serpent's head. Ask *Abraham*, he will tell you, It is 'Melchizedek King of Salem,' King of Peace (Gen. 14:18, KJV). *Jacob* will tell you, He is Shiloh of the tribe of Judah. *Isaiah* will tell you, 'Immanuel,' 'Wonderful, Counselor, The mighty God, The everlasting Father, The Prince of Peace' (Isa. 7:14; 9:6, KJV). *Jeremiah* will tell you, The Branch of David, 'the Lord our Righteousness' (Jer. 23:6, KJV). *Daniel* will tell you, He is the Messiah. *Hosea* will tell you, He is 'the Lord God of hosts; the Lord is His memorial' (Hosea 12:5, KJV). *John the Baptist* will tell you, He is 'the Lamb of God, which taketh away the sin of the world' (John 1:29, KJV). *The great Jehovah* has proclaimed from His throne, 'This is my beloved Son' (Matt. 3:17, KJV). *We, His disciples*, declare, This is Jesus, the Messiah, the Prince of life, the Redeemer of the world. And *the prince of the powers of darkness* acknowledges Him, saying, 'I know thee who thou art, the Holy One of God' (Mark 1:24, KJV)."[48]

So much evidence, yet the rulers wouldn't accept Christ's divinity. Trying to silence the crowd, the rulers themselves got accused of fomenting trouble. Jesus passed unnoticed into the Temple, where He lingered only a short time. It was late, so He withdrew quietly to Bethany, and when the people searched for Him to place Him upon the throne, they could not find Him.

Two groups of people met that day: one group moving toward Jerusalem singing praises and the other coming out from Jerusalem to reject their Saviour. Two groups then, two groups now.

Preten- tious Foliage

Now the next day, when they had come out from Bethany, He was hungry. And seeing from afar a fig tree having leaves, He went to see if perhaps He would find something on it.

Mark 11:12, 13.

The morning after the triumphal entry, while returning to the Temple from Bethany, Jesus passed a fig orchard. Being hungry, He spied a tree whose full foliage promised fruit. It was too early for figs, but it is the nature of a fig tree to bear fruit before leaves. "When He came to it, He found nothing but leaves, for it was not the season for figs. In response Jesus said to it, 'Let no one eat fruit from you ever again.' And His disciples heard it" (Mark 11:13, 14). The cursing of the fig tree astonished the disciples. Always before Jesus had restored and healed, never destroyed. Why had He done it? Jesus linked the earlier parable of the fig tree with the act of cursing the fig tree. The fig tree represented the Jewish nation. Their lack of concern for the welfare of those perishing in sin around them while they had great light was but part of their downfall. In His curse appeared the result of the previous parable. Even after the gardener pleaded for more time, Israel determined its own destruction by rejecting Christ.

"The Jewish religion, with its magnificent temple, its sacred altars, its mitered priests and impressive ceremonies, was indeed fair in the outward appearance, but humility, love, and benevolence were lacking." [49] The other trees in the orchard represented the Gentile nations. Leafless, they raised no expectation of fruit, so they were not the disappointment the Jewish nation was. They made no pretension of serving God. In fact, they did not as yet know God and His ways. But their time would come. To know truth and boast of God's favor, yet yield no fruit is to receive the curse of God. Jesus came to Israel searching for "self-sacrifice and compassion, zeal for God, and a deep yearning of soul for the salvation of their fellow men. Had they kept the law of God, they would have done the same unselfish work that Christ did. But love to God and man was eclipsed by pride and self-sufficiency. They brought ruin upon themselves by refusing to minister to others." [50]

Are we likewise failing as we strive to keep the law while refusing to reach out to minister to others? Are we nothing but leaves? Where is the gospel fruit?

Divinity Flashed Through Humanity

Then He taught, saying to them, "Is it not written, 'My house shall be called a house of prayer for all nations'? But you have made it a 'den of thieves.'"

Mark 11:17.

Jesus had cleansed the Temple at the beginning of His Judean ministry in the spring of A.D. 28. Now with piercing eyes He looked once again over the desecrated outer court. "The condition of things was even worse than before. The outer court of the temple was like a vast cattle yard. With the cries of the animals and the sharp chinking of coin was mingled the sound of angry altercation between traffickers, and among them were heard the voices of men in sacred office. The dignitaries of the temple were themselves engaged in buying and selling and the exchange of money. So completely were they controlled by their greed of gain that in the sight of God they were no better than thieves."[51]

Everyone stared at Him. "Priest and ruler, Pharisee and Gentile, looked with astonishment and awe upon Him who stood before them with the majesty of heaven's King. Divinity flashed through humanity, investing Christ with a dignity and glory He had never manifested before. Those standing nearest Him drew as far away as the crowd would permit. Except for a few of His disciples, the Saviour stood alone. Every sound was hushed. The deep silence seemed unbearable. Christ spoke with a power that swayed the people like a mighty tempest: 'It is written, my house shall be called the house of prayer; but ye have made it a den of thieves.' His voice sounded like a trumpet through the temple. The displeasure of His countenance seemed like consuming fire."[52] Jesus stood as Master and King, directly asserting His rightful ownership of the Temple courts and clearly showing the majesty the crowd the previous day had wished to bestow upon Him.

Three years previously the priests had fled in terror before Christ, and they had lived with the shame of that panic-stricken retreat ever since. They had determined that never again would they surrender their dignity and flee from such a humble Man. "Yet they were now more terrified than before, and in greater haste to obey His command. There were none who dared question His authority. Priests and traders fled from His presence, driving their cattle before them."[53]

If Jesus were to come to your church lobby, what noise would greet Him— praise, or the noise of common everyday conversation? Think about your attitude of worship in His house.

Offensive Shouts of Rejoicing

But when the chief priests and scribes saw the wonderful things that He did, and the children crying out in the temple and saying, "Hosanna to the Son of David!" they were indignant. Matt. 21:15.

The priests and traders fleeing the Temple encountered those coming with their sick. As their terror subsided, the priests quietly returned, curious to know what Jesus was doing. "Upon entering, they stood transfixed before the wonderful scene. They saw the sick healed, the blind restored to sight, the deaf receive their hearing, and the crippled leap for joy. The children were foremost in the rejoicing. Jesus had healed their maladies; He had clasped them in His arms, received their kisses of grateful affection, and some of them had fallen asleep upon His breast as He was teaching the people."[54] "Baby voices were lisping the praises of the mighty Healer. Yet with the priests and elders all this did not suffice to overcome their prejudice and jealousy."[55] Such sounds alienated the Temple rulers. Frantically they appealed to Jesus to stop the noise and quiet the acclamations of praise. "Do You hear what these are saying?" they asked Jesus (Matt. 21:16). "Yes," He replied. "Have you never read, 'Out of the mouth of babes and nursing infants You have perfected praise'?" (verse 16). Jesus aimed a powerful rebuke at the religious leaders of Israel. The quotation of Psalm 8:2 should have aroused in them the realization that current events were Scripture being fulfilled.

"The priests and rulers of Israel refused to herald His glory, and God moved upon the children to be His witnesses. Had the voices of the children been silent, the very pillars of the temple would have sounded the Saviour's praise."[56] The same men who had licensed the illegal trafficking and noise in the Temple courtyards could not understand or tolerate the ministry of mercy or the sound of praises sung to the Lord. "Jesus had taken His position as guardian of the temple. . . . Never before had His words and works possessed so great power. He had done marvelous works throughout Jerusalem, but never before in a manner so solemn and impressive. In the presence of the people who had witnessed His wonderful works, the priests and rulers dared not show Him open hostility. Though enraged and confounded by His answer, they were unable to accomplish anything further that day."[57] Jesus retired to Bethany to spend Monday night among friends.

We too will still find solace, peace, and healing for our spiritual woes in His presence.

"NEITHER WILL I TELL YOU"

Now when He came into the temple, the chief priests and the elders of the people confronted Him as He was teaching.

Matt. 21:23.

Jesus returned to the Temple Tuesday morning to teach. The priests and elders confronted Him, demanding, "By what authority are You doing these things? And who gave You this authority?" (Matt. 21:23). It was a common question asked of all who might be prophets of God. No person could teach the people without rabbinical permission unless he was such a prophet. In that instance, leadership expected the prophet to provide evidence of his or her divine commission. The religious rulers had raised the same question with John the Baptist only three and one-half years before (John 1:19). Now the priests sought to find in Jesus' response something to condemn Him by. If He claimed to be from God, they would deny it. Jesus knew they would not recognize in His works God's divine character. He knew they wished instead to stir up the people against Him. As a result He evaded their question and aimed one at them, the approved procedure in rabbinical debate.

"I also will ask you one thing, which if you tell Me, I likewise will tell you by what authority I do these things: The baptism of John—where was it from? From heaven or from men?" (Matt. 21:24, 25). If they attempted to explain the mission of John the Baptist, they would find themselves forced to answer their own question to Jesus. The core of both questions involved their ability to evaluate divine credentials. Hurriedly they drew aside and conferred with each other. They were in a dilemma. If they honestly answered that John's ministry was from heaven, then Jesus would most likely ask why they did not believe John when he confessed Jesus as the Messiah. But if they said John's ministry was only human, they would bring upon themselves the wrath of those people who believed John to have been a divine prophet.

"With intense interest the multitude awaited the decision. They knew that the priests had professed to accept the ministry of John, and they expected them to acknowledge without a question that he was sent from God. But after conferring secretly together, the priests decided not to commit themselves. Hypocritically professing ignorance, they said, 'We cannot tell.' 'Neither tell I you,' said Christ, 'by what authority I do these things.' "[58]

How much evidence do you require before you acknowledge Jesus as the Messiah?

TAX COLLECTORS AND HARLOTS

Jesus said to them, "Assuredly, I say to you that tax collectors and harlots enter the kingdom of God before you." Matt. 21:31.

Many of those who had anxiously awaited the result of the questioning of Jesus were finally to become His disciples, first drawn toward Him by His words on that eventful day. The scene in the temple court was never to fade from their minds." [59] Jesus now presented a parable. "But what do you think? A man had two sons, and he came to the first and said, 'Son, go, work today in my vineyard.' He answered and said, 'I will not,' but afterward he regretted it and went. Then he came to the second and said likewise. And he answered and said, 'I go, sir,' but he did not go. Which of the two did the will of his father?" (Matt. 21:28-31). "In this parable the father represents God, the vineyard the church. By the two sons are represented two classes of people. The son who refused to obey the command, saying, 'I will not,' represented those who were living in open transgression, who made no profession of piety, who openly refused to come under the yoke of restraint and obedience which the law of God imposes. . . . In the son who said, 'I go, sir,' and went not, the character of the Pharisees was revealed." [60] The priests and Pharisees did not see the underlying truth in Christ's words, but they answered from logic. The son who did the will of His father was "the first," they replied.

Jesus stated, "Assuredly, I say to you that tax collectors and harlots enter the kingdom of God before you." "Many today claim to obey the commandments of God, but they have not the love of God in their hearts to flow forth to others. Christ calls them to unite with Him in His work for the saving of the world, but they content themselves with saying, 'I go, sir.' They do not go. They do not cooperate with those who are doing God's service. They are idlers. . . . There is no such thing as a truly converted person living a helpless, useless life. It is not possible for us to drift into heaven. . . . Those who refuse to cooperate with God on earth would not cooperate with Him in heaven. It would not be safe to take them to heaven." [61]

Being a "pseudo-Christian" is professing to be a son or daughter of God, yet failing to do His will. Profession without action is valueless.

WICKED VINE-DRESSERS

Then He began to speak to them in parables.

Mark 12:1.

Jesus said, "Hear another parable: There was a certain landowner [God] who planted a vineyard [the national symbol of Israel] and set a hedge [the divine law] around it, dug a winepress in it and built a tower [the holy Temple]. And he leased it to vinedressers [the priests and teachers] and went into a far country. Now when vintage-time drew near, he sent his servants [prophets] to the vinedressers, that they might receive its fruit [the fruits of character]. And the vinedressers took his servants, beat one, killed one, and stoned another. Again he sent other servants, more than the first, and they did likewise to them. Then last of all he sent his son [Jesus] to them, saying, 'They will respect my son.' But when the vinedressers saw the son, they said among themselves, 'This is the heir. Come, let us kill him and seize his inheritance' [the Sanhedrin was even then meeting, seeking ways to put Jesus to death]. . . . Therefore, when the owner of the vineyard comes, what will he do to those vinedressers?" (Matt. 21:33-40). The priests again failed to see themselves in the story. "They said to Him, 'He will destroy those wicked men miserably, and lease his vineyard to other vinedressers who will render him the fruits in their seasons'" (verse 41). Their own mouths pronounced their doom for seeking to put to death the Son of God.

The parable of the vineyard has a lesson for the church of today. "There are many whose names are on the church books, but who are not under Christ's rule. They are not heeding His instruction or doing His work. . . . They are doing no positive good; therefore they are doing incalculable harm." [62] The Lord wants us to appreciate the plan of redemption. Having the high privilege of being called God's children, we should rejoice in the service opportunities that come our way. "To praise God in fullness and sincerity of heart is as much a duty as is prayer." [63] We are to be faithful workers in the Lord's vineyard, showing our gratitude for His blessings through our tithes and offerings, and serving Him through personal ministry for others. Each of us is to work for the salvation of our fellow humans.

God has a place and a work for all. The whole earth is the Lord's vineyard.

275

The Chief Corner- stone

Have you not even read this Scripture: "The stone which the builders rejected has become the chief cornerstone. This was the Lord's doing, and it is marvelous in our eyes"?

Mark 12:10, 11.

The religious leaders instantly recognized the Messianic passage found in Psalm 118:22. The story of the chief cornerstone had a place in the actual history of Israel. "While it had a special application at the time of Christ's first advent, and should have appealed with special force to the Jews, it has also a lesson for us. When the temple of Solomon was erected, the immense stones for the walls and the foundation were entirely prepared at the quarry; after they were brought to the place of building, not an instrument was to be used upon them; the workmen had only to place them in position. For use in the foundation, one stone of unusual size and peculiar shape had been brought; but the workmen could find no place for it, and would not accept it. It was an annoyance to them as it lay unused in their way. Long it remained a rejected stone. But when the builders came to the laying of the corner, they searched for a long time to find a stone of sufficient size and strength, and of the proper shape, to take that particular place, and bear the great weight which would rest upon it. Should they make an unwise choice for this important place, the safety of the entire building would be endangered. . . .

"Several stones had at different times been chosen, but under the pressure of immense weights they had crumbled to pieces. Others could not bear the test of the sudden atmospheric changes. But at last attention was called to the stone so long rejected. It had been exposed to the air, to sun and storm, without revealing the slightest crack. The builders examined this stone. It had borne every test but one. If it could bear the test of severe pressure, they decided to accept it for the cornerstone. The trial was made. The stone was accepted, brought to its assigned position, and found to be an exact fit. In prophetic vision, Isaiah was shown that this stone was a symbol of Christ."[64]

"Now when the chief priests and Pharisees heard His parables, they perceived that He was speaking of them. But when they sought to lay hands on Him, they feared the multitudes, because they took Him for a prophet" (Matt. 21:45, 46).

A firm foundation, He can save and support—but only you can choose to let Him do so.

THE WEDDING GARMENT

But when the king came in to see the guests, he saw a man there who did not have on a wedding garment. So he said to him, "Friend, how did you come in here without a wedding garment?" And he was speechless.

Matt. 22:11, 12.

Jesus now related the parable of the wedding feast. The Jews understood the marriage feast symbolism to represent the joys of the Messianic kingdom. Three invitations went out for people to attend the feast. The original Jewish invitation (the first in the parable) came through the Old Testament prophets. John the Baptist extended the second one to Israel, then Jesus and eventually the disciples after the crucifixion and resurrection of Christ. The invitees didn't even bother to make excuses for not attending. The third call of the parable involved the Gentiles. God wanted those in the highways of life to have the chance to join the church.

The king (God) entered into the wedding hall filled with guests to determine who might stay. "In a special sense [this] represents the work of the investigative judgment."[65] Only those who have put on the wedding garment have the right to remain. "By the wedding garment in the parable is represented the pure, spotless character which Christ's true followers will possess."[66] The righteousness of Christ, His character, God imputes to all who receive Him as their personal Saviour. "When we submit ourselves to Christ, the heart is united with His heart, the will is merged in His will, the mind becomes one with His mind, the thoughts are brought into captivity to Him; we live His life. This is what it means to be clothed with the garment of His righteousness."[67]

"The man who came to the feast without a wedding garment represents the condition of many in our world today. They profess to be Christians, and lay claim to the blessings and privileges of the gospel; yet they feel no need of a transformation of character. They have never felt true repentance for sin. They do not realize their need of Christ or exercise faith in Him. . . . They think that they are good enough in themselves, and they rest upon their own merits instead of trusting in Christ."[68]

"There will be no future probation in which to prepare for eternity. It is in this life that we are to put on the robe of Christ's righteousness. This is our only opportunity to form characters for the home which Christ has made ready for those who obey His commandments."[69]

THE ROMAN COIN

Tell us, therefore, what do You think? Is it lawful to pay taxes to Caesar, or not?

Matthew 22:17.

The chief priests and Pharisees now sent agents to trap Jesus through still another question. "They did not send the old Pharisees whom Jesus had often met, but young men, who were ardent and zealous, and whom, they thought, Christ did not know. These were accompanied by certain of the Herodians, who were to hear Christ's words, that they might testify against Him at His trial. The Pharisees and Herodians had been bitter enemies, but they were now one in enmity to Christ."[70] "The question really involved the problem as to whether a man could be a good Jew and yet submit to Roman authority."[71] If Jesus said it was unlawful to pay tribute to Rome, the occupation authorities could arrest Him for inciting rebellion. But if He said it was lawful to render tribute, the priests planned to accuse Him of opposing God's law. Jesus cut through their duplicity by replying, "Why do you test Me, you hypocrites? Show Me the tax money" (Matt. 22:18).

So they brought Him a denarius. One side had the image of the emperor and the other that of a pagan deity. Conquered nations might mint copper coins, but Rome reserved the right to make all silver ones. Jewish coins bore the symbol of an olive or palm tree in keeping with the second commandment, which allowed no image to take the place of God. Looking at the denarius, Jesus said, "'Whose image and inscription is this?' They said to Him, 'Caesar's.' And He said to them, 'Render therefore to Caesar the things that are Caesar's, and to God the things that are God's'" (verses 20, 21).

God is the supreme authority. When human laws seek to contravene divine ones, then God's laws must take precedence. "Jesus sets forth the fundamental principle that determines the Christian's relationship to the state. He is not to ignore the just claims of the state upon him, because there are certain things which are Caesar's."[72] The Jews had not rendered to God what was rightly His. As a result of their unfaithfulness they now lived under the power of a foreign nation. "When they had heard these words, they marveled, and left Him and went their way" (verse 22). The multitude understood the teaching and saw the underlying principle clearly.

We are not to ignore the just claims of the state or those owed to God.

WHAT ABOUT THE RESUR- RECTION?

You are mistaken, not knowing the Scriptures nor the power of God. For in the resurrection they neither marry nor are given in marriage, but are like angels of God in heaven.

Matt. 22:29, 30.

When they saw the awkward position of the Pharisees, the Sadducees attempted to question Jesus. "The Sadducees denied the existence of angels, the resurrection of the dead, and the doctrine of a future life, with its rewards and punishments. On all these points they differed with the Pharisees. Between the two parties the resurrection was especially a subject of controversy."[73] For this reason the Sadducees naturally rejected Jesus' teachings. It greatly distressed them when He raised Lazarus from the dead, since it refuted their disbelief in a resurrection. Now they came with a crafty question. If Jesus should agree with them, He would offend the Pharisees. But if He should disagree, they could then ridicule His teachings.

Sadducees believed that the immortal body must mimic the mortal state in substance. If raised from the dead, the person must consist of flesh and blood and must resume where he or she had left off at death. By their reasoning, if life did exist following resurrection to the kingdom of God, it must be a continuation of the same existence a person experienced while upon earth. They carried it further to include individual earthly relationships and their survival in heaven. Quoting the marriage law from Deuteronomy 25, the Sadducees conjectured a problem for a woman with seven separate husbands. Which would be her husband in heaven? The question was one of speculative theology. Because they prided themselves on their knowledge of the Scriptures, Jesus' answer shocked them. "You are mistaken, not knowing the Scriptures nor the power of God."

Human beings cannot reason out God. "The secret things belong to the Lord our God, but those things which are revealed belong to us and to our children forever" (Deut. 29:29). "The Sadducees forgot that a God powerful enough to raise men from the dead also had the wisdom and power to set up anew a perfect order of society in the perfect new earth. Furthermore, all who are saved will be contented and happy with the glorious new order of things, even though they cannot fully realize in this life what the future will bring forth (see 1 Cor. 2:9)."[74]

Likewise, we should not concern ourselves with such questions.

279

WHICH IS THE GREAT COMMAND- MENT?

Then one of them, a lawyer, asked Him a question, testing Him, and saying, "Teacher, which is the great command- ment in the law?" Matt. 22:35, 36.

The Pharisees now made one final attempt to dis- credit Jesus. The rabbis had long tried to rank the commandments of God into a strict hierarchy of importance. They could then spend hours debating which commandment took precedence and under which condition the higher command might supersede the lower. Jesus taught that the commandments of God were not separate precepts but that humanity must keep them as a whole. "Then one of them, a lawyer, asked Him a question, testing Him, and saying, 'Teacher, which is the great commandment in the law?' Jesus said to him, 'You shall love the Lord your God with all your heart, with all your soul, and with all your mind. This is the first and great commandment. And the second is like it: "You shall love your neighbor as yourself." On these two commandments hang all the Law and the Prophets'" (Matt. 22:35-40).

"The first four of the Ten Commandments are summed up in the one great precept, 'Thou shalt love the Lord thy God with all thy heart.' The last six are in- cluded in the other, 'Thou shalt love thy neighbor as thyself.' Both these com- mandments are an expression of the principle of love. The first cannot be kept and the second broken, nor can the second be kept while the first is broken."[75] The Pharisees put great stock in the first four commandments, assuming that they were more important than the last six. Believing that, they sometimes neg- lected their fellow human beings and practical religion. Jesus' response amazed the scribe. Realizing that Christ demonstrated great understanding, he replied, "Well said, Teacher. You have spoken the truth" (Mark 12:32).

"He knew that the Jewish religion consisted in outward ceremonies rather than inward piety. He had some sense of the worthlessness of mere ceremonial offerings, and the faithless shedding of blood for expiation of sin. Love and obe- dience to God, and unselfish regard for man, appeared to him of more value than all these rites."[76] Jesus united all of human duty into one lesson derived from Deuteronomy 6:4, 5 and Leviticus 19:18. But one thing remained for the scribe to understand: "He needed to recognize the divine character of Christ, and through faith in Him receive power to do the works of righteousness."[77]

The law points out our duty to God and humanity, but it is through Christ alone that we gain the power and pardon to keep it.

CHRIST CANNOT BE DAVID'S SON

The Lord said to my Lord, "Sit at My right hand, till I make Your enemies Your footstool."

Ps. 110:1.

The Pharisees had gathered closely about Jesus as He answered the scribe's question. Now, turning to them, He asked, "How can they say that the Christ is the Son of David? Now David himself said in the Book of Psalms, 'The Lord said to my Lord, "Sit at My right hand, till I make Your enemies Your footstool."' David therefore calls Him 'Lord'; how is He then his Son?" (Luke 20:41-44). Jesus designed the question to have them evaluate whether He was merely a human being or the Son of God. "When Jesus revealed His divinity by His mighty miracles, when He healed the sick and raised the dead, the people had inquired among themselves, 'Is not this the Son of David?' The Syrophoenician woman, blind Bartimaeus, and many others had cried to Him for help, 'Have mercy on me, O Lord, thou Son of David' (Matt. 15:22, KJV). While riding into Jerusalem He had been hailed with the joyful shout, 'Hosanna to the Son of David: Blessed is he that cometh in the name of the Lord' (Matt. 21:9, KJV). And the little children in the temple had that day echoed the glad ascription. But many who called Jesus the Son of David did not recognize His divinity. They did not understand that the Son of David was also the Son of God." [78]

If Christ was the Son of David, then why did David call Him Lord? The priests could not answer Him, "nor from that day on did anyone dare question Him anymore" (Matt. 22:46). Only one possible answer to the question existed. "The One who was to come as Messiah would have existed prior to His incarnation on this earth. As David's 'Lord,' Messiah was none other than the Son of God; as David's 'Son,' Messiah was the Son of man. . . . Obviously the Jewish leaders were unprepared to answer this question because of their erroneous concepts of the Messiah. . . . They could not very well answer the question without admitting that Jesus of Nazareth was the Messiah, the Son of God. In asking this question, then, Jesus brought the Pharisees and scribes face to face with the central idea of His mission to earth, for this question would undoubtedly, if faced sincerely and intelligently, have led to the recognition of His Messiahship." [79]

Was Jesus more than human, and are you prepared to accept Him as the Son of God as well as the Son of David?

TITHE OF MINT, ANISE, AND CUMMIN

Woe to you, scribes and Pharisees, hypocrites! For you pay tithe of mint and anise and cummin, and have neglected the weightier matters of the law: justice and mercy and faith. Matt. 23:23.

The crowd closely followed the Temple debate. "There stood the young Galilean, bearing no earthly honor or royal badge. Surrounding Him were priests in their rich apparel, rulers with robes and badges significant of their exalted station, and scribes with scrolls in their hands, to which they made frequent reference. Jesus stood calmly before them, with the dignity of a king. As one invested with the authority of heaven, He looked unflinchingly upon His adversaries, who had rejected and despised His teachings, and who thirsted for His life. They had assailed Him in great numbers, but their schemes to ensnare and condemn Him had been in vain. Challenge after challenge He had met, presenting the pure, bright truth in contrast to the darkness and errors of the priests and Pharisees."[80] Jesus now directly condemned the scribes and Pharisees.

They loved their positions and showed partiality. Although they professed to obey Scripture, they secretly ignored what they forced others to observe. While they made a great show of piety by stressing human tradition, they neglected justice, mercy, and faith. Coveting the title "rabbi" and wearing phylacteries containing small strips of parchment bound about their head and wrists that they felt would cause the law of God to take firmer hold on their hearts and minds (taking literally the admonition found in Deuteronomy 6:8), they defrauded widows and distorted the Word of the Lord. To draw attention to their pious natures they enlarged the tassels on their religious robes. "They were so exclusive as to think that the kingdom of heaven was a sort of private club into which only men who measured up to their standards might secure admission."[81]

As Christ laid each fault bare, the people realized that their leadership had beguiled them. They had allowed them to require such things as straining their drinking water for small unclean insects. Seven times Jesus called such false teachers "hypocrites."

False teachers still exist among today's churches, and "these denunciations are given as a warning to all who 'outwardly appear righteous unto men, but within' 'are full of hypocrisy and iniquity.'"[82]

HER WHOLE LIVELIHOOD

Now Jesus sat opposite the treasury and saw how the people put money into the treasury.

Mark 12:41.

Divine pity marked the countenance of the Son of God as He cast one lingering look upon the temple and then upon His hearers. In a voice choked by deep anguish of heart and bitter tears He exclaimed, 'O Jerusalem, Jerusalem, thou that killest the prophets, and stonest them which are sent unto thee, how often would I have gathered thy children together, even as a hen gathereth her chickens under her wings, and ye would not!' . . . Pharisees and Sadducees were alike silenced. Jesus summoned His disciples, and prepared to leave the temple, not as one defeated and forced from the presence of his adversaries, but as one whose work was accomplished. He retired a victor from the contest."[83]

As Jesus passed the Court of the Women, He happened to notice a poor widow. Halting His disciples, He watched as she moved furtively toward the collection boxes. Hesitatingly she approached the boxes, fearful that others would criticize her small offering. They put in large amounts with great theatrics while her gift seemed to her so small. Hurriedly she cast in her two lepta. Her two coins totaled a fraction of one U.S. cent."[84] Jesus said, "Assuredly, I say to you that this poor widow has put in more than all those who have given to the treasury; for they all put in out of their abundance, but she out of her poverty put in all that she had, her whole livelihood" (Mark 12:44). The woman heard His words of commendation and "tears of joy filled her eyes as she felt that her act was understood and appreciated."[85]

"In the sight of Heaven it is not really the size of a gift that counts, but the motive that prompts it. Heaven is interested only in the amount of love and devotion the gift represents, not its monetary value. That is the only basis on which God rewards men, as Jesus so pointedly illustrated by the parable of the Laborers in the Vineyard (see . . . Matt. 20:15)."[86]

It is the motive and not the monetary value that heaven marks in its ledger. What motive prompts your offerings to God?

"Sir, We Wish to See Jesus"

Sir, we wish to see Jesus. John 12:21.

In His closing remarks to the scribes and Pharisees, Jesus referred to the Temple as "your house" (Matt. 23:38), while just the day before He had called it "my house" (Matt. 21:13). It was not a misstatement. They and the nation now stood in the midst of the prophetic week of Daniel 9:27. The sacrifice and oblation were about to cease as type met antitype in the sacrifice of the Lamb of God. The Jewish nation had sealed its fate when it rejected Jesus as the Messiah. In town for the Passover were many proselytes from other countries who were restricted to the Court of the Gentiles. As Jesus prepared to leave the Temple precincts forever, Philip approached Andrew with a request and together they went to Jesus.

Many of the Greek proselytes had heard of His triumphal entry into Jerusalem, and they wanted to know the truth regarding His ministry. Passing into the outer court, Jesus held a personal interview with them. He explained that a kernel of wheat must die completely if it is to spring up and bear fruit. Just so, He must die to bring forth fruit for the kingdom of God. Christ's sacrifice would gather many of all nations, and He became lost in thought as His work of redemption passed before His eyes. Jesus, standing in the very shadow of the cross, submitted all to the will of His Father. "But for this purpose I came to this hour. Father, glorify Your name" (John 12:27, 28). A voice from heaven declared, "I have both glorified it and will glorify it again" (verse 28). God's name had been glorified in the ministry and life of Jesus and would be glorified in His death. "Now God again set His seal to the mission of His Son."[87] Christ said, "And I, if I am lifted up from the earth, will draw all peoples to Myself." In the request of the Greeks for an audience, Jesus saw that nations other than the Jews would accept His sacrifice. "These men came from the West to find the Saviour at the close of His life, as the wise men had come from the East at the beginning."[88] "Alas for those who knew not the time of their visitation! Slowly and regretfully Christ left forever the precincts of the temple."[89]

We may sum up the whole of salvation in the request, "Sir, we wish to see Jesus." Once you have seen Him—really seen Him—you will never be the same. Share Him with others!

NOT ONE STONE LEFT UPON ANOTHER

Then Jesus went out and departed from the temple, and His disciples came up to show Him the buildings of the temple. Matt. 24:1.

The words of Jesus "See! Your house is left to you desolate" left the priests with a sense of impending doom. They also worried Jesus' disciples. "As they passed with Him out of the temple, they called His attention to its strength and beauty (Mark 13:1). The stones of the temple were of the purest marble, of perfect whiteness, and some of them of almost fabulous size. A portion of the wall had withstood the siege by Nebuchadnezzar's army. In its perfect masonry it appeared like one solid stone dug entire from the quarry. How those mighty walls could be overthrown, the disciples could not comprehend."[1] "Josephus compares the white stone walls of the Temple to the beauty of a snow-covered mountain . . . , and gives the fabulous size of some of the stones used in its construction—45 by 5 by 6 cubits (about 66 by 7 by 9 feet)."[2] Jesus led His disciples down the steep descent of the Kidron Valley and then up the western slope of the Mount of Olives to a panoramic view of the city of Jerusalem and the Temple Mount. Here, overlooking the pride and joy of all Jewish faithful, Peter, Andrew, James, and John asked Him to clarify His words. "Tell us, when will these things be? And what will be the sign of Your coming, and of the end of the age?" (Matt. 24:3).

"The disciples posed their question with the Messianic messages of the Old Testament prophets in their minds. But they, in common with other Jews, did not fully understand that God's promises could be fulfilled to Israel only upon the fulfillment of the necessary conditions."[3] They believed, as did most Jews, that the Messiah would disappear for a brief period of time only to reappear from a location no one could determine. After such a "second coming" the Messianic kingdom would from that day on rule forever. Jesus knew the final destruction of the massive Temple walls in A.D. 70 by Roman legions under Titus (despite his attempts to save it) would not occur by human hands. "Angels of God were sent to do the work of destruction, so that one stone was not left one upon another that was not thrown down."[4]

Christ's words can be trusted! Our faith should strengthen as we consider prophecy yet to be fulfilled.

"WHAT WILL BE THE SIGN OF YOUR COMING?"

"Tell us, when will these things be? And what will be the sign of Your coming, and of the end of the age?"

Matt. 24:3.

Jesus now pulled aside the curtain of the future so the disciples might glimpse history. The same disciples, who were still having difficulty comprehending what would transpire just days from now, suddenly received an overview of the next two millennia. The scenes He opened to them must have been overwhelming, and only upon later reflection would they understand many of them.

"Take heed that no one deceives you. For many will come in My name, saying, 'I am the Christ,' and will deceive many" (Matt. 24:4, 5). The Jewish nation had always been susceptible to anyone claiming to be the Messiah. Again and again Jesus had emphasized that His disciples must watch, for there would come false christs (verses 4-6, 11, 23-26, 36, 42-46). The words of Jesus were accurately fulfilled. Josephus tells us that just prior to the destruction of Jerusalem many claimed to be the nation's salvation and that such false messiahs deceived many (*War* 6. 5. 2). "Between His death and the siege of Jerusalem many false messiahs appeared. But this warning was given also to those who live in this age of the world. The same deceptions practiced prior to the destruction of Jerusalem have been practiced through the ages, and will be practiced again."[5]

"And you will hear of wars and rumors of wars. See that you are not troubled; for all these things must come to pass, but the end is not yet" (Matt. 24:6). "Prior to the destruction of Jerusalem, men wrestled for the supremacy. Emperors were murdered. Those supposed to be standing next the throne were slain. There were wars and rumors of wars."[6] "For nation will rise against nation, and kingdom against kingdom. And there will be famines, pestilences, and earthquakes in various places. All these are the *beginning* of sorrows" (verses 7, 8). "Jewish and Roman writers describe the period from A.D. 31-70 as a time of great calamities. . . . A particularly severe famine in Judea about A.D. 44 is alluded to in Acts 11:28. There were altogether four major famines during the reign of Claudius, A.D. 41-54. . . . There was a series of major earthquakes between A.D. 31 and A.D. 70. The worst of these were in Crete (46 or 47), Rome (51), Phrygia (60), and Campania (63). Tacitus (*Annuals* xvi. 10-13) also speaks of particularly severe hurricanes and storms in the year 65."[7]

Fulfilled prophecy confirms future prophecy and builds trust.

THE ABOMINA-TION OF DESOLATION

"Therefore when you see the 'abomination of desolation,' spoken of by Daniel the prophet, standing in the holy place"
(whoever reads, let him understand),
"then let those who are in Judea flee to the mountains."
Matt. 24:15, 16.

Jesus continued His discourse on future events. "Then they will deliver you up to tribulation and kill you, and you will be hated by all nations for My name's sake" (Matt. 24:9). Those who took His name, "Christians," would suffer for their faith. Peter and John (Acts 4:3-7, 21) and Peter and James (Acts 12:1-4) endured persecution at the hands of the authorities. Tradition tells us that Andrew was martyred in Greece. First Jews, then Gentiles, hounded the early Christian church. Jesus predicted that despite such opposition the gospel would go to the entire world. "Thirty years after Christ spoke these words Paul affirmed that the gospel had gone to all the world . . . , confirming the literal fulfillment of this prediction in his day. . . . The complete fulfillment of this prediction of our Lord is yet to be realized."[8]

After outlining a general history of the age to come, Jesus gave His disciples a sign of the coming destruction of Jerusalem less than 40 years distant. "But when you see Jerusalem surrounded by armies, then know that its desolation is near. Then let those who are in Judea flee to the mountains, let those who are in the midst of her depart, and let not those who are in the country enter her" (Luke 21:20, 21). Jews consider idols "abominations." "The event foretold is obviously the destruction of Jerusalem by the Romans in A.D. 70, at which time the symbols of pagan Rome were set up within the Temple area."[9] Daniel prophesied, "And forces shall be mustered by him, and they shall defile the sanctuary fortress; then they shall take away the daily sacrifices, and place there the abomination of desolation" (Dan. 11:31).

As Roman standards encircled the city of Jerusalem in siege, Christians watched and waited. "During a temporary respite, when the Romans unexpectedly raised their siege of Jerusalem, all the Christians fled, and it is said that not one of them lost his life."[10] Christians did not postpone their flight to gather personal belongings. The Romans returned with a vengeance. "One million people perished during and after the siege of the city and 97,000 more were taken captive. . . . The stubborn defense of the city so infuriated the Roman soldiers, that when they finally entered, their desire for revenge knew no bounds."[11]

We can trust Jesus to provide His children an escape.

GREAT TRIBULATION

For then there will be great tribulation, such as has not been since the beginning of the world until this time, no, nor ever shall be.

Matt. 24:21.

Following the fall of Jerusalem would come "long centuries of darkness, centuries for His church marked with blood and tears and agony. Upon these scenes His disciples could not then endure to look, and Jesus passed them by with a brief mention."[12] "The history of the early church testified to the fulfillment of the Saviour's words. . . . Paganism foresaw that should the gospel triumph, her temples and altars would be swept away; therefore she summoned her forces to destroy Christianity. The fires of persecution were kindled."[13]

Satan attempted to destroy the infant Christian church through fierce opposition. Wild beasts tore early Christians apart or they were set afire as entertainment in arenas. Driven from their homes, their possessions confiscated, many hid in catacombs beneath the hills of Rome. Although living their physical lives in darkness, the lights of faith and hope burned within them. Persecution continued for nearly three centuries. Paul expressed it best when he wrote that "all who desire to live godly in Christ Jesus will suffer persecution" (2 Tim. 3:12). "And unless those days were shortened, no flesh would be saved; but for the elect's sake those days will be shortened" (Matt. 24:22). Now was seen the fulfillment of Christ's prophecy: "You will be betrayed even by parents and brothers, relatives and friends; and they will put some of you to death. And you will be hated by all for My name's sake" (Luke 21:16, 17).

Slowly a more sinister threat replaced the open warfare against Christianity. The church not shaken by fire and sword was to be watered down by stealth and secrecy. Pagan rituals, as well as errors based on human theories, slowly crept into it. The simple gospel became embellished with pomp and pageant. Still, compromise between Christianity and paganism did not end persecution. The "Dark Ages," 1,260 years of religious supremacy and persecution as foretold in Daniel 7:25 and Revelation 13:5-7, began in A.D. 538. Believers transferred their faith from Christ to human leadership. Leaders changed the day of worship from Sabbath to the first day of the week.

The Creator's law contains the fourth commandment, setting forever the seventh day as the true day of worship.

THE WATCHFUL SERVANT

Watch therefore, for you do not know when the master of the house is coming. Mark 13:35.

Jesus exhorted His disciples to watch for His second coming. He wanted His followers to understand that while the time of His return was a secret known only to His Father in heaven, the manner of His coming would not be hidden. "But of that day and hour no one knows, not even the angels of heaven, but My Father only" (Matt. 24:36). The entire discourse of Matthew 24 deals with time. Jesus repeatedly told His disciples to be prepared!

God would reveal signs to aid those living in the last days. "But in those days, after that tribulation, the sun will be darkened, and the moon will not give its light; the stars of heaven will fall, and the powers in the heavens will be shaken" (Mark 13:24, 25). Matthew writes: "Immediately after the tribulation of those days the sun will be darkened, and the moon will not give its light; the stars will fall from heaven, and the powers of the heavens will be shaken" (Matt. 24:29). Church historians agree that the reign of the medieval church ended in 1798, when the pope died in exile after a French army entering Rome under orders from Napoleon took him captive. Although the church soon selected a new pope, the Papacy no longer had the influence it once wielded.

Immediately after the tribulation, the first of the signs given to herald the second coming of Christ appeared. On May 19, 1780, there took place a darkening of the sun that became known as the Dark Day. "Since the time of Moses no period of darkness of equal density, extent, and duration has ever been recorded. The description of this event, as given by eyewitnesses, is but an echo of the words of the Lord, recorded by the prophet Joel, twenty-five hundred years previous to their fulfillment: 'The sun shall be turned into darkness, and the moon into blood, before the great and the terrible day of the Lord come' (Joel 2:31, KJV)." [14] That same evening the moon resembled blood.

One of the largest star showers ever recorded occurred on November 13, 1833. "These two phenomena, of 1780 and 1833, exactly fulfilled Jesus' predictions, for they came at the specified time." [15]

Are you watching for the Master and noting the signs of the times?

LIGHTNING FLASHES

"For as the lightning comes from the east and flashes to the west, so also will the coming of the Son of Man be."

Matt. 24:27.

Christ is coming with clouds and with great glory. A multitude of shining angels will attend Him. He will come to raise the dead, and to change the living saints from glory to glory. He will come to honor those who have loved Him, and kept His commandments, and to take them to Himself. He has not forgotten them nor His promise." [16] Jesus "stated plainly to His disciples that He Himself could not make known the day or the hour of His second appearing. Had He been at liberty to reveal this, why need He have exhorted them to maintain an attitude of constant expectancy? There are those who claim to know the very day and hour of our Lord's appearing. Very earnest are they in mapping out the future. But the Lord has warned them off the ground they occupy. The exact time of the second coming of the Son of man is God's mystery." [17]

On that wonderful day we will meet face-to-face the angels responsible for guarding us during their earthly sojourn. When the trumpet sounds, the dead in Christ will rise incorruptible. "For the Lord Himself will descend from heaven with a shout, with the voice of an archangel, and with the trumpet of God. And the dead in Christ will rise first. Then we who are alive and remain shall be caught up together with them in the clouds to meet the Lord in the air. And thus we shall always be with the Lord" (1 Thess. 4:16, 17). We will finally see Jesus, our very best friend. "Behold, I tell you a mystery: We shall not all sleep, but we shall all be changed—in a moment, in the twinkling of an eye, at the last trumpet. For the trumpet will sound, and the dead will be raised incorruptible, and we shall be changed" (1 Cor. 15:51, 52).

John witnessed "a great multitude which no one could number, of all nations, tribes, peoples, and tongues, standing before the throne and before the Lamb, clothed with white robes, with palm branches in their hands" (Rev. 7:9). A heavenly messenger told him that "these are the ones who come out of the great tribulation, and washed their robes and made them white in the blood of the Lamb" (verse 14).

"A little longer, and He will present us 'faultless before the presence of his glory with exceeding joy' (Jude 24, KJV)." [18]

THE DAYS OF NOAH?

But as the days of Noah were, so also will the coming of the Son of Man be. Matt. 24:37.

Our Lord compares the condition of the earth during the last days to that of the antediluvian world. "Christ does not here bring to view a temporal millennium, a thousand years in which all are to prepare for eternity."[19] Jesus' parables (the sheep and the goats, the wheat and the tares, the dragnet) repeatedly show that judgment takes place before His return. When He comes, it will be to claim those covered by His righteousness and judged worthy. Jesus emphasized repeatedly that now is the time heaven has granted us to get ready. Our world is not moving closer to a millennium of glory, but is constantly edging closer to the wickedness that caused the destruction of the antediluvian world.

"Then the Lord saw that the wickedness of man was great in the earth, and that every intent of the thoughts of his heart was only evil continually" (Gen. 6:5). Despite Noah's warnings, people went about their usual round of daily activities in total disregard of the prophecy of their soon destruction. Those living in our day will also feel little concern for the world's fate. His appearance will be as a thief in the sense that most will not be watching for it. "The crisis is stealing gradually upon us."[20] Jesus repeatedly told His disciples and now tells us, "Take heed" (Matt. 24:4); "Watch" (verse 42); "Be ready" (verse 44). He is even "at the doors" (verse 33). It takes no genius to realize that our world has surely reached the same wicked condition that existed in the days of Noah.

"The teaching known as the 'secret rapture,' according to which the saints are to be secretly snatched away from this earth prior to the visible return of Christ, is wholly unscriptural. Its advocates appeal to the statements of Christ in Matthew 24:39-41 as proof. But these verses teach no such thing. The 'coming' of Matthew 24 is always, without exception, the literal, visible appearance of Christ (see verses 3, 27, 30, 39, 42, 44, 46, 48, 50). . . . Everything of the nature of a 'secret' coming Christ attributed to the false christs (verses 24-26)."[21] Many will be discouraged and lose faith in God when He does not whisk them to safety prior to the last plagues.

The gospel will go to the whole world, but the whole world will not be converted. Sadly, too few will heed the warning and obey His commandments. As it was in the days of Noah . . .

WISE AND FOOLISH

The kingdom of heaven shall be likened to ten virgins. Matt. 25:1.

Evening descended upon the Mount of Olives. "In full view is a dwelling house lighted up brilliantly as if for some festive scene. The light streams from the openings, and an expectant company wait around, indicating that a marriage procession is soon to appear."[22] Jesus drew a parallel. Ten virgins waited for a bridegroom. Five wise virgins had purchased extra oil because no one could know how long the festivities would last. Five foolish virgins showed up with just the oil in their lamps. As the bridegroom took his time, all ten maidens fell asleep. At midnight someone announced, "The bridegroom cometh." All ten rose and trimmed the wick on their lamps. But the foolish now discovered theirs empty of oil—and they had no reserve! The wise could not share, for they needed all their oil to get themselves through the evening. The foolish rushed to purchase oil, and while they were gone the bridegroom arrived. Those ready and waiting went in with Him to the wedding feast. When the foolish maids returned they found themselves shut out. Desperately they pounded upon the door and begged, " 'Lord, Lord, open to us!' But he answered and said, 'Assuredly, I say to you, I do not know you' " (Matt. 25:11, 12).

The Bridegroom is Christ. The wedding feast is His return to take us home to the marriage supper of the Lamb. "The two classes of watchers represent the two classes who profess to be waiting for their Lord. They are called virgins because they profess a pure faith. By the lamps is represented the Word of God. The psalmist says, 'Thy word is a lamp unto my feet, and a light unto my path' (Ps. 119:105, KJV). The oil is a symbol of the Holy Spirit."[23] Every virgin sleeps prior to the coming of the Bridegroom! The foolish maidens were attracted to the gospel and the theory of truth, but they had put off preparation, neglecting to change their lives to conform to Christ's teachings. "Both parties were taken unawares; but one was prepared for the emergency, and the other was found without preparation."[24] A crisis will reveal one's character. The foolish maidens' spiritual development had been superficial and inadequate. Preparation begins now, for waiting until midnight is perilous.

When your probation closes, it is too late to acquire the oil needed to accompany the Bridegroom. Daily we must let the Spirit fill us. Then we will be prepared to meet Him.

THE PARABLE OF THE TEN TALENTS

For the kingdom of heaven is like a man traveling to a far country. Matt. 25:14.

The parable of the ten virgins stressed personal preparation for the Lord's coming. The parable of the ten talents emphasized our responsibility to witness to others. In it a man journeyed to a distant country. Before leaving, he gave three servants varying amounts of capital to invest. Jesus has traveled to that far country of heaven to prepare a place for us. We are to spend our time and talents in working for the Lord. Each of us has a task we might do for the Lord. "Not more surely is the place prepared for us in the heavenly mansions than is the special place designated on earth where we are to work for God." [25]

"The development of all our powers is the first duty we owe to God and to our fellow men." [26] The amount of the gift each servant received is not the important part of the parable. Taking the gifts the Lord has given you and expanding them to His glory is critical. "A noble character is earned by individual effort through the merits and grace of Christ. God gives the talents, the powers of the mind; we form the character. It is formed by hard, stern battles with self. Conflict after conflict must be waged against hereditary tendencies. We shall have to criticize ourselves closely, and allow not one unfavorable trait to remain uncorrected." [27] It was a duty the slothful servant refused.

"A character formed according to the divine likeness is the only treasure that we can take from this world to the next. Those who are under the instruction of Christ in this world will take every divine attainment with them to the heavenly mansions. And in heaven we are continually to improve. How important, then, is the development of character in this life." [28] But what should we do? "We should do as Christ did. Wherever He was, in the synagogue, by the wayside, in the boat thrust out a little from the land, at the Pharisee's feast or the table of the publican, He spoke to men of the things pertaining to the higher life." [29] "Character is power. The silent witness of a true, unselfish, godly life carries an almost irresistible influence." [30] "The Lord in His distribution of gifts is testing character." [31]

"By faithfulness in little duties, we are to work on the plan of addition, and God will work for us on the plan of multiplication." [32]

"YOU DID IT UNTO ME"

And the King will answer and say to them, "Assuredly, I say to you, inasmuch as you did it to one of the least of these My brethren, you did it to Me."
Matt. 25:40.

Jesus' last parable outlines, appropriately enough, the requirements of the judgment. In plain language He explains that at the close of the millennium those sinners on His left will "go away into everlasting punishment, but the righteous into eternal life" (Matt. 25:46). What decides whether we are a sheep or a goat? "Eternal destiny will be determined by what they have done or have neglected to do for Him in the person of the poor and the suffering."[33] God will test all to see whether they have true religion or not. "Pure and undefiled religion before God and the Father is this: to visit orphans and widows in their trouble, and to keep oneself unspotted from the world" (James 1:27). The spirit of Christ is an attitude of selflessness. The righteous will naturally exhibit this tendency and will be surprised when Christ commends them for their efforts. (Matt. 25:37-40).

"Genuine love for God reveals itself in love for God's suffering children. True religion involves more than passive assent to dogmas."[34] Today's world emphasizes materialism and self. Such a philosophy is 180 degrees away from the life of a dedicated follower of Christ. True Christians should be more concerned with the salvation of neighbors than their stock portfolio or business. God calls all of us to be workers with Him. "In the great judgment day, those who have not worked for Christ, who have drifted along thinking of themselves, caring for themselves, will be placed by the Judge of the whole earth with those who did evil. They receive the same condemnation."[35]

"Many feel that it would be a great privilege to visit the scenes of Christ's life on earth, to walk where He trod, to look upon the lake beside which He loved to teach, and the hills and valleys on which His eyes so often rested. But we need not go to Nazareth, to Capernaum, or to Bethany, in order to walk in the steps of Jesus. We shall find His footprints beside the sickbed, in the hovels of poverty, in the crowded alleys of the great city, and in every place where there are human hearts in need of consolation."[36]

"In doing as Jesus did when on earth, we shall walk in His steps."[37]

SATAN ENTERED JUDAS

Then Satan entered Judas, surnamed Iscariot, who was numbered among the twelve. So he went his way and conferred with the chief priests and captains, how he might betray Him to them. Luke 22:3, 4.

Jesus knew Judas's heart. "For Jesus knew from the beginning who they were who did not believe, and who would betray Him" (John 6:64). Judas had steadily drawn away from Jesus' ministry. "In all that Christ said to His disciples, there was something with which, in heart, Judas disagreed. Under his influence the leaven of disaffection was fast doing its work. The disciples did not see the real agency in all this; but Jesus saw that Satan was communicating his attributes to Judas, and thus opening up a channel through which to influence the other disciples."[38] The disciple had not fully hardened to his task of betrayal even after meeting with the priests and scribes for a second time. He still had time to repent of his act. Not until the Passover Supper did Judas finally cross the line and totally resist the Saviour's tender call for repentance. Although Judas had never surrendered fully to Christ, Jesus did not expose his duplicity; instead, "Jesus hungered for his soul. He felt for him such a burden as for Jerusalem when He wept over the doomed city. His heart was crying, How can I give thee up? The constraining power of that love was felt by Judas."[39] Jesus knew a traitor existed within His followers, yet His love for the man never wavered. The inner turmoil of concealing what he was doing, yet knowing full well that Jesus read his heart, must have wrenched Judas's soul.

The first contact between Judas and the priests had been during the feast at Bethany. While Jesus was dining with Simon, Judas was counting the silver given him to betray his Lord. "A little before the Passover, Judas had renewed his contract with the priests to deliver Jesus into their hands. Then it was arranged that the Saviour should be taken at one of His resorts for meditation and prayer. Since the feast at the house of Simon, Judas had had opportunity to reflect upon the deed which he had covenanted to perform, but his purpose was unchanged. For thirty pieces of silver—the price of a slave—he sold the Lord of glory to ignominy and death."[40]

Resisting the Saviour's plea for repentance is dangerous. You are either for Him or . . .

"GO AND PREPARE THE PASSOVER"

Then came the Day of Unleavened Bread, when the Passover must be killed. And He sent Peter and John, saying, "Go and prepare the Passover for us, that we may eat."

Luke 22:7, 8.

And He said, 'Go into the city to a certain man, and say to him, "The Teacher says, 'My time is at hand; I will keep the Passover at your house with My disciples.'"' So the disciples did as Jesus had directed them; and they prepared the Passover" (Matt. 26:18, 19). The Jews celebrated the Passover yearly in the month of Abib, now called Nisan. On the tenth each Jewish family set aside a lamb. On the fourteenth they sacrificed the lamb at twilight and ate it that same evening. They roasted the lamb whole over a fire and consumed it with unleavened bread and bitter herbs. The feast represented the "passing over" of the angel of the Lord. On that night the firstborn of Pharaoh died, and he "thrust out" the Israelites before the morning of the fifteenth day.

By the time of Jesus the original rules had modified. The priests killed the lambs, and the people took them home for roasting. Participants sat or reclined around tables set in the prescribed manner with wine, herbs, and unleavened bread. The significance of the Passover lamb centered in the promise of Christ, "the Lamb of God who takes away the sin of the world!" (John 1:29). "For indeed Christ, our Passover, was sacrificed for us" (1 Cor. 5:7). God instructed Moses that the people were not to break any bone in the sacrificial lamb's body (Ex. 12:46; Num. 9:12). "For these things were done that the Scripture should be fulfilled, 'Not one of His bones shall be broken'" (John 19:36).

"In the upper chamber of a dwelling at Jerusalem, Christ was sitting at table with His disciples. They had gathered to celebrate the Passover. The Saviour desired to keep this feast alone with the twelve. He knew that His hour was come; He Himself was the true paschal lamb, and on the day the Passover was eaten He was to be sacrificed. He was about to drink the cup of wrath; He must soon receive the final baptism of suffering. But a few quiet hours yet remained to Him, and these were to be spent for the benefit of His beloved disciples."[41]

As His mission came to a climax, Jesus longed for His disciples to understand that God is about love and sacrifice for others.

A LIFE OF UNSELFISH SERVICE

Now there was also a dispute among them, as to which of them should be considered the greatest. Luke 22:24.

The interviews between Jesus and His disciples were usually seasons of calm joy, highly prized by them all. The Passover suppers had been scenes of special interest; but upon this occasion Jesus was troubled. His heart was burdened, and a shadow rested upon His countenance. As He met the disciples in the upper chamber, they perceived that something weighed heavily upon His mind, and although they knew not its cause, they sympathized with His grief."[42] Custom required a minimum of 10 persons be present to eat the Passover together. Jesus studied the 12 men surrounding Him. He longed to save them the coming heartbreak, but looking into their faces He saw they were not prepared to bear His message. His words remained upon His lips and the silence became pervasive. The disciples grew uneasy. Glancing at one another, they wondered whom their Lord would favor that night.

Even during the last scenes of His earthly ministry, the disciples contended for the best spots. "The whole life of Christ had been a life of unselfish service. 'Not to be ministered unto, but to minister' (Matt. 20:28, KJV), had been the lesson of His every act. But not yet had the disciples learned the lesson."[43] As they milled about, they remembered the attempt by James and John to claim seats of honor in the kingdom, and the thought again filled them with jealousy. Judas's criticism of the two brothers had been severest of all, and he now pushed forward. As Jesus seated Himself, "Judas pressed next to Christ on the left side; John was on the right. If there was a highest place, Judas was determined to have it, and that place was thought to be next to Christ. And Judas was a traitor."[44] "In view of events so soon to occur, it was tragic that the disciples should have been arguing about rank in an imaginary kingdom that Christ did not come to establish."[45] Jesus had repeatedly taught, "Whoever desires to become great among you, let him be your servant" (Matt. 20:26; cf. 18:4; Mark 9:35). But they ignored His plain instruction and forgot the whole selfless example of Jesus' ministry in their jealous desire for honor and position.

What more could Jesus do to show that humble, loving service for others constitutes true greatness in heaven?

He Girded Himself

Jesus . . . rose from supper and laid aside His garments, took a towel and girded Himself.
John 13:3, 4.

The disciples noticed that no foreign servant waited to perform the menial task of washing the feet. Someone had laid out a pitcher, basin, and towel, but "each of the disciples, yielding to wounded pride, determined not to act the part of a servant. All manifested a stoical unconcern, seeming unconscious that there was anything for them to do. By their silence they refused to humble themselves."[46] Jesus had waited to see what His disciples might do. "Then He, the divine Teacher, rose from the table. Laying aside the outer garment that would have impeded His movements, He took a towel, and girded Himself."[47] "After that, He poured water into a basin and began to wash the disciples' feet, and to wipe them with the towel with which He was girded" (John 13:5).

Shame filled the disciples. How could they have allowed their Master to assume the position they should have accepted? When Jesus reached Peter he refused to let Jesus serve him. "You shall never wash my feet!" he told his Master (verse 8). Jesus answered, "If I do not wash you, you have no part with Me" (verse 8). "The service which Peter refused was the type of a higher cleansing. Christ had come to wash the heart from the stain of sin. In refusing to allow Christ to wash his feet, Peter was refusing the higher cleansing included in the lower. He was really rejecting his Lord."[48] Foot washing symbolizes cleansing from sins that have occurred since our baptism. It shows a spirit of Christian fellowship in service to one another. And it indicates humble acceptance of the service necessary to work for the Lord. As an act, foot washing isn't significant. The symbolic removal of sin by confession and sincere repentance that leads to a spirit of communion with Christ is the key element.

Jesus longed to rescue Judas. "When the Saviour's hands were bathing those soiled feet, and wiping them with the towel, the heart of Judas thrilled through and through with the impulse then and there to confess his sin. But he would not humble himself. He hardened his heart against repentance; and the old impulses, for the moment put aside, again controlled him. . . . Judas was satisfied that there was nothing to be gained by following Christ. After seeing Him degrade Himself, as he thought, he was confirmed in his purpose to disown Him . . ."[49]

Does pride keep you from following your Lord in service to others?

AN ORDINANCE OF SERVICE

If I then, your Lord and Teacher, have washed your feet, you also ought to wash one another's feet. For I have given you an example, that you should do as I have done to you. John 13:14, 15.

Jesus moved around the table in clockwise fashion, washing the dusty, soiled feet of His disciples. Judas had been first to have his feet washed. "John, toward whom Judas had felt so much bitterness, was left till the last. But John did not take this as a rebuke or slight."[50] Instead, the disciple saw plainly the life and lessons of Christ exemplified in His humble act. The lesson was plain: "through love serve one another" (Gal. 5:13). Jesus came to show us the Father. God stands forever in service to others. The mission He imparted to His Son was one of ministry. "The only distinction is found in devotion to the service of others."[51] The world values and stresses gratification and glorification of self, but heaven emphasizes the need to uplift and support the welfare of others. The whole world needs our ministry. Surrounding us are the poor, the sick, and the helpless, and it is the blessed duty of every Christian to be a servant to fellow humanity.

The act of washing their feet impressed the disciples. They still did not understand the spiritual significance of the act, but Christ's humble, compassionate service moved them. Jesus replaced His outer garment and resumed His seat. "Do you know what I have done to you? You call me Teacher and Lord, and you say well, for so I am. If I then, your Lord and Teacher, have washed your feet, you also ought to wash one another's feet. For I have given you an example, that you should do as I have done to you" (John 13:12-15). Jesus here instituted the ritual He enjoined all disciples to emulate prior to partaking of the Lord's Supper. "The ordinance of feet washing is an ordinance of service. This is the lesson the Lord would have all learn and practice."[52] "This ordinance is Christ's appointed preparation for the sacramental service. While pride, variance, and strife for supremacy are cherished, the heart cannot enter into fellowship with Christ. We are not prepared to receive the communion of His body and His blood. Therefore it was that Jesus appointed the memorial of His humiliation to be first observed."[53]

Christ summons us to serve others. All Christians are to be servants to their neighbors.

This Is My Body

And He took bread, gave thanks and broke it, and gave it to them.

Luke 22:19.

Christ was standing at the point of transition between two economies and their two great festivals. He, the spotless Lamb of God, was about to present Himself as a sin offering, that He would thus bring to an end the system of types and ceremonies that for four thousand years had pointed to His death. As He ate the Passover with His disciples, He instituted in its place the service that was to be the memorial of His great sacrifice. The national festival of the Jews was to pass away forever. The service which Christ established was to be observed by His followers in all lands and through all ages." [54]

On the paschal table before Jesus rested unleavened cakes and unfermented Passover wine. "These emblems Christ employs to represent His own unblemished sacrifice. Nothing corrupted by fermentation, the symbol of sin and death, could represent the 'Lamb without blemish and without spot' (1 Peter 1:19, KJV)." [55] Judas was present at the table. By serving him, Jesus demonstrated that the observance of the Lord's Supper cannot be restricted. "None should exclude themselves from the Communion because some who are unworthy may be present. Every disciple is called upon to participate publicly, and thus bear witness that he accepts Christ as a personal Saviour." [56]

Jesus picked up the bread and blessed it. Breaking the unleavened bread into pieces, He distributed it to His disciples, saying, "Take, eat; this is My body which is broken for you; do this in remembrance of Me" (1 Cor. 11:24). Many take His statement literally, but it is in the figurative sense that the bread symbolizes His broken flesh. "That Jesus spoke figuratively regarding the 'bread' becomes transparently evident from Luke 22:20 . . . , 'This cup is the new testament in my blood.' If the bread actually became His very body, by the same process the 'cup' must literally have become the 'new testament.' The verb 'is' in the phrase 'this is my body' is used in the sense of 'represents,' as it is in Mark 4:15-18; Luke 12:1; Galatians 4:24." [57] Jesus said during His ministry, "I am the living bread which came down from heaven. If anyone eats of this bread, he will live forever; and the bread that I shall give is My flesh, which I shall give for the life of the world" (John 6:51).

To eat His flesh is to appropriate His life by faith, receiving Him as a personal Saviour who forgives us and makes us complete in Him.

THE NEW COVENANT IN MY BLOOD

Likewise He also took the cup after supper, saying, "This cup is the new covenant in My blood, which is shed for you." Luke 22:20.

Picking up the paschal cup, containing the pure juice of the vine, probably diluted with water according to Jewish custom, Christ offered thanks. Then, passing it to His disciples, He said, "Drink from it, all of you. For this is My blood of the new covenant, which is shed for many for the remission of sins" (Matt. 26:27, 28). Jesus wanted none to miss any opportunity to drink from the cup. Where the bread represents His body, the drink symbolizes His blood that Christ shed for the pardon of all that accept His sacrifice in faith and believe in His atonement for their sins (Heb. 9:15). Only a blood sacrifice could purge human sin. The blood of a sacrificial animal ratified the original covenant between God and His people (Ex. 24:5-7). Jesus' shed blood is the promise of the kingdom and the hope of our salvation through faith in His word.

The Communion service should be a time not of sorrow but rather of joy. It should direct our thoughts to His second coming. "For as often as you eat this bread and drink this cup, you proclaim the Lord's death till He comes" (1 Cor. 11:26). "The ordinance of the Lord's table significantly links the first advent with the second."[58] When we meet to commemorate His death we recall His words: "I will not drink of the fruit of the vine until the kingdom of God comes" (Luke 22:18). John remembered them: "Let us be glad and rejoice and give Him glory, for the marriage of the Lamb has come. . . . Blessed are those who are called to the marriage supper of the Lamb!" (Rev. 19:7-9).

"The ordinances that point to our Lord's humiliation and suffering are regarded too much as a form. They were instituted for a purpose. Our senses need to be quickened to lay hold of the mystery of godliness. It is the privilege of all to comprehend, far more than we do, the expiatory sufferings of Christ. 'As Moses lifted up the serpent in the wilderness,' even so has the Son of man been lifted up, 'that whosoever believeth in him should not perish, but have eternal life' (John 3:14, 15, KJV)."[59]

"To the cross of Calvary, bearing the dying Saviour, we must look. Our eternal interests demand that we show faith in Christ."[60]

A Piece
of Dipped
Bread

*And having dipped
the bread, He gave
it to Judas Iscariot,
the son of Simon.
John 13:26.*

Judas had been looking for a suitable time and place to betray his Lord. For that reason Jesus had waited until the last moment to give Peter and John instructions on how to prepare the Passover observance. Late in the day the two returned from their errand. Only then did the remaining disciples learn the location of the upper room. Judas had no chance to lay plans to capture Jesus in the upper room.

"Judas the betrayer was present at the sacramental service. He received from Jesus the emblems of His broken body and His spilled blood. He heard the words, 'This do in remembrance of me.' And sitting there in the very presence of the Lamb of God, the betrayer brooded upon his own dark purposes, and cherished his sullen, revengeful thoughts."[61] "At the Passover the case of Judas was decided. Satan took control of heart and mind. He thought that Christ was either to be crucified, or would have to deliver Himself out of the hands of His enemies. At all events, he would make something out of the transaction, and make a sharp bargain by betraying his Lord."[62]

Judas was convinced that Jesus knew of his actions—especially when Christ said, "You are not all clean" (John 13:11). "One of you will betray Me" (verse 21). Fear seized the disciples, for they distrusted themselves. "With the most painful emotion, one after another inquired, 'Lord, is it I?' But Judas sat silent."[63] The disciples lay around the table on their left sides, facing inward. John, whom Jesus loved, leaned back upon His chest, for he reclined to Jesus' right. Peter motioned for John to ask Jesus who the traitor might be. "John in deep distress at last inquired, 'Lord, who is it?' And Jesus answered, 'He that dippeth his hand with me in the dish, the same shall betray me. . . .' And now the silence of Judas drew all eyes to him. Amid the confusion of questions and expressions of astonishment, Judas had not heard the words of Jesus in answer to John's question. But now, to escape the scrutiny of the disciples, he asked as they had done, 'Master, is it I?' Jesus solemnly replied, 'Thou hast said.'"[64] After he received the piece of bread, Judas quickly rose and went out into the night to sell His Master.

The priests purchased Jesus with Temple money used to buy sacrifices. How fitting that they unknowingly bought the greatest sacrifice for humanity in such a manner.

BELIEVE IN ME

Let not your heart be troubled; you believe in God, believe also in Me.

John 14:1.

The disciples thought Jesus to be instructing Judas to buy something needed for their feast or perhaps to give money to the poor when He said, "What you do, do quickly" (John 13:27). Leaving the upper room, Judas hurried to the priests for his third and final visit. Jesus now plainly told the others He would be leaving them. "Little children, I shall be with you a little while longer. You will seek Me; and as I said to the Jews, 'Where I am going, you cannot come'" (verse 33). "The disciples could not rejoice when they heard this. Fear fell upon them. They pressed close about the Saviour. Their Master and Lord, their beloved Teacher and Friend, He was dearer to them than life. . . . Now He was to leave them, a lonely, dependent company. Dark were the forebodings that filled their hearts."[65]

But Jesus did not allow them to remain in this state. Instead He turned their thoughts to the heavenly home. "Let not your heart be troubled; you believe in God, believe also in Me. . . . I go to prepare a place for you. And if I go and prepare a place for you, I will come again and receive you to Myself; that where I am, there you may be also" (John 14:1-3). "While He was building mansions for them, they were to build characters after the divine similitude."[66] It is to be the work of every believer today.

Thomas was perplexed. "Lord, we do not know where You are going, and how can we know the way?" Jesus replied, "I am the way, the truth, and the life. No one comes to the Father except through Me. If you had known Me, you would have known My Father also; and from now on you know Him and have seen Him" (verses 5-7). Philip now said, "Lord, show us the Father, and it is sufficient for us" (verse 8). "Amazed at his dullness of comprehension, Christ asked with pained surprise, 'Have I been so long time with you, and yet hast thou not known me, Philip? Is it possible that you do not see the Father in the works he does through me? Do you not believe that I came to testify of the Father?'"[67]

Philip's question is one every human being must answer in his or her own heart. Do you believe in Christ and in the Father who sent Him?

ASK ANYTHING IN MY NAME

If you ask anything in My name, I will do it. John 14:14.

The Saviour's promise to His disciples is a promise to His church to the end of time. God did not design that His wonderful plan to redeem men should achieve only insignificant results. All who will go to work, trusting not in what they themselves can do, but in what God can do for and through them, will certainly realize the fulfillment of His promise." [68] We find the secret to success in this life through relying upon the name of Jesus. "The prayer of the humble supplicant He presents as His own desire in that soul's behalf. Every sincere prayer is heard in heaven. It may not be fluently expressed; but if the heart is in it, it will ascend to the sanctuary where Jesus ministers, and He will present it to the Father without one awkward, stammering word, beautiful and fragrant with the incense of His own perfection. The path of sincerity and integrity is not a path free from obstruction, but in every difficulty we are to see a call to prayer." [69]

More is involved in praying in His name than using it to close a prayer. Prayer is the science of knowing God. To pray in Christ's name means that we accept His character, manifest His spirit, and do His works. Our Saviour's promise is conditional. "If you love Me," He tells us, "keep My commandments" (John 14:15). He saves human beings not in sin, but from sin. Those who love Him will show their love by obedience (1 John 3:22). "All true obedience comes from the heart. It was heart work with Christ. And if we consent, He will so identify Himself with our thoughts and aims, so blend our hearts and minds into conformity to His will, that when obeying Him we shall be but carrying out our own impulses. The will, refined and sanctified, will find its highest delight in doing His service. When we know God as it is our privilege to know Him, our life will be a life of continual obedience. Through an appreciation of the character of Christ, through communion with God, sin will become hateful to us." [70]

"Those who decide to do nothing in any line that will displease God will know, after presenting their case before Him, just what course to pursue. And they will receive not only wisdom, but strength." [71]

ANOTHER HELPER

And I will pray the Father, and He will give you another Helper. John 14:16.

On this last night with His disciples, Jesus promised them He would send Another to remain with them forever. The term He used was *parakletos*, or Comforter. Literally translated, it means "one called alongside." Jesus had been their comfort and friend during His earthly sojourn, and now He would bestow on them a gift. Seven weeks, or 50 days, after this Passover, the disciples would gather to celebrate the Feast of Weeks, or Pentecost. At that time the Holy Spirit would descend with great power (Acts 2:1-4), and they would fearlessly proclaim the gospel of Jesus Christ.

The Spirit would do more than comfort the disciples. He would also teach (John 14:26), enabling them to recall the lessons Jesus had given them. Parables would suddenly seem clearer. Christ's mission to humanity and Jesus' words would take on deeper significance. The Spirit would testify of Christ (John 15:26) and "convict the world of sin, and of righteousness, and of judgment" (John 16:8). He would convict human beings of their need for salvation and that they could attain it only through Christ's sacrifice. Guiding men and women into all truth and showing things yet to come (verse 13), the Spirit would glorify Christ (verse 14) by illuminating the plan of salvation. Christ could have given His followers no greater gift.

"Before this the Spirit had been in the world; from the very beginning of the work of redemption He had been moving upon men's hearts. But while Christ was on earth, the disciples had desired no other helper. Not until they were deprived of His presence would they feel their need of the Spirit, and then He would come. The Holy Spirit is Christ's representative, but divested of the personality of humanity, and independent thereof. Cumbered with humanity, Christ could not be in every place personally. Therefore it was for their interest that He should go to the Father, and send the Spirit to be His successor on earth. No one could then have any advantage because of his location or his personal contact with Christ. By the Spirit the Saviour would be accessible to all. In this sense He would be nearer to them than if He had not ascended on high."[72]

His promise is for future disciples as well: "I will pray the Father, and He will give you another Helper, that He may abide with you forever" (John 14:16).

"IF YOU LOVE ME"

He who has My commandments and keeps them, it is he who loves Me.

John 14:21.

Today many quote Romans 6:14 as saying that we are under a "dispensation of grace" because Christ nailed the commandments to the cross. They claim that obedience to the commandments is legalism and that those who keep the commandments of God "minimize" Christ's sacrifice on the cross. It is a strange belief considering the emphasis Jesus placed upon obedience to the commandments during His last hours with His disciples. The law of God is eternal and unchanging. Breaking the law brought death upon humanity. Jesus would not set aside the basis of God's government, but He would save us from transgression's penalty. "For the wages of sin is death, but the gift of God is eternal life in Christ Jesus our Lord" (Rom. 6:23).

"Now by this we know that we know Him, if we keep His commandments. He who says, 'I know Him,' and does not keep His commandments, is a liar, and the truth is not in him. But whoever keeps His word, truly the love of God is perfected in him. By this we know that we are in Him. He who says he abides in Him ought himself also to walk just as He walked" (1 John 2:3-6). How did Jesus walk? He tells us: "The Father has not left Me alone, for I always do those things that please Him" (John 8:29). "If you keep My commandments, you will abide in My love, just as I have kept My Father's commandments and abide in His love" (John 15:10). He says, "I delight to do Your will, O my God, and Your law is within my heart" (Ps. 40:8).

"What shall we say then? Shall we continue in sin [breaking the law] that grace [His unmerited favor to us] may abound? Certainly not!" (Rom. 6:1, 2). "What then? Shall we sin because we are not under the law but under grace? Certainly not!" (verse 15). If there is no law to break, there is no need of grace. By violating the law, we place ourselves under condemnation. Only when we repent and ask forgiveness through the merit of Christ's shed blood can He impart grace to us. His grace does not give us license to continue sinning.

Are we under grace? Yes, thank God! Are we still required to render loving obedience to God's law? If you love Him, the answer must be yes! Interestingly, the final conflict between Satan and Christ will be over commandment keeping (Rev. 12:17; 14:12).

A NEW COMMAND-MENT

A new command-ment I give to you, that you love one another; as I have loved you, that you also love one another. John 13:34.

Now, in the last moments with His disciples, Jesus focused upon those things He wanted them to remember. First, they must not feel deserted. After His crucifixion and burial they would see Him again. "Therefore you now have sorrow; but I will see you again and your heart will rejoice, and your joy no one will take from you" (John 16:22).

Jesus now gave His disciples what He called a "new" commandment. It wasn't really new, for Moses had already presented it to the Israelites. "You shall not take vengeance, nor bear any grudge against the children of your people, but you shall love your neighbor as yourself: I am the Lord" (Lev. 19:18). Christ told His disciples that the commandment of Leviticus 19 was to be broadened. "By His revelation of His Father's character Jesus had opened to men a new concept of the love of God. The new command enjoined men to preserve the same relationship with one another that Jesus had cultivated with them and mankind generally. Where the old commandment enjoined men to love their neighbors as themselves, the new urged them to love as Jesus had loved. The new was, in fact, more difficult than the old, but grace for its accomplishment was freely provided."[73]

John the beloved disciple understood what Jesus was saying for later he would write in 1 John 4:19: "We love Him because He first loved us." "By this we know that we love the children of God, when we love God and keep His commandments. For this is the love of God, that we keep His commandments. And His commandments are not burdensome" (1 John 5:2, 3). "Followers of great teachers reflect the characteristics of their teachers. Love was one of the principal attributes of Jesus. Jesus' life had been a practical demonstration of love in action. A manifestation of this same kind of love by the disciples of Jesus would give evidence of their relationship and close association with their Master. It is love rather than profession that marks the Christian."[74]

We are not capable of such love, for it is a gift from God. Love is long-suffering, kind, content, humble, civil, not self-seeking, mild, and pure. It rejoices not in sin but in truth, bears long, believes, hopes and endures all things, never fails. Such love is the greatest of all gifts! (1 Cor. 13:4-8).

SINGING PRAISES TO THE LAMB

And when they had sung a hymn, they went out to the Mount of Olives.

Mark 14:26.

Accorging to the Mishnah . . . , the ritual of the Passover meal was as follows: (1) The head of the family or group celebrating the supper together mixed the first cup of wine, and passed it to the others, pronouncing a blessing upon the day and upon the wine. (2) He then performed a ritual washing of his hands. (3) The table was then spread. Foods served at the paschal meal consisted of the paschal lamb, the unleavened bread, the bitter herbs, lettuce and other vegetables, and a relish sauce called *charoseth,* made of almonds, dates, figs, raisins, spice, and vinegar. At this stage some of the vegetables were eaten as an appetizer. (4) A second cup of wine was then passed around the circle, and the head of the family explained the meaning of the Passover. (5) The first part of the Passover hallel, consisting of Psalms 113 and 114, was sung. (6) The participants then ate of the Passover meal. The head of the family gave thanks for and broke the unleavened cakes, and distributed a portion to each guest. Portions of the paschal lamb were then eaten. (7) The third cup of wine was passed, and the benediction over the meal pronounced. (8) A fourth cup of wine was passed, after which all united in the second part of the hallel, consisting of Psalms 115 to 118."[75]

"Before leaving the upper chamber, the Saviour led His disciples in a song of praise. His voice was heard, not in the strains of some mournful lament, but in the joyful notes of the Passover hallel: 'O praise the Lord, all ye nations: praise him, all ye people. For his merciful kindness is great toward us: and the truth of the Lord endureth for ever. Praise ye the Lord' (Ps. 117, KJV). After the hymn, they went out. Through the crowded streets they made their way, passing out of the city gate toward the Mount of Olives."[76] Psalm 118, a part of the hallel, says: "God is the Lord, and He has given us light. . . . You are my God, and I will praise You; You are my God, I will exalt You. Oh, give thanks to the Lord, for He is good! For His mercy endures forever" (Ps. 118:27-29).

"Praise to God and the Lamb will be in our hearts and on our lips; for pride and self-worship cannot flourish in the soul that keeps fresh in memory the scenes of Calvary."[77]

THREE DENIALS BEFORE SUNRISE

But Peter said to Him, "Even if all are made to stumble, yet I will not be." Mark 14:29.

As the little group left Jerusalem, Jesus sadly announced, "All of you will be made to stumble because of Me this night, for it is written: 'I will strike the Shepherd, and the sheep of the flock will be scattered'" (Matt. 26:31). In the upper room Jesus had stated that Peter would deny his Lord. Now He repeated the prediction. Peter once again protested his Lord's claim. But he wasn't alone in vowing to follow Christ come what may. "They all said likewise" (Mark 14:31). Still not understanding their own weaknesses, they tended to discount the words of the One who knew for certain what would happen in the future.

"When Peter said he would follow His Lord to prison and to death, he meant it, every word of it; but he did not know himself. Hidden in his heart were elements of evil that circumstances would fan into life. Unless he was made conscious of his danger, these would prove his eternal ruin. The Saviour saw in him a self-love and assurance that would overbear even his love for Christ. . . . Peter needed to distrust himself, and to have a deeper faith in Christ."[78] "How true was the Saviour's friendship for Peter! how compassionate His warning! But the warning was resented. In self-sufficiency Peter declared confidently that he would never do what Christ had warned him against. 'Lord,' he said, 'I am ready to go with thee to prison and to death.' His self-confidence proved his ruin. He tempted Satan to tempt him, and he fell under the arts of the wily foe. When Christ needed him most, he stood on the side of the enemy, and openly denied his Lord."[79]

Jesus had prayed that Peter's faith might not fail. Satan possessed Judas and now had designs on Peter. Christ made the disciple aware of his enemy when He said, "Simon, Simon! Indeed, Satan has asked for you, that he may sift you as wheat" (Luke 22:31). If only Peter had remembered his experience on the Sea of Galilee. When he took his eyes off Christ he had started to sink beneath the waves. The hand of Christ waited to save him, but he needed to ask for salvation. "Lord, save me" (Matt. 14:30) should have been his plea now.

It should likewise be ours when tempted to believe we can defeat the devil in our own strength.

THE TRUE VINE

I am the vine, you are the branches.

John 15:5.

Slowly the group made its way to the foot of the Mount of Olives. "The Saviour had been explaining to His disciples His mission to the world, and the spiritual relation to Him which they were to sustain. Now He illustrates the lesson. The moon is shining bright, and reveals to Him a flourishing grapevine. Drawing the attention of the disciples to it, He employs it as a symbol. 'I am the true Vine,' He says. Instead of choosing the graceful palm, the lofty cedar, or the strong oak, Jesus takes the vine with its clinging tendrils to represent Himself. The palm tree, the cedar, and the oak stand alone. They require no support. But the vine entwines about the trellis, and thus climbs heavenward. So Christ in His humanity was dependent upon divine power. 'I can of mine own self do nothing,' He declared (John 5:30, KJV)."[80]

Israel had long ago adopted the vine as its national symbol. "At the entrance to the temple was a vine of gold and silver, with green leaves and massive clusters of grapes executed by the most skillful artists. This design represented Israel as a prosperous vine."[81] The Jews based salvation upon national heritage. Jesus now explained to His disciples that only a living and vital connection, by faith in Him as personal Saviour, would enable them to grow spiritually. The branch must maintain a constant link with the vine or it dies. By drawing upon the strength of the vine itself, the branch may flourish and yield fruit. "When we live by faith on the Son of God, the fruits of the Spirit will be seen in our life; not one will be missing."[82]

The Christlike character shows the world those who are branches of Christ. One who takes the name of "Christian" must display the fruits of righteousness (Phil. 1:11). "A profession of religion places men in the church, but the character and conduct show whether they are in connection with Christ."[83] Men and women may fake a vital connection to Christ and profess great piety. While it may gain them a place in the church, trial and test will eventually prune away such fruitless branches. It is meaningless to have your name registered on church books if you are not growing in Jesus.

"There can be no life without growth. As long as there is life there is need of continual development. Character development is the work of a lifetime."[84]

NOT OF THIS WORLD

If the world hates you, you know that it hated Me before it hated you.

John 15:18.

In this last meeting with His disciples, the great desire which Christ expressed for them was that they might love one another as He had loved them. . . . To the disciples this commandment was new; for they had not loved one another as Christ had loved them. . . . The command to love one another had new meaning in the light of His self-sacrifice. The whole work of grace is one continual service of love, of self-denying, self-sacrificing effort. During every hour of Christ's sojourn upon the earth, the love of God was flowing from Him in irrepressible streams. All who are imbued with His Spirit will love as He loved."[85]

Brotherly love characterizes the true disciple. The world is not our home, and shortly its full fury will turn against us. But it should not surprise us. As the world's Redeemer, Christ constantly endured apparent failure. He seemed to accomplish little of the work He longed to do in uplifting and saving. At every turn Satanic influences blocked His way. Christ said, "Blessed are you when they revile and persecute you, and say all kinds of evil against you falsely for My sake. Rejoice and be exceedingly glad, for great is your reward in heaven, for so they persecuted the prophets who were before you" (Matt. 5:11, 12). Those who live consistently righteous lives will encounter persecution. The world cannot stand the rebuke of a life devoted to God (1 John 3:13, 14).

Those who profess to worship God but do not understand His character and twist His Word "do not know Him" (John 15:21). "Therefore, to him who knows to do good and does not do it, to him it is sin" (James 4:17). But the Word of God is plain and the example of His Son is clear. Jesus is the way, the truth, the life (John 14:6). "In the judgment men will be condemned not because they have been in error but because they 'have neglected heaven-sent opportunities for learning what is truth' (*The Desire of Ages*, p. 490)."[86] The disciples finally learned the lesson of love, eliminated all rivalry from among them (Luke 22:24; Acts 2:2), and became courageous in the face of persecution (Acts 5:41; 2 Cor. 4:8-12).

His grace is also sufficient for you, for His strength is made perfect in weakness (2 Cor. 12:9).

THIS IS ETERNAL LIFE

And this is eternal life, that they may know You, the only true God, and Jesus Christ whom You have sent.

John 17:3.

Jesus told His disciples, "Whatever you ask the Father in My name He will give you" (John 16:23). "For the Father Himself loves you, because you have loved Me, and have believed that I came forth from God" (verse 27). Jesus intercedes with the Father for us. "Therefore He is also able to save to the uttermost those who come to God through Him, since He always lives to make intercession for them" (Heb. 7:25). God loves the entire world (John 3:16), but when men and women respond with love to His Son, He pours a greater manifestation of that love upon those who love Jesus.

John 17 is Jesus' longest recorded prayer. It divides into three natural parts: (1) the prayer for Himself (verses 1-5); (2) the prayer for His disciples (verses 6-19); and (3) the prayer for all believers (verses 20-26). Jesus raised His eyes toward His heavenly Father when He prayed, something unusual, since most Jews turned their eyes toward the Temple. Jesus' prayer starts with the words: "Father, the hour has come. Glorify Your Son, that Your Son also may glorify You" (verse 1). The Father and the Son were intimately linked in the plan of salvation. As Jesus would be glorified when lifted up at the cross and again at His resurrection, so God would be glorified in the completion of the mission Jesus came to do on earth. Salvation comes not simply by knowing about Jesus but through following Him. Both knowledge and development of a Christian character are essential to eternal life. Romans 10:13 says: "For 'whoever calls on the name of the Lord shall be saved.'" Such knowledge of Christ is vital! We do not want to repeat what the Lord said about ancient Israel: "My people are destroyed for lack of knowledge. Because you have rejected knowledge, I also will reject you from being priest for Me; because you have forgotten the law of your God, I also will forget your children" (Hosea 4:6). Salvation involves more than simple knowledge, however.

We must first gain knowledge of Him and then love Him enough to follow Him through obedience. Obedience shows our love for the One who loved us first. Eternal life is simply a bonus.

A PRAYER FOR US

Sanctify them by Your truth. Your word is truth.

John 17:17.

About to leave His disciples, Jesus committed their safekeeping to His Father. "Now I am no longer in the world, but these are in the world, and I come to You. Holy Father, keep through Your name those whom You have given Me, that they may be one as We are" (John 17:11). Jesus continued, "I do not pray that You should take them out of the world, but that You should keep them from the evil one" (verse 15). The disciples had a mission to accomplish. Chosen to take the gospel to the world, they first needed to develop Christlike characters. How would they do that? Christ answered, "Sanctify them by Your truth. Your word is truth" (verse 17). In other words, "Make them holy [an attribute of God] by Your truth."

Humanity has long sought to know what constitutes truth. Even Pilate asked Jesus, "What is truth?" (John 18:38). Jesus says: "If you abide in My word, you are My disciples indeed. And you shall know the truth, and the truth shall make you free" (John 8:31, 32). "The Word of God is declared to be 'truth.' The Scriptures reveal to us the character of God and of Jesus Christ. We become new creatures by making the truths of the Word of God a part of the life."[87]

If knowledge is important, so is character development. In His lesson of the True Vine, Jesus said, "If anyone does not abide in Me, he is cast out as a branch and is withered; and they gather them and throw them into the fire, and they are burned" (John 15:6). Such a statement strikes at the heart of the concept "once saved, always saved." "It is possible for those who have been in Christ to sever their connection with Him and be lost (see . . . Heb. 6:4-6). Salvation is conditional upon abiding in Christ until the end."[88] "If you would become acquainted with the Saviour, study the Holy Scriptures."[89] "It is heart work. Bible sanctification is not the spurious sanctification of today, which will not search the Scriptures, but trusts to good feelings and impulses rather than to the seeking for truth as for hidden treasure. Bible sanctification is to know the requirements of God and to obey them."[90]

Scripture refers to people who believe they are saved and can do whatever they like without worry about the consequences as "having a form of godliness but denying its power. And from such people turn away!" (2 Tim. 3:5).

THERE WAS A GARDEN

When Jesus had spoken these words, He went out with His disciples over the Brook Kidron, where there was a garden, which He and His disciples entered. John 18:1.

In company with His disciples, the Saviour slowly made His way to the garden of Gethsemane. The Passover moon, broad and full, shone from a cloudless sky. The city of pilgrims' tents was hushed into silence. Jesus had been earnestly conversing with His disciples and instructing them; but as He neared Gethsemane, He became strangely silent. He had often visited this spot for meditation and prayer; but never with a heart so full of sorrow as upon this night of His last agony."[91] Gethsemane derived its name from the olive groves that covered the slopes of the Mount of Olives. The name meant "oil press" in Aramaic, and the lower western slope of the mount contained a garden.

Arriving at the entrance, Jesus left eight of the disciples just inside the gate. Taking Peter, James, and John, Jesus moved even farther into the secluded recesses of the garden. They had seen Christ's glory on the Mount of Transfiguration and Jesus now desired them with Him during His struggle. Many times they had accompanied Him only to pray for a time before drifting off into sleep. This time Jesus wanted them to stay awake and pray with Him. "Stay here and watch," He entreated.

"He went a little distance from them—not so far but that they could both see and hear Him—and fell prostrate upon the ground. He felt that by sin He was being separated from His Father. The gulf was so broad, so black, so deep, that His spirit shuddered before it. This agony He must not exert His divine power to escape. As man He must suffer the consequences of man's sin. As man He must endure the wrath of God against transgression."[92] "He is tempted to fear" He will be "shut . . . out forever from His Father's love. Feeling how terrible is the wrath of God against transgression, He exclaims, 'My soul is exceeding sorrowful, even unto death.'"[93] Now Satan arrived at the scene of the struggle.

Some of the weight of sin upon Christ came from you and me. Not a day should pass that we do not thank Him. When seemingly overwhelmed with pain and sorrow, we should go to dark Gethsemane and see our Saviour anew. Rejoice! He loved you enough to suffer for you.

"Stay Here and Watch With Me"

Then He came to the disciples and found them sleeping. Matt. 26:40.

In agony Jesus "clings to the cold ground, as if to prevent Himself from being drawn farther from God. The chilling dew of night falls upon His prostrate form, but He heeds it not. From His pale lips comes the bitter cry, 'O my Father, if it be possible, let this cup pass from me.' Yet even now He adds, 'Nevertheless not as I will, but as thou wilt.'"[94] "Terrible was the temptation to let the human race bear the consequences of its own guilt, while He stood innocent before God. If He could only know that His disciples understood and appreciated this, He would be strengthened."[95]

Longing for human companionship, Jesus stumbled to where He had left His disciples, only to find them sleeping (Mark 14:37, 38). "Fainting and exhausted, He staggered back to the place of His former struggle. His suffering was even greater than before. As the agony of soul came upon Him, 'his sweat was as it were great drops of blood falling down to the ground.'"[96] "Now His voice was heard on the still evening air, not in tones of triumph, but full of human anguish. The words of the Saviour were borne to the ears of the drowsy disciples, 'O my Father, if this cup may not pass away from me, except I drink it, thy will be done.'"[97]

Jesus again returned to His disciples. When they awoke and saw His face covered with blood, it frightened them. "So His visage was marred more than any man, and His form more than the sons of men" (Isa. 52:14). Once more leaving them, Jesus collapsed to the ground. "The awful moment had come—that moment which was to decide the destiny of the world. The fate of humanity trembled in the balance. Christ might even now refuse to drink the cup apportioned to guilty man. It was not yet too late. He might wipe the bloody sweat from His brow, and leave man to perish in his iniquity. He might say, Let the transgressor receive the penalty of his sin, and I will go back to My Father."[98] But Jesus recognized that without Him sinners would perish. Left alone, the human race would find itself helpless against sin's power. If He shrank from His sacrifice, it would doom humanity, and in that moment "His decision is made. He will save man at any cost to Himself."[99]

What do you and I owe Him? More than we can possibly repay!

"LET THIS CUP PASS"

O My Father, if it is possible, let this cup pass from Me.

Matt. 26:39.

Intensely heaven watched the struggle of their beloved Commander. "They saw their Lord enclosed by legions of satanic forces, His human nature weighed down with a shuddering, mysterious dread. Everywhere He may look is a horror of great darkness beyond the measurement of human minds. And there was silence in heaven; no harp was touched. Could mortals have viewed the amazement of the angelic host as they watched in silent grief the Father separating His beams of light, love, and glory from the beloved Son, they would better understand how offensive sin is in His sight."[1] "The human nature of Christ was like unto ours, and suffering was more keenly felt by Him; for His spiritual nature was free from every taint of sin. Therefore His desire for the removal of suffering was stronger than human beings can experience. How intense was the desire of the humanity of Christ to escape the displeasure of an offended God, how His soul longed for relief, is revealed in the words 'O my Father, if this cup may not pass away from me, except I drink it, thy will be done.'"[2]

"The worlds unfallen and the heavenly angels had watched with intense interest as the conflict drew to its close. Satan and his confederacy of evil, the legions of apostasy, watched intently this great crisis in the work of redemption. The powers of good and evil waited to see what answer would come to Christ's thrice-repeated prayer. Angels had longed to bring relief to the divine sufferer, but this might not be."[3] God did not forget His Son. "In this awful crisis, when everything was at stake, when the mysterious cup trembled in the hand of the sufferer, the heavens opened, a light shone forth amid the stormy darkness of the crisis hour, and the mighty angel who stands in God's presence, occupying the position from which Satan fell, came to the side of Christ. The angel came not to take the cup from Christ's hand, but to strengthen Him to drink it, with the assurance of the Father's love."[4] "Gabriel is sent to strengthen the divine Sufferer, and brace Him to tread His bloodstained path. And while the angel supports His fainting form, Christ takes the bitter cup, and consents to drink its contents."[5]

"For wages of sin is death, but the gift of God is eternal life in Christ Jesus our Lord" (Rom. 6:23). Amen.

SLEEPING SENTINELS

Then an angel appeared to Him from heaven, strengthening Him.
Luke 22:43.

The Garden of Eden, with its foul blot of disobedience, is to be carefully studied and compared with the Garden of Gethsemane, where the world's Redeemer suffered superhuman agony when the sins of the whole world were rolled upon Him. . . . Adam did not stop to calculate the result of his disobedience."[6] "The Son of God prayed in agony. Great drops of blood gathered upon His face and fell to the ground. Angels were hovering over the place, witnessing the scene, but only one was commissioned to go and strengthen the Son of God in His agony. There was no joy in heaven. The angels cast their crowns and harps from them and with the deepest interest silently watched Jesus. They wished to surround the Son of God, but the commanding angels suffered them not, lest, as they should behold His betrayal, they should deliver Him; for the plan had been laid, and it must be fulfilled."[7]

God suffered the separation and felt the pangs of heartache as intensely as did His only-begotten Son. The message Gabriel brought did not seek to relieve Christ of His burden but rather to strengthen Him. "He pointed Him to the open heavens, telling Him of the souls that would be saved as the result of His sufferings. He assured Him that His Father is greater and more powerful than Satan, that His death would result in the utter discomfiture of Satan, and that the kingdom of this world would be given to the saints of the Most High. He told Him that He would see the travail of His soul, and be satisfied, for He would see a multitude of the human race saved, eternally saved."[8]

Peter, James, and John witnessed the form of an angel bowing over their prostrate Master. They saw him take Jesus' head and rest it upon his own chest, then point heavenward. After hearing the sweet tones of his voice speak comforting words, they drifted off again into sleep. Unable to comprehend their Master's suffering and anguish, they do not see the coming storm about to shatter their feeble faith.

How few of us go to dark Gethsemane with our Lord to watch and pray. We fail because we are rather more like Peter, James, and John, the sleeping disciples. As a result we are a sleeping church. When admonished to watch lest we fall into temptation, many of us slumber.

LANTERNS, TORCHES, AND WEAPONS

Then Judas, having received a detachment of troops, and officers from the chief priests and Pharisees, came there with lanterns, torches, and weapons. John 18:3.

A s Jesus returned a third time to find the disciples sleeping He heard the footsteps and saw the torchlight of the mob searching for Him. Judas led them right to the spot where he knew the Master would be. With calm dignity Jesus faced the crowd, and as they approached He asked, "Whom are you seeking?" They answered, "Jesus of Nazareth." He replied, "I am He." "As these words were spoken, the angel who had lately ministered to Jesus moved between Him and the mob. A divine light illuminated the Saviour's face, and a dovelike form overshadowed Him. In the presence of this divine glory, the murderous throng could not stand for a moment. They staggered back. Priests, elders, soldiers, and even Judas, fell as dead men to the ground. The angel withdrew, and the light faded away. Jesus had opportunity to escape, but He remained, calm and self-possessed. As one glorified He stood in the midst of that hardened band, now prostrate and helpless at His feet."[9] Quickly they scrambled to their feet. Again Jesus asked, "Whom are you seeking?" Again they told Him, "Jesus of Nazareth." Jesus repeated, "I have told you that I am He. Therefore, if you seek Me, let these go their way." Jesus, wishing to shield His disciples, proposed that the mob let them leave in peace.

Judas had not forgotten his role. "When the mob entered the garden, he had led the way, closely followed by the high priest. To the pursuers of Jesus he had given a sign, saying, 'Whomsoever I shall kiss, that same is he: hold him fast' (Matt. 26:48, KJV). Now he pretends to have no part with them. Coming close to Jesus, he takes His hand as a familiar friend. With the words, 'Hail, Master,' he kisses Him repeatedly, and appears to weep as if in sympathy with Him in His peril."[10] Looking at him with pitying eyes, Jesus says, "Judas, are you betraying the Son of man with a kiss?" Judas stiffened, stubborn and defiant. At the touch of Judas, the crowd grew bold and seized Christ. The Temple police brought cords, and they "proceeded to bind those precious hands that had ever been employed in doing good."[11] The disciples watched in the flickering torchlight as the mob jostled and held their Lord. The scene was truly unbelievable.

Whom are you seeking?

MALCHUS

Then Simon Peter, having a sword, drew it and struck the high priest's servant, and cut off his right ear. The servant's name was Malchus.
John 18:10.

The account of the arrest of Jesus in the book of John is unique. "John, who was personally acquainted with the high priest (see John 18:15), identifies the servant as Malchus. . . . Malchus may have been one of those who 'laid hands on Jesus' Matt. 26:50, KJV)." [12] Jesus stood calmly in their midst. It amazed the disciples that their Master would allow Himself to be taken. Now disappointment swept over them as Jesus let the mob bind His hands.

"Peter in his anger rashly drew his sword and tried to defend his Master, but he only cut off an ear of the high priest's servant. When Jesus saw what was done, He released His hands, though held firmly by the Roman soldiers, and saying, 'Suffer ye thus far,' He touched the wounded ear, and it was instantly made whole." [13] "Peter's rash act could easily have been construed by the Jewish leaders as evidence that Jesus and His disciples were a band of dangerous revolutionaries, and this charge might have been pressed against Him as valid proof that His death was in the public interest." [14] The only defense a Christian may make is to use the "sword of the Spirit, which is the word of God" (Eph. 6:17). Christians are not to use or condone force (Matt. 5:39). "We do not defend the life-giving gospel by killing men for whom Christ died. The supreme evidence of Christian love is willingness to die for others (see John 15:13)." [15]

Facing the priests and Temple police, Jesus fixed them with a searching glance. "The words He spoke they would never forget as long as life should last." [16] "Have you come out, as against a robber, with swords and clubs? When I was with you daily in the temple, you did not try to seize Me. But this is your hour, and the power of darkness" (Luke 22:52, 53). Then turning to Peter, He said, "Put your sword in its place, for all who take the sword will perish by the sword. Or do you think that I cannot now pray to My Father, and He will provide Me with more than twelve legions of angels? How then could the Scriptures be fulfilled, that it must happen thus?" (Matt. 26:52-54).

At least 80,000 angels stood ready to deliver their Commander, yet He chose to surrender and die for you and me.

FATHER-IN-LAW TO CAIAPHAS

And they led Him away to Annas first, for he was the father-in-law of Caiaphas who was high priest that year. John 18:13.

The disciples were terrified as they saw Jesus permit Himself to be taken and bound. They were offended that He should suffer this humiliation to Himself and them. They could not understand His conduct, and they blamed Him for submitting to the mob. In their indignation and fear, Peter proposed that they save themselves. Following this suggestion, 'they all forsook him, and fled.'"[17] Jesus had already foreseen such a reaction (John 16:32). He meekly submitted to the Temple police roughly shoving Him along the path to Jerusalem while brave Peter fled with the rest of the disciples.

"Over the brook Kedron, past gardens and olive groves, and through the hushed streets of the sleeping city, they hurried Jesus. It was past midnight, and the cries of the hooting mob that followed Him broke sharply upon the still air. The Saviour was bound and closely guarded, and He moved painfully. But in eager haste His captors made their way with Him to the palace of Annas, the ex-high priest. Annas was the head of the officiating priestly family, and in deference to his age he was recognized by the people as high priest. . . . The less-experienced Caiaphas might fail of securing the object for which they were working. His [Annas'] artifice, cunning, and subtlety must be used on this occasion; for, at all events, Christ's condemnation must be secured."[18]

Annas first tried to prove that Jesus had been secretly formulating plans to overthrow Rome. Jesus denied the charge. "I spoke openly to the world. I always taught in synagogues and in the temple, where the Jews always meet, and in secret I have said nothing" (John 18:20). His accusers were guiltier than He, for their secret midnight seizure was illegal. Israelite law considered a man innocent until proven guilty. They had also violated their law by binding His hands, signifying conviction of a crime. "Annas was silenced by the decision of the answer. Fearing that Christ would say something regarding his course of action that he would prefer to keep covered up, he said nothing more to Him at this time. One of his officers, filled with wrath as he saw Annas silenced, struck Jesus on the face, saying, 'Answerest Thou the high priest so?'"[19] The former high priest knew that speed was vital before public opinion could rally to Jesus' defense, so he ordered the prisoner taken at once to the Sanhedrin.

How often a wrong position is covered by a need to speed "justice."

320

BEFORE THE SANHEDRIN ONE LAST TIME

And those who had laid hold of Jesus led Him away to Caiaphas the high priest, where the scribes and the elders were assembled. Matt. 26:57.

"It was now early morning, and very dark; by the light of torches and lanterns the armed band with their prisoner proceeded to the high priest's palace. Here, while the members of the Sanhedrin were coming together, Annas and Caiaphas again questioned Jesus, but without success."[20] The assembly did not summon Joseph of Arimathaea and Nicodemus, because it knew they would defend Jesus. "When the council had assembled in the judgment hall, Caiaphas took his seat as presiding officer. On either side were the judges, and those specially interested in the trial. The Roman soldiers were stationed on the platform below the throne. At the foot of the throne stood Jesus. Upon Him the gaze of the whole multitude was fixed. The excitement was intense. Of all the throng He alone was calm and serene. The very atmosphere surrounding Him seemed pervaded by a holy influence."[21] Jesus had already endured two preliminary hearings: first before Annas, and again before Annas and Caiaphas. Now He stood before the ecclesiastical body of the Jewish nation to be arraigned.

The Sanhedrin consisted almost equally of Pharisees and Sadducees, and neither party cherished any love for the other. Caiaphas feared Jesus might play upon points of contention and lock the two groups in endless debate and argument. His seemingly impossible task was to steer clear of any topic that might create dissension. The arraignment must avoid three rather obvious charges: 1. Jesus had denounced the scribes and priests and labeled them hypocrites and murderers, but Sadducees routinely called Pharisees these names and worse. This charge was mute. 2. Witnesses might claim Jesus had no regard for Jewish tradition. Again Pharisee and Sadducee disagreed among themselves on the observance of certain traditions, and besides, the Romans cared little for Jewish tradition. 3. Witnesses could claim Jesus broke the Sabbath. Examination of this claim would show the true character of His work, and that they must also avoid at all costs. Any charges brought this night must excite no controversy, and Caiaphas was a rather inexperienced Sanhedrin president. Many feared he would fail to get a conviction. The universe now witnessed the greatest travesty of justice ever seen.

In the midst of turmoil, Jesus stood serene, totally trusting His Father. What faith!

SILENT AS A LAMB (ISAIAH 53:7)

But Jesus kept silent. Matt. 26:63.

As Caiaphas now looked upon the prisoner, he was struck with admiration for His noble and dignified bearing. A conviction came over him that this Man was akin to God. The next instant he scornfully banished the thought. Immediately his voice was heard in sneering, haughty tones demanding that Jesus work one of His mighty miracles before them. But his words fell upon the Saviour's ears as though He heard them not." [22] False witnesses next claimed Jesus had incited rebellion against Rome, but their testimony proved confusing and ineffective. The priests charged that Jesus had threatened the Temple when He said, "Destroy this temple, and in three days I will raise it up" (John 2:19). He had of course referred to the death and resurrection of His own body (verse 21), but the Jews took the statement literally. "The Romans had engaged in rebuilding and embellishing the Temple, and they took great pride in it; any contempt shown to it would be sure to excite their indignation. Here Romans and Jews, Pharisees and Sadducees, could meet; for all held the Temple in great veneration. On this point two witnesses were found whose testimony was not so contradictory as that of the others had been." [23]

By now it was almost 4:00 a.m. The trial had been in progress for almost an hour with no result. The Mishnah stated that capital offense trials must take place during daylight to allow the accused the opportunity to call defense witnesses. But the Sanhedrin did not want that. They had "determined to settle the case, and put Jesus in the custody of the Romans, before anyone should have opportunity to speak in His defense." [24] "Patiently Jesus listened to the conflicting testimonies. No word did He utter in self-defense. At last His accusers were entangled, confused, and maddened. The trial was making no headway; it seemed that their plottings were to fail. Caiaphas was desperate. One last resort remained; Christ must be forced to condemn Himself. The high priest started from the judgment seat, his face contorted with passion, his voice and demeanor plainly indicating that were it in his power he would strike down the prisoner before him. 'Answerest Thou nothing?' he exclaimed; 'what is it which these witness against thee?' " [25]

" 'He was oppressed, and he was afflicted, yet he opened not his mouth: he is brought as a lamb to the slaughter, and as a sheep before her shearers is dumb, so he openeth not his mouth' (Isa. 53:7, KJV)." [26]

DEATH SENTENCE

Then the high priest tore his clothes, saying, "He has spoken blasphemy!" Matt. 26:65.

At last, Caiaphas, raising his right hand toward heaven, addressed Jesus in the form of a solemn oath: 'I adjure thee by the living God, that thou tell us whether thou be the Christ, the Son of God.' To this appeal Christ could not remain silent. . . . His own relation to the Father was called in question. He must plainly declare His character and mission." [27] "Every ear was bent to listen, and every eye was fixed on His face as He answered, 'Thou hast said.' A heavenly light seemed to illuminate His pale countenance as He added, 'Nevertheless I say unto you, Hereafter shall ye see the Son of man sitting on the right hand of power, and coming in the clouds of heaven.' For a moment the divinity of Christ flashed through His guise of humanity. The high priest quailed before the penetrating eyes of the Saviour. That look seemed to read his hidden thoughts, and burn into his heart. Never in afterlife did he forget that searching glance of the persecuted Son of God." [28]

Tearing his priestly robes in pretended horror, Caiaphas demanded that the assembly condemn the prisoner for blasphemy. "The charge of *blasphemy,* on the basis of which Caiaphas demanded the death penalty (Matt. 26:65, 66), was invalid. According to *Sanhedrin* 7. 5, Soncino ed. of the Talmud (p. 378), 'The blasphemer is punished only if he utters [the divine] Name' itself, that is *Yahweh* (Jehovah), and the punishment for blasphemy was death by hanging (*ibid.* 6. 4 [p. 300]) or stoning (*ibid.* 7. 4 [p. 359]). Jesus did not use the sacred name for God." [29] The technicality made no difference to Caiaphas. Jesus would never leave the chambers without receiving a death sentence. "They answered and said, 'He is deserving of death.' Then they spat in His face and beat Him; and others struck Him with the palms of their hands, saying, 'Prophesy to us, Christ! Who is the one who struck You?' " (Matt. 26:66-68).

Caiaphas broke more than one law to gain a conviction. Christ had told Moses, "Do not uncover your heads nor tear your clothes, lest you die, and wrath come upon all the people" (Lev. 10:6). "Everything worn by the priest was to be whole and without blemish. By those beautiful official garments was represented the character of the great antitype, Jesus Christ. Nothing but perfection, in dress and attitude, in word and spirit, could be acceptable to God." [30]

By tearing his priestly robes Caiaphas himself committed blasphemy. "Standing under the condemnation of God, he pronounced sentence upon Christ as a blasphemer." [31]

THE LOOK THAT BROKE A HEART

And the Lord turned and looked at Peter. So Peter went out and wept bitterly. Luke 22:61, 62.

After deserting their Master in the garden, two of the disciples had ventured to follow, at a distance, the mob that had Jesus in charge. These disciples were Peter and John. The priests recognized John as a well-known disciple of Jesus, and admitted him to the hall, hoping that as he witnessed the humiliation of his Leader, he would scorn the idea of such a one being the Son of God. John spoke in favor of Peter, and gained an entrance for him also. In the court a fire had been kindled; for it was the coldest hour of the night, being just before the dawn." [32] Peter, though trying to remain inconspicuous, warmed himself by the fire. "As the light flashed upon Peter's face, the woman who kept the door cast a searching glance upon him. She had noticed that he came in with John, she marked the look of dejection on his face, and thought that he might be a disciple of Jesus." [33] She said, " 'You also were with Jesus of Nazareth.' But he denied it, saying, 'I neither know nor understand what you are saying.' And he went out on the porch, and a rooster crowed" (Mark 14:67, 68).

A second servant girl commented to those nearby, "This is one of them" (verse 69). Peter pretended he didn't hear, but she continued to press him. His denial, "Woman, I do not know Him" (Luke 22:57), he now coupled with an oath. "An hour had passed, when one of the servants of the high priest, being a near kinsman of the man whose ear Peter had cut off, asked him, 'Did not I see thee in the garden with him?' 'Surely thou art one of them: for thou art a Galilean, and thy speech agreeth thereto.' At this Peter flew into a rage. . . . Peter now denied his Master with cursing and swearing. Again the cock crew. Peter heard it then, and he remembered the words of Jesus, 'Before the cock crow twice, thou shalt deny me thrice' (Mark 14:30, KJV)." [34] At that moment Jesus turned from His judges and looked full into the face of His disciple. Peter saw no anger in His expression, only sorrow, pity, and forgiveness. His heart breaking, Peter fled into the night.

Real danger exists in overestimating our abilities apart from Christ. It is equally risky to try to follow the Lord from a distance.

A KEENER ANGUISH

When morning came, all the chief priests and elders of the people plotted against Jesus to put Him to death. Matt. 27:1.

Peter ran out into the darkness not knowing where he went nor really caring. "The sight of that pale, suffering face, those quivering lips, that look of compassion and forgiveness, pierced his heart like an arrow. . . . He pressed on in solitude and darkness."[35] The disciple found himself drawn to Gethsemane. Devastated, he "prostrated himself where he had seen His Saviour's prostrate form. He remembered with remorse that he was asleep when Jesus prayed during those fearful hours. His proud heart broke, and penitential tears moistened the sod so recently stained with the bloody sweat-drops of God's dear Son. He left the garden a converted man."[36]

"The record indicates that all three denials were made during the first trial before the Sanhedrin, which took place between about 3:00 and 5:00 a.m. The first light of dawn would become visible about 4:00 at this season of the year, in the latitude of Jerusalem, and sunrise would be about 5:30."[37] The Sanhedrin could not by Jewish law try a prisoner at night. Therefore the authorities took Jesus to a guardroom until daylight. "While in the guardroom, awaiting His legal trial, He was not protected. The ignorant rabble had seen the cruelty with which He was treated before the council, and from this they took license to manifest all the satanic elements of their nature. Christ's very nobility and godlike bearing goaded them to madness. His meekness, His innocence, His majestic patience, filled them with hatred born of Satan. Mercy and justice were trampled upon. Never was [a] criminal treated in so inhuman a manner as was the Son of God. But a keener anguish rent the heart of Jesus; the blow that inflicted the deepest pain no enemy's hand could have dealt. While He was undergoing the mockery of an examination before Caiaphas, Christ had been denied by one of His own disciples."[38]

The Sanhedrin reassembled at dawn, and again guards roughly jostled Jesus into the council room. Many now present had not heard Him the night before. Again they asked, "Are You then the Son of God?" Jesus remained silent but finally said, " 'You rightly say that I am.' And they said, 'What further testimony do we need? For we have heard it ourselves from His own mouth' " (Luke 22:70, 71).

And the Jewish Sanhedrin condemned Him to death in the light of the new day.

BLOOD MONEY

"I have sinned by betraying innocent blood." Matt. 27:4.

That Jesus allowed Himself to be bound and taken from Gethsemane shocked Judas. Anxiously he waited for the Master to free Himself, "but as hour after hour went by, and Jesus submitted to all the abuse heaped upon Him, a terrible fear came to the traitor that he had sold his Master to His death." [39] As he stared in horror about him in the judgment hall Judas felt that he had started a tragic chain of events that nothing could stop.

"Suddenly a hoarse voice rang through the hall, sending a thrill of terror to all hearts: He is innocent; spare Him, O Caiaphas! The tall form of Judas was now seen pressing through the startled throng. His face was pale and haggard, and great drops of sweat stood on his forehead. Rushing to the throne of judgment, he threw down before the high priest the pieces of silver that had been the price of his Lord's betrayal. Eagerly grasping the robe of Caiaphas, he implored him to release Jesus, declaring that He had done nothing worthy of death. Caiaphas angrily shook him off, but was confused, and knew not what to say. The perfidy of the priests was revealed. It was evident that they had bribed the disciple to betray his Master." [40] Their bribe had directly violated the laws of Moses (Ex. 23:8).

Anguish overwhelmed Judas. "I have sinned by betraying innocent blood," he cried. The high priest, recovering his composure, scornfully answered, "What is that to us? You see to it!" Throwing himself at the feet of Jesus, Judas acknowledged before all that Christ was the Son of God. He pleaded with Christ to spare Himself. Jesus neither reproached nor condemned Judas. Instead, looking at him with compassion, He said, "For this hour came I into the world." "A murmur of surprise ran through the assembly. With amazement they beheld the forbearance of Christ toward His betrayer. Again there swept over them the conviction that this Man was more than mortal. . . . Judas saw that his entreaties were in vain, and he rushed from the hall exclaiming, It is too late! It is too late! He felt that he could not live to see Jesus crucified, and in despair went out and hanged himself." [41]

Judas sold his Master for 30 pieces of silver. What price would you have taken to deny Him? Many are shocked at the suggestion they would sell out their Lord. Does your lifestyle deny Him now?

A TRAVESTY OF JUSTICE

And they bound Jesus, led Him away, and delivered Him to Pilate. Mark 15:1.

Jesus now stood sentenced to death by the highest court of the land. To carry out the sentence the Sanhedrin must hand Him over to Roman authorities. "When the condemnation of Jesus was pronounced by the judges, a satanic fury took possession of the people. The roar of voices was like that of wild beasts. The crowd made a rush toward Jesus, crying, He is guilty, put Him to death! Had it not been for the Roman soldiers, Jesus would not have lived to be nailed to the cross of Calvary. He would have been torn in pieces before His judges, had not Roman authority interfered, and by force of arms restrained the violence of the mob.

"Heathen men [the Romans] were angry at the brutal treatment of one against whom nothing had been proved. The Roman officers declared that the Jews in pronouncing condemnation upon Jesus were infringing upon the Roman power, and that it was even against the Jewish law to condemn a man to death upon his own testimony. This intervention brought a momentary lull in the proceedings; but the Jewish leaders were dead alike to pity and to shame.

"Priests and rulers forgot the dignity of their office, and abused the Son of God with foul epithets. They taunted Him with His parentage. They declared that His presumption in proclaiming Himself the Messiah made Him deserving of the most ignominious death. The most dissolute men engaged in infamous abuse of the Saviour. An old garment was thrown over His head, and His persecutors struck Him in the face, saying, 'Prophesy unto us, Thou Christ, Who is he that smote Thee?' When the garment was removed, one poor wretch spat in His face.

"The angels of God faithfully recorded every insulting look, word, and act against their beloved Commander. One day the base men who scorned and spat upon the calm, pale face of Christ will look upon it in its glory, shining brighter than the sun."[42] John witnessed the entire travesty of a trial. "He was not questioned, for he did not assume a false character, and thus lay himself liable to suspicion. He sought a retired corner secure from the notice of the mob, but as near Jesus as it was possible for him to be. Here he could see and hear all that took place at the trial of his Lord."[43]

Angels still record every word and act we commit for or against Jesus.

A DECEIVER OF THE PEOPLE

Then the whole multitude of them arose and led Him to Pilate. Luke 23:1.

Pilate was aroused early in the morning, at approximately 6:00 or soon thereafter."[44] "In the judgment hall of Pilate, the Roman governor, Christ stands bound as a prisoner. About Him are the guard of soldiers, and the hall is fast filling with spectators. Just outside the entrance are the judges of the Sanhedrin, priests, rulers, elders, and the mob. . . . But these Jewish officials would not enter the Roman judgment hall. According to their ceremonial law they would be defiled thereby, and thus prevented from taking part in the feast of the Passover. . . . They did not see that Christ was the real Passover lamb, and that, since they had rejected Him, the great feast had for them lost its significance."[45]

The Roman procurator was not in a good mood. His sleep interrupted, he wanted to deal with the disturbance as quickly as possible. But when he saw Jesus, he stopped short. Expecting a hardened criminal, instead "he saw no sign of guilt, no expression of fear, no boldness or defiance. He saw a man of calm and dignified bearing, whose countenance bore not the marks of a criminal, but the signature of heaven. Christ's appearance made a favorable impression upon Pilate. . . . He had heard of Jesus and His works. . . . He resolved to demand of the Jews their charges against the prisoner."[46]

Turning to the priests, Pilate asked, "Who is this Man, and wherefore have ye brought Him? What accusation bring ye against Him?" They answered, "Jesus of Nazareth, a deceiver of the people." Again Pilate demanded, "What accusation bring ye against this Man?" The priests refused to respond. "What is your sentence?" he persisted. "Death," they replied, "but we cannot lawfully put a man to death. Trust us, this man deserves to die. We will take responsibility for the act." "Pilate was not a just or a conscientious judge; but weak though he was in moral power, he refused to grant this request. He would not condemn Jesus until a charge had been brought against Him. The priests were in a dilemma. They saw that they must cloak their hypocrisy under the thickest concealment. They must not allow it to appear that Christ had been arrested on religious grounds. Were this put forward as a reason, their proceedings would have no weight with Pilate."[47]

Labeling Jesus a deceiver of the people, the priests sought to trick Pilate by hiding their true intent.

"ARE YOU THE KING OF THE JEWS?"

Now Jesus stood before the governor. Matt. 27:11.

As the priests could not enter the Praetorium, Pilate went out to them and asked their charges against the prisoner. The priests, and Caiaphas in particular, presented a threefold accusation against Jesus: " 'We found this fellow perverting the nation, and forbidding to give tribute to Caesar, saying that he himself is Christ a King' (Luke 23:2, KJV). Three charges, each without foundation."[48] Their claims did not fool Pilate. Turning to Jesus, he asked, " 'Are You the King of the Jews?' Jesus said to him, 'It is as you say' " (Matt. 27:11).

Caiaphas immediately seized upon Jesus' words as a confession. The crowd took up the call for death. The bedlam in the square confused Pilate. Facing Jesus, Pilate inquired, "Do You not hear how many things they testify against You?" (verse 13). "He stood unmoved by the fury of the waves that beat about Him. It was as if the heavy surges of wrath, rising higher and higher, like the waves of the boisterous ocean, broke about Him, but did not touch Him. He stood silent, but His silence was eloquence. It was a light shining from the inner to the outer man. Pilate was astonished at His bearing."[49]

Moving into the Praetorium and taking Jesus aside, Pilate asked Him, "Are You the King of the Jews?" Jesus knew the Holy Spirit was striving with Pilate, so He answered, " 'Are you speaking for yourself about this, or did others tell you this concerning Me?' Pilate answered, 'Am I a Jew? Your own nation and the chief priests have delivered You to me. What have You done?' " (John 18:34, 35). Jesus told Pilate His kingdom did not threaten Rome. " 'If My kingdom were of this world, My servants would fight, so that I should not be delivered to the Jews; but now My kingdom is not from here.' Pilate therefore said to Him, 'Are You a king then?' Jesus answered, 'You say rightly that I am a king. For this cause I was born, and for this cause I have come into the world, that I should bear witness to the truth. Everyone who is of the truth hears My voice.' Pilate said to Him, 'What is truth?' And when he had said this, he went out again to the Jews, and said to them, 'I find no fault in Him at all' " (verses 36-38).

"The way, the truth, and the life" (John 14:6) stood before Pilate, yet for expediency's sake he failed to recognize truth. Today many make the same mistake.

"THIS MAN IS A GALILEAN"

When Pilate heard of Galilee, he asked if the Man were a Galilean. Luke 23:6.

When Pilate said, "I find no fault in Him at all," it enraged the priests and elders. "They loudly denounced Pilate, and threatened him with the censure of the Roman government. They accused him of refusing to condemn Jesus, who, they affirmed, had set Himself up against Caesar." [50] The crowd now murmured that Jesus had preached sedition against Rome. Some yelled, "He stirs up the people, teaching throughout all Judea, beginning from Galilee to this place" (Luke 23:5). "When he [Pilate] heard that Christ was from Galilee, he decided to send Him to Herod, the ruler of that province, who was then in Jerusalem. By this course, Pilate thought to shift the responsibility of the trial from himself to Herod. He also thought this a good opportunity to heal an old quarrel between himself and Herod. And so it proved. The two magistrates made friends over the trial of the Saviour." [51]

"Pilate was faced with a dilemma. He was fully convinced of Jesus' innocence and had publicly announced his decision to this effect. His own determination to release Jesus was exceeded only by the determination of the Jewish authorities to have the Saviour crucified. During Pilate's past tenure of about five years as procurator of Judea (which then included Samaria), he had made himself most unpopular with the Jews, and he feared that to displease them further would endanger his office. He knew well the treachery of some of the Jewish leaders. He knew also that their hatred of Jesus was due to malice alone. Pilate therefore must have felt that he was cutting the Gordian knot by sending Jesus to Herod, hoping thereby to maintain the good will of the Jewish authorities and at the same time evade responsibility for the death of one who was obviously innocent." [52]

Although a stubborn, inflexible, and harsh man, Pilate was enough of a politician to understand that to retain his position he had no choice but to compromise justice. His conscience and duty told him he should release Jesus, but his desire to retain his influence and position argued against it.

So it is today with individuals who sacrifice principle for personal gain. Scripture said of Jesus: "He will bring forth justice for truth. He will not fail nor be discouraged, till He has established justice in the earth; and the coastlands shall wait for His law" (Isa. 42:3, 4). Amen.

SHOW ME A MIRACLE

Then Herod, with his men of war, treated Him with contempt and mocked Him, arrayed Him in a gorgeous robe, and sent Him back to Pilate. Luke 23:11.

The Jews detested Herod. Half Samaritan and half Idumaean, he professed belief in Judaism because of political expediency. He knew that he should be in Jerusalem to keep up appearances, but he had no desire to observe the festival. Pilate handed Jesus over to the soldiers and they had dragged Him through the crowd to Herod's judgment hall. The client king was glad to have the opportunity to finally meet Jesus.

"A large company of the priests and elders had accompanied Christ to Herod. And when the Saviour was brought in, these dignitaries, all speaking excitedly, urged their accusations against Him. But Herod paid little regard to their charges. He commanded silence, desiring an opportunity to question Christ. He ordered that the fetters of Christ should be unloosed, at the same time charging His enemies with roughly treating Him. Looking with compassion into the serene face of the world's Redeemer, he read in it only wisdom and purity. He as well as Pilate was satisfied that Christ had been accused through malice and envy."[53] Although he questioned Jesus at length, Herod received no reply. The king promised to release Christ immediately if He would perform a simple miracle. "Of all things they [the priests] most dreaded an exhibition of His power."[54] But Jesus remained silent.

"Herod was irritated by this silence. It seemed to indicate utter indifference to his authority."[55] After Jesus' failure to comply with the royal request for a miracle, "Herod's face grew dark with passion. Turning to the multitude, he angrily denounced Jesus as an impostor. Then to Christ he said, If You will give no evidence of Your claim, I will deliver You up to the soldiers and the people. They may succeed in making You speak. If You are an impostor, death at their hands is only what You merit; if You are the Son of God, save Yourself by working a miracle.' No sooner were these words spoken than a rush was made for Christ. . . . Jesus was dragged this way and that, Herod joining the mob in seeking to humiliate the Son of God. Had not the Roman soldiers interposed, and forced back the maddened throng, the Saviour would have been torn in pieces."[56] Someone placed a discarded royal robe upon Him, and the crowd bowed and mocked Him.

Often we treat with contempt what we do not understand.

"I Have Found No Fault in This Man"

"Having examined Him in your presence, I have found no fault in this Man concerning those things of which you accuse Him."

Luke 23:14.

It was now 8:00 a.m., and Pilate felt even more distressed. Having been awakened early this Friday morning and having to deal with the duplicity of the Jewish leaders was bad enough, but his solution to the problem had not worked and Herod had returned the prisoner to his own court. "You have brought this Man to me, as one who misleads the people," he told the Jewish leaders. "And indeed, having examined Him in your presence, I have found no fault in this Man concerning those things of which you accuse Him; no, neither did Herod, for I sent you back to him; and indeed nothing deserving of death has been done by Him. I will therefore chastise Him and release Him" (Luke 23:14-16).

"Here Pilate showed his weakness. He had declared that Jesus was innocent, yet he was willing for Him to be scourged to pacify His accusers. He would sacrifice justice and principle in order to compromise with the mob. This placed him at a disadvantage. . . . Had he carried out his convictions of right, the Jews would not have presumed to dictate to him. Christ would have been put to death, but the guilt would not have rested upon Pilate. But Pilate had taken step after step in the violation of his conscience. He had excused himself from judging with justice and equity, and he now found himself almost helpless in the hands of the priests and rulers. His wavering and indecision proved his ruin."[57] "Satan and his angels were tempting Pilate and trying to lead him on to his own ruin. They suggested to him that if he did not take part in condemning Jesus others would; the multitude were thirsting for His blood; and if he did not deliver Him to be crucified, he would lose his power and worldly honor, and would be denounced as a believer on the impostor."[58]

For a second time Jesus remained silent, Herod's cast-off royal robe draped over His shoulders. The Roman guard who had twice shielded Him from being torn apart by the mob surrounded Him. Pilate saw the seething mob and the Saviour standing quietly before him. The contrast between the two was striking. Somehow he must act to keep the peace or lose his position.

Too often we sacrifice principle for expediency. Those who do so throw it away at their own risk and at society's peril.

A TROUBLING DREAM

While he was sitting on the judgment seat, his wife sent to him, saying, "Have nothing to do with that just Man, for I have suffered many things today in a dream because of Him." Matt. 27:19.

Pilate faced a dilemma, but God did not leave him without guidance. God sent a message warning him not to do what he contemplated. "The wife of Pilate had been visited by an angel from heaven, and in a dream she had beheld the Saviour and conversed with Him. Pilate's wife was not a Jew, but as she looked upon Jesus in her dream, she had no doubt of His character or mission. She knew Him to be the Prince of God. . . . She heard the condemnation pronounced by Pilate, and saw him give Christ up to His murderers. She saw the cross uplifted on Calvary. She saw the earth wrapped in darkness, and heard the mysterious cry, 'It is finished.' Still another scene met her gaze. She saw Christ seated upon the great white cloud, while the earth reeled in space, and His murderers fled from the presence of His glory. With a cry of horror she awoke, and at once wrote to Pilate words of warning. While Pilate was hesitating as to what he should do, a messenger pressed through the crowd, and handed him the letter from his wife, which read: 'Have thou nothing to do with that just man: for I have suffered many things this day in a dream because of him.' Pilate's face grew pale. He was confused by his own conflicting emotions. But while he had been delaying to act, the priests and rulers were still further inflaming the minds of the people. Pilate was forced to action."[59]

A custom the Romans followed during Jewish festivals allowed for the release of one condemned prisoner as a conciliatory gesture to the conquered provinces. The Romans had in prison a convicted revolutionary sentenced to die. Pilate now thought of a plan. By contrasting the hardened criminal Barabbas with the Son of man he might yet gain Jesus' release.

Pilate now asked the crowd, "Whom do you want me to release to you? Barabbas, or Jesus who is called Christ?" (Matt. 27:17). The crowd shouted, "Barabbas! Barabbas!" Thinking they had not heard the question correctly, Pilate again demanded, "'What then shall I do with Jesus who is called Christ?' They all said to him, 'Let Him be crucified!'" (verse 22).

We still each have to make the choice. Which will it be—Barabbas or Christ?

SCOURGED

So then Pilate took Jesus and scourged Him. John 19:1.

Pilate's ruse failed because "much of Jesus' popular support had come from Galilee and Peraea, where He had recently labored, and pilgrims from these regions probably slept outside the city and had not as yet entered at this early hour. One thing the leaders greatly feared was an attempt on the part of such friendly pilgrims to liberate Jesus. . . . The mob before his [Pilate's] judgment seat was made up mostly, if not altogether, of men who were unfriendly or at least indifferent toward Jesus." [60]

Now the procurator demanded of the crowd in response to their call for crucifixion, "Why, what evil has He done?" (Matt. 27:23). "Pilate, representing the power of imperial Rome, was arguing the question with the rabble of Jerusalem! Not only so; he was being worsted in the argument." [61] Still trying to save Jesus, he argued, "I have found no reason for death in Him. I will therefore chastise Him and let Him go" (Luke 23:22). "Jesus was taken, faint with weariness and covered with wounds, and scourged in the sight of the multitude." [62] "The Roman scourge . . . was a cruel instrument of torture. To its leather lashes were attached pieces of metal or bone to increase the suffering. It was used not only for punishment but also for the extraction of confessions (Acts 22:24). Criminals condemned to be executed were usually scourged . . . before they were put to death, as was done in the case of Jesus. (Matt. 27:26; Mark 15:15; John 19:1). The victim was stripped to the waist, usually bound to a post with his hands tied together, and the scourge applied to the back with lacerating blows." [63]

"The law of Moses provided for flogging (Deut. 25:1-3). Forty stripes were the maximum penalty. It was customary to administer no more than 39 strokes—withholding the last implied mercy." [64] "When Pilate gave Jesus up to be scourged and mocked, he thought to excite the pity of the multitude," [65] but prophecy had decreed Jesus should be "despised and rejected by men, a Man of sorrows and acquainted with grief. And we hid, as it were, our faces from Him; He was despised, and we did not esteem Him" (Isa. 53:3). "I gave My back to those who struck Me, and My cheeks to those who plucked out the beard; I did not hide My face from shame and spitting" (Isa. 50:6). "But He was wounded for our transgressions, He was bruised for our iniquities; the chastisement of our peace was upon Him, and by His stripes we are healed" (Isa. 53:5).

"BEHOLD THE MAN!"

Then Jesus came out, wearing the crown of thorns and the purple robe. And Pilate said to them, "Behold the Man!" John 19:5.

Jesus still wore the purple gown Herod had given Him. A Roman soldier wove a crown of thorns and roughly forced it down upon His brow. After placing a reed in His hand, the soldiers led Him out onto the porch in full view of the crowd. They did it to mock the Jews. "Occasionally some wicked hand snatched the reed that had been placed in His hand, and struck the crown upon His brow, forcing the thorns into His temples, and sending the blood trickling down His face and beard."[66] Summoning Barabbas, Pilate presented the two men side by side and pointing to Jesus solemnly announced, "Behold, I am bringing Him out to you, that you may know that I find no fault in Him."

"There stood the Son of God, wearing the robe of mockery and the crown of thorns. Stripped to the waist, His back showed the long, cruel stripes, from which the blood flowed freely. His face was stained with blood, and bore the marks of exhaustion and pain; but never had it appeared more beautiful than now. The Saviour's visage was not marred before His enemies. Every feature expressed gentleness and resignation and the tenderest pity for His cruel foes. . . . Some of the spectators were weeping. As they looked upon Jesus, their hearts were full of sympathy. Even the priests and rulers were convicted that He was all that He claimed to be. The Roman soldiers that surrounded Christ were not all hardened; some were looking earnestly into His face for one evidence that He was a criminal or dangerous character. From time to time they would turn and cast a look of contempt upon Barabbas."[67]

It amazed Pilate that the people showed no sympathy for the innocent Man. Had his eyes been opened to the struggle between good and evil, he would have seen that "Satan led the cruel mob in its abuse of the Saviour. It was his purpose to provoke Him to retaliation if possible, or to drive Him to perform a miracle to release Himself, and thus break up the plan of salvation."[68] "Behold the Man!" was a great truth Pilate unknowingly proclaimed for "the One before him, the eternal Word . . . , had become man. . . . He was, indeed, the Son of man . . . , but also the Son of God. . . . His incarnation and death won for us eternal salvation."[69]

Wonder of wonders, He suffered for you and me.

"You Are Not Caesar's Friend"

"If you let this Man go, you are not Caesar's friend. Whoever makes himself a king speaks against Caesar." John 19:12.

Jesus bore every verbal insult, every slur against His parentage, every blow from a curled fist, every stripe laid upon His back. "Nothing could have induced Christ to leave His honor and majesty in heaven, and come to a sinful world, to be neglected, despised, and rejected by those He came to save, and finally to suffer upon the cross, but eternal, redeeming love, which will ever remain a mystery."[70] Pilate sought to release Jesus, but the mob shouted, "We have a law, and according to our law He ought to die, because He made Himself the Son of God" (John 19:7). The procurator knew little of Christ's mission, but he did believe in a supreme being. Studying Him more intently now, he wondered if perhaps the prisoner was not divine. Taking Jesus back into the judgment hall, he questioned Him further. "Where are You from?" Jesus answered nothing. "Then Pilate said to Him, 'Are You not speaking to me? Do You not know that I have power to crucify You, and power to release You?'" (verses 9, 10). Jesus answered, "You could have no power at all against Me unless it had been given you from above. Therefore the one who delivered Me to you has the greater sin" (verse 11). "By this Christ meant Caiaphas, who, as high priest, represented the Jewish nation."[71] "Thus the pitying Saviour, in the midst of His intense suffering and grief, excused as far as possible the act of the Roman governor who gave Him up to be crucified. What a scene was this to hand down to the world for all time! What a light it sheds upon the character of Him who is the Judge of all the earth!"[72]

Bringing Jesus onto the porch one last time, Pilate appealed to the crowd as it chanted, Crucify Him! Crucify Him! "If you let this Man go, you are not Caesar's friend. Whoever makes himself a king speaks against Caesar" (verse 12). "The Jews had at last struck upon an argument that was to prove successful. Their reply was a threat, for if the emperor should learn that Pilate had attempted to shield a pretender to the title of king, the governor's position would be in danger. Fear for his safety led Pilate to forget the religious awe with which he had regarded the prisoner."[73]

Condoning evil while not actively participating in it does not wash away the stain of sin.

THE PLACE OF THE SKULL

And He, bearing His cross, went out to a place called the Place of a Skull, which is called in Hebrew, Golgotha.

John 19:17.

Seated upon the judgment seat, Pilate asked, " 'Shall I crucify your King?' The chief priests answered, 'We have no king but Caesar!' " (John 19:15). "Thus by choosing a heathen ruler, the Jewish nation had withdrawn from the theocracy. They had rejected God as their king. Henceforth they had no deliverer. They had no king but Caesar. To this the priests and teachers had led the people. For this, with the fearful results that followed, they were responsible. A nation's sin and a nation's ruin were due to the religious leaders." [74] Giving in and washing his hands of the blood of the innocent prisoner, Pilate issued the sentence of execution that the priests and rulers demanded.

At 8:00 a.m. the Roman soldiers responsible for carrying out the sentence of the court took charge of Him. Another flogging preceded the Crucifixion. "Jesus had scarcely passed the gate of Pilate's house when the cross which had been prepared for Barabbas was brought out and laid upon His bruised and bleeding shoulders. Crosses were also placed upon the companions of Barabbas, who were to suffer death at the same time with Jesus." [75] Blood flowed from His back as every step taken with the cruel instrument of torture pressed it down into His lacerated muscles. Drops of blood dripped to the ground and marked His passage. "The Saviour had borne His burden but a few rods when, from loss of blood and excessive weariness and pain, He fell fainting to the ground. When Jesus revived, the cross was again placed upon His shoulders and He was forced forward. He staggered on for a few steps, bearing His heavy load, then fell as one lifeless to the ground. He was at first pronounced to be dead, but finally He again revived." [76]

"The disciples and believers from the region round about joined the throng that followed Jesus to Calvary. The mother of Jesus was also there, supported by John, the beloved disciple. Her heart was stricken with unutterable anguish; yet she, with the disciples, hoped that the painful scene would change, and Jesus would assert His power, and appear before His enemies as the Son of God." [77] Roman soldiers pushed back the immense Passover crowd that jeered and heckled the three men struggling beneath their crosses. Each step led them closer to Golgotha and the painful ordeal of crucifixion.

How light our crosses appear when we understand the weight of His.

SIMON OF CYRENE

Now as they came out, they found a man of Cyrene, Simon by name. Him they compelled to bear His cross. Matt. 27:32.

The Romans probably tried Jesus in the Tower of Antonia located directly north of the Temple. The Gospels say Calvary was outside the city gates near a garden (John 19:41) and a conspicuous place (Mark 15:40; Luke 23:49). Most believe Calvary was but a few hundred feet beyond the North City wall. " 'That he might sanctify the people with his own blood,' Christ 'suffered without the gate' (Heb. 13:12, KJV). For the transgression of the law of God, Adam and Eve were banished from Eden. Christ, our substitute, was to suffer without the boundaries of Jerusalem. He died outside the gate, where felons and murderers were executed." [78] The Sheep Gate stood near the northeast corner of the city not far from the Temple. Through it for centuries had passed sacrificial offerings. Now it opened for the great Antitype, the Lamb of God.

"The priests and rulers felt no compassion for their suffering victim; but they saw that it was impossible for Him to carry the instrument of torture farther." [79] Cyrene was a large Greek city located in what is modern-day Libya, North Africa. Cyrenian Jews, Alexandrian Jews, and Libertines from Cilicia and Asia had their own synagogue in Jerusalem called the Synagogue of the Freedmen (Acts 6:9). "At this time a stranger, Simon a Cyrenian, coming in from the country, meets the throng. He hears the taunts and ribaldry of the crowd; he hears the words contemptuously repeated, Make way for the King of the Jews! He stops in astonishment at the scene; and as he expresses his compassion, they seize him and place the cross upon his shoulders." [80] "The cross he [Simon] was forced to bear became the means of his conversion. His sympathies were deeply stirred in favor of Jesus; and the events of Calvary, and the words uttered by the Saviour, caused him to acknowledge that He was the Son of God." [81]

"Faint from His recent ordeal, Jesus was unable to bear His cross, as custom required. Jesus' disciples might have come forward and offered to do so, but fear held them back from any demonstration of allegiance to Him. What a privilege it was for Simon to bear that cross, and thus to have a share with Jesus in His sufferings!" [82]

"Today, it is our privilege to bear the cross of Jesus by remaining true to principle in the face of unpopularity, slighting remarks, and abuse." [83]

"Father, Forgive Them"

*Then Jesus said,
"Father, forgive them,
for they do not know
what they do."
Luke 23:34.*

Of the multitude that followed the Saviour to Calvary, many had attended Him with joyful hosannas and the waving of palm branches as He rode triumphantly into Jerusalem. But not a few who had then shouted His praise, because it was popular to do so, now swelled the cry of 'Crucify Him, crucify Him.'"[84] The sympathies expressed by certain women along the road to the cross drew Christ's compassion. "As Jesus falls fainting beneath the cross, they break forth into mournful wailing."[85] Jesus knew they lamented Him, not as the Son of God, but merely from human pity for one condemned to death. Looking down through time, He saw Jerusalem's destruction. "In that terrible scene, many of those who were now weeping for Him were to perish with their children."[86] Even in His anguish, the thought stirred Jesus' heart. "Daughters of Jerusalem, do not weep for Me," He said, "but weep for yourselves and for your children" (Luke 23:28).

When they arrived at the place of execution, the soldiers offered their prisoners a vinegar wine mixed with frankincense and myrrh. After tasting the mixture, Jesus refused it. He would allow nothing to cloud His mind. "His faith must keep fast hold upon God. This was His only strength. To becloud His senses would give Satan an advantage."[87] The guards wrestled the thieves into position and bound them with ropes to the crosses, but Jesus offered no resistance. His mother had followed Him and seen Him faint beneath the load of the cross. She had longed to bathe His brow, but it was not possible. Now she saw Him willingly lay down upon the cross and extend His hands. His hands ever outstretched in blessing He now placed upon the wooden bar of the cross. "The hammer and the nails were brought, and as the spikes were driven through the tender flesh, the heart-stricken disciples bore away from the cruel scene the fainting form of the mother of Jesus. The Saviour made no murmur of complaint. His face remained calm and serene, but great drops of sweat stood upon His brow. . . . While the soldiers were doing their fearful work, Jesus prayed for His enemies, 'Father, forgive them; for they know not what they do.'"[88]

Thank God that the prayer for those Gentile soldiers embraced the entire world and our culpability in crucifying Him. His only thought was of forgiveness! Precious Lord, forgive us!

BETWEEN EARTH AND HEAVEN

And when they had come to the place called Calvary, there they crucified Him. Luke 23:33.

"A s soon as Jesus was nailed to the cross, it was lifted by strong men, and with great violence thrust into the place prepared for it. This caused the most intense agony to the Son of God."[89] The manner of Christ's death was Roman. "In submitting to this form of death Christ humbled Himself utterly (Phil. 2:8). A curse was supposed to rest upon those who were crucified (Deut. 21:23; Gal. 3:13). . . . The lingering death upon a cross was horrible indeed, for victims commonly lived for many hours, sometimes several days."[90] The weight of one's body placed great pressure upon the arms and ribs, making it difficult to breathe. In a desperate attempt to breathe, the condemned forced himself higher with his legs. The continuous up-and-down effort, coupled with the difficulty in breathing and the strain upon the muscles, eventually resulted in death by asphyxiation or total exhaustion and shock.

"It is said that those crucified sometimes died from exposure and exhaustion after about 12 hours, though in other cases death did not come for two or three days. Mark (chap. 15:25) states that Jesus was crucified at the third hour, by Jewish reckoning, or about 9:00 a.m."[91] Four Roman guards now unknowingly fulfilled prophecy. They each took an article of Christ's clothing. When they came to His seamless tunic, woven in one piece from the top down, "they said therefore among themselves, 'Let us not tear it, but cast lots for it, whose it shall be,' that the Scripture might be fulfilled which says: 'They divided My garments among them, and for My clothing they cast lots' [Psalm 22:18]. Therefore the soldiers did these things" (John 19:24).

Roman authority had decreed a death sentence, and Roman soldiers maintained a guard to see that it got carried out. Our world's Creator hung between heaven and earth upon a cruel instrument of torture. Those He had come to rescue from sin stood at the foot of His cross and mocked Him. His naked form was exhibited for all to see.

"Behold Him hanging upon the cross those dreadful hours of agony until the angels veil their faces from the horrid scene, and the sun hides its light, refusing to behold. Think of these things, and then ask, Is the way too strait? No, no."[92]

"HE SAVED OTHERS— LET HIM SAVE HIMSELF"

"Let Him save Himself if He is the Christ." Luke 23:35.

As Jesus hung upon the cross, the priests and rulers mocked Him. "Thou that destroyest the temple, and buildest it in three days, save thyself. If thou be the Son of God, come down from the cross. Likewise also the chief priests mocking him, with the scribes and elders, said, He saved others; himself he cannot save. If he be the King of Israel, let him now come down from the cross, and we will believe him. He trusted in God; let him deliver him now, if he will have him: for he said, I am the Son of God" (Matt. 27:40-43, KJV). "*If thou be the Christ . . .*" "These words are reminiscent of the challenge uttered by Satan as he approached Christ in the wilderness of temptation. . . . To all appearances, Jesus could not possibly be the Son of God. Even His disciples had completely lost hope that He might be."[93]

"Not one word did Jesus answer to all this. Even while the nails were being driven through His hands and the sweat-drops of agony were forced from His pores, from the pale quivering lips of the innocent sufferer a prayer of pardoning love was breathed for His murderers."[94] "At the baptism and at the transfiguration the voice of God had been heard proclaiming Christ as His Son. Again, just before Christ's betrayal, the Father had spoken, witnessing to His divinity. But now the voice from heaven was silent. No testimony in Christ's favor was heard. Alone He suffered abuse and mockery from wicked men. . . . And Satan with his angels, in human form, was present at the cross. The archfiend and his hosts were cooperating with the priests and rulers. . . . Jesus, suffering and dying, heard every word."[95]

The words were a direct fulfillment of prophecy. Anyone searching the Scriptures would finally understand Christ's mission when they read "All those who see Me ridicule Me; they shoot out the lip, they shake the head, saying, 'He trusted in the Lord, let Him rescue Him; let Him deliver Him, since He delights in Him!'" (Ps. 22:7, 8). "This is the word which the Lord has spoken concerning him: 'The virgin, the daughter of Zion, has despised you, laughed you to scorn; the daughter of Jerusalem has shaken her head behind your back!'" (Isa. 37:22).

"Christ's refusal to save Himself was the supreme demonstration of divine love. . . . It is precisely because Jesus chose not to save Himself at this moment that He can save others."[96]

KING OF THE JEWS

Now Pilate wrote a title and put it on the cross.

John 19:19.

Matthew reports the sign read: "This is Jesus the king of the Jews" (Matt. 27:37). Mark tells us it said only "The king of the Jews" (Mark 15:26) and Luke states it read: "This is the king of the Jews" (Luke 23:38). John gives the full inscription, explaining that it "was written in Hebrew (Aramaic), the common language of the people, in Greek, the language of learning and culture, and in Latin, the official language of the Roman Empire."[97] The inscription read: "Jesus of Nazareth, the king of the Jews" (John 19:19).

During the trial, the Jews had shouted, "Away with Him, away with Him! Crucify Him!" (verse 15). Pilate had asked them pointedly, "Shall I crucify your King?" The chief priests had answered, "We have no king but Caesar!" It was customary to place the crime of the individual deemed worthy of death upon the cross above them so bystanders might note the penalty for transgressing Rome's will. But they listed no offense for Jesus other than the title "King of the Jews." "The inscription was a virtual acknowledgment of the allegiance of the Jews to the Roman power. It declared that whoever might claim to be the King of Israel would be judged by them worthy of death. The priests had overreached themselves. When they were plotting the death of Christ, Caiaphas had declared it expedient that one man should die to save the nation. Now their hypocrisy was revealed. In order to destroy Christ, they had been ready to sacrifice even their national existence."[98]

Going to Pilate, they demanded he change the sign. They said, "Do not write, 'The King of the Jews,' but, 'He said, "I am the King of the Jews"'" (verse 21). Coldly he answered, "What I have written, I have written" (verse 22). "A higher power than Pilate or the Jews had directed the placing of that inscription above the head of Jesus. In the providence of God it was to awaken thought, and investigation of the Scriptures. The place where Christ was crucified was near to the city. Thousands of people from all lands were then at Jerusalem, and the inscription declaring Jesus of Nazareth the Messiah would come to their notice. It was a living truth, transcribed by a hand that God had guided."[99]

Today we read: "Jesus Our Saviour, King of kings."

"REMEMBER ME, LORD"

Then he said to Jesus, "Lord, remember me when You come into Your kingdom."
Luke 23:42.

To Jesus in His agony on the cross there came one gleam of comfort. It was the prayer of the penitent thief. Both the men who were crucified with Jesus had at first railed upon Him; and one under his suffering only became more desperate and defiant. But not so with his companion. . . . He had seen and heard Jesus, and had been convicted by His teaching, but he had been turned away from Him by the priests and rulers."[100] Conviction arose again within him that Jesus must be the Christ.

"Then one of the criminals who were hanged blasphemed Him, saying, 'If You are the Christ, save Yourself and us.' But the other, answering, rebuked him, saying, 'Do you not even fear God, seeing you are under the same condemnation? And we indeed justly, for we receive the due reward of our deeds; but this Man has done nothing wrong.' Then he said to Jesus, 'Lord, remember me when You come into Your kingdom'" (Luke 23:39-42). Those at the foot of the cross caught the words of the thief to Jesus. The soldiers gambling for Christ's garments stopped and listened. "Quickly the answer came. Soft and melodious the tone, full of love, compassion, and power the words: 'Verily I say unto thee today, Thou shalt be with Me in paradise.'"[101] "As He spoke the words of promise, the dark cloud that seemed to enshroud the cross was pierced by a bright and living light. To the penitent thief came the perfect peace of acceptance with God."[102]

"Christ did not promise that the thief should be with Him in Paradise that day. He Himself did not go that day to Paradise. He slept in the tomb, and on the morning of the resurrection He said, 'I am not yet ascended to my Father' (John 20:17, KJV). But on the day of the crucifixion, the day of apparent defeat and darkness, the promise was given. 'Today' while dying upon the cross as a malefactor, Christ assures the poor sinner, Thou shalt be with Me in Paradise."[103] "To the last of His work Christ is a sin-pardoner. At deepest midnight . . . lo there shines amid the moral darkness with distinct brightness the faith of a dying sinner as he lays hold upon a dying Saviour."[104]

"Such faith may be represented by the eleventh hour laborers who receive as much reward as do those who have labored for many hours."[105]

"WOMAN, BEHOLD YOUR SON!"

When Jesus therefore saw His mother, and the disciple whom He loved standing by, He said to His mother, "Woman, behold your son!" Then He said to the disciple, "Behold your mother!" And from that hour that disciple took her to his own home. John 19:26, 27.

Christ, bearing the sin of the world, seemed to be deserted; but He was not wholly left alone. John stood close by the cross. Mary had fainted in her anguish, and John had taken her to his house away from the harrowing scene. But he saw that the end was near, and he brought her again to the cross."[106] Now "as the eyes of Jesus wandered over the multitude about Him, one figure arrested His attention. At the foot of the cross stood His mother, supported by the disciple John. She could not endure to remain away from her Son."[107]

Looking at His grief-stricken mother, He said to her, "Woman, behold your son!" Then shifting His gaze to John, His most beloved disciple, He said, "Behold your mother." Throughout His life Jesus had ever been the dutiful, obedient, attentive, loving son. Now, at the end of that life, Jesus remembered with compassion His mother. "The relationship between John and Jesus was more intimate than that between Jesus and the other disciples . . . , and John could therefore carry out the duties of a son more faithfully than they. That Jesus entrusted His mother to a disciple is acknowledged as evidence that Joseph no longer lived, and is thought by some to indicate that Mary had no other sons of her own, at least in a position to care for her. Jesus' older brothers, sons of Joseph by a former marriage . . . , did not, at this time, believe in Him, and He may have felt that their attitude toward Mary would have been critical and unsympathetic, as it had been toward Him."[108]

"John understood Christ's words, and accepted the trust. He at once took Mary to his home, and from that hour cared for her tenderly. . . . The perfect example of Christ's filial love shines forth with undimmed luster from the mist of ages. For nearly thirty years Jesus by His daily toil had helped bear the burdens of the home. And now, even in His last agony, He remembers to provide for His sorrowing, widowed mother."[109]

"The same spirit will be seen in every disciple of our Lord. Those who follow Christ will feel that it is a part of their religion to respect and provide for their parents."[110]

THE SIXTH TO THE NINTH HOUR

"Into Your hands I commit My spirit."

Luke 23:46.

The guilt of every human being since Adam pressed down upon Jesus. A sense of the Father's wrath against sin filled Him with dismay. "The withdrawal of the divine countenance from the Saviour in this hour of supreme anguish pierced His heart with a sorrow that can never be fully understood by man. So great was this agony that His physical pain was hardly felt."[111] Jesus could not see beyond the tomb. He feared that sin was so loathsome to the Father it would separate Him permanently from the One He loved most. "The Father was with His Son. Yet His presence was not revealed. . . . In the thick darkness, God veiled the last human agony of His Son. . . . Through long hours of agony Christ had been gazed upon by the jeering multitude. Now He was mercifully hidden by the mantle of God. The silence of the grave seemed to have fallen upon Calvary."[112]

At 3:00 p.m. the cloud of darkness lifted from the people but remained covering the cross. Lightning lashed the hilltop. Jesus cried out something, but His voice was indistinct in the wind. "Eli, Eli, lama sabachthani?" "My God, My God, why have You forsaken Me?" (Matt. 27:46). As the cloud lifted from His spirit, Jesus again felt physical pain, and said, "I thirst." The Roman soldiers, touched with pity, lifted up to His parched and quivering lips a sponge dipped in vinegar, fulfilling another prophecy: "They also gave me gall for my food, and for my thirst they gave me vinegar to drink" (Ps. 69:21).

For six hours Jesus hung suspended between heaven and earth. "Suddenly the gloom lifted from the cross, and in clear, trumpetlike tones, that seemed to resound throughout creation, Jesus cried, 'It is finished.' 'Father, into thy hands I commend my spirit.' A light encircled the cross, and the face of the Saviour shone with a glory like the sun. He then bowed His head upon His breast, and died."[113] "When Christ cried, 'It is finished,' God's unseen hand rent the strong fabric composing the veil of the temple from top to bottom. The way into the holiest of all was made manifest. God bowed His head satisfied. Now His justice and mercy could blend. . . . 'It is finished. The human race shall have another trial.' The redemption price was paid, and Satan fell like lightning from heaven."[114]

"God Himself was crucified with Christ; for Christ was one with the Father."[115]

NO VEIL
BETWEEN

Therefore He is also able to save to the uttermost those who come to God through Him, since He always lives to make intercession for them. Heb. 7:25.

As Jesus bowed His head upon His breast and died, the priests were officiating in the Temple. The people had gathered for the 3:00 p.m. sacrifice (the ninth hour). The blood of the sacrificial lamb, representative of Jesus, waited to be spilt. As the Passover pilgrims watched, the priest raised his knife to take the life of the innocent lamb. Meanwhile those around the cross on Golgotha who witnessed the final scene of Christ's death "stood paralyzed, and with bated breath gazed upon the Saviour. Again darkness settled upon the earth, and a hoarse rumbling, like heavy thunder, was heard. There was a violent earthquake. The people were shaken together in heaps. The wildest confusion and consternation ensued. In the surrounding mountains, rocks were rent asunder, and went crashing down into the plains. Sepulchers were broken open, and the dead were cast out of their tombs. Creation seemed to be shivering to atoms. Priests, rulers, soldiers, executioners, and people, mute with terror, lay prostrate upon the ground."[1] As the earth trembled, God the Father drew near the Temple mount. An unseen hand tore from top to bottom the thick tapestry separating the holy from the Most Holy. The multitude gazed into the previously unseen place once filled with God's glory. "The most holy place of the earthly sanctuary is no longer sacred."[2]

"The same hand that traced on the wall the characters that recorded Belshazzar's doom and the end of the Babylonian kingdom rent the veil of the Temple from top to bottom, opening a new and living way for all, high and low, rich and poor, Jew and Gentile. From henceforth people might come to God without priest or ruler."[3] Jesus by His own blood had "entered the Most Holy Place once for all, having obtained eternal redemption" (Heb. 9:12). As the knife fell from the priest's hand, the sacrificial lamb escaped into the crowd. Type had met antitype. The true Lamb of God had taken away the world's sin.

No longer must humanity approach the Father through an earthly priest. Now it had a heavenly High Priest who "with His own blood . . . entered the Most Holy Place once for all, having obtained eternal redemption" (Heb. 9:12).

"TRULY THIS WAS THE SON OF GOD"

So when the centurion saw what had happened, he glorified God, saying, "Certainly this was a righteous Man!"

Luke 23:47.

The captain of the Roman guard at the Crucifixion was not a Jewish proselyte. Raised in a culture that stressed Roman invincibility, he gave little thought to the fate of any Jew. As the leader of 50 to 100 trained members of a legion, the centurion had found himself garrisoned in the empire's worst frontier posting. Synonymous with uprising and riot, Palestine was a hotbed of murder and intrigue. Repeatedly he had had to put down insurrections caused by successive "messiahs," each boasting they would save the Jewish nation from Roman oppression. Yet in the midst of the turmoil he encountered something that changed his life. He had to carry out the death sentence of a man called Jesus.

"When the darkness had lifted from the cross, and the Saviour's dying cry had been uttered, immediately another voice was heard, saying, 'Truly this was the Son of God' (Matt. 27:54, KJV). These words were said in no whispered tones. All eyes were turned to see whence they came. Who had spoken? It was the centurion, the Roman soldier. The divine patience of the Saviour, and His sudden death, with the cry of victory upon His lips, had impressed this heathen. In the bruised, broken body hanging upon the cross, the centurion recognized the form of the Son of God. He could not refrain from confessing his faith. Thus again evidence was given that our Redeemer was to see of the travail of His soul. Upon the very day of His death, three men, differing widely from one another, had declared their faith—he who commanded the Roman guard, he who bore the cross of the Saviour, and he who died upon the cross at His side."[4]

Evening approached, and with it an unearthly silence. Most of those around the cross drifted off to their homes. The crowd that had shouted "Crucify Him, crucify Him" had sobered. As the gloom lifted, many were convinced that the priests had condemned an innocent person. "The veil of the temple, rent so mysteriously, changed the religious ideas of many of the Jewish priests, and a large company changed their faith."[5] Many more believed that in Jesus they had surely beheld the divine Son of God crucified.

Millions today must decide His divinity and thousands proclaim with the Roman centurion, "Truly this was the Son of God."

THEY SHALL LOOK ON HIM WHOM THEY PIERCED

One of the soldiers pierced His side with a spear, and immediately blood and water came out. John 19:34.

If a man has committed a sin deserving of death, and he is put to death, and you hang him on a tree, his body shall not remain overnight on the tree, but you shall surely bury him that day" (Deut. 21:22, 23). The Jewish leaders hated Jesus even in death. "They feared the results of that day's work. Not on any account would they have had His body remain on the cross during the Sabbath. The Sabbath was now drawing on, and it would be a violation of its sanctity for the bodies to hang upon the cross. So, using this as a pretext, the leading Jews requested Pilate that the death of the victims might be hastened, and their bodies be removed before the setting of the sun."[6]

Pilate agreed and issued the order. The Roman soldiers broke the legs of the two thieves to hasten their death, but upon reaching Jesus they discovered that He was already dead, something most unusual. Most victims of crucifixion lingered for days. Jesus had hung upon the cross for only six excruciating hours. Touched by what they had seen during His death, the soldiers refrained from breaking His limbs. They had fulfilled the law of the Passover offering that stated, "They shall leave none of it until morning, nor break one of its bones" (Num. 9:12). The Lamb of God was not to have even one of His bones broken. "He guards all his bones; not one of them is broken" (Ps. 34:20).

Wishing confirmation that Jesus was really dead, the priests urged a soldier to thrust a spear into His side. Had Jesus been living still, the wound would have been instantly fatal. Jesus did not die of the spear thrust or the pain of the cross—"He died of a broken heart. His heart was broken by mental anguish. He was slain by the sin of the world."[7] The soldier's action completed yet another prophecy: "And I will pour on the house of David and on the inhabitants of Jerusalem the Spirit of grace and supplication; then they will look on Me whom they pierced. Yes, they will mourn for Him as one mourns for his only son, and grieve for Him as one grieves for a firstborn" (Zech. 12:10).

Those present that day will see it all again! "Behold, He is coming with clouds, and every eye will see Him, even they who pierced Him" (Rev. 1:7).

THE TOMB OF JOSEPH

After this, Joseph of Arimathea . . . asked Pilate that he might take away the body of Jesus; and Pilate gave him permission. John 19:38.

The death of their Master devastated the disciples. "They looked upon His closed eyelids and drooping head, His hair matted with blood, His pierced hands and feet, and their anguish was indescribable. Until the last they had not believed that He would die; they could hardly believe that He was really dead. Overwhelmed with sorrow, they did not recall His words foretelling this very scene."[8] Although they wished to claim His body, John and the women of Galilee did not know how to proceed. Treason against Rome was a high crime, and the charge carried with it burial in a special ground reserved for criminals against the state. Joseph of Arimathea and Nicodemus now used their positions to make sure Jesus would not be buried dishonorably.

Jesus died about 3:00 p.m., and sunset would arrive about 6:30 p.m. at that time of year and at that latitude. Having influence, "Joseph went boldly to Pilate, and begged from him the body of Jesus. For the first time, Pilate learned that Jesus was really dead. Conflicting reports had reached him in regard to the events attending the crucifixion, but the knowledge of Christ's death had been purposely kept from him. . . . Upon hearing Joseph's request, he therefore sent for the centurion who had charge at the cross, and learned for a certainty of the death of Jesus. He also drew from him an account of the scenes of Calvary, confirming the testimony of Joseph."[9]

Even while John worried about His Lord's burial, Joseph returned with the order to release the body, and Nicodemus, anticipating the success of Joseph's mission to Pilate, came with 72 pounds of costly embalming spices. "The most honored in all Jerusalem could not have been shown more respect in death. The disciples were astonished to see these wealthy rulers as much interested as they themselves in the burial of their Lord."[10] Isaiah had prophesied: "And they made His grave with the wicked—but with the rich at His death, because He had done no violence, nor was any deceit in His mouth" (Isa. 53:9).

The courage of Joseph and Nicodemus during the hour of crisis should give strength to all Christians who face an unknown future. The Lord has servants in unknown quarters. Servants yet to come forward to aid Christians in their battles with Satan.

HE RESTED OVER THE SABBATH DAY

And they rested on the Sabbath according to the commandment. Luke 23:56.

Their hopes dashed, the three disciples "gently and reverently . . . removed with their own hands the body of Jesus from the cross."[11] "Now in the place where He was crucified there was a garden, and in the garden a new tomb in which no one had yet been laid" (John 19:41). The new sepulcher had been excavated for the family of Joseph of Arimathea, and now he gave it over to his Lord. Arriving at the tomb, Joseph, Nicodemus, and John "straightened the mangled limbs, and folded the bruised hands upon the pulseless breast. The Galilean women came to see that all had been done that could be done for the lifeless form of their beloved Teacher. Then they saw the heavy stone rolled against the entrance of the tomb, and the Saviour was left at rest."[12]

As the huge stone closed the entrance to the tomb to protect it from theft, it seemed to the disciples that all hope for a lost world had also died. Humanity must surely be sealed forever in sin, for those He created and sought to redeem had killed the Son of God. "But they need not have feared; for I saw that the angelic host watched with untold interest in the resting place of Jesus, earnestly waiting for the command to act their part in liberating the King of glory from His prison house."[13] Not only was their hope gone, but now the disciples feared for their very lives. If the enemies of Christ could put the Master to death, might not the same evil men return and finish the job by killing His followers also? "They felt assured that such hatred as had been manifested against the Son of God would not end with Him. Lonely hours they spent in weeping over their disappointment. . . . In their sorrow and disappointment, they doubted whether He had not deceived them. Even His mother wavered in her faith in Him as the Messiah."[14]

"At the setting of the sun on the evening of the preparation day the trumpets sounded, signifying that the Sabbath had begun. The Passover was observed as it had been for centuries, while He to whom it pointed had been slain by wicked hands, and lay in Joseph's tomb."[15] Jesus slept, but those who plotted His death were about to appreciate the bitterness of what they had done.

Even in death, Christ rested on the seventh-day Sabbath.

GRAVE ROBBERS

The chief priests and Pharisees gathered together to Pilate, saying, ". . . Command that the tomb be made secure until the third day, lest His disciples come by night and steal Him away."
Matt. 27:62-64.

The Sabbath had become a disaster for the priests and rulers. They heard the name "Jesus" on every street corner. "Many had come from far to find Him who had healed the sick and raised the dead. On every side was heard the cry, We want Christ the Healer! . . . The friendly hands of Jesus of Nazareth, that never refused to touch with healing the loathsome leper, were folded on His breast. The lips that had answered his petition with the comforting words, 'I will; be thou clean' (Matt. 8:3, KJV), were now silent. Many appealed to the chief priests and rulers for sympathy and relief, but in vain. Apparently they were determined to have the living Christ among them again. . . . But they were driven from the temple courts, and soldiers were stationed at the gates to keep back the multitude that came with their sick and dying, demanding entrance. The sufferers who had come to be healed by the Saviour sank under their disappointment. The streets were filled with mourning."[16] Where now were those who had cried, "Crucify Him, Crucify Him!"?

To retain the people's favor, the priests had killed Christ. Now they had lost their goal by the very action they thought would secure it. They found themselves forced to believe they had put the Messiah to death, and the thought drove them insane. The priests now feared Jesus' prophecies, for "He had said that He would rise again the third day, and who could say that this also would not come to pass? They longed to shut out these thoughts, but they could not."[17] Going to Pilate, they asked him to guard the tomb. "Pilate was as unwilling as were the Jews that Jesus should rise with power to punish the guilt of those who had destroyed Him, and he placed a band of Roman soldiers at the command of the priests. Said he, 'Ye have a watch: go your way, make it as sure as ye can. So they went, and made the sepulchre sure, sealing the stone, and setting a watch' (Matt. 27:65, 66, KJV)."[18] "A guard of one hundred soldiers was then stationed around the sepulcher to prevent it from being tampered with. The priests did all they could to keep Christ's body where it had been laid. He was sealed as securely in His tomb as if He were to remain there through all time."[19]

"The very efforts made to prevent Christ's resurrection are the most convincing arguments in its proof."[20]

JESUS

MINISTRY TO THE CHURCH
Christ Our Redeemer

Resurrection to Ascension, A.D. 31

Matthew 28

Mark 16

Luke 24

John 20; 21:24, 25

The Desire of Ages, pp. 779-835

THE FIRST DAY OF THE WEEK

Now after the Sabbath, as the first day of the week began to dawn, Mary Magdalene and the other Mary came to see the tomb. Matt. 28:1.

Twilight came at 4:00 a.m. and the sun rose at 5:30 a.m. on that Jerusalem Sunday. Mary had spent the Sabbath hours mourning with family and friends at her home in Bethany, two miles distant. "Christ was still a prisoner in His narrow tomb. The great stone was in its place; the Roman seal was unbroken; the Roman guards were keeping their watch. And there were unseen watchers. Hosts of evil angels were gathered about the place. Had it been possible, the prince of darkness with his apostate army would have kept forever sealed the tomb that held the Son of God. But a heavenly host surrounded the sepulcher. Angels that excel in strength were guarding the tomb, and waiting to welcome the Prince of life." [21]

"He who died for the sins of the world was to remain in the tomb the allotted time. He was in that stony prison house as a prisoner of divine justice. He was responsible to the Judge of the universe. He was bearing the sins of the world, and His Father only could release Him. . . . But prophecy had pointed out that on the third day Christ would rise from the dead. . . . His body was to come forth from the tomb untarnished by corruption." [22]

"Before anyone had reached the sepulcher, there was a great earthquake. The mightiest angel from heaven, he who held the position from which Satan fell, received his commission from the Father, and clothed with the panoply of heaven, he parted the darkness from his track. His face was like the lightning, and his garments white as snow. As soon as his feet touched the ground it quaked beneath his tread. The Roman guard were keeping their weary watch when this wonderful scene took place, and they were enabled to endure the sight, for they had a message to bear as witnesses of the resurrection of Christ. The angel approached the grave, rolled away the stone as though it had been a pebble, and sat upon it. The light of heaven encircled the tomb, and the whole heaven was lighted by the glory of the angels. Then his voice was heard, 'Thy Father calls Thee; come forth.' " [23]

An angelic host welcomed the resurrected Jesus with songs of praise. His resurrection is every bit as important to our salvation as was His death!

FIRSTFRUITS

Your dead shall live; together with my dead body they shall arise. Awake and sing, you who dwell in dust; for your dew is like the dew of herbs, and the earth shall cast out the dead. Isa. 26:19.

An earthquake marked the hour when Christ laid down His life, and another earthquake witnessed the moment when He took it up in triumph. . . . When He shall come to the earth again, He will shake 'not the earth only, but also heaven' (Heb. 12:26, KJV)."[24] "At the death of Jesus the soldiers had beheld the earth wrapped in darkness at midday; but at the resurrection they saw the brightness of the angels illuminate the night, and heard the inhabitants of heaven singing with great joy and triumph: Thou hast vanquished Satan and the powers of darkness; Thou hast swallowed up death in victory!

"Christ came forth from the tomb glorified, and the Roman guard beheld Him. Their eyes were riveted upon the face of Him whom they had so recently mocked and derided. In this glorified Being they beheld the prisoner whom they had seen in the judgment hall, the one for whom they had plaited a crown of thorns. This was the One who had stood unresisting before Pilate and Herod, His form lacerated by the cruel scourge. This was He who had been nailed to the cross, at whom the priests and rulers, full of self-satisfaction, had wagged their heads, saying, 'He saved others; himself he cannot save' (Matt. 27:42, KJV). This was He who had been laid in Joseph's new tomb. The decree of heaven had loosed the captive. Mountains piled upon mountains over His sepulcher could not have prevented Him from coming forth."[25]

"Christ arose from the dead as the first fruits of those that slept. He was the antitype of the wave sheaf, and His resurrection took place on the very day when the wave sheaf was to be presented before the Lord. . . . The sheaf dedicated to God represented the harvest. So Christ the first fruits represented the great spiritual harvest to be gathered for the kingdom of God. His resurrection is the type and pledge of the resurrection of all the righteous dead. 'For if we believe that Jesus died and rose again, even so them also which sleep in Jesus will God bring with him' (1 Thess. 4:14, KJV)."[26]

What a wondrous day awaits us when the graves open and the dead in Christ also rise to immortality!

The Bribe

When they had assembled with the elders and consulted together, they gave a large sum of money to the soldiers. Matt. 28:12.

As the light of the angels shone brighter than the sun around the tomb of Jesus, the Roman guard collapsed to the ground. They were powerless to prevent Christ's resurrection. Satan's angels also witnessed the resurrection of Jesus, and they bitterly complained to Satan that their captive had been taken from them. Their period of apparent triumph over Christ had been short-lived. "For as Jesus walked forth from His prison house a majestic conqueror, Satan knew that after a season he must die, and his kingdom pass unto Him whose right it was. . . . Satan bade his servants go to the chief priests and elders. Said he, 'We succeeded in deceiving them, blinding their eyes and hardening their hearts against Jesus. . . . Now hold it before them that if it becomes known that Jesus is risen, they will be stoned by the people for putting to death an innocent man.' "[27]

The guards "were making their way to Pilate, but . . . the chief priests and rulers sent for them to be brought first into their presence. A strange appearance those soldiers presented. Trembling with fear, their faces colorless, they bore testimony to the resurrection of Christ. . . . The faces of the priests were as those of the dead. Caiaphas tried to speak. His lips moved, but they uttered no sound. The soldiers were about to leave the council room, when a voice stayed them. Caiaphas had at last found speech. Wait, wait, he said. Tell no one the things you have seen. A lying report was then given to the soldiers. 'Say ye,' said the priests, 'His disciples came by night, and stole Him away while we slept.' "[28] The priests wanted the guards to admit dereliction of duty. Sleeping at one's post or loss of a prisoner were both offenses punishable by death.

"In order to silence the testimony they feared, the priests promised to secure the safety of the guard, saying that Pilate would not desire to have such a report circulated any more than they did. The Roman soldiers sold their integrity to the Jews for money."[29] The priests told Pilate the invented story, but when he questioned the guards in private, they feared for their lives and did not dare conceal the story. Pilate agreed to let the matter drop at the priests' insistence.

The cover-up was in place, and none of the participants would ever know peace again.

THE THREE WOMEN

Now when the Sabbath was past, Mary Magdalene, Mary the mother of James, and Salome bought spices, that they might come and anoint Him. Mark 16:1.

Christ rested in the tomb on the Sabbath day, and when holy beings of both heaven and earth were astir on the morning of the first day of the week, He rose from the grave. . . . But this fact does not consecrate the first day of the week, and make it a Sabbath. Jesus, prior to His death, established a memorial of the breaking of His body and the spilling of His blood for the sins of the world, in the ordinance of the Lord's supper. . . . And the repentant believer, who takes the steps required in conversion, commemorates in his baptism the death, burial, and resurrection of Christ. He goes down into the water in the likeness of Christ's death and burial, and he is raised out of the water in the likeness of His resurrection—not to take up the old life of sin, but to live a new life in Christ Jesus."[30]

But now the women came to the tomb. "As they walked, they recounted Christ's works of mercy and His words of comfort. But they remembered not His words, 'I will see you again' (John 16:22, KJV)."[31] Approaching the sepulcher, they wondered aloud, "Who will roll away the stone from the door of the tomb for us?" As they arrived at the burial place they noticed light shining about the tomb. Entering, they discovered that the body of Jesus was not inside. Not knowing what to do next, they realized, for the first time, that they were not alone. "A young man clothed in shining garments was sitting by the tomb. It was the angel who had rolled away the stone. He had taken the guise of humanity that he might not alarm these friends of Jesus. Yet about him the light of the heavenly glory was still shining, and the women were afraid."[32]

Turning, he told them that Jesus had risen and that they must notify the disciples. Then he invited them to view the empty tomb again. Another angel, also present in human form, reminded them of the words of Jesus: "The Son of man must be delivered into the hands of sinful men, and be crucified, and the third day rise again." Suddenly they grasped the importance of the news. He had risen! Forgetting the now-useless spices they had brought, they raced with joy to tell the eleven.

He is risen should be our great message to the world.

JOHN, THE SPRINTER

Then she ran and came to Simon Peter, and to the other disciple, whom Jesus loved, and said to them, "They have taken away the Lord out of the tomb, and we do not know where they have laid Him." John 20:2.

Mary had not heard the good news the other three women had already discovered. Having arrived ahead of them, she immediately ran to Peter and John with what she had seen. "The incident related in verses 3-10 remarkably reflects the different temperaments of Peter and John. John was quiet, reserved, deep feeling . . . ; Peter was impulsive, zealous, and forward. . . . Each reacted in his characteristic fashion upon the receipt of the news from Mary."[33] Both disciples immediately set out for the sepulcher.

John soon outdistanced Peter. We must remember that Peter, even though he had spent his life in hard physical outdoor labor, was older than John was. "And he [John], stooping down and looking in, saw the linen cloths lying there; yet he did not go in" (John 20:5). Hesitating, John did not go inside, but Peter was never one to be called timid. "Then Simon Peter came, following him, and went into the tomb; and he saw the linen cloths lying there, and the handkerchief that had been around His head, not lying with the linen cloths, but folded together in a place by itself. Then the other disciple [John], who came to the tomb first, went in also; and he saw and believed" (verses 6-8). "He did not yet understand the scripture that Christ must rise from the dead; but he now remembered the Saviour's words foretelling His resurrection. It was Christ Himself who had placed those graveclothes with such care. . . . In His sight who guides alike the star and the atom, there is nothing unimportant. Order and perfection are seen in all His work."[34]

Peter was not as quick to understand that his Lord had risen. Luke tells us that Peter "departed, marveling to himself at what had happened" (Luke 24:12). Neither disciple comprehended the prophecy that stated: "For You will not leave my soul in Sheol, nor will You allow Your Holy One to see corruption" (Ps. 16:10). Scripture tells us Peter and John "went away again to their own homes" (John 20:10). What good news the "disciple whom Jesus loved" must have carried home to the mother of Jesus. He could report that her Son lived! What a thrill it must have been to carry hope to those who loved Him!

It is still a thrill to share Him with others.

MARY MAGDALENE

Now when He rose early on the first day of the week, He appeared first to Mary Magdalene. Mark 16:9.

Mary had followed Peter and John back to the garden. Now they had returned to Jerusalem while she remained behind. "As she looked into the empty tomb, grief filled her heart. Looking in, she saw the two angels. . . . 'Woman, why weepest thou?' they asked her. 'Because they have taken away my Lord,' she answered, 'and I know not where they have laid him.' . . . Another voice addressed her, 'Woman, why weepest thou? whom seekest thou?' Through her tear-dimmed eyes, Mary saw the form of a man, and thinking that it was the gardener, she said, 'Sir, if thou have borne him hence, tell me where thou hast laid him, and I will take him away.' If this rich man's tomb was thought too honorable a burial place for Jesus, she herself would provide a place for Him." [35]

Jesus' first appearance after His death wasn't to Peter, John, or even His own mother, but to Mary Magdalene. Mary, who had loved Him so much for His forgiveness and love that she had anointed His body with expensive perfume before burial. Staying at the cross until the very end, she had followed the body to the sepulcher, was first to the tomb on Sunday morning, and had lingered behind in tears when the news was confirmed that her Master was missing. To Mary, Jesus came first!

"But now in His own familiar voice Jesus said to her, 'Mary.' Now she knew that it was not a stranger who was addressing her, and turning she saw before her the living Christ. In her joy she forgot that He had been crucified. Springing toward Him, as if to embrace His feet, she said, 'Rabboni.' But Christ raised His hand, saying, Detain Me not; 'for I am not yet ascended to my Father: but go to my brethren, and say unto them, I ascend unto my Father, and your Father; and to my God, and your God.' " [36] Jesus had not forbidden her to touch His resurrected body, but rather He wished "first to ascend to His Father, there to receive the assurance that His sacrifice has been accepted. . . . After His temporary ascension Jesus permitted, without protest, the act He now asked Mary to postpone." [37] Hurrying to the disciples, she told them that she had seen Jesus, but they did not believe her.

Do you believe He has risen? Your answer is critical to your acceptance of Him.

"I HAVE NOT YET ASCENDED"

Jesus said to her, "Do not cling to Me, for I have not yet ascended to My Father." John 20:17.

When He closed His eyes in death upon the cross, the soul of Christ did not go at once to heaven, as many believe, or how could His words be true—'I am not yet ascended to my Father'? The spirit of Jesus slept in the tomb with His body, and did not wing its way to heaven, there to maintain a separate existence. . . . All that comprised the life and intelligence of Jesus remained with His body in the sepulcher; and when He came forth it was as a whole being; He did not have to summon His spirit from heaven. He had power to lay down His life and to take it up again." [38] "When Christ was crucified, it was His human nature that died. Deity did not sink and die; that would have been impossible." [39]

"Jesus immediately ascended to heaven and presented Himself before the throne of God, showing the marks of shame and cruelty upon His brow, His hands and feet. But He refused to receive the coronet of glory, and the royal robe, and He also refused the adoration of the angels as He had refused the homage of Mary, until the Father signified that His offering was accepted. He also had a request to prefer concerning His chosen ones upon earth. He wished to have the relation clearly defined that His redeemed should hereafter sustain to heaven, and to His Father. . . . God's answer to this appeal goes forth in the proclamation: 'Let all the angels of God worship him.' Every angelic commander obeys the royal mandate, and Worthy, worthy is the Lamb that was slain; and that lives again a triumphant conqueror! echoes and re-echoes through all heaven. The innumerable company of angels prostrate themselves before the Redeemer. The request of Christ is granted." [40]

"To the believer, death is but a small matter. Christ speaks of it as if it were of little moment. 'If a man keep my saying, he shall never see death,' 'he shall never taste death.' To the Christian, death is but a sleep, a moment of silence and darkness. . . . The same power that raised Christ from the dead will raise His church, and glorify it with Him, above all principalities, above all powers, above every name that is named, not only in this world, but also in the world to come." [41]

At Christ's second coming all the dead in Christ shall hear His voice, and come forth to glorious, immortal life.

"Go to Galilee"

Then Jesus said to them, "Do not be afraid. Go and tell My brethren to go to Galilee, and there they will see Me."

Matt. 28:10.

As the news about the risen Saviour spread, Satan had a counterfeit prepared. The Roman guard told all who would listen that the disciples had spirited Christ's body away during the night. While the people of Jerusalem seemed willing to accept their claim, God made sure that people would not think this important event in our salvation was nothing more than a lie. Those who came back to life with Jesus testified to His resurrection. Just as predicted, many priests still did not believe—even after the evidence of those raised from the dead (Luke 16:27-31).

The disciples found it equally hard to accept the women's message. The disciples "had heard so much of the doctrines and the so-called scientific theories of the Sadducees that the impression made on their minds in regard to the resurrection was vague. They scarcely knew what the resurrection from the dead could mean. They were unable to take in the great subject."[42] The proof of Christ's resurrection appeared in what the angel had said to the women: "But go, tell His disciples—and Peter—that He is going before you into Galilee; there you will see Him, as He said to you" (Mark 16:7). Only those who had been with Christ would have recognized the words and instructions as His, and they referred to Peter! "Jesus' mention of him by name was an indication that, in spite of his mistakes, Peter was still acknowledged and included among Jesus' closest friends, because he had sincerely repented."[43]

Jesus sent three messages to His disciples: the first carried by the women who talked with the angels at the tomb (verse 6); the second by Mary Magdalene (John 20:17); and the third by the same women when Jesus met them on the way to the disciples and they worshiped Him (Matt. 28:9, 10). It is important to note that Jesus now accepted the homage of the women that He had forbidden Mary to express earlier. Between the two appearances Jesus had ascended to His Father and had His sacrifice approved of. The disciples needed to exercise faith. His messages required them to not only believe, but to act upon that belief by going to Galilee.

Often we are in essence directed to "go to Galilee." We must then remember His words and exercise faith.

ROAD TO EMMAUS

Now behold, two of them were traveling that same day to a village called Emmaus. Luke 24:13.

L ate in the afternoon of the day of the resurrection, two of the disciples were on their way to Emmaus, a little town eight miles from Jerusalem. These disciples had had no prominent place in Christ's work, but they were earnest believers in Him. They had come to the city to keep the Passover, and were greatly perplexed by the events that had recently taken place. They had heard the news of the morning in regard to the removal of Christ's body from the tomb, and also the report of the women who had seen the angels and had met Jesus. They were now returning to their homes to meditate and pray. Sadly they pursued their evening walk, talking over the scenes of the trial and the crucifixion. Never before had they been so utterly disheartened. Hopeless and faithless, they were walking in the shadow of the cross. They had not advanced far on their journey when they were joined by a stranger, but they were so absorbed in their gloom and disappointment that they did not observe him closely."[44] The other Person walked with them for the better part of two hours as they slowly journeyed home.

Opening the discussion, Jesus asked, "What kind of conversation is this that you have with one another as you walk and are sad?" Cleopas, one of the two, replied, "The things concerning Jesus of Nazareth, who was a Prophet mighty in deed and word before God and all the people, and how the chief priests and our rulers delivered Him to be condemned to death, and crucified Him." The two men feared that somehow they might have been mistaken to have believed in Jesus and His claims, yet they had not given up all hope in Him as Messiah. "A supposed faith in Christ that is not firmly rooted in the teachings of the Scriptures cannot possibly remain steadfast when the storms of doubt blow."[45]

Then Jesus, beginning with the first five books of the Bible, outlined for them the prophecies regarding His mission and death. "Misguided men who deprecate the Old Testament reveal little knowledge of the high esteem in which Christ held those sacred, inspired writings."[46]

"Those who study and believe the Old Testament, written by the hand of Moses and others, will find Christ therein. . . . Christ Himself warned that those who minimize the importance and value of the Old Testament do not really believe in Him (see . . . John 5:47)."[47]

"ABIDE WITH US"

Then they drew near to the village where they were going. . . . But they constrained Him, saying, "Abide with us, for it is toward evening, and the day is far spent."
Luke 24:28, 29.

Jesus continued to expound Scripture as they walked along in gathering darkness. Slowly the two comprehended the humanity of Jesus and His mission of suffering to rescue humanity. They now realized that the sacrifice of Christ and His shed blood ratified the age-old covenant. With great care Jesus pointed out the passages referring to His death and resurrection. Those texts included: Genesis 3:15; Exodus 12:5; Numbers 21:9; 24:17; Deuteronomy 18:15; Psalm 22:1, 8, 16, 18; Isaiah 7:14; 9:6, 7; 50:6; 53; Jeremiah 23:5; Micah 5:2; Zechariah 9:9; 12:10; 13:7; and Malachi 3:1; 4:2.

"The disciples were weary, but the conversation did not flag. Words of life and assurance fell from the Saviour's lips. But still their eyes were holden. . . . But little did they yet suspect who their traveling companion was. . . . They thought that He was one of those who had been in attendance at the great feast, and who was now returning to his home. He walked as carefully as they did over the rough stones, now and then halting with them for a little rest. Thus they proceeded along the mountainous road, while the One who was soon to take His position at God's right hand . . . walked beside them."[48]

As the men reached their homes it appeared as if their new friend would continue on, so they urged Him to stay with them. They prepared simple fare and placed it before their guest. "Now He puts forth His hands to bless the food. The disciples start back in astonishment. Their companion spreads forth His hands in exactly the same way as their Master used to do. They look again, and lo, they see in His hands the print of nails. Both exclaim at once, It is the Lord Jesus! He has risen from the dead!"[49] Forgetting their weariness, they joyfully retraced their steps to Jerusalem to tell the disciples.

"Had the disciples failed to press their invitation, they would not have known that their traveling companion was the risen Lord. Christ never forces His company upon anyone. He interests Himself in those who need Him. Gladly will He enter the humblest home, and cheer the lowliest heart. But if men are too indifferent to think of the heavenly Guest, or ask Him to abide with them, He passes on."[50]

A MESSAGE OF HOPE

Now as they said these things, Jesus Himself stood in the midst of them.

Luke 24:36.

The disciples had witnessed amazing things in the past 72 hours, and they found it just a little overwhelming and hard to believe. "Trouble seemed crowding upon trouble. On the sixth day of the week they had seen their Master die; on the first day of the next week they found themselves deprived of His body, and they were accused of having stolen it away for the sake of deceiving the people. They despaired of ever correcting the false impressions that were gaining ground against them. They feared the enmity of the priests and the wrath of the people. They longed for the presence of Jesus, who had helped them in every perplexity." [51] Little did the 10 men realize that that very night they would see even greater things.

The sun was just setting as Cleopas and his friend invited their new acquaintance to join them in a meal. Following the interrupted meal, darkness cloaked the Shephelah, or hill country. The moon rose late that spring night, so a return trip to Jerusalem over treacherous footpaths would be in total darkness. "The night is dark, but the Sun of Righteousness is shining upon them. Their hearts leap for joy. They seem to be in a new world. Christ is a living Saviour. . . . They carry the greatest message ever given to the world, a message of glad tidings upon which the hopes of the human family for time and for eternity depend." [52]

"On reaching Jerusalem the two disciples enter at the eastern gate, which is open at night on festal occasions. The houses are dark and silent, but the travelers make their way through the narrow streets by the light of the rising moon. They go to the upper chamber where Jesus spent the hours of the last evening before His death. Here they know that their brethren are to be found. Late as it is, they know that the disciples will not sleep till they learn for a certainty what has become of the body of their Lord." [53] It is now Monday morning by Jewish reckoning. Knocking quietly, they give their names. Someone unbars the door and allows them to slip into the room. Quickly the door shuts behind them. Out of breath and excited, they tell of meeting the Lord on the road to Emmaus.

Suddenly, there exists a third Person standing among them. All eyes turn toward the Stranger. Your eyes should also turn to the Saviour.

"PEACE BE WITH YOU"

Then, the same day at evening, being the first day of the week, when the doors were shut where the disciples were assembled, for fear of the Jews, Jesus came and stood in the midst. John 20:19.

The two disciples from Emmaus had just finished their tale when another Man stood before them. "Every eye is fastened upon the Stranger. No one has knocked for entrance. No footstep has been heard. The disciples are startled, and wonder what it means. Then they hear a voice which is no other than the voice of their Master. Clear and distinct the words fall from His lips, 'Peace be unto you.' "[54] Immediately they fear the figure. Some think they have seen a spirit. We must remember that they were the same group of men who, under other desperate conditions, had thought they had witnessed a spirit walking on the Sea of Galilee.

"Why are you troubled?" Jesus said. "And why do doubts arise in your hearts? Behold My hands and My feet, that it is I Myself. Handle Me and see, for a spirit does not have flesh and bones as you see I have" (Luke 24:38, 39). Approaching them, Jesus stretched out His hands for them to observe the marks of the nails in His wrists between the long bones of His arms. He lifted the hem of His garment so that they might observe the holes in His feet. Jesus wanted them to use all of their senses to assure themselves that He was real. He certainly looked like the Master, and they recognized His distinct voice. Also they could touch and know that the cruel nail marks were present in His resurrected body. As they struggled to understand the experience, Jesus asked them, " 'Have you any food here?' So they gave Him a piece of a broiled fish and some honeycomb. And He took it and ate in their presence" (verses 41-43).

"The resurrection of Jesus was a type of the final resurrection of all who sleep in Him. The countenance of the risen Saviour, His manner, His speech, were all familiar to His disciples. As Jesus arose from the dead, so those who sleep in Him are to rise again. We shall know our friends, even as the disciples knew Jesus."[55]

"In the face radiant with the light shining from the face of Jesus, we shall recognize the lineaments of those we love."[56] "Amen. Even so, come, Lord Jesus!" (Rev. 22:20).

DOUBTING THOMAS

So he said to them, "Unless I see in His hands the print of the nails . . . and put my hand into His side, I will not believe."

John 20:25.

Thomas had not been present when Jesus first appeared to the disciples. Despite their claims, he refused to believe Jesus was alive. A week passed, and Thomas felt more wretched than ever. He told his fellow disciples, "Unless I see in His hands the print of the nails . . . and put my hand into His side, I will not believe" (John 20:25). The disciples had made the upper chamber a home for themselves and met there with some regularity. One evening, eight days after Jesus showed Himself to the 10, Thomas decided to join them. Suddenly Jesus appeared, greeting them with the words "Peace to you!" No one had told Jesus of Thomas' unbelief, but turning to the disciple, Jesus said, " 'Reach your finger here, and look at My hands; and reach your hand here, and put it into My side. Do not be unbelieving, but believing.' And Thomas answered and said to Him, 'My Lord and my God!' " (verses 27, 28).

"God ever provides men with sufficient evidence on which to base faith, and those who are willing to accept it can always find their way to Him. At the same time God does not compel men to believe against their will, for in so doing He would deprive them of the right to make their own choice. Were all men like Thomas, later generations could never come to a saving knowledge of the Saviour. In fact, none but the few hundred who actually saw the risen Lord with their natural eyesight would have believed in Him. But for all who do receive Him by faith and believe on His name . . . Heaven reserves a special blessing—'Blessed are they that have not seen, and yet have believed' (John 20:29, KJV)."[57]

"Jesus, in His treatment of Thomas, gave His followers a lesson regarding the manner in which they should treat those who have doubts upon religious truth, and who make those doubts prominent. He did not overwhelm Thomas with words of reproach, nor did He enter into a controversy with him; but, with marked condescension and tenderness, He revealed Himself unto the doubting one."[58]

"Persistent controversy will seldom weaken unbelief, but rather put it upon self-defense, where it will find new support and excuse. Jesus, revealed in His love and mercy as the crucified Saviour, will wring from many once unwilling lips the acknowledgment of Thomas, 'My Lord, and my God.' "[59]

BREAKFAST BY THE SEA

After these things Jesus showed Himself again to the disciples at the Sea of Tiberias. John 21:1.

As Passover closed, seven disciples retraced their steps toward home—Galilee. Now they returned to the scenes of their association with Christ. Memories came flooding back as they descended to the shores of Galilee. "The evening was pleasant, and Peter, who still had much of his old love for boats and fishing, proposed that they should go out upon the sea and cast their nets. In this plan all were ready to join; they were in need of food and clothing, which the proceeds of a successful night's fishing would supply. So they went out in their boat, but they caught nothing. All night they toiled, without success. . . . At length the morning dawned. The boat was but a little way from the shore, and the disciples saw a stranger standing upon the beach." [60]

Calling out to them, the stranger asked, "Children, have you any food?" They answered no. Fishing had been poor, and now daylight was upon them and prospects were not good. "Cast the net on the right side of the boat, and you will find some," the Man suggested. After they had thrown the net from the side closest to Jesus, the disciples could not pull in the bountiful catch. John remembered a time when someone had asked them to cast their nets to one side and they had broken under that catch (Luke 5:1-11). Turning to Peter, John said, "It is the Lord!" Impetuous Peter, putting on his outer garment (for he had stripped down to work the nets), immediately jumped overboard and swam to shore. The six others struggled to bring the catch the final 100 yards to shore, and Peter joined them in hauling it up the beach. A small fire of coals burned near the shore, and fish cooked upon it with bread nearby. Jesus had made them breakfast! He knew they were hungry and tired. Once again He was reminding them of their first call to be "fishers of men." "While they were doing His work, He would provide for their needs. And Jesus had a purpose in bidding them cast their net on the right side of the ship. On that side He stood upon the shore. That was the side of faith. If they labored in connection with Him—His divine power combining with their human effort—they could not fail of success." [61]

Neither can we.

"DO YOU LOVE ME?"

He said to him the third time, "Simon, son of Jonah, do you love Me?" . . . And he said to Him, "Lord, You know all things; You know that I love You." Jesus said to him, "Feed My sheep."

John 21:17.

That Peter had dishonored his Master was common knowledge among the others, and they distrusted him. While eating together in silence around the fire, Jesus turned to Peter and said, "Simon, son of Jonah, do you love [Greek, *agape*] Me more than these?" Jesus used the word *agape*, or love of the highest form. Peter recalled his rash words: "Even if all are made to stumble because of You, I will never be made to stumble." Now, not so self-assured, he replied, "Yes, Lord; You know that I love [Greek, *phileo*] You." Peter replied with the term *phileo*, or love based on emotion or common friendship. The Master replied, "Feed My lambs." Again Jesus asked, "Simon, son of Jonah, do you love *[agape]* Me?" "Yes, Lord," Peter answered. "You know that I love [*phileo*, "have affection for") You." After saying to him, "Tend My sheep," Jesus asked a third time: "Simon, son of Jonah, do you *phileo* [love Me as a friend]?" Peter felt hurt. How could he convince Jesus he loved Him when the Master clearly doubted his friendship? Appealing to Jesus, Peter humbly asked Him to read his heart. All thoughts of boasting were gone. He didn't even answer the question with the word "Yes."

Instead he answered, "Lord, You know all things; You know that I love [*phileo*] You." Peter remembered the three denials of his Lord. Now he had received three chances to affirm, before all the others, that he was loyal and had repented of his mistake. Once again Jesus said, "Feed My sheep."

"The question that Christ had put to Peter was significant. He mentioned only one condition of discipleship and service. 'Lovest thou Me?' He said. This is the essential qualification. Though Peter might possess every other, yet without the love of Christ he could not be a faithful shepherd over the Lord's flock."[62] Christ never elevated Peter to a position of superiority over the other disciples. In fact, Peter himself attested, "The elders who are among you I exhort, *I who am a fellow elder* and a witness of the sufferings of Christ, and also a partaker of the glory that will be revealed" (1 Peter 5:1).

There is only one Chief Shepherd and only one Rock upon which the church is founded—Christ Himself, and the sheep and lambs are His!

PETER'S DEATH

"Follow Me."

John 21:19.

Jesus beckoned Peter to accompany Him down the beach, away from those gathered near the fire. "Before His death, Jesus had said to him, 'Whither I go, thou canst not follow me now; but thou shalt follow me afterwards.' To this Peter had replied, 'Lord, why cannot I follow thee now? I will lay down my life for thy sake' (John 13:36, 37, KJV). . . . Peter had failed when the test came. . . . That he might be strengthened for the final test of his faith, the Saviour opened to him his future. He told him that after living a life of usefulness, when age was telling upon his strength, he would indeed follow his Lord."[63] Using graphic terms, even to the stretching out of his hands, Jesus told Peter that he also would be crucified for following his Lord. Quietly and with great love Jesus told His disciple, "Follow Me." Once Peter would have tried to do things his way, but now he understood he must not run before the Lord—he must wait upon Him.

Looking behind them, Peter saw John following at a distance. Curious, Peter asked, "But Lord, what about this man?" Jesus replied, "If I will that he remain till I come, what is that to you? You follow Me." Jesus was not telling Peter that John would live until the Second Coming. Exiled to the Isle of Patmos, John the beloved would live to be an old man. He would write the book of Revelation and the beautiful sentiments contained in his three Epistles. Peter, "the once restless, boastful, self-confident disciple, became subdued and contrite. He followed his Lord indeed—the Lord he had denied. The thought that Christ had not denied and rejected him was to Peter a light and comfort and blessing. He felt that he could be crucified from choice, but it must be with his head downward. And he who was so close a partaker of Christ's sufferings will also be a partaker of His glory when he shall 'sit upon the throne of his glory.' "[64]

"How many today are like Peter! They are interested in the affairs of others, and anxious to know their duty, while they are in danger of neglecting their own. It is our work to look to Christ and follow Him. We shall see mistakes in the lives of others, and defects in their character. Humanity is encompassed with infirmity. But in Christ we shall find perfection. Beholding Him, we shall become transformed."[65] Never turn your eyes from Jesus!

THE GREAT COMMISSION

"Go therefore and make disciples of all the nations, baptizing them in the name of the Father and of the Son and of the Holy Spirit, teaching them to observe all things that I have commanded you; and lo, I am with you always, even to the end of the age." Amen.

Matt. 28:19, 20.

Jesus called a meeting upon a mountain in Galilee, and all the believers that the disciples could contact now gathered to hear Him. "They made their way to the place of meeting by circuitous routes, coming in from every direction, to avoid exciting the suspicion of the jealous Jews. With wondering hearts they came, talking earnestly together of the news that had reached them concerning Christ. At the time appointed, about five hundred believers were collected in little knots on the mountainside, eager to learn all that could be learned from those who had seen Christ since His resurrection. From group to group the disciples passed, telling all they had seen and heard of Jesus, and reasoning from the Scriptures as He had done with them. Thomas recounted the story of his unbelief, and told how his doubts had been swept away. Suddenly Jesus stood among them."[66]

For many it was their first encounter with Jesus. Jesus reassured His disciples that He had accomplished His mission. He had made the sacrifice for humanity, purchasing salvation by the blood of God's own Son. The Father had accepted the sacrifice, and the atonement was complete. Jesus now left those disciples and all future disciples with a Great Commission (Matt. 28:18-20). He assigned all disciples to take the message of a crucified and risen Saviour to all. This message was not for the Jews only, but was global. His followers were to preach the gospel of the kingdom "in all the world as a witness to all the nations" (Matt. 24:14).

All who take the name "Christian" assume responsibility for spreading the good news of salvation through Jesus Christ. "It is a fatal mistake to suppose that the work of saving souls depends alone on the ordained minister. All to whom the heavenly inspiration has come are put in trust with the gospel. All who receive the life of Christ are ordained to work for the salvation of their fellow men. For this work the church was established, and all who take upon themselves its sacred vows are thereby pledged to be coworkers with Christ."[67]

Every human being is our mission, and the world is our mission field.

CARRIED UP INTO HEAVEN

And He led them out as far as Bethany, and He lifted up His hands and blessed them. Now it came to pass, while He blessed them, that He was parted from them and carried up into heaven.

Luke 24:50, 51.

Following the mountainside meeting in Galilee, the disciples returned to Jerusalem. Jesus now spent 40 wonderful days with them. He explained the plan of salvation in the light of the cross so they now understood the nature of Christ's mission to save fallen humanity. Christ carried the minds of the disciples beyond the tomb to a living Saviour. Now the time had come for them to take the gospel to all nations. Jesus must leave them, and He chose His parting location with care. The Mount of Olives had always held a special place in His heart.

Reaching the crest of Olivet and looking down upon Jerusalem for the last time, He passed a little way over the summit and down the eastern slope toward Bethany. Here He paused, and the disciples gathered around Him. "Christ had sojourned in the world for thirty-three years; He had endured its scorn, insult, and mockery; He had been rejected and crucified."[68] What would be His reaction to those He came to save? Would He withdraw His love from those who had rejected His sacrifice? Would He leave His disciples with no thought for their welfare? No! "Beams of light seemed to radiate from His countenance as He looked lovingly upon them. He upbraided them not for their faults and failures; words of the deepest tenderness were the last that fell upon their ears from the lips of their Lord. With hands outstretched in blessing, and as if in assurance of His protecting care, He slowly ascended from among them, drawn heavenward by a power stronger than any earthly attraction. As He passed upward, the awe-stricken disciples looked with straining eyes for the last glimpse of their ascending Lord. A cloud of glory hid Him from their sight; and the words came back to them as the cloudy chariot of angels received Him, 'Lo, I am with you alway, even unto the end of the world.'"[69]

Jesus would never leave them nor desert us. The marks of His love are permanently engraved in His hands and feet, and He has hidden us in Him. We may take heart that whatever happens, His promise "to be with us always" is ours until the very end of our world and beyond.

GOD'S RIGHT HAND

So then, after the Lord had spoken to them, He was received up into heaven, and sat down at the right hand of God. Mark 16:19.

Christ had ascended to heaven in the form of humanity. The disciples had beheld the cloud receive Him. The same Jesus who had walked and talked and prayed with them; who had broken bread with them; who had been with them in their boats on the lake; and who had that very day toiled with them up the ascent of Olivet—the same Jesus had now gone to share His Father's throne. And the angels had assured them that the very One whom they had seen go up into heaven would come again even as He had ascended. He will come 'with clouds; and every eye shall see him' (Rev. 1:7, KJV). . . . 'The Son of man shall come in his glory, and all the holy angels with him, then shall he sit upon the throne of his glory' (Matt. 25:31, KJV)." [70]

The disciples returned to Jerusalem changed individuals. Those who saw them would have expected them to be dejected by the death of their Master, but they were triumphant. The disciples knew Jesus had overcome the grave and death and that He had ascended to the Father as a representative of the human race. As such, He was a friend to all who confessed His name, having promised to represent them before His Father. Heaven seemed very close to the disciples, and they did not feel deserted or forgotten. While they were still in this world of shadow and turmoil, they knew that God was preparing a heavenly place for them. Jesus had promised to return and take them home with Him. His death and resurrection were the surety of His promise. It would not be long before they would gaze once again upon that face they loved. They knew in their hearts that once again they would hear His words of life as they fell from the lips of their Lord and Master. Trusting in the Lord, they willingly did His work while they waited.

"Therefore be patient, brethren, until the coming of the Lord. See how the farmer waits for the precious fruit of the earth, waiting patiently for it until it receives the early and latter rain. You also be patient. Establish your hearts, for the coming of the Lord is at hand" (James 5:7, 8).

HEAVEN WELCOMES HOME ITS KING

Lift up your heads, O you gates! And be lifted up, you everlasting doors! And the King of glory shall come in.

Ps. 24:7.

All heaven was waiting the hour of triumph when Jesus should ascend to His Father. Angels came to receive the King of glory and to escort Him triumphantly to heaven. After Jesus had blessed His disciples, He was parted from them and taken up. And as He led the way upward, the multitude of captives who were raised at His resurrection followed. A multitude of the heavenly host were in attendance, while in heaven an innumerable company of angels awaited His coming. As they ascended to the Holy City, the angels who escorted Jesus cried out, 'Lift up your heads, O ye gates; and be ye lifted up, ye everlasting doors; and the King of glory shall come in.' The angels in the city cried out with rapture, 'Who is this King of glory?' The escorting angels answered in triumph, 'The Lord strong and mighty, the Lord mighty in battle! Lift up your heads, O ye gates; even lift them up, ye everlasting doors; and the King of glory shall come in!' Again the waiting angels asked, 'Who is this King of glory?' and the escorting angels answered in melodious strains, 'The Lord of hosts, He is the King of glory.' And the heavenly train passed into the city of God."[71]

As Moses was about to die upon Mount Nebo, God granted him a vision. From the birth of Jesus in Bethlehem to His death upon the cross, the life of Christ passed before the great Hebrew leader. Witnessing future events, he saw the triumph of Christ. He "beheld Him coming forth a conqueror, and ascending to heaven escorted by adoring angels and leading a multitude of captives. He saw the shining gates open to receive Him, and the host of heaven with songs of triumph welcoming their Commander. And it was there revealed to him that he himself would be one who should attend the Saviour, and open to Him the everlasting gates. As he looked upon the scene, his countenance shone with a holy radiance. How small appeared the trials and sacrifices of his life when compared with those of the Son of God! how light in contrast with the 'far more exceeding and eternal weight of glory'! (2 Cor. 4:17, KJV)."[72]

Jesus wishes to welcome us to those same celestial courts. Then "He shall see the labor of His soul, and be satisfied" (Isa. 53:11). What a homecoming awaits us!

A GREAT HIGH PRIEST

For Christ has not entered the holy places made with hands, which are copies of the true, but into heaven itself, now to appear in the presence of God for us.

Heb. 9:24.

When Jesus at His ascension entered by His own blood into the heavenly sanctuary to shed upon His disciples the blessings of His mediation, the Jews were left in total darkness to continue their useless sacrifices and offerings. The ministration of types and shadows had ceased. That door by which men had formerly found access to God was no longer open. The Jews had refused to seek Him in the only way whereby He could then be found, through the ministration in the sanctuary in heaven. Therefore they found no communion with God. To them the door was shut. They had no knowledge of Christ as the true sacrifice and the only mediator before God; hence they could not receive the benefits of His mediation. The condition of the unbelieving Jews illustrates the condition of the careless and unbelieving among professed Christians, who are willingly ignorant of the work of our merciful High Priest." [73]

"But Christ came as High Priest of the good things to come, with the greater and more perfect tabernacle not made with hands, that is, not of this creation. Not with the blood of goats and calves, but with His own blood He entered the Most Holy Place once for all, having obtained eternal redemption" (Heb. 9:11, 12). The law of God is eternal and immutable. If God could have abridged or abrogated it, Christ need not have died. It required Jesus' death to save humanity from sin. The blood of Christ redeems us!

"The great truth taught by the stipulation that the shedding of blood was required for forgiveness was that the salvation of man would one day require the death of the Son of God. . . . Every animal sacrifice pointed forward to the supreme sacrifice of the 'Lamb of God, which taketh away the sin of the world' (John 1:29, KJV)." [74] "Except for the vicarious death of Christ the plan of salvation would never have become a reality. Even those saved in Old Testament times were saved by virtue of the sacrifice to come (Heb. 9:15). They were saved as they looked forward in faith, even as men find salvation today by looking backward to the death of Christ." [75]

We gain salvation not by observing ceremonial laws but through faith in the atoning blood of Jesus Christ.

Blessing and Honor and Glory and Power

And every creature which is in heaven and on the earth and under the earth and such as are in the sea, and all that are in them, I heard saying: "Blessing and honor and glory and power be to Him who sits on the throne, and to the Lamb, forever and ever!" Rev. 5:13.

There is the throne, and around it the rainbow of promise. There are cherubim and seraphim. The commanders of the angel hosts, the sons of God, the representatives of the unfallen worlds, are assembled. The heavenly council before which Lucifer had accused God and His Son, the representatives of those sinless realms over which Satan had thought to establish his dominion—all are there to welcome the Redeemer. They are eager to celebrate His triumph and to glorify their King. But He waves them back. Not yet; He cannot now receive the coronet of glory and the royal robe. He enters into the presence of His Father. He points to His wounded head, the pierced side, the marred feet; He lifts His hands, bearing the print of nails. He points to the tokens of His triumph; He presents to God the wave sheaf, those raised with Him as representatives of that great multitude who shall come forth from the grave at His second coming. . . . He declares, Father: it is finished. I have done Thy will, O My God. I have completed the work of redemption. If Thy justice is satisfied, 'I will that they also, whom thou hast given me, be with me where I am' (John 17:24, KJV). The voice of God is heard proclaiming that justice is satisfied. . . . The Father's arms encircle His Son, and the word is given, 'Let all the angels of God worship him' (Heb. 1:6, KJV)."[76]

No words can describe that scene as heaven publicly reinstates the Son of God to the place of honor and glory He voluntarily left upon becoming a man. "Christ ascended to heaven bearing a sanctified, holy humanity. He took this humanity with Him into the heavenly courts, and through the eternal ages He will bear it, as the One who has redeemed every human being in the city of God, the One who has pleaded before the Father, 'I have graven them upon the palms of my hands.'"[77]

"If we are wounded and bruised, if we meet with difficulties that are hard to manage, let us remember how much Christ suffered for us."[78]

"YOU SHALL RECEIVE POWER"

But you shall receive power when the Holy Spirit has come upon you; and you shall be witnesses to Me in Jerusalem, and in all Judea and Samaria, and to the end of the earth.

Acts 1:8.

Satan did not easily surrender our world's dominion just because Christ succeeded in His mission to ransom humanity. "Satan again counseled with his angels, and with bitter hatred against God's government told them that while he retained his power and authority upon earth their efforts must be tenfold stronger against the followers of Jesus. They had prevailed nothing against Christ but must overthrow His followers, if possible. In every generation they must seek to ensnare those who would believe in Jesus. He related to his angels that Jesus had given His disciples power to rebuke them and cast them out, and to heal those whom they should afflict. Then Satan's angels went forth like roaring lions, seeking to destroy the followers of Jesus."[79]

Christ did not leave the disciples defenseless in the face of the renewed onslaught of Satan and his legions. Jesus had promised them power, and in obedience to Christ's command, they waited in Jerusalem for the promise of the Father—the outpouring of the Spirit. But they did not wait in idleness. The record says that they were "continually in the temple praising and blessing God" (Luke 24:53). The first disciples "prepared themselves for their work. Before the day of Pentecost they met together, and put away all differences. They were of one accord. They believed Christ's promise that the blessing would be given, and they prayed in faith. They did not ask for a blessing for themselves merely; they were weighted with the burden for the salvation of souls. The gospel was to be carried to the uttermost parts of the earth, and they claimed the endowment of power that Christ had promised. Then it was that the Holy Spirit was poured out, and thousands were converted in a day. So it may be now. Instead of man's speculations, let the Word of God be preached. Let Christians put away their dissension, and give themselves to God for the saving of the lost. Let them in faith ask for the blessing, and it will come."[80]

"The outpouring of the Spirit in apostolic days was the 'former rain,' and glorious was the result. But the 'latter rain' will be more abundant (Joel 2:23, KJV)."[81]

IT ALL COMES DOWN TO BELIEF IN HIM!

And truly Jesus did many other signs in the presence of His disciples, which are not written in this book; but these are written that you may believe that Jesus is the Christ, the Son of God, and that believing you may have life in His name.

John 20:30, 31.

This is the disciple who testifies of these things, and wrote these things; and we know that his testimony is true. And there are also many other things that Jesus did, which if they were written one by one, I suppose that even the world itself could not contain the books that would be written. Amen" (John 21:24, 25). John explained that he could have told much more about the 3½-year ministry of Jesus: His physical description, other miracles He performed, and the marvelous teachings He presented. Many of those reading his writings knew of other signs Jesus had done. They have been lost to us through the years. But John, in presenting to the world the Saviour he had followed, did not intend to present a full and detailed history. John chose certain "signs" to share with his readers that formed the underlying basis for the message he sought to convey. The disciple's message was simple. He wanted us to understand that the historical man Jesus was and is the Son of God, the Messiah, the living Creator and crucified Saviour. The disciple shared with us the plan of salvation. He wanted us to believe in Jesus as the Christ, the Son of God, and that believing, we might have life in His name.

Ellen White reminds us that "angels of God were commissioned to guard with special care the sacred, important truths which were to serve as an anchor to the disciples of Christ through every generation."[82] "And this is eternal life, that they may know You, the only true God, and Jesus Christ whom You have sent" (John 17:3). The humble Carpenter from Nazareth had certainly changed the world! No one has made a greater contribution to earth's history than He. Almost 2,000 years have passed since He lived His remarkable life, and yet He has had a greater impact upon society than any other person who ever lived.

What would be humanity's history had He not chosen to live among us? The Gospel writers unanimously state that Jesus of Nazareth was "God in human flesh"! Amen.

WHAT MUST WE DO?

But the end of all things is at hand; therefore be serious and watchful in your prayers. 1 Peter 4:7. Therefore do not cast away your confidence, which has great reward. Heb. 10:35.

Before Christ came to the world, His home was in the kingdom of glory, among beings that had never fallen. They loved Him, and He might have stayed there and rejoiced in their love. But He did not do this. He left the royal courts, and went without the camp, bearing the reproach of sin. He came to a world all marred and seared by the curse to save the lost sheep; and He gathered into His divine bosom all that would come to Him. He was a Man of sorrows and acquainted with grief. He trod the rugged path of self-denial Himself, and so set us an example. This was the work of Christ for us. Had He not done this, we should have been left to perish without hope in God. We find here a duty that rests upon all alike; not one of us is excused. Those who see the preciousness of the Saviour's love as He hung upon the cross, those who understand its value as there revealed, will be in earnest; they will be anxious to become colaborers with Christ in seeking for the lost and perishing. We are not placed here merely to seek our own gratification. There are sinners to be saved, and they are all about us. . . . The perils of the last days are about us; and we should have such an intense love for souls for whom Christ died that we cannot remain at home. . . . We are not to think that there is no responsibility resting upon us. . . . The nearer our lives approach to the life of Christ, the more helpful shall we be to those around us, and the more happiness we can bring into their lives. We are called upon to labor understandingly for fallen humanity. And by and by, when the Man of Nazareth shall 'see of the travail of his soul, and be satisfied,' we shall enter into the joy of our Lord. But let us be faithful in the work that is committed to us; for it is only to those who have done well that the 'Well done' will be spoken." [83]

God bless you in the coming year as you share with others your story of what the Bright and Morning Star has done for you.

He was born in an obscure village, the child of a peasant woman. He grew up in another obscure village, where He worked in a carpenter shop until He was 30.

Then for three years He was an itinerant preacher. He never had a family or owned a home. He never set foot inside a big city. He never traveled 200 miles from the place He was born. He never wrote a book or held an office. He did none of the things that usually accompany greatness.

While He was still a young man, the tide of popular opinion turned against Him. His friends deserted Him. He was turned over to His enemies and went through the mockery of a trial. He was nailed to a cross between two thieves. While He was dying, His executioners gambled for the only piece of property He had—His coat. When He was dead, He was taken down and laid in a borrowed grave.

Nineteen centuries have come and gone, and today He is the central figure for much of the human race. All of the armies that ever marched, and all the navies that ever sailed, and all the parliaments that ever sat, and all the kings that ever reigned, put together, have not affected the life of man upon this earth as powerfully as this One Solitary Life.

Anonymous

SOURCE REFERENCES

On the following pages are listed the source references for the 1,086 excerpts appearing in this volume. The key below indicates the abbreviations used for the various books, pamphlets, and periodicals.

AA	*The Acts of the Apostles*
1BC	*The Seventh-day Adventist Bible Commentary,* vol. 1 (2BC, etc., for vols. 2-7)
BD	*Seventh-day Adventist Bible Dictionary* (1979)
COL	*Christ's Object Lessons*
DA	*The Desire of Ages*
Ev	*Evangelism*
EW	*Early Writings*
FE	*Fundamentals of Christian Education*
GC	*The Great Controversy*
MB	*Thoughts From the Mount of Blessing*
MH	*The Ministry of Healing*
1MR	Ellen G. White *Manuscript Releases,* vol. 1 (2MR, etc., for vols. 2-21)
MYP	*Messages to Young People*
PK	*Prophets and Kings*
PP	*Patriarchs and Prophets*
RH	*Review and Herald*
SC	*Steps to Christ*
SDAH	*The Seventh-day Adventist Hymnal*
1SM	*Selected Messages,* book 1 (2SM, etc., for books 2, 3)
1SP	*Spirit of Prophecy,* vol. 1 (2SP, etc., for vols. 1-4)
SR	*The Story of Redemption*
ST	*Signs of the Times*
1T	*Testimonies for the Church,* vol. 1 (2T, etc., for vols. 2-9)
TM	*Testimonies to Ministers and Gospel Workers*
UL	*The Upward Look*
YI	*Youth's Instructor*

Resources

January

1 DA 20
2 AA 39
3 Ev 615
4 *Ibid.*
5 DA 19
6 5BC 901
7 DA 26
8 SDAH 337
9 1SM 22
10 DA 32
11 DA 37
12 5BC 672
13 DA 98
14 GC 493, 494
15 DA 234
16 DA 693
17 DA 694
18 DA 779
19 DA 793
20 DA 832
21 DA 99
22 7BC 399
23 5BC 682
24 5BC 685
25 5BC 690
26 PK 481
27 5BC 286
28 5BC 39
29 5BC 38
30 DA 44
31 *Ibid.*
32 5BC 698
33 ST July 30, 1896
34 GC 313
35 GC 315
36 DA 50
37 DA 52
38 DA 55
39 *Ibid.*
40 5BC 288
41 DA 60
42 DA 63
43 RH Dec. 24, 1872
44 5BC 289
45 RH Dec. 24, 1872
46 DA 65
47 DA 67
48 DA 66
49 YI Feb. 1, 1873
50 MYP 78
51 DA 69
52 DA 86
53 *Ibid.*
54 DA 90
55 DA 88
56 5BC 712
57 DA 71

58 *Ibid.*
59 5BC 707
60 DA 77
61 5BC 708
62 DA 81
63 DA 82
64 DA 74
65 DA 73
66 Ev 378
67 DA 109; italics supplied
68 YI Aug. 22, 1901
69 YI Jan. 1874
70 FE 402
71 DA 70
72 DA 87
73 DA 74
74 DA 363
75 DA 107
76 DA 104
77 DA 215
78 DA 107
79 DA 109
80 *Ibid.*
81 DA 110
82 DA 111
83 5BC 302
84 DA 111

February

1 DA 111
2 DA 112
3 DA 113
4 *Ibid.*
5 DA 115
6 5BC 725
7 DA 117
8 DA 123
9 DA 147
10 DA 118
11 DA 119
12 *Ibid.*
13 DA 123
14 1SM 282
15 DA 125
16 DA 126
17 DA 129
18 DA 131
19 *Ibid.*
20 1SM 289
21 DA 49
22 DA 686
23 3T 480
24 5BC 719
25 5BC (EGW) 1077; italics supplied

26 DA 136
27 DA 137
28 DA 138
29 *Ibid.*
30 DA 139
31 *Ibid.*
32 5BC 277
33 GC 347
34 DA 139
35 DA 141
36 SC 91
37 *Ibid.*
38 4T 534
39 4T 533
40 DA 150, 151
41 DA 152
42 2SP 99
43 DA 145
44 DA 147
45 *Ibid.*
46 *Ibid.*
47 5BC 922
48 *Ibid.*
49 *Ibid.*
50 DA 149
51 DA 148, 149
52 DA 150
53 DA 155
54 *Ibid.*
55 DA 157
56 BD 1103
57 DA 157
58 DA 158
58 *Ibid.*
60 *Ibid.*
61 DA 165
62 *Ibid.*
63 DA 168
64 *Ibid.*
65 DA 172
66 *Ibid.*
67 *Ibid.*
68 DA 175
69 DA 176
70 DA 177
71 *Ibid.*
72 5BC 930
73 DA 178
74 *Ibid.*
75 8T 332
76 DA 179
77 5BC 932
78 DA 179
79 5T 224, 225
80 5T 224
81 DA 181
82 BD 972
83 DA 188

84 DA 193

March

1 PP 204
2 *Ibid.*
3 PP 500
4 DA 183
5 *Ibid.*
6 *Ibid.*
7 DA 183, 184
8 DA 184
9 *Ibid.*
10 *Ibid.*
11 DA 187
12 DA 187, 188
13 TM 390
14 TM 391
15 DA 189
16 DA 190
17 5BC 941
18 DA 190
19 DA 191
20 3T 217
21 DA 192
22 MH 26
23 DA 194
24 *Ibid.*
25 AA 106, 107
26 DA 196
27 DA 197
28 DA 198
29 5BC 944
30 5BC 943, 944
31 DA 199
32 DA 200
33 *Ibid.*
34 DA 214, 215
35 DA 215
36 DA 216
37 DA 224
38 5BC 948
39 DA 201, 202
40 DA 203
41 DA 119
42 DA 204
43 DA 205
44 DA 206
45 5BC 950, 951
46 DA 207
47 *Ibid.*
48 5BC 953
49 DA 407
50 DA 212
51 MB 2
52 DA 232
53 DA 213
54 DA 232

[55] Ibid.
[56] DA 236
[57] 5BC 729
[58] DA 237
[59] DA 239
[60] DA 240
[61] Ibid.
[62] DA 252
[63] Ibid.
[64] DA 261
[65] DA 253
[66] RH July 19, 1887
[67] DA 254
[68] Ibid.
[69] DA 253
[70] DA 244
[71] DA 244, 245
[72] DA 245
[73] MH 20, 21
[74] 5BC (EGW) 1134
[75] 8BC 383
[76] DA 249
[77] DA 246
[78] Ibid.
[79] DA 249
[80] 5BC 739
[81] Ibid.
[82] DA 251
[83] MH 481
[84] DA 255
[85] DA 256
[86] 5BC 570
[87] Ibid.
[88] MH 29
[89] MH 22
[90] MH 19
[91] 5BC 571
[92] 5BC (EGW) 1130
[93] DA 260
[94] DA 208
[95] 5BC 571
[96] MH 509
[97] DA 32
[98] DA 263
[99] Ibid.
[100] DA 266
[101] DA 265
[102] Ibid.
[103] DA 266
[104] DA 267
[105] DA 269
[106] DA 271
[107] 5BC 582
[108] DA 273
[109] Ibid.
[110] Ibid.

APRIL

[1] DA 284
[2] DA 285
[3] 5BC 586, 587
[4] MB 3
[5] 5BC 587
[6] Ibid.
[7] SC 51
[8] 2T 202
[9] DA 295
[10] DA 296
[11] DA 294
[12] 5BC 595
[13] 5BC 596
[14] 5BC 595
[15] Ibid.
[16] 5T 224
[17] DA 294
[18] Ibid.
[19] ST May 20, 1897
[20] DA 298, see also MB 4
[21] MB 4
[22] 5BC 323
[23] DA 299
[24] MB 6
[25] 5BC 324
[26] DA 300
[27] Ibid.
[28] MB 11
[29] DA 301
[30] MB 14
[31] MB 15
[32] MB 17
[33] MB 19
[34] COL 312
[35] MB 23
[36] 6T 262
[37] MB 24, 25
[38] 5BC 327
[39] MB 26
[40] Ibid.
[41] 2T 437, 438
[42] MB 36
[43] Ibid.
[44] DA 306
[45] 5BC 330
[46] MB 37
[47] MB 36, 37
[48] MB 38
[49] MB 39
[50] DA 307
[51] MB 43
[52] MB 48
[53] DA 308
[54] 5BC 332
[55] 5BC 333
[56] DA 309
[57] ST Sept. 4, 1884
[58] MB 56, 57
[59] DA 310
[60] MB 59, 60
[61] MB 70
[62] MB 72
[63] 5BC 341
[64] 5BC 344
[65] MB 81
[66] MB 86, 87
[67] RH May 28, 1895
[68] Ibid.
[69] MB 84
[70] MB 124
[71] MB 125
[72] MB 129
[73] MB 138
[74] MB 141
[75] MB 148
[76] DA 314
[77] MB 150
[78] DA 316
[79] DA 317
[80] MH 65
[81] MH 31
[82] MH 66
[83] DA 321
[84] DA 327
[85] DA 152
[86] 5BC 757
[87] DA 318
[88] 5BC 757
[89] DA 318, 319

MAY

[1] DA 143
[2] DA 406. 407
[3] DA 321
[4] DA 87
[5] 5BC 400
[6] COL 23
[7] COL 22
[8] DA 322
[9] COL 34
[10] COL 42
[11] COL 59, 60
[12] COL 33
[13] COL 63
[14] COL 65
[15] COL 67
[16] COL 77
[17] COL 77, 78
[18] 5BC 409
[19] COL 95
[20] 5BC 409
[21] COL 102
[22] COL 71
[23] COL 72
[24] COL 74
[25] COL 123
[26] 5BC 412
[27] 5BC 411
[28] COL 115
[29] COL 116, 117
[30] 5BC 411
[31] RH, Aug. 1, 1899
[32] COL 125
[33] COL 126
[34] COL 128
[35] COL 133
[36] DA 329
[37] DA 330
[38] Ibid.
[39] DA 333
[40] DA 334
[41] DA 335
[42] DA 336
[43] RH, July 14, 1910
[44] Ibid.
[45] MH 99
[46] DA 339
[47] DA 340
[48] DA 274
[49] 6T 173
[50] DA 275
[51] 5BC 583
[52] DA 278
[53] DA 279
[54] DA 280
[55] Ibid.
[56] DA 342
[57] DA 343
[58] Ibid.
[59] DA 143
[60] DA 347
[61] COL 125
[62] DA 349
[63] Ev 58
[64] RH, Feb. 1, 1898
[65] DA 351
[66] DA 355
[67] DA 215
[68] DA 216
[69] DA 217
[70] DA 218
[71] Ibid.
[72] DA 220
[73] Ibid.
[74] DA 241
[75] DA 242
[76] Ibid.
[77] DA 359
[78] DA 361
[79] DA 362
[80] DA 363
[81] DA 221
[82] RH, Mar. 11, 1873
[83] DA 222
[84] Ibid.
[85] RH, Apr. 8, 1873
[86] Ibid.
[87] Ibid.
[88] DA 223
[89] DA 224
[90] DA 224, 225

JUNE

[1] DA 364
[2] DA 365
[3] DA 371
[4] DA 367
[5] *Ibid.*
[6] DA 368
[7] DA 369
[8] DA 377
[9] DA 718, 719
[10] 5BC 415
[11] DA 378, 379
[12] DA 378
[13] DA 381
[14] *Ibid.*
[15] *Ibid.*
[16] ST Aug. 11, 1898
[17] *Ibid.*
[18] DA 381
[19] 5BC 417
[20] DA 382
[21] *Ibid.*
[22] DA 384
[23] 5BC 965
[24] DA 385
[25] 5BC 967
[26] DA 391
[27] DA 393
[28] DA 392
[29] 5BC (EGW) 1135
[30] DA 393
[31] 5BC 622
[32] *Ibid.*
[33] DA 396
[34] DA 399
[35] DA 400
[36] DA 401
[37] *Ibid.*
[38] DA 403
[39] 5BC 627
[40] DA 404
[41] 5BC 424
[42] DA 405
[43] BD 873
[44] DA 409
[45] DA 406
[46] DA 406, 407
[47] DA 407
[48] DA 408
[49] DA 409
[50] BD 481
[51] *Ibid.*
[52] COL 212, 213
[53] DA 410
[54] DA 411
[55] DA 412
[56] 5BC 429
[57] 5BC 430
[58] DA 412
[59] 5BC 431
[60] DA 413
[61] DA 415
[62] DA 30
[63] DA 416
[64] BD 250
[65] DA 417
[66] *Ibid.*
[67] DA 419
[68] DA 420
[69] DA 421
[70] EW 162
[71] EW 164
[72] DA 425
[73] DA 427
[74] DA 428
[75] DA 429
[76] 5BC 634
[77] DA 431
[78] GC 513
[79] GC 510

JULY

[1] 5BC 442
[2] 5BC 443
[3] DA 435
[4] DA 437
[5] 5BC 449
[6] COL 251
[7] COL 245
[8] 5BC 450
[9] 5 BC 635
[10] DA 438
[11] DA 439
[12] DA 448
[13] BD 1084
[14] DA 449
[15] DA 450
[16] *Ibid.*
[17] DA 452
[18] 5BC 978
[19] DA 459
[20] DA 454
[21] DA 455
[22] DA 459
[23] 5BC 982
[24] *Ibid.*
[25] 5BC (EGW) 1136
[26] DA 460
[27] 5BC 985
[28] MH 88
[29] *Ibid.*
[30] MH 89
[31] DA 462
[32] *Ibid.*
[33] DA 463, 464
[34] DA 464
[35] DA 467
[36] DA 469, 470
[37] DA 470
[38] DA 471
[39] *Ibid.*
[40] DA 472
[41] DA 474
[42] DA 475
[43] DA 480
[44] 5BC 1004
[45] ST Dec. 4, 1893
[46] DA 478, 479
[47] ST Dec. 4, 1893
[48] DA 483
[49] 5BC 453
[50] DA 487
[51] DA 488
[52] DA 294
[53] 5BC 777
[54] *Ibid.*
[55] DA 488
[56] ST Dec. 10, 1894
[57] DA 498
[58] 5BC 783
[59] COL 378
[60] 5BC 783
[61] DA 499
[62] DA 503
[63] 5BC 784
[64] DA 503
[65] DA 504
[66] DA 524
[67] DA 525
[68] 5BC 1007
[69] COL 140
[70] 5BC 346
[71] 5BC 789
[72] COL 143
[73] COL 142
[74] COL 142, 143
[75] DA 408, 409
[76] 5BC 795
[77] 5BC 796

AUGUST

[1] DA 634
[2] COL 365
[3] BD 580
[4] COL 214
[5] DA 584
[6] DA 586
[7] COL 216
[8] 5BC 801
[9] 5BC 802
[10] DA 360
[11] 5BC 803
[12] 5BC 804
[13] 5BC 808
[14] COL 222
[15] 5BC 809
[16] COL 223
[17] COL 235
[18] 5BC 811
[19] COL 237
[20] *Ibid.*
[21] 5BC 812
[22] *Ibid.*
[23] COL 185
[24] COL 187
[25] *Ibid.*
[26] RH June 30, 1896
[27] COL 188, 189
[28] COL 189
[29] COL 190
[30] RH June 30, 1896
[31] COL 192
[32] *Ibid.*
[33] COL 193, 194
[34] MH 163
[35] COL 206
[36] 5BC 817
[37] COL 367
[38] 5BC 826
[39] COL 369
[40] COL 373
[41] COL 262
[42] 5BC 831
[43] COL 263
[44] *Ibid.*
[45] *Ibid.*
[46] 5BC 833; italics supplied
[47] COL 270, 271
[48] 5BC 837
[49] SC 52
[50] 5BC 838
[51] COL 370
[52] 5BC 838
[53] COL 373
[54] DA 526
[55] DA 527
[56] DA 528
[57] DA 529
[58] 5BC 1015
[59] DA 536
[60] DA 539
[61] *Ibid.*
[62] DA 540, 541
[63] DA 541, 542
[64] 5BC 839
[65] *Ibid.*
[66] *Ibid.*
[67] DA 506
[68] DA 507
[69] DA 508, 509
[70] 5BC 844
[71] COL 165
[72] COL 172
[73] COL 173
[74] COL 174
[75] COL 175
[76] COL 154
[77] 5BC 848
[78] *Ibid.*
[79] 5BC 454
[80] BD 290, 291
[81] DA 511
[82] DA 511, 512

[83] DA 515
[84] DA 518
[85] 5BC 458
[86] 2T 680
[87] DA 523

SEPTEMBER
[1] COL 394
[2] COL 396
[3] 5BC 464
[4] COL 402
[5] 5BC 465
[6] DA 548
[7] *Ibid.*
[8] 5BC 466
[9] DA 550; italics supplied
[10] 5BC 466
[11] RH Mar. 15, 1887
[12] 5BC 641
[13] RH Mar. 15, 1887
[14] 5BC 764
[15] DA 552
[16] DA 553
[17] DA 553, 554
[18] DA 555
[19] DA 557, 558
[20] 5BC 517
[21] DA 557
[22] DA 568
[23] DA 559
[24] DA 566
[25] *Ibid.*
[26] DA 568
[27] DA 559
[28] DA 560
[29] *Ibid.*
[30] DA 565
[31] DA 567
[32] DA 763
[33] 5BC 764
[34] DA 568
[35] DA 559, 560
[36] DA 563
[37] DA 563, 564
[38] DA 565
[39] DA 717
[40] *Ibid.*
[41] DA 719
[42] DA 569
[43] DA 570
[44] DA 571
[45] DA 572
[46] DA 575
[47] 5BC 470
[48] DA 578, 579; italics supplied
[49] DA 583
[50] *Ibid.*
[51] DA 589
[52] DA 590, 591

[53] DA 592
[54] *Ibid.*
[55] COL 273
[56] DA 593
[57] *Ibid.*
[58] DA 594
[59] *Ibid.*
[60] COL 275, 276
[61] COL 279, 280
[62] COL 304
[63] COL 299
[64] DA 597, 598
[65] 5BC 480
[66] COL 310
[67] COL 312
[68] COL 315
[69] COL 319
[70] DA 601
[71] 5BC 481
[72] 5BC 482
[73] DA 603
[74] 5BC 483
[75] DA 607
[76] DA 608
[77] *Ibid.*
[78] DA 608, 609
[79] 5BC 484, 485
[80] DA 610
[81] 5BC 489
[82] TM 79
[83] DA 620
[84] 5BC 648
[85] DA 615
[86] 5BC 649
[87] DA 625
[88] DA 621
[89] DA 626

OCTOBER
[1] DA 627
[2] 5BC 495
[3] 5BC 497
[4] 5BC (EGW) 1099
[5] DA 628
[6] *Ibid.*
[7] 5BC 497
[8] 5BC 498
[9] 5BC 499
[10] *Ibid.*
[11] *Ibid.*
[12] DA 630, 631
[13] GC 39
[14] GC 308
[15] 5BC 502
[16] DA 632
[17] DA 632, 633
[18] DA 632
[19] DA 633
[20] DA 636
[21] 5BC 504
[22] COL 405

[23] COL 406
[24] COL 412
[25] COL 327
[26] COL 329
[27] COL 331
[28] COL 332
[29] COL 338
[30] COL 340
[31] COL 355
[32] COL 360
[33] DA 637
[34] 5BC 513
[35] DA 641
[36] DA 640
[37] *Ibid.*
[38] DA 720
[39] DA 645
[40] DA 716
[41] DA 642
[42] DA 642, 643
[43] DA 642
[44] DA 644
[45] 5BC 868
[46] DA 644
[47] *Ibid.*
[48] DA 646
[49] DA 645
[50] *Ibid.*
[51] DA 650
[52] 5BC (EGW) 1138
[53] DA 650
[54] DA 652
[55] DA 653
[56] DA 656
[57] 5BC 522, 523
[58] 5BC 523
[59] DA 660
[60] *Ibid.*
[61] DA 653
[62] ST Dec. 24, 1894
[63] DA 654
[64] *Ibid.*
[65] DA 662
[66] DA 663
[67] *Ibid.*
[68] DA 667
[69] *Ibid.*
[70] DA 668
[71] *Ibid.*
[72] DA 669
[73] 5BC 1032
[74] *Ibid.*
[75] 5BC 521
[76] DA 672, 673
[77] DA 661
[78] DA 673
[79] 5BC (EGW) 1123
[80] DA 674, 675
[81] DA 575
[82] DA 676
[83] *Ibid.*

[84] 5BC 1042
[85] DA 677, 678
[86] 5BC 1044
[87] 5BC 1053
[88] 5BC 1042
[89] SC 88
[90] 5BC (EGW) 1147
[91] DA 685
[92] DA 686
[93] DA 685
[94] DA 687
[95] DA 688
[96] DA 689
[97] DA 690
[98] *Ibid.*
[99] DA 693

NOVEMBER
[1] ST Dec. 9, 1897
[2] *Ibid.*
[3] DA 693
[4] *Ibid.*
[5] ST Dec. 9, 1897
[6] 6MR 336, 337
[7] SR 210
[8] DA 693, 694
[9] DA 694
[10] DA 695, 696
[11] DA 696
[12] 5BC 527
[13] DA 696
[14] 5BC 527
[15] 5BC 869
[16] DA 697
[17] *Ibid.*
[18] DA 698
[19] DA 700
[20] DA 703
[21] DA 703, 704
[22] DA 704, 705
[23] DA 706
[24] 5BC 538
[25] DA 706
[26] *Ibid.*
[27] *Ibid.*
[28] DA 707
[29] 5BC 539
[30] DA 709
[31] *Ibid.*
[32] DA 710
[33] DA 710, 711
[34] DA 712
[35] DA 713
[36] ST Nov. 11, 1897
[37] 5BC 531
[38] DA 710
[39] DA 721
[40] DA 721, 722
[41] DA 722
[42] DA 715
[43] DA 711, 712

[44] 5BC 539
[45] DA 723
[46] DA 724
[47] DA 725
[48] DA 726
[49] *Ibid.*
[50] DA 727, 728
[51] DA 728
[52] 5BC 874
[53] DA 729
[54] *Ibid.*
[55] DA 730
[56] DA 730, 731
[57] DA 731, 732
[58] SR 218, 219
[59] DA 732. 733
[60] 5BC 545
[61] *Ibid.*
[62] DA 734
[63] BD 988
[64] 5BC 377
[65] DA 735
[66] DA 734
[67] DA 735
[68] DA 734
[69] 5BC 1061
[70] 2T 207
[71] DA 737
[72] DA 736
[73] 5BC 1061
[74] DA 737, 738
[75] SR 220
[76] SR 220, 221
[77] SR 220
[78] DA 741
[79] SR 221
[80] DA 742
[81] 5BC (EGW) 1107
[82] 5BC 547

[83] *Ibid.*
[84] DA 743
[85] *Ibid.*
[86] *Ibid.*
[87] DA 746
[88] DA 744
[89] DA 745
[90] BD 250
[91] 5BC 548
[92] 1T 241
[93] 5BC 548
[94] ST Aug. 21, 1879
[95] DA 746, 749
[96] 5BC 548
[97] *Ibid.*
[98] DA 745
[99] DA 745, 746
[100] DA 749
[101] DA 750
[102] DA 751
[103] *Ibid.*
[104] 5BC (EGW) 1124
[105] 5BC (EGW) 1125
[106] 5BC (EGW) 1149
[107] DA 752
[108] 5BC 1063
[109] DA 752
[110] *Ibid.*
[111] DA 753
[112] DA 754
[113] DA 756
[114] 5BC (EGW) 1150
[115] ST Mar. 26, 1894

DECEMBER
[1] DA 756
[2] DA 757
[3] 12 MR 392
[4] DA 770

[5] 12MR 387
[6] DA 771
[7] DA 772
[8] *Ibid.*
[9] DA 773
[10] *Ibid.*
[11] DA 774
[12] *Ibid.*
[13] EW 180, 181
[14] EW 180
[15] DA 774
[16] DA 776
[17] DA 777
[18] SR 228, 229
[19] DA 778
[20] *Ibid.*
[21] DA 779
[22] 5BC (EGW) 1114
[23] 5BC (EGW) 1110
[24] DA 780
[25] DA 780, 781
[26] DA 785, 786
[27] EW 182, 183
[28] DA 781, 782
[29] DA 782
[30] 3SP 204
[31] DA 788
[32] DA 788, 789
[33] 5BC 1065
[34] DA 789
[35] DA 789, 790
[36] DA 790
[37] 5BC 1066
[38] 3SP 203, 204
[39] UL 260
[40] 3SP 202, 203
[41] DA 787
[42] DA 793
[43] 5BC 658
[44] DA 795

[45] 5BC 882
[46] 5BC 883
[47] *Ibid.*
[48] DA 800
[49] *Ibid.*
[50] *Ibid.*
[51] DA 794
[52] DA 801
[53] DA 802
[54] DA 802, 803
[55] DA 804
[56] *Ibid.*
[57] 5BC 1067
[58] 3SP 222
[59] *Ibid.*
[60] DA 810
[61] DA 811
[62] DA 815
[63] *Ibid.*
[64] YI Dec. 22, 1898
[65] DA 816
[66] DA 818, 819
[67] DA 822
[68] DA 830
[69] DA 830, 831
[70] DA 832
[71] EW 190, 191
[72] PP 476
[73] GC 430
[74] 7BC 455
[75] 5BC 523
[76] DA 834
[77] 5BC (EGW) 1125
[78] *Ibid.*
[79] EW 191, 192
[80] DA 827
[81] *Ibid.*
[82] EW 196, 197
[83] ST Dec. 3, 1885